More Praise for

GIVEN UP *for* DEAD

"*Given Up for Dead* is the riveting account of a small ⌐rrison of Marines, sailors, and civilian workers who handed th̶̶̶̶̶̶ ̶ e their first defeat of World War II in the Pacific. It is r̶̶̶̶̶̶ re-searched, and told with brilliance and sensiti̶̶ ̶s book will serve as a lasting tribute to a r̶̶ ̶up of men."
—General P. X. Kelley, USMC (Ret.), 2̶̶ ̶̶̶̶arine Corps

"[*Given Up for Dead* is] a gripping ac̶̶ ̶̶ear, concise . . . at times like a thriller."
                    —*Pittsburgh Post-Gazette*

"*Given Up for Dead* is a welcome find. . . . It is the fifteen days of siege forming the core of the book that most readers are quite likely to remember most vividly. . . . By producing a nuanced account instead of a jingoistic, gung-ho glorification of a distant battle in a long-ago war, Sloan has added a valuable book to World War II literature."
                    —*Milwaukee Journal Sentinel*

"A powerful new narrative . . . Sloan does an outstanding job in telling the story of these heroes . . . and giving a critical analysis of the various commanders' actions."
                    —*Flint Journal*

GIVEN UP
for DEAD

America's Heroic Stand

at Wake Island

Bill Sloan

Bantam Books

GIVEN UP FOR DEAD
AMERICA'S HEROIC STAND AT WAKE ISLAND
A Bantam Book

PUBLISHING HISTORY
Bantam hardcover edition published October 2003
Bantam trade paperback edition / October 2004

Published by Bantam Dell
A Division of Random House, Inc.
New York, New York

Book design by Virginia Norey

Library of Congress Catalog Card Number: 2003057801

Bantam Books and the rooster colophon are
registered trademarks of Random House, Inc.

ISBN 0-553-38194-6

Manufactured in the United States of America
Published simultaneously in Canada

BVG   10   9   8   7   6   5   4   3   2   1

CONTENTS

CONTENTS

AUTHOR'S NOTE

During forty-five years as a journalist, editor, and author, I've encountered hundreds of good stories—but only a few truly great ones. The story of Wake Island definitely belongs in the latter category because it symbolizes the heights to which the human spirit can rise in the worst imaginable conditions. It's a story of misery and suffering, blood and death, defeat and despair, but it's also one of resourcefulness, tenacity, comradeship, and incredible courage.

Truthfully, I stumbled onto it quite by accident. The project started early in 2001 with a phone call from my agent, Jim Donovan, who asked if I knew of any World War II stories most Americans might not have heard before.

A few days later, I mentioned Jim's inquiry to Floyd Wood, an old friend and avid history buff. "Help me out here," I said, kidding. "What's the most heroic 'untold story' you can think of about World War II?"

The first two words out of Floyd's mouth were: "Wake Island."

I faintly recalled Wake as one of those small Pacific outposts that fell to the Japanese early in the war. But my hazy recollections didn't include a single detail. Floyd quickly filled me in.

"It was actually a victory of sorts—at least the first part of the battle was," he explained. "When the Japanese came to invade the island, the Marines played possum until the invasion fleet moved in close to shore. Then they opened up on them with their five-inch batteries and the few planes they had and sank or damaged a lot of enemy ships. The Japanese had to call off the invasion and limp back to Kwajalein to regroup. It was the first time they'd been stopped anywhere."

Floyd lent me a copy of a book called *The Story of Wake Island,* originally published in 1947 and written by Colonel James P. S. Devereux, who commanded the Marine detachment on Wake. It was the kind of story that made the hair stand up on the back of your neck if there was an iota of patriotism in your makeup.

I learned from the book that over 1,100 civilian construction workers had been trapped on Wake when the war broke out, and a search of the Internet turned up a civilian survivors' organization, located in Boise, Idaho. I reached the group's president, Chalas Loveland, who, in turn, gave me the name and number of Franklin D. Gross, an ex-Marine in Independence, Missouri, who published a quarterly newsletter for military survivors of Wake.

Frank Gross turned out to be a "walking directory" of Wake Island veterans and a gold mine of information on individual stories of valor and heroism, some of which had never been fully told before.

Frank put me in touch with one Wake veteran who was practically a neighbor of mine. A retired Marine colonel named Bryghte D. Godbold had been a captain and strongpoint commander on Wake, and he lived just a few miles from my home in Dallas. When I did my initial interview with Godbold in June 2001, he was the first Wake Islander I'd met face-to-face.

Not all the news was encouraging. Many Wake veterans had died within the past few years, and former Sergeant Charles Holmes of Bonham, Texas, who compiled one of the nation's most extensive collections of Wake Island memorabilia, had been dead for more than a decade. No one seemed to know what had happened to Holmes's collection in the interim, and numerous inquiries failed to turn up any information on its whereabouts.

But when Gross mentioned former Private First Class Wiley Sloman, then living in Harlingen in the Lower Rio Grande Valley, my excitement level soared. Here was just what I'd been searching for—an ordinary young Marine with a truly extraordinary story. Here was a virtually unknown saga of personal courage and nail-biting drama that could form the catalyst for a broader look at the Wake Islanders' valiant stand against impossible odds, the flawed command decisions that sealed their fate, and the forced surrender that none of them wanted.

A crewman on a five-inch battery that sank the first major Japanese warship in the Pacific, Sloman had been shot through the head and left for dead on the battlefield. He lay there for three days, until he was found clinging to life by a burial detail collecting enemy corpses.

As soon as I heard Sloman's story from his own lips, I knew what the title of my Wake Island book should be:

Given Up for Dead.

In late 1941 and early 1942, the battle for Wake was viewed as an event of immense historical import, but in later years it faded into an obscure footnote on the Pacific war. In this book dozens of young Americans from every corner of the country and every type of background bring their epic struggle back to life. Day by day and hour by hour, they describe how they endured, adjusted, fought on—and survived—in circumstances as horrific as any nightmare.

Many of them were little more than boys when they fought for their lives and their nation's honor in America's first real battle of World War II. But they were fully ready to die at their guns, and, in fact, most were sad or angry that they weren't given that right. Now they're old men, grateful for their lives but still gripped by conflicting feelings, still harboring a sense of regret that they weren't allowed to choose death above the dishonor of surrender.

For the most part, other Wake Island books have been broad overviews by military commanders or professional historians. *Given Up for Dead,* on the other hand, places the reader down in the sweat, smoke, and grime of foxholes and gun pits, where bullets whine, bombs explode, coral splinters fly, blood spurts, rats bite, men scream, and death is never more than inches away.

The saga of Wake is an old story—in many cases, an overlooked or never-heard story—but one you aren't soon likely to forget. I believe the men who defended Wake Island sixty-plus years ago merit a permanent spot in our national consciousness, along with the heroes of Bunker Hill, the Alamo, Gettysburg, San Juan Hill, and the Argonne Forest.

I've never met a group of men that I admired more. If this book can help them achieve the respect and remembrance they deserve from present and future generations of Americans, I could ask for nothing else.

Many people helped make this great story a reality. Without Frank Gross's contacts and his constant willingness to solve puzzles and provide information, I'd never have gotten to first base. I lost count of the hours I spent with Wiley Sloman, both in person and on the phone. When he died suddenly just as the manuscript was nearing completion, I lost not only an invaluable source but a true friend as well.

John Johnson, Walter Bowsher, Bryghte Godbold, Artie Stocks, Jack Hearn, Robert Bourquin, Ralph Holewinski, Tom Kennedy, Jack Skaggs, Clifton Sanders, Mackie Wheeler, Glenn Tripp, John Kinney, Robert Hanna, David Kliewer, Richard Gilbert, Ernest Rogers, and many other Wake Islanders and their relatives graciously shared their time and personal recollections with me.

June Faubion, secretary-treasurer of the Survivors of Wake, Guam and Cavite, Inc., was particularly helpful—and hospitable—before and during my trip to Boise to interview civilian survivors. While I was there, in addition to giving me a super interview, John Rogge lent me several priceless documents to make copies. Glenn Newell, Chalas Loveland, Ed Doyle, J. J. Coker, and Glen Walden were other civilians who set aside time for lengthy interviews.

Career Marine Ed Borne provided a wealth of information, including contact information for Dr. Shigeyoshi Ozeki, who came ashore with the Japanese landing force and later helped save the lives of wounded Americans. Before his death in October 2002, Dr. Ozeki answered my questions with thoughtfulness and insight and also put me in touch with Hisao Tsuji, another Japanese Wake survivor. Between them, they helped give me an entirely different point of view on the battle.

My special thanks goes to my farsighted agent, Jim Donovan; my friend and historical guru, Floyd Wood; my talented and perceptive editor at Bantam, John Flicker; and my wife and copyeditor extraordinaire, Lana Henderson Sloan.

There are others, from Jeff Hunt, curator of the Museum of the Pacific

War in Fredericksburg, Texas, to Lena Kaljot, photo historian at the Marine Corps Historical Center in Washington, to the nice lady at Kinko's in Boise, all of whom deserve a word of appreciation. To everyone who helped, whether your name is listed here or not, my sincere thanks.

Bill Sloan
Dallas, Texas
2003

*

*With the omnipresent surf in the background,
this monument to Wake's Marines stands
sentinel on the island today.*
(Courtesy Artie Stocks)

U.S. Military Personnel
Killed in Action at Wake Island
or who Died in POW Camps

U.S. Marine Corps

Agar, Paul R.
Allen, Jack V.

Bailey, William
Beaver, Darrell L.
Bedell, Henry A.
Bertels, Alton J.
Boyle, Hugh L.

Comin, Howard D.
Commers, Joseph F.
Conderman, Robert J.
Couch, Winslow
Culp, Joseph C.

Davidson, Carl R.
DeSparr, Marshall E.
Double, John F.

Edwards, Robert P.
Elrod, Henry T.

Farrar, Herbert D.
Fleming, Manton L.

Garr, Robert F. Jr.
Gilley, Ernest N. Jr.
Gleichauf, William A.
Graves, George A.
Guthrie, Frank A.

Haley, Gifford L.
Halstead, William C.
Hannum, Earl R.
Hemmelgarn, Paul F.
Himelrick, John R.
Holden, Frank J.
Houde, Severe R.
Hunt, Quince A.

Katchak, John
King, Curtis P.
Koontz, Benjamin D.

Lane, Lloyd G.
Locklin, Eugene D.

Marlowe, Clovis R.
Marshall, Gordon L.
McBride, James E.
Mitwalsky, Robert W.

Nanninga, Henry D.

Phipps, Ralph E.
Pickett, Ralph H.
Pratt, Robert M.
Puckett, Ray V.
Purvis, Gordon W.

Reed, Alvey A.
Renner, Francis J.

Stevens, Robert L.
Stockton, Maurice E.
Sutton, Mack P.

Taylor, Dale K.
Tokryman, Paul
Tucker, William M.

Venable, Alexander B. Jr.

Wilsford, Clyde D.
Wiskochil, Robert I.
Wright, Johnalson E.

Zurchauer, Robert Jr.

U.S. Navy

Barnes, James E.
Bird, Edwin A.

Franklin, Theodore D.

Gonzales, Roy J.

Hodgkins, Ray K. Jr.

Kidd, Franklin B.
Kilcoyne, Thomas P.

Lambert, John W.
Lechler, William R.

McCoy, William H.

Williams, Harold R.
Wolney, George J.

This monument was erected in memory
of the civilians killed on Wake
during and after the battle.
(Courtesy Artie Stocks)

American Civilians Executed
on Wake Island After the U.S. Surrender

Abbott, Cyrus W. Jr.
Allen, Horace L.
Anderson, Norman A.
Andre, Roland A.
Anvick, Allen E.

Baasch, Carl A.
Bellanger, George
Bowcutt, Don R.
Boyce, Dolphia (Dave) M.

Cantry, Charles A.
Carlson, Stanley A.
Cavanagh, Allen A.
Chambers, David B.
Chard, Donley D.
Church, Carleton G.
Cormier, Louis H.
Cox, Karl L.
Cummings, David E.
Cunha, James A.

Davis, Joseph R.
Dean, George W.
Dobyns, Harold L.
Dogger, Martin H.
Dreyer, Henry M.
Dunn, Joseph M.
Fenex, Jack A.
Flint, Howard A.
Fontes, Glenn B.
Forsberg, Floyd F.
Francis, Dale G.
French, Albert P.
Froberger, Lawrence G.

Gerdin, William P.
Gibbs, Charles A.
Goembel, Clarence R.

Haight, Ralph E.
Haines, William H.
Hansen, John Vernon
Harris, George
Harvey, Wilber C.
Hastie, Frank
Hettcik, Howard L.
Hochstein, Ernest A.
Hofmeister, Julius M.
 (Babe)*

Jensen, George A.
Jones, Alfred A.

Keeler, Ora K.
Kelly, Martin T.
Kennedy, Thomas F.
Kidwell, Charles A. Jr.
Kroeger, Woodrow W.

Light, Rolland E.
Ling, Henry C.
Lythgoe, Eugene

Marshall, Irving E.
Martin, John
McDaniel, James B.
McInnes, Thomas L.
Migacz, Frank
Migacz, Melvin
Miller, Irvin E.
Mitchell, Howard H.
Mitchell, Wayne E.
Mittendorf, Joseph F.
Mueller, Carl W.
Myers, Richard B.

Omstead, Clifford A.

Páse, Gordon H.
Pratt, Archie H.
Preston, Donald W.

Rankin, Morton B.
Ray, William H.
Reynolds, William H.
Robbins, Sheldon G.

Schemel, Charles H.
Schottler, Herman
Shank, Lawton E. (M.D.)
Shepard, Orbin R.
Sherman, Glenwood H.
Shriner, Gould H.
Sigman, Russell J.
Simpers, William T.
Smith, Charles E.
St. John, Francis C.
Stone, Willis C.
Streblow, Alvin L.
Stringer, Wesley W.
Susee, Arthur J.

Tart, Lacy F.
Thompson, Glenn H.
Tucker, Earl E.
Vancil, Vernon
Vant, Glen
Van Valkenberg, Ralph W.
Villines, Charles M.

Williamson, Frank E.
Wilper, Redmond J.
Woods, Charles

Yuen, Harry T. K.

---

* Hofmeister was beheaded in March 1942; all others were killed by machine gun fire on October 7, 1943. Another unidentified civilian was reportedly beheaded in the summer of 1942, and a survivor of the machine gun massacre, also unidentified, was reportedly hacked to death on October 8, 1943.

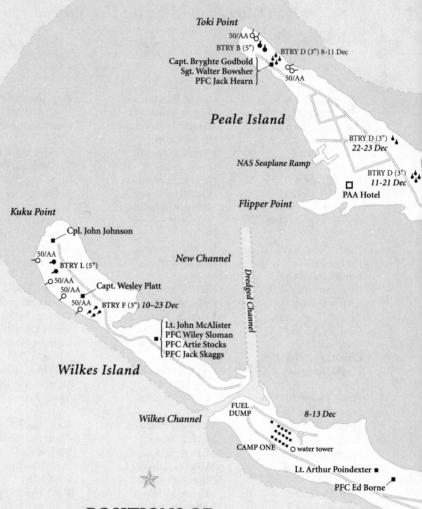

Toki Point

50/AA

BTRY B (5")

Capt. Bryghte Godbold
Sgt. Walter Bowsher
PFC Jack Hearn

BTRY D (3") 8-11 Dec

50/AA

Peale Island

BTRY D (3")
22-23 Dec

NAS Seaplane Ramp

BTRY D (3")
11-21 Dec

Flipper Point

PAA Hotel

Kuku Point

Cpl. John Johnson

New Channel

50/AA

BTRY L (5")

50/AA

Capt. Wesley Platt

50/AA

50/AA

BTRY F (3") 10–23 Dec

Lt. John McAlister
PFC Wiley Sloman
PFC Artie Stocks
PFC Jack Skaggs

Wilkes Island

Wilkes Channel

FUEL
DUMP

8-13 Dec

CAMP ONE

water tower

Lt. Arthur Poindexter

PFC Ed Borne

POSITIONS OF
VARIOUS PERSONNEL ON WAKE
ON THE MORNING
OF DECEMBER 23, 1941

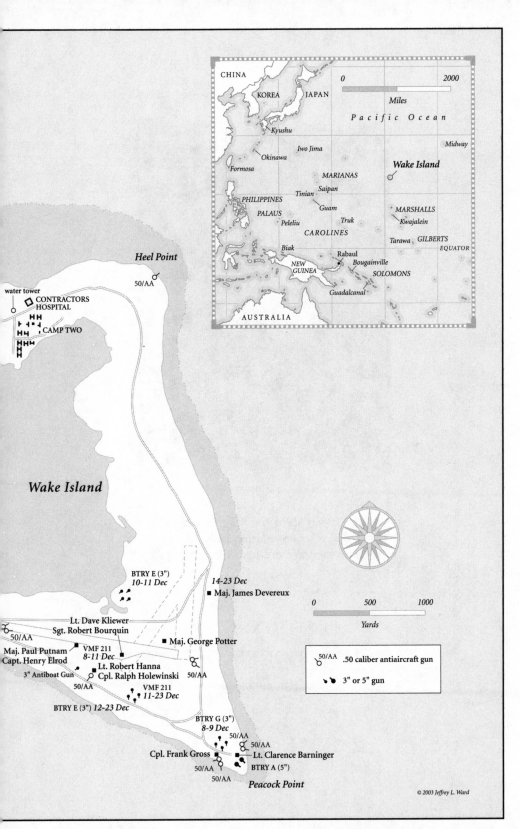

Heel Point

50/AA

water tower

CONTRACTORS
HOSPITAL

CAMP TWO

CHINA

KOREA   JAPAN

Kyushu

Iwo Jima

Midway

Okinawa

Formosa

MARIANAS

Saipan

Tinian

PHILIPPINES   Guam

PALAUS

Peleliu   Truk

CAROLINES

Biak

NEW
GUINEA

AUSTRALIA

Pacific Ocean

0   2000

Miles

Wake Island

MARSHALLS

Kwajalein

Tarawa   GILBERTS

EQUATOR

Rabaul

Bougainville

SOLOMONS

Guadalcanal

Wake Island

BTRY E (3")
10-11 Dec

14-23 Dec
■ Maj. James Devereux

Lt. Dave Kliewer
Sgt. Robert Bourquin

50/AA

Maj. Paul Putnam
Capt. Henry Elrod

3" Antiboat Gun

VMF 211
8-11 Dec

■ Maj. George Potter

Lt. Robert Hanna
Cpl. Ralph Holewinski

50/AA

50/AA

VMF 211
11-23 Dec

BTRY E (3") 12-23 Dec

BTRY G (3")
8-9 Dec

50/AA   50/AA

Cpl. Frank Gross   Lt. Clarence Barninger

50/AA   BTRY A (5")

50/AA

Peacock Point

0   500   1000

Yards

50/AA   .50 caliber antiaircraft gun

3" or 5" gun

© 2003 Jeffrey L. Ward

⋆

Wiley Sloman (third row, third from right) *is
shown with other new Marines on his graduation
from boot camp at San Diego in November 1939.*

PROLOGUE

Wilkes Island, Wake Atoll
December 26, 1941

The almost-naked young man with the bullet hole in his head groaned as he emerged from the depths of prolonged unconsciousness. He opened his eyes, blinking and trying to focus on something that might help him remember who he was, where he was, and what had happened to him.

His senses slowly came back to him through the feverish pounding in his skull as he struggled to assemble the jigsaw-puzzle pieces of his own identity:

His name was Wiley W. Sloman and he was a private first class in the First Defense Battalion of the U.S. Marine Corps, assigned to a five-inch gun crew on Wake Island. Roughly a month ago, he'd celebrated his twentieth birthday.

By rights, he figured he should be dead already. A more rational person probably would have just given up and said to hell with it. But Sloman hadn't been rational since the Japanese soldier shot him, so he just kept hanging on. Sometimes he could feel himself slipping away, but then he'd shake it off somehow, unsure what motivated him to cling to life.

It wasn't hope. As far as he could tell, his buddies had given him up for dead. They'd left him on the coral embankment, and there was no reason to think they were ever coming back. It wasn't fear or courage, either. It was more like some survival instinct that was beyond his control.

The sun was high and bright. Sloman felt its rays reflecting off his bed of coral, and he wondered if his head would go right on hurting even after he died. It was humid, too, the way it always was on Wake, but the sticky heat didn't bother him like it usually did. On the contrary, he was shivering, and the sweat on his skin felt cold.

At first, Sloman thought the roaring in his ears was part of the ferocious pain in his head. Then he realized it was the surf pounding on the beach fifty yards away. It was the same damn surf that had kept them from hearing the Japanese bombers that first day.

It was the surf, too, that had covered up the sound of the enemy landing craft the night of the invasion. The roar of it had been so constant for so long that it scarcely registered anymore as an identifiable sound. But now, as Sloman fully awakened, he noticed the dried blood on his left arm and shoulder, and he tried to move his left hand. It was no use. The hand might as well have belonged to somebody else. Like the whole left side of his body, it was paralyzed.

He was stripped down to his underwear, he noticed, and his uniform was nowhere in sight. It puzzled him a little, but he didn't really care one way or the other. It wasn't as if some cute girl was likely to stroll past on her way to the beach and see him in this sorry, embarrassing state. Just a year ago, Sloman had been loafing around in San Diego, going to artillery school and waiting for the Marine Corps to make up its mind where it was going to send him. The beaches there had been filled with cute girls, but there were no women at all on Wake.

What did bother Sloman, though, was that his rifle was gone, too. A Marine and his rifle were supposed to be inseparable. There was nothing worse than losing your rifle—not even losing your helmet. Marine Gunner Clarence McKinstry, the red-bearded mountain of a man who ran Sloman's Battery L, would be plenty pissed off if he found out.

He'd been having dreams about McKinstry that had nothing to do with the missing rifle. At least he thought they were dreams. Two or three times, he seemed to hear McKinstry talking to him, reassuring him.

"Just hang on, kid," McKinstry kept saying. "We're gonna get you out of here. We're gonna get you to a hospital."

"Why're you being so nice all of a sudden?" Sloman demanded. "Last time you said anything to me, you were threatening to shoot me in the ass if I didn't keep moving."

"Aw, hell, I wasn't talking to you," McKinstry said. "I was talking to those other guys."

McKinstry hadn't been the only one to visit Sloman's dreams as he lay there abandoned and unable to move. His mother had dropped in on him a couple of times to tell him she loved him. On one visit, she'd brought along old Doc Danforth, the family physician who'd delivered Sloman on a November day in 1921, to take a look at his wound. Since Danforth had been dead for quite a while, his appearance raised disquieting questions in Sloman's mind about whether he was dead himself.

Sloman's gaze moved a few feet farther away to the dead Japanese strewn in tangled heaps all around him, several of them so close he could have reached out and touched them with his good right hand. He didn't know how long they'd been there, but their bodies were swollen and stinking in the heat. Swarms of flies buzzed around them, intent on their work. They were all over Sloman, too, especially his head, but he didn't have the strength to shoo them away.

He sank back on his bed of coral and closed his eyes again. God, his head hurt. He needed to think of something to get his mind off the pain, the flies, and the enemy corpses. Anything.

He dimly remembered that it was Christmastime. The enemy invaders had sneaked ashore in the early hours of December 23, and the Marines had fought them until the afternoon sun was beaming down. They'd been whipping them pretty damn good, too, when the bullet slammed into Sloman's head an inch above his left temple and exited two inches farther back.

Ever since then, he'd drifted through an endless twilight fog, mostly in a comalike state. Sometimes he emerged briefly into semiconsciousness, but at best his mental processes had ranged from hazy to nonexistent. Now, for the first time since lapsing into shock—and for reasons he couldn't explain—he was awake. Plenty addled and confused but fully conscious. His time sense was still screwed up, but he was sure it had to be at least the next day after the invasion. That would mean it was Christmas Eve.

Back home in Texas City, Texas, his family—a large, close-knit clan that took fierce pride in its Irish roots—would be gathering around the Christmas tree. There'd be presents wrapped in crinkly tissue paper and bright ribbon. His mother would be cooking a big turkey with all the trimmings and baking one of her famous angelfood cakes and big pans of hot rolls. The house would be full of people, some singing Christmas carols, others grinning and sipping eggnog. It had been that way as far back as Sloman could remember, right up to the last Christmas he'd spent at home two years ago, when he was fresh out of boot camp.

Since he was the youngest of five children, the holiday had always been a big deal for Sloman, especially the year he'd just turned ten and got the big, shiny $12 bicycle. The bike was secondhand, of course. That had been in the rock-bottom depths of the Depression, after his dad had lost his long-shoreman's job and was making a living by buying live crabs fresh out of the nets and reselling them to a seafood market in Houston. Nobody in the Sloman family could afford a brand-new bike—but the used one was the prettiest thing Wiley had ever seen. While everybody else was in the crowded house, talking, laughing, stuffing themselves with food, and generally making merry, he'd ridden about fifty miles up and down the street. The bike was a little big for him, and he'd had to stretch his legs to reach the pedals, but that didn't matter. Pretty soon his legs got longer and stronger, and then it was easy.

It had been nearly two and a half hours after midnight when they'd first heard the motors of the Japanese landing barges. The weather was misty and the dark sky was spitting rain. By then, even if the gun crews could have seen the barges in the pitch blackness, the invaders were too close for the Marines to bring their five-inch batteries to bear. Minutes later, the first enemy troops had splashed ashore.

The enemy had landed about a hundred men on Wilkes Island, the strip of coral and brush next to Wake proper where Sloman was stationed, and only sixty American defenders were there to meet them. Over the next eight or nine hours, however, the Marines had put up a serious fight. Sloman clearly remembered that he and his mates were mopping up the last small pockets of Japanese resistance on Wilkes at the moment he was hit.

In the blur that followed, he could hear the voices of the Marines around him.

"Looks like Sloman got his, Mac," he heard his buddy, PFC Gordon Marshall, tell Gunner McKinstry. "You can have his rifle if you want it."

So that was what happened to the damned rifle, Sloman thought. Well, at least McKinstry couldn't give him a hard time about losing it.

Then, after what had seemed a terribly long interval, Sloman heard a yell from another battery mate, PFC Bill Raymond, who'd been firing beside him when he was hit:

"Hey, Sloman's not dead yet. Get a medic over here."

A Navy corpsman named Ernest Vaale appeared from somewhere and put a bandage on Sloman's wound. As Vaale worked, Sloman noticed that the shoulder of his sweatshirt, where he'd been resting his head, was drenched with blood. He also saw a glob of gray brain tissue there.

That can't be my brains, he'd told himself calmly, *because I'm still alive. People can't live when their brains have been blown out.*

Sloman didn't want to pass out again, but he closed his eyes for a while because the glare of the sun made the throbbing in his head worse. When he opened them again, he was startled to see his company commander, Captain Wesley Platt, leaning over him. Platt was the man who'd led the Marines' counterattack on Wilkes and one of the most fearless officers Sloman had ever known. For a second, he wondered if Platt was really there or if he was dreaming again.

Then he saw other figures moving around nearby. Some of them were uniformed Japanese. They were loading up the enemy dead and starting to haul them away.

"Hey, son, can you hear me?" Platt asked in his soft South Carolina drawl.

"Yes, sir," Sloman whispered.

"Sorry you got left out here," the captain said. "But don't worry, we're going to get you taken care of."

As Platt and another Marine loaded him onto a stretcher, Sloman tried to smile. "This is one helluva way to spend Christmas Eve," he mumbled.

Platt shook his head. "I'm afraid you've lost a chunk of time there, son," he said. "Christmas Eve and Christmas Day have both come and gone."

"How'd you find me?" Sloman asked.

"McKinstry told us where to look," Platt said. "Don't you remember him coming out here?"

As he felt himself being lifted and carried on the stretcher, the young Marine with the ugly wound in his head began to drift off again. It would be a relief to go back to sleep, especially in a bed away from the flies and the smell of death, but he battled to stay awake until he could figure out what was going on.

He saw that the Japanese in the burial detail had weapons, while Platt and the other Marines were unarmed. It took a moment to comprehend what this meant, but as his memory cleared a little more, he understood. The Marines had surrendered, and the Japanese were in control. Despite killing or capturing every invader on Wilkes, the Marines had been forced to lay down their weapons and give up.

Sloman couldn't believe it. He couldn't understand it, either. How could such a thing happen? Marines never surrendered. Not ever. Not under any circumstances. Certainly not after they'd won the battle.

*

A Navy dive bomber over Wake Island.
(The Mariners' Museum/Corbis)

A Place at the
Ends of the Earth

In the four-plus centuries since they were first discovered—and promptly forgotten again—the tiny specks of land identified on maps as Wake Island have been described in many unflattering terms.

After finding and circling the atoll in October 1568, Spanish explorer Alvaro de Mendaña de Neyra dismissed it as "useless." The barrier reef surrounding it, coupled with the fierce, unpredictable local currents, made a landing too risky, he decided. In disgust, he sailed away without going ashore, despite the fact that he was short of food and water, had been searching for land for days, and many of his crew were sick with scurvy.

The next officially recorded sighting of Wake didn't take place until 1796, when a British merchant ship, the *Prince William Henry*, came upon it by accident. The ship's captain, Samuel Wake, knew nothing of Mendaña's earlier visit, so he christened the little landmass "Wake" in honor of himself. But he, too, wanted no part of the reef and the currents, and he departed without ever setting foot on the island that still bears his name.

To understand the treacherous conditions surrounding Wake, picture a towering underwater mountain—a long-extinct volcano—with only the uppermost tips of its crater protruding above the sea. Completely surrounding it about a hundred yards offshore is a jagged coral reef formed over tens of thousands of years. Until a channel was blasted through the reef in the mid-1930s, it continued to make Wake one of the most inaccessible points on the globe.

Much of the reef lurks less than two feet below sea level, and except in a man-made opening, only very small, flat-bottomed boats could safely pass over it. To compound the danger, the ocean's depth just beyond the reef suddenly plunges thousands of feet down the almost perpendicular sides of the submerged prehistoric mountain. This creates perpetually rough seas that send huge waves pounding shoreward.

Even in relatively modern times, ships found no safe anchorage at Wake, and—like those of Mendaña and Samuel Wake—any vessel that ventured near it inevitably did so at its peril. In all likelihood, the reef and the tides claimed numerous small craft over the centuries. But their most notable victim was the German passenger ship *Libelle*, which crashed on the reef and broke to pieces in March 1866 after being blown off course en route from Honolulu to Hong Kong. The *Libelle*'s anchor and other remnants of the doomed ship were found on Wake seventy-five years later.

On October 15, 1941, some seven weeks before the outbreak of World War II in the Pacific, Major James P. S. Devereux arrived on Wake to take command of its small Marine garrison. Devereux's feelings about the place were remarkably similar to those expressed by Mendaña 373 years earlier. The major referred to Wake as "a spit-kit of sand and coral without any reason for being." Many of Devereux's men added their own appraisals: "uninviting," "lonely," "barren," "oppressive," "desolate," "flat and ugly," and "nothing but sand and rocks," to list a few of the milder ones. But Tech Sergeant Charles Holmes, a career Marine from the rolling prairies of North Texas, may have summed it up better than anyone. On first impression, he said, Wake struck him as "the most isolated place in the world."

Unlovely as it was, however, PFC Wiley Sloman was actually glad to be there when he finally made it ashore on November 1, 1941. He would have much preferred to stay at Midway, where he'd been stationed previously, but under the circumstances, he was glad to be anywhere as long as there was land under his feet.

On his way out from Pearl on the U.S.S. *Castor,* the ship had hit some really nasty weather, and almost everybody on board was seasick except Sloman, who wasn't bothered at all by the rough seas. Not only had he been around plenty of salt water and ships as a kid growing up on the Texas coast, but his great-grandfather had traveled around the world as captain of a three-masted sailing ship, and Sloman figured maybe he'd inherited some of the old man's seaworthiness. But his healthy state turned out to be small comfort when he was assigned to torpedo watch during the worst part of the storm. Then, after reaching Wake, the *Castor* had sailed around the atoll for four days waiting for the ground swells to ease off before anybody could go ashore.

Sloman grabbed a spot on the first motor launch to leave the *Castor,* but he quickly learned that the easy life he'd enjoyed on Midway was a thing of the past. He barely got off the launch before they handed him a jackhammer and put him to work cutting holes in the coral to mount corner posts for the Marines' tents. "From then on until the war started, we didn't get much rest," he said. "On Midway, it was good duty, and we were usually through by noon. On Wake, reveille was at 5:00 A.M., and we worked our tails off all day."

Wake Atoll is actually made up of three small islands grouped around a shallow lagoon that was once the crater of the extinct volcano. V-shaped Wake proper, the largest of the three, is separated by narrow channels from Wilkes and Peale islands, just to the west. Together, they form a rough horseshoe shape with its open end pointing west. Peale forms the tip of the upper or northern leg of the horseshoe and Wilkes forms the tip of the lower or southern leg.

Wilkes Island took its name from Lieutenant Charles Wilkes, captain of the U.S. Navy sloop *Vincennes* and leader of an expedition that visited Wake briefly in 1841. Peale Island was named for Titian R. Peale, a well-known naturalist of the day, who was along on the same expedition. Wilkes's and Peale's opinions of the place were pretty typical, it seems. Peale found it to be "very unpleasant," and Wilkes dismissed it as "unfit for human habitation."

Beyond shimmering-white beaches studded with coral boulders, a low bank rises toward a few slight ridges. Much of the interior is covered with a dense, junglelike growth of brush, vines, and scrubby trees. Most of the native trees grow no more than twelve to fifteen feet tall, and, in 1941, the stately palms that proliferate naturally on most tropical Pacific isles were notably absent. Even in the interior, the terrain remains predominantly flat. The highest point of land is only about twenty-one feet above sea level. On an average of every fifteen years or so, tidal waves sweep across Wake during typhoon season. When they do, every inch of the atoll is subject to flooding.

All three islands put together constitute less than three square miles of land area—about 2,600 acres—in the vast reaches of the western Pacific. Wake is just over 2,000 miles due west of Honolulu. Midway lies nearly 1,200 miles to the northeast, and Guam is almost 1,400 miles farther west. The closest significant points of land are the Marshall, Mariana, and Caroline islands, which were mandated to Japanese control after World War I. In 1941, these islands bristled with hostile armaments and were anything but friendly territory. Major Japanese air bases on Kwajalein Atoll were just over 600 miles away; the giant Japanese naval installation at Truk was only slightly farther.

Except for multitudes of seabirds, including one totally wingless variety, and a particularly bold species of rat (which probably came ashore originally as refugees from some doomed ship), Wake has no native population. For all but the past seventy or so years of its history, the atoll has been totally devoid of human habitation. In addition to its remoteness, its reefs, and its currents, Wake is a "desert island" in the truest sense of the term. It has no natural source of fresh water. When the first permanent residents arrived in the mid-1930s, installing desalinization equipment for seawater and building systems to catch and store rainwater were among their most urgent priorities.

Yet despite all its drawbacks, Wake generated interest in Washington as early as Spanish-American War days, both as a possible site for a trans-Pacific cable station and as a stopping point for U.S. naval units bound for the Far East. Since the British still had a vague claim to the island, and Japanese fishermen also showed up from time to time, U.S. military leaders took steps to solidify Wake's status as American territory.

On Independence Day 1898, an American fleet carrying troops to the Philippines stopped off at Wake. Major General Francis Greene located a break in the barrier reef and went ashore, where he tied a small American flag to a tree limb and claimed the island for the United States. The following January, the U.S. Navy gunboat *Bennington* visited Wake, and its captain, Commander Edward Taussig, installed a more permanent flag and formally declared Wake a U.S. possession.

Within a few years, the cable station idea was scrapped, after Wake's lack of fresh water came to light, and the cable route was altered in favor of Midway and Guam. By this time, as a result of the U.S. victory over Spain, the United States had acquired a Pacific empire that stretched from Hawaii to the Philippines. Some military planners toyed with the idea of establishing a chain of strategic forward bases to protect these new holdings. If it ever happened, Wake was ideally situated to become part of that chain.

Still, Wake was destined to remain virtually untouched by the outside world—and virtually unknown to the American public—for another three decades. In Washington, the acquisitive imperialism that dominated political thinking during the Spanish-American War era gave way to rigid, head-in-the-sand isolationism following World War I. The size, strength, and influence of America's military diminished steadily through the 1920s and early 1930s. Military leaders lost most of their fiscal clout with an increasingly isolationist Congress. The lawmakers balked at appropriating money for anything related to arms, least of all new bases on faraway islands, and the Great Depression that descended on the country in 1929 made the situation infinitely worse. Domestic recovery was the battle cry, and to hell with vague threats in Europe and Asia.

Then, in 1933, Hitler came to power in Berlin, FDR was inaugurated as president in Washington, and the national political pendulum gradually began to swing back in the opposite direction. But the about-face from isolationism to military preparedness would be an agonizingly slow process—especially for the War Department, the Navy Department, and the admirals and generals.

By the early 1930s, the U.S. Navy had shrunk to little more than a third its size at the end of World War I, and much of what was left of it was old, rusty, and obsolete. The new president, who had served as an assistant secretary of the Navy in 1917 and 1918, was shocked when he discovered its deplorable condition. The Army hadn't fared much better, and the U.S. Marine Corps was barely a shadow of what it had once been.

"When I entered the Marines in June 1939, there were just 16,300 men in the Corps," recalled Corporal John Johnson, who came to Wake as a nineteen-year-old machine gunner from Missouri and later fought with Wiley Sloman on Wilkes. "That was less men than the New York City Police Department."

The change in national attitude would take years to run its course—a delay the depleted military could ill afford. Not until war was painfully imminent would the public and the politicians finally embrace the need for all-out mobilization.

In the meantime, occasional subterfuge by America's military establishment would be essential if the country was to avoid total calamity, or so the military minds in Washington believed. One of the major beneficiaries of that subterfuge—as well as one of the major victims of the delay—was to be Wake Island.

The first small step toward turning Wake into a formidable Pacific fortress came with almost no fanfare and little public notice. On December 29, 1934, while much of Washington was shut down for the Christmas–New Year holidays, FDR signed an executive order placing Wake under the direct jurisdiction of the Navy Department. The Navy, in turn, quickly declared the atoll a bird sanctuary and announced a stringent set of rules to protect its feathered throngs.

It was all a ruse, of course. The Navy's real interest was in airplanes, not birds. A little over two months later, on March 11, 1935, Pan American Airways announced plans to establish the world's first regularly scheduled passenger service from California to the Orient via its soon-to-be-famous "China Clipper" route. One day later, the Navy gave the airline permission to build docking, fueling, and lodging facilities for its Clippers and their passengers on three remote Pacific islands: Wake, Midway, and Guam.

Japan protested loudly when the news broke. The militarists in Tokyo strongly suspected what most private American citizens of the period would never have guessed—that Wake was quietly being groomed for future military use. It was, after all, closer to Tokyo than it was to Honolulu.

It was also much nearer to Japan's home islands than Midway, Johnston, or Palmyra, other links in a defensive chain envisioned by Washington as a protective westward shield for Hawaii. While being a mere three- or four-hour bomber flight from the big Japanese bases at Truk and Kwajalein made Wake a prominent target, it also gave the atoll enormous offensive potential. Wake wasn't nearly as exposed or vulnerable to attack as Guam, which was in the middle of the Mariana Islands and encircled by Japanese bases—a fact that had already caused U.S. planners to write off Guam as an immediate loss if war came.

To Japan, all these factors made any U.S. attempt to tamper with Wake's centuries-old status as vacant specks of coral in the middle of nowhere a threat to be reckoned with. Pan Am's Clippers would be the first planes on Wake, true, but the Navy's own PBYs would be next, and the Army's B-17s wouldn't be far behind.

In Tokyo's view, a fortified Wake would be nothing less than a dagger aimed at the very heart of its empire—and thus a target of the highest priority. News of the deal between the U.S. Navy and Pan Am prompted Japanese naval strategists to revise their war plans. Wake would now have to be seized within the first few days of conflict.

Quietly, unobtrusively, an ominous sequence of events had been set in motion. The attack on Pearl Harbor was still more than six and a half years away. But the clock was ticking.

In the second half of the 1930s, most Americans were blissfully unaware that relations between the United States and Japan had been on a downward spiral for decades. Their mental images of the Japanese were still drawn more from the characters in *Madame Butterfly*—tragically beautiful geishas and funny little slant-eyed men who bowed a lot—than from current reality. Few of them realized that expansion-minded warlords had seized control of Japan's destiny prior to the Russo-Japanese War of 1904. Fewer still knew that Tokyo had been actively preparing for hostilities with America for the better part of three decades.

Japan's increasingly aggressive posture had caused military leaders in Washington to draw up a tentative battle plan for a U.S.-Japanese conflict as early as 1906, while Teddy Roosevelt was still in the White House. They foresaw a strong possibility of both the Philippines and Hawaii being overrun quickly in such a war.

The planners predicted that it would take at least six months for the United States to retaliate effectively, giving the Japanese time to firmly entrench themselves in the captured territories. Even then, America's military supply lines would be stretched over more than 13,000 miles of ocean and hostile territory. Well-defended naval bases and fueling stations in the western Pacific could help offset this huge disadvantage—and no U.S. possession was better suited for this purpose than Wake.

After World War I, with Germany eliminated as a sea power, the U.S. War and Navy departments quickly focused on Japan as America's most likely future adversary. In the summer of 1919, their concern prompted Navy Secretary Josephus Daniels to divide the Navy into two separate battle fleets for the first time in the nation's history. One of them was to be permanently assigned to the Pacific.

In February 1922, after more than a little arm-twisting by Secretary of State Charles Evans Hughes, Japan agreed to sign the Washington Naval Treaty, which limited Japan to just 300,000 tons of capital ships while allowing the U.S. and Britain 500,000 tons each. Japan accepted these limitations in exchange for an American promise not to fortify the Philippines, Guam, or any other U.S. possession west of Hawaii.

The agreement clearly included "useless" little Wake Island.

Neither side, as it turned out, had much interest in honoring the terms of the agreement. But over the next decade or so, the treaty would prove considerably more damaging to the United States than to its future foe. The restrictions it imposed were viewed as a serious defeat by high-ranking Navy officers because they set strict tonnage ceilings on U.S. aircraft carriers and battleships. In exchange, all America got was a negligible tonnage margin for smaller, less powerful vessels. Washington diplomats, lawmakers, and bureaucrats, however, maintained that Japan's hands had been successfully tied and allowed the treaty to be used as a license for complacency and military neglect. The Atlantic and Pacific fleets were again combined into one downsized U.S. Fleet. Without bases to support naval operations in the western Pacific and faced by deep budget cuts after the Great Depression began in 1929, the fleet lost its power to operate effectively—much less aggressively—in the Far East. Tokyo's militants, meanwhile, kept right on priming their arsenal for war.

On the morning of May 9, 1935, when the chartered steamer *North Haven* arrived at Wake, the stage was set for America to abandon its end of the bargain as well. Piled in the *North Haven*'s hold and lashed to her decks were a hundred freightcar loads of materials and equipment for the new Pan Am facilities on Wake, and in her cabins were construction crews ready to put them to use. Wake's transformation was about to begin in earnest, and it would never be the same again.

"Wake Island Is Stirred to Life," read the headline in *The New York Times* of May 13, 1935.

By that time, 113 construction workers under the supervision of William Grooch, a Pan Am manager with experience in remote areas and primitive circumstances, were hard at work. The airline first planned to locate its facilities on Wilkes Island, which was adjacent to a natural break in the reef and seemed the most convenient place to ferry equipment and workers ashore. But Charles R. Russell, the expedition's chief engineer, quickly ruled out Wilkes as a suitable building site for the "airport village" envisioned by Pan Am.

The beach on Wilkes was strewn with scores of large coral boulders, and the interior was largely covered with almost impenetrable masses of trees and brush. Suitable building sites were scarce, and even moving supplies was difficult. More important, though, Russell could tell that Wilkes had been inundated by seawater not many years ago. The vegetation was just as thick on parts of Peale Island, but the flood danger was considerably less, so Peale was selected as the site for Pan Am's base.

Wake didn't yield willingly to civilization. It resisted every inch of progress, and the vagaries of the place turned the simplest tasks into backbreaking ordeals. The *North Haven* couldn't simply drop anchor on the north side of Peale and unload her supplies directly onto the chosen atoll.

The ocean there was too deep and the winds too strong for that. The workers ended up having to unload their goods on Wilkes, after all, then ferry them across the lagoon to Peale. It took more than a week of eighteen-hour days and large doses of dynamite to widen the shallow channel between Wilkes and Wake proper to allow a motor launch and lighter to transport material through it. Workmen also constructed a short-haul railroad to speed the material-moving process.

Meanwhile, others hacked with axes and machetes at the junglelike growth where the Pan Am "village" would rise and built a 400-foot-long redwood seaplane dock in the lagoon. Facing the dock, they erected an attractive, crescent-shaped compound of neat white buildings, which encompassed quarters for airline employees, various workshops, offices, storerooms, and other facilities.

Towering over the development were the cross-shaped, fifty-foot-tall antennas without which future Pan Am flights might never have been able to locate tiny Wake. The antennas were capable of picking up radio signals from planes as much as 2,200 miles away.

In August 1935, the first Pan Am seaplane to reach Wake skimmed across the lagoon and taxied up to the new dock. The pilot complained, however, that too many dangerous obstacles remained around the just-completed marine runway. Many more weeks of dynamiting would be necessary before landing conditions were considered safe enough for scheduled service to begin.

A month earlier, the *North Haven* had returned to San Francisco, where it was reloaded with the components of two complete prefabricated hotels, one for Midway and the other for Wake. When the single-story, forty-five-room Pan American Airways Inn was completed on Peale in May 1936, it became the centerpiece of what the men who built it had come to call "PAAville." The hotel featured comfortable screened verandas, ceiling fans, handsome wicker furniture, a well-appointed art deco dining room, tall drinks served by white-jacketed waiters, tennis courts, and other amenities specifically designed to make the hot tropical climate less oppressive to well-heeled air travelers bound to and from the Orient.

That October, Pan Am officially inaugurated its "sky highway" to Asia with two Clipper flights each week, one eastbound and one westbound. At long last, the first Americans other than a few score military personnel and construction workers began finding their way to "the most isolated spot in the world."

There were no tourist-class seats available on the Clippers. Most of their pampered passengers were top-level executives, wealthy adventurers, high government officials, or celebrities. Each paid around $1,800, the equivalent of two years' salary for a typical American wage earner of the period, for the privilege of flying across the Pacific.

The trip from California to Hong Kong took approximately sixty hours of actual flying time, assuming the planes encountered no serious weather delays. Normally, a round trip consumed a minimum of twelve days, and safety concerns required that the trips be broken up into daily segments averaging about a thousand miles with a stopover each night. The Clippers usually arrived at midafternoon and departed the next morning, which didn't leave passengers with a lot of time to kill on Wake.

Nevertheless, Pan Am went to considerable lengths to offer various diversions. Regardless of the season, it was almost always warm enough for swimming, and passengers had ample opportunity to take a dip in a protected pool during their rest stop. They could also take rides in a glass-bottomed boat and view the lagoon's "remarkable collections" of rare tropical fish. Archery, skeet shooting, and an extensive library were available, as well.

Airline officials even tried to utilize Wake's boisterous, burgeoning rat population as a form of entertainment. Clipper passengers were given a pamphlet called "Welcome to Wake," which invited them to pick up air rifles at the Pan Am office and join nightly rat-hunting expeditions. Or, if guests preferred to make it a spectator sport, they could merely watch while the airline's Guamanian houseboys attacked the pesty rodents with rocks and sticks.

These forays scarcely caused a dent in the rat population. With human food available in large quantities for the first time in their existence on Wake, the rats proliferated wildly, swarming through the developed areas of Peale, invading the buildings, and raiding the Pan Am flower and vegetable gardens. They had absolutely no fear of humans, and when hundreds of U.S. servicemen and civilian construction workers reached the atoll a few years later, the problem grew even worse. During the siege of Wake, few Marines were spared the unsavory experience of waking up at night in their foxholes to find small, furry visitors sharing their beds or slithering across their faces.

For bird-watchers, however, Wake was a genuine treasure. This fact was heavily emphasized by Pan Am, along with the excellent fishing in the lagoon, in a none-too-successful effort to promote its most remote outpost as a tourist attraction. To try to increase the occupancy rate at Wake's PAA Inn, which was usually empty for five nights out of every seven, the airline advertised special package deals for anyone willing to stay there for a couple of weeks.

There were few takers, but those who did vacation at Wake got a close-up look at some of the world's rarest—and strangest—feathered creatures. There was, for example, a small, red-eyed bird called a peewee that had to hop wherever it went because it couldn't fly.

Major Walter Bayler, a Marine communications specialist temporarily assigned to Wake in December 1941 to install radio equipment, described the flightless peewee as "just a fluffy ball of feathers with no wings and no tail." The robin-size fowl was indigenous to Australia, and Bayler and other officers used to speculate on how peewees could have reached distant Wake Island in the first place. Nobody was able to offer any plausible solution to the puzzle.

Bayler termed the bosun bird, another extremely rare Wake denizen, "a clumsy, raucous nuisance," whose chief claim to fame was that it "can fly backwards—and often does." Except for its peculiar "reverse gear," the pigeon-size bosun bird's two most striking features were its bloodred beak and two bright vermillion tailfeathers that grew up to twenty inches long.

Wake's aptly named pirate bird had a "villainous face and a disposition to match," Bayler observed, adding: "His racket has the true piratical touch. He hovers high in the air on wide graceful wings till he sees some smaller bird below him capture a morsel of food. Then he swoops down on his victim so fiercely that he frightens the smaller bird into regurgitating his meal. The pirate bird neatly picks it out of the air and bolts it himself."

But to the Marines charged with Wake's defense, the worst thing about the pirate birds was their tendency to fly together in neat, close-order formations. From a distance, the birds could bear an unnerving resemblance to a squadron of Japanese bombers.

Above left: *PFCs Merle Swartz (left) and Artie Stocks on leave in Hawaii in the spring of 1941 before shipping out to Wake.*
(Courtesy Artie Stocks)

Above right: *Just out of boot camp, new Marine Jack Skaggs poses in his dress blues in September 1940. He was still seventeen years old at the time.*
(Courtesy Jack Skaggs)

★ 2 ★

A Massive Awakening

Thanks to Pan Am's hefty investment, steadily advancing technology, and the active interest of the U.S. Navy, Wake had finally become an inhabited place—but just barely. By early 1937, there were about enough full-time residents to field two teams for a baseball game. Except for a twelve-member ground staff, headed by airport manager George Bicknell, and a few carpenters and groundskeepers who stayed on to do landscaping and minor construction, everyone else had left and gone back to the States.

Beyond the boundaries of "PAAville" and the other facilities on Peale, the atoll remained basically untouched by civilization or human hands. Actually, since there was as yet no bridge connecting Peale to Wake proper, both it and Wilkes remained inaccessible to airline passengers. There was nothing to attract them to the other islands, anyway—just more sand, coral, dense undergrowth, and desolation.

Only on the two evenings a week when an eastbound or westbound Clipper was moored at the dock in the lagoon, and the hotel was filled with overnight guests, was there a semblance of normal human activity on Peale. The rest of the time, even around the Pan Am compound, the days dragged, and all of them seemed the same. At best, the routine was boringly repetitive; at worst, the loneliness and isolation could be demoralizing.

For their own physical and mental well-being, it soon became obvious that airline personnel shouldn't be left on Wake for more than six months at a stretch. At first, Chinese domestics were hired to cook, clean, and wait tables at the hotel, but when their terms of service ended, most quit, and it was difficult to find replacements. To keep the staff up to strength, Pan Am turned to Chamorros, natives of Guam, who were more acclimated to life on a small, out-of-the-way island. For the most part, the Chamorros didn't like Wake much better than the Chinese had, but they were in greater need of good-paying jobs, so most of them toughed it out.

Life on Wake continued in this obscure, limited sense for the better part of four years. Now and then, small contingents of strangers came calling by ship or seaplane. Engineers conducted surveys and took measurements; mapmakers drew maps and charts; military observers looked around, made copious notes, and took photographs.

On the atoll itself, nothing changed materially throughout the final years of the 1930s. But in the power centers of Washington, it was a much different story. After nearly twenty years in the driver's seat, the isolationists were finally losing their chokehold on military spending, and FDR's forces in the House and Senate were gaining strength. In May 1938, they succeeded in passing the Naval Expansion Act, authorizing some 200,000 additional tons of U.S. warships and a naval air arm of at least 3,000 planes.

The following month, Navy Secretary Claude Swanson appointed Admiral Arthur J. Hepburn, outgoing commander of the U.S. Fleet, to chair an elite, five-member board to study the need for new naval bases and fortifications. By December 1, 1938, the board had completed what became known as the Hepburn Report. It recommended enlarging a dozen existing bases and building eighteen brand-new ones. Near the top of the list of proposed new bases was Wake Island.

Strategically, the report concluded, Wake was "next in importance" to Midway as a base for aircraft, submarines, land-based forces, and fleet support facilities in the mid-Pacific. In the board's judgment, only Pearl Harbor itself ranked higher in importance than Midway. In other words, Wake had the third-highest priority in the entire Pacific region.

The Hepburn Report portrayed Hawaii as the cornerstone of U.S. naval power in the Pacific and as a potent barrier against any attack on the American mainland. Patrol planes conducting continuous surveillance from a fortified Wake were seen, in turn, as vital cogs in Hawaii's defense. They could provide an early warning of hostile movements by Japan and give U.S. land- and carrier-based planes time to get into the air to counter a Japanese threat to Hawaii.

The report urged Congress to appropriate $7.5 million for initial base development on Wake—and to put a rush on it. The isolationists in Congress were far from ready to capitulate, however. In early 1939, such powerful Republican leaders as FDR-hating Congressman Hamilton Fish of New York did their best to scuttle enabling legislation for the proposed new bases. Fish accused Roosevelt of creating war hysteria and unnecessarily provoking Japan.

A revised version of the bill won final approval in April 1939, but in a political trade-off to gain enough middle-of-the-road "yea" votes for building or expanding bases at Wake, Midway, and ten other sites, Guam became a sacrificial lamb. All mention of Guam was deleted from the legislation, and it would never again be seriously considered as a defendable outpost in the event of war.

Wake wasn't out of the woods yet, either. It still had to get past the capricious congressional funding process. Early in 1940, the House Appropriations Committee cut nearly $4 million from the $9.6 million request for Wake and trimmed the requests for Midway, Palmyra, and Johnston islands in similar fashion. In return for restoring the other cuts, Georgia Congressman Carl Vinson, chairman of the House Naval Affairs Committee, offered to let the base on Wake "go by the board," and his offer was accepted.

For several months, the Wake project wallowed in limbo and looked to be dead, but Navy brass and their allies in Congress kept looking for a way to bring it back to life. They found it in a rash of defense-related bills rushed through Congress in the spring of 1940. One of these was a catchall measure allowing the Navy to spend $144 million on nearly a score of widely scattered naval aviation facilities. Among the funding, apparently unnoticed by isolationist watchdogs, was $7.6 million designated for

"Naval Air Station, Wake Island." Purposely, no doubt, the bill's spending provisions were vaguely worded, allowing the money to be used for "aviation shore facilities...buildings...accessories and defense facilities."

This time, the Navy took no chances on congressional second thoughts. Within weeks, it awarded $30 million worth of contracts—including the Wake project—to a consortium of private U.S. construction companies operating under the name Contractors Pacific Naval Air Bases.

Other legislative hurdles and bureaucratic stumbling blocks still lay ahead before the full $20 million was appropriated to complete the project. It would take six more months before the first nail could be driven, the first concrete poured, or the first excavation blasted into the coral. Worse yet, two long, pivotal years had been lost and could never be reclaimed.

But the machinery had been set in motion, and there was no turning back now. A massive awakening was about to take place on Wake Island.

Release of the Hepburn Report marked the first time in a quarter century that Navy brass had openly advocated a tougher, more aggressive U.S. posture in the Pacific. But the admirals were well aware that the pendulum of public opinion hadn't yet swung completely over to their side, so they were still treading lightly. They put heavy emphasis on the defensive value of having a fully operational base in the far western Pacific, and—almost as important from the strategists' point of view—denying the use of Wake to the enemy.

What they pointedly didn't mention during their prolonged fight for approval and funding was that a fortified Wake also offered intriguing offensive possibilities. Forward-thinking naval strategists could see air power becoming the dominant factor in future sea battles—and Wake serving as a sort of "stationary aircraft carrier" capable of launching raids against any number of enemy targets.

In the Army, too, top military planners clearly foresaw a major offensive role for Wake in War Plan Orange, the "grand strategy" they were devising to deal with the growing Japanese menace in the Pacific. Dozens of America's new B-17 heavy bombers, the most powerful warplanes the world had yet seen, were already rolling off the assembly lines at Boeing Aircraft.

From an airbase on Wake, the "Flying Fortresses" could utilize their 2,000-mile range to strike virtually any point in the Japanese empire.

The Marines, meanwhile, were developing their own special plans for Wake. In May 1939, Marine Colonel Harry Pickett had been dispatched to Wake, Midway, and Johnston islands to draw up proposed antiaircraft and shore defense systems for the new bases. A month later, Major General Thomas Holcomb, the Marines Corps commandant, approved the organizational outline for a new "Wake Island Defense Detachment."

The outline called for Wake to be garrisoned by a force of 510 Marines equipped with three three-inch antiaircraft batteries of four guns each, three five-inch shore batteries of two guns each, two dozen .50-caliber machine guns, and two dozen .30-caliber machine guns. Despite minor shifts in strategy, periodic juggling and reorganization of units, and other assorted tweakings by the brass, Wake's defenses would be composed of these same basic elements when the first Japanese attack came thirty months later. There would be one key difference, however: considerably fewer men.

Everywhere the generals and admirals looked, as tensions steadily mounted between mid-1939 and late 1941, the problem was inevitably the same: They could plot and plan until hell froze over, but until more armaments could be produced and more men recruited for military service, there wouldn't be enough of either to go around.

By now, it was unnervingly clear that America could never defend its Pacific interests against this prospective enemy called "Orange" with an antiquated, undersized fleet; a critical shortage of state-of-the-art aircraft; and a Marine Corps smaller than the New York Police Department.

On September 1, 1939, Hitler's well-oiled war machine smashed across the Polish frontier and plunged Europe into the abyss of World War II. As Nazi Panzer divisions roared across the flat countryside toward Warsaw, and Polish resistance crumbled under their tanks and the Luftwaffe's dive bombers, a new word entered America's vocabulary: "blitzkrieg."

Britain and France immediately declared war on Germany—they had no other choice—but Poland fell in just three weeks.

Overnight, Tokyo's ambitions and aggressions seemed far less important to official Washington than they had a few weeks earlier. Even among
the most ardent preparedness advocates, the threat of a war with Japan in
the Pacific had to be relegated to back-burner status in the face of the con-
flagration raging on the opposite side of the world. To most typical grass-
roots Americans, Japan had never been a significant cause of worry,
anyway.

For a military establishment struggling to overcome two decades of de-
cline, deterioration, and forced downsizing, the crisis in Europe posed a
monstrous dilemma. Many of the admirals and generals remained convinced that the Japanese threat was real and growing, but FDR's Washington was determined to do everything possible to help the Allies withstand
Hitler's relentless onslaught.

In the spring of 1940, German armies overran Denmark, Norway, Bel-
gium, Luxembourg, and the Netherlands in quick succession. France itself
collapsed in a matter of days. By mid-June, the Nazis were holding a victory celebration in Paris, and Britain stood alone while bombs rained
down on London.

Horror and disbelief gripped America. As Allied resistance withered in
Europe, the last pretenses of U.S. neutrality quickly dissolved. FDR designated the United States as "the great arsenal of democracy," and, with minimal resistance, Congress approved sending billions of dollars' worth of
arms to Britain. Yet in this atmosphere, getting men and materiel committed to budding defensive operations in the Pacific was like pulling teeth.

Behind the scenes, however, Roosevelt was still committed to halting
Japanese aggression in China and protecting vulnerable British, Dutch,
and French territories in the Far East, as well as those of the United States.
Even more than FDR, Secretary of State Cordell Hull advocated an increasingly hard line in dealing with Tokyo. Hull was a straitlaced, highly
principled Tennessean who despised duplicity, and because American
cryptographers had cracked Japan's top-secret diplomatic code, he knew
beyond doubt that Japanese officials had been lying to him consistently
and could never be trusted again.

On September 27, 1940, when Japan signed a treaty aligning itself with

Germany and Italy and creating the Berlin-Rome-Tokyo Axis, it was the last straw as far as Hull was concerned. He had little difficulty persuading Roosevelt to declare severe economic sanctions against Japan unless it withdrew from the alliance with Hitler and Mussolini.

Ten months later, in July 1941, when Japanese forces occupied what was then French Indochina, Roosevelt announced a total embargo on all American oil shipments to petroleum-starved Japan. At the same time, he froze all of Japan's assets in the United States and completely suspended all U.S. trade with the country. Shipments to Japan of other vital materials, such as scrap iron, had already been cut off in an effort to force it to pull out of China.

From Tokyo's point of view, these were nothing short of acts of war, and shutting off the flow of U.S. oil was the final blow that made armed conflict with America unavoidable. From that point on, no amount of negotiations could narrow the widening gulf between the two nations. Japan's survival as a modern power depended on securing adequate petroleum, and the quickest way to do that in the face of the U.S. embargo was to seize the oil-rich Dutch East Indies, now virtually defenseless after the fall of the Netherlands. But the Imperial Cabinet, dominated by War Minister Hideki Tojo and militant Foreign Minister Yosuke Matsuoka, knew that America would never stand still for this.

The solution: Strike America first in a massive surprise attack, cripple its Pacific Fleet, decimate its air force, overrun its island bases, and destroy its ability to retaliate. Then grab as much of Asia as necessary.

After long delay and against tremendous odds—and in the midst of this precarious scenario—the funding had been secured for a major base on Wake Island. But building adequate fortifications, assembling sufficient weaponry, and finding enough trained personnel to keep it safely in U.S. hands in the face of a Japanese attack would be a herculean task.

The first phase of that task took place on the docks in Honolulu during the first three weeks of December 1940. On Pier 31A, stevedores labored day and night to load vast quantities of equipment and supplies aboard a Navy transport named the U.S.S. *William Ward Burrows*. There were 2,000 tons of it in all—trucks, tractors, bulldozers, cement mixers, generators, water distillation plants, refrigeration units, stacks of lumber and structural steel, barrels of oil and gasoline, thousands of cases of dynamite, and mountains of food.

When the hold of the *Burrows* was filled to capacity, more cargo was stacked on her decks. When the decks wouldn't hold any more, the stevedores turned their attention to a 40-by-100-foot wooden barge attached to the *Burrows* by a towline. It was called the *Wake No. 1*, and soon it was also groaning under tons of heavy equipment.

In the words of Captain Ross Dierdorff, the *Burrows*'s skipper, the ship, the barge, and an accompanying fifty-five-foot tug, the *Pioneer*, carried "everything needed to set up a self-sustaining community for eighty men and to pave the way for hundreds more."

On the morning after Christmas, several dozen construction workers, some of them still wearing leis and nursing hangovers from the previous night's merriment, kissed their wives and girlfriends good-bye and boarded the *Burrows* for the voyage to Wake Island. The trip was no picnic. It took two weeks to cover the 2,000 miles, and the barge broke loose from the ship twice in heavy seas. By the time the workers reached Wake and started the gigantic job of unloading their supplies and machinery, it was January 8, 1941.

The "Pioneer Party" of contractors aboard the *Burrows* were the first of 1,146 civilian workers who would be brought to Wake over the next few months to tackle one of the most gargantuan rush jobs in U.S. military history. Their major assignments included building an airfield capable of handling the largest military planes of the day, cutting a new channel through Wilkes Island, dredging the lagoon to remove dangerous coral heads, and constructing roads, barracks, storage facilities, workshops, and a hospital.

Unfortunately, however, there were no provisions in their contract for gouging out bunkers, revetments, gun emplacements, and other fortifications in the coral. The structures most crucial to Wake's defense would be left largely up to the Marines—and the first of them wouldn't reach Wake until seven months later.

Within days of the contractors' arrival, the little atoll was transformed from one of the most uneventful spots on the globe to one of the busiest. Workmen swarmed over all three islands, dredging, dynamiting, bulldozing, and building in all directions.

The man in charge of this hectic flurry of activity was construction superintendent Nathan Dan Teters, a native Ohioan with an engineering degree from Washington State College. Teters had served as an Army sergeant during World War I, and by all accounts, he was as rugged as any of the men who worked for him. A strapping Irishman with both a stubborn streak and an infectious sense of humor, he was described by one naval officer as someone "who would be good to have along in a fight." Most of the men who worked under him on Wake considered him a "real good boss."

Teters was an experienced engineer who ran his own contracting company for a while, then went broke and joined the Morrison-Knudsen Company, a fast-growing construction firm based in Boise, Idaho. He was such a valued hand that M-K made a major exception to its rules and allowed him to take his wife, Florence, with him to Wake. Mrs. Teters was one of only three women on the island, but with tensions steadily mounting, she and the other two—wives of Pan Am supervisors—were evacuated in early November 1941.

M-K's rise had been fueled by work on the Boulder and Grand Coulee dam projects, and by the end of the 1930s, it was recognized as one of the nation's leaders in the field of heavy construction. In 1940, M-K became one of the companies forming the consortium known as Contractors Pacific Naval Air Bases. When the firm was assigned to handle the $20 million chore of turning a desert island into a bastion of U.S. power in the Pacific, Teters was named to run the show. He was answerable only to Lieutenant Commander Elmer B. Greey, the Navy's resident officer in charge, and M-K Vice President George Youmans, stationed in Hawaii. For everybody else concerned—civilian and military alike—Teters's word was law where the CPNAB construction on Wake was concerned.

The *William Ward Burrows* paid six more visits to Wake between January and November 1941, each time bringing additional men and equipment.

The Navy also pressed three other cargo ships—the *Regulus,* the *Sirius,* and the *Kaula*—into service in its crash program of base-building. But most of the nearly 43,000 tons of construction materials delivered during this time came aboard pairs of barges drawn by deep-sea tugboats on tedious, monthlong round trips from Pearl Harbor.

Yet even with this constant flow of supplies, there was the inescapable problem of "hurry up and wait." Many times from May 1941 on, construction came to a near standstill on Wake because workmen ran out of essential materials. By August, the M-K workforce had swelled to 800 men, and more were on the way, but Teters found it increasingly difficult to keep all his crews busy.

Nevertheless, their transformation of the atoll by late that summer was almost miraculous. There were now two large camps that faced each other across the widest part of the lagoon at the ends of the northern and southern legs of Wake proper. Camp One, the "tent city" just across the channel from Wilkes Island, was where the contractors had originally been housed, but it was now occupied by the Marines. As military field quarters went, it was fairly comfortable. The wood-framed, wood-decked tents stood in neat rows, their sides screened to let the breezes blow through, and electricity was provided by on-site generators. Nearby were a fully equipped mess hall, a post exchange, and an officers' club with iceboxes full of beer.

By comparison, however, Camp Two, which the civilians now called home, represented true luxury where only a wasteland had existed a few months before. Located on Wake proper adjacent to Peale Island and connected to the Pan Am facilities on Peale by a new causeway, Camp Two consisted of permanent wooden barracks that were superior in comfort and amenities to those on most stateside military bases of the period. The camp also included a modern hospital, a well-stocked commissary, a barbershop, an outdoor movie theater, an ice-cream parlor, tennis courts, and even a small, protected swimming pool in the lagoon. Military personnel were allowed to use the amenities at Camp Two and could reach them via a new seven-mile-long road of crushed coral that curved around the lagoon to connect the two camps.

East of Camp One, down on the fattest part of the base of Wake's V, the new airfield was nearing completion. Its 200-foot-wide main runway was just a shade less than a mile long and could handle the largest existing military aircraft. Adjacent to the airfield were eight partially underground magazines made of reinforced concrete. Barracks for pilots and crew members, as well as various shops and warehouses, were under construction nearby. Near the east end of the runway was an aboveground gasoline storage tank with a 25,000-gallon capacity.

Over on Peale, meanwhile, next to the PAA Inn, a new seaplane ramp jutted into the lagoon near where barracks and a hospital for the new naval air station were being built. Dredges were working in the lagoon to clear more landing area for seaplanes.

Little work had been done on Wilkes so far, except for building one road that ran the length of the island, but a submarine base was planned there. In preparation, a whole new channel was being cut through the island to allow better access to the lagoon, and the existing channel was also being deepened and widened. There was still no bridge connecting Wilkes to Wake proper, but small boats were used to ferry men and materials back and forth, and construction was about to begin on several powder magazines. The only prominent structures on Wilkes were a couple of aboveground fuel storage tanks belonging to Pan Am.

Considering that Wake's full development was originally envisioned as a two- to three-year project for CPNAB, the first months of work had produced impressive results. The problem, though, was one of skewed priorities—the old cart-before-the-horse situation. The gun emplacements, earthworks, underground shelters, camouflage, aerial patrols, beach defenses, and air raid warning equipment needed to protect all this other construction from the impact of a sudden attack were nowhere in sight.

Back at Pearl, an increasingly nervous Navy hierarchy was doing all it could to speed up the actual fortification of Wake. On April 18, 1941, Admiral Husband E. Kimmel, commander in chief of the U.S. Pacific Fleet, expressed his fear that defensive efforts had started too late.

It seems ironic that Kimmel, who would be blamed for the Navy's lack of preparedness in the disaster of December 7 and forced to resign afterward, should sound such a strident warning more than seven months before the Japanese attack.

"The strategic importance of Wake is increasingly evident, as one inquires into the means by which the Pacific Fleet may carry on offensive operations to the westward," Kimmel wrote in a letter to Admiral Harold R. Stark, chief of naval operations. "If Wake be defended, then for the Japanese to reduce it would require extended operations of their naval forces in an area where we might be able to get at them. . . . We should try, by every possible means, to get the Japanese to expose naval units. In order to do this, we must provide objectives that require such exposure."

One of the immediate steps urged by Kimmel was to place a substantial Marine force on Wake no later than June 1. But it was June 23 before Stark even issued an order to send elements of the First Marine Defense Battalion to Wake "as soon as practicable." Almost two more months would elapse before the first small group of Marines—173 enlisted men and 5 officers—finally reached the island on August 19.

Corporals Frank Gross and John Johnson were among that first "Pioneer Platoon" of Marines. The two young Missourians found that six five-inch guns, salvaged from World War I–era Navy cruisers, had already been delivered to Wake for use as shore batteries, but there were no platforms or protective emplacements for them. Virtually no other work of a defensive nature had been completed, either.

At first, the atmosphere on Wake was peaceful and relaxed. As far as Gross, Johnson, and the rest of their group knew, there was no threat of war out there in the middle of nowhere, and there was no sense of urgency about anything. They had plenty of free time to fish, swim, explore the beaches, and play cards. The pushing didn't start until Major Devereux showed up two months later. "Then all hell broke loose," said Gross. "We didn't get but one other day off until the shooting started."

About that time, Gross wrote a letter to his sister back home, reassuring her that he was in absolutely no danger. "The war's in Europe," he told her confidently. "The further I get out in the Pacific, the further I get away from it."

The carrier U.S.S. Enterprise *delivered the planes and pilots of Marine Fighter Squadron VMF-211 to Wake on December 4, 1941.*
(National Archives)

Too Little and Too Late

At the time he reached Wake Island on October 15, 1941, aboard the U.S.S. *Regulus,* Major James Patrick Sinnot Devereux had been a Marine for eighteen years and a commissioned officer for sixteen. Born in 1903 in Cuba, where his father was a U.S. Army medical officer, Devereux had served in China, the Philippines, Nicaragua, Pearl Harbor, and various stateside posts. He'd been stationed on the Yangtze River and at the U.S. Legation in Peking as conflict intensified between China and Japan, and he'd seen action in the "banana wars" of Central America, but he'd never had a tougher mission than the one facing him now.

His assignment was to take command of the elements of the First Marine Defense Battalion that had begun arriving on Wake two months earlier and get them and their weaponry into shape to repel an attack as soon as humanly possible. For all practical purposes, that meant starting from scratch and struggling against odds that increased with each passing day.

Devereux stood barely five feet five inches tall, and his thin mustache and flawless dress gave him a rather dapper look, but he had a well-established reputation as a no-nonsense commander, a stickler for regulations, and a tough-as-nails taskmaster. He missed his wife, Mary, and his seven-year-old son, Paddy, who had stayed at the family home in Maryland when he shipped out for the Pacific in January 1941, but he also enjoyed being a Marine officer and liked looking the part. One of the major assets he brought to Wake was his consummate skill as an artillery tactician. Another was total dedication to planning and preparation. His established leadership style and ability won him respect wherever he went from the men he led—if sometimes grudgingly.

"He wasn't a particularly warm guy, and he didn't get overly chummy with his men," said Corporal Frank Gross, "but the better you got to know him, the more you trusted his judgment. He just struck you as somebody who knew what he was doing."

Bryghte D. Godbold, a scholarly twenty-six-year-old captain from Alabama who served as Devereux's strongpoint commander on Peale Island, described his superior officer as "quiet and reserved with impeccable character." The major wasn't particularly charismatic or companionable, but men who served with him came to realize that they could trust his word implicitly. He wanted things run the right way, but he wasn't a meddler who tried to tell his junior officers how to do their job.

While he was desperately striving to bolster Wake's defenses, however, Devereux picked up a highly unflattering nickname. By the time PFC Wiley Sloman got to Wake, Devereux had been there for a couple of weeks, and he was driving the men really hard. One of the first cracks Sloman heard from the Marines who'd been there for a while was that Devereux's initials—JPS—stood for "just plain shit." Sloman interpreted it as more of a description of the kind of grind Devereux was putting the men through than a putdown of the major himself.

That grind consisted of twelve hours or more a day, seven days a week, of bone-wearying labor, and it continued without letup through November into early December. There were no drills, no training, no target practice—just the endless drudgery of gouging out holes in the coral for machine gun emplacements, digging pits for ack-ack batteries, filling and stacking sandbags, building platforms for the five-inch guns and their range finders, and so on into the night.

Someone found out that Sloman had experience as a carpenter—actually just a few things he'd picked up working summers on a building crew when he was a kid—and that meant extra work and responsibility for the young Texan. From that day on, Sloman spent a lot of his time sawing boards, driving nails, and overseeing construction details.

Many of the Marines' requests for lumber and other building materials were denied because most was reserved for structures at the naval air station. On Peale, the Marines couldn't get enough timbers to support the sides of a magazine they were trying to build for artillery shells. The walls collapsed, prompting Lieutenant Woodrow Kessler, the sharp-spoken commander of Battery B, to complain that all the ammunition for his five-inch guns was stuck "around in little holes covered with tar paper" and unprotected from anything more serious than rain.

Meanwhile, there wasn't enough camouflage netting, so the Marines cut strips of burlap and doused them with various kinds of paint. They also cut bushes and clumps of brush and nailed them to boards that were placed around the guns, then moved when it was time to fire them. Lieutenant John A. McAlister, who commanded Sloman's Battery L on Wilkes, proved he had a creative streak to go with his hot temper by planting fast-growing vines to help cover his five-inchers.

The Marine Defense Battalions, first organized and activated in 1940, were designed as small, flexible units capable of meeting and countering various hostile actions. In the official language of the Corps, they were responsible for "rendering our bases relatively secure against air raids, hit-and-run surface attacks, or even minor landings."

Each battalion was seen as a highly versatile force, able to provide anti-aircraft protection and stand off attacks by lighter men-of-war and transports. In the event of a landing by enemy ground forces, battalion personnel were expected to leave their artillery batteries and "fight on the beaches with individual weapons in the tradition that every Marine, first and last, is an infantryman."

It sounded good on paper, but some glaring problems developed when these theories were put in practice. Among the most critical was a severe shortage of manpower. The official recommended strength of a defense battalion was originally set at 939 enlisted men and 43 officers, but fewer than one-third that number were on Wake when Devereux got there. Ideally, one full battalion would be assigned to each of the new Pacific island bases, but the First Defense Battalion ended up being divided between

Wake and Midway, and—as Sloman's experience illustrated—its components were shifted around hither and yon in the summer and fall of 1941.

When Sloman, along with 199 other enlisted men and 9 officers, disembarked from the U.S.S. *Castor* on November 1 and 2, Wake's defense battalion contingent grew to 15 officers and 373 enlisted men. There would be no further additions. As it stood, one three-inch antiaircraft battery was entirely without personnel, and each of the other two batteries could man only three of its four guns. In other words, only six of the twelve ack-ack guns could be utilized, and there was far less than half the personnel needed to man the twenty-four .50-caliber antiaircraft machine guns and the thirty .30-caliber ground-defense machine guns. Only the crews of the three five-inch seacoast batteries were anywhere near full strength. Of all the batteries on the island, only Godbold's three-inchers on Peale had their full training complement of 62 men and 2 officers, and that was less than half the 140 men and 4 officers authorized by a U.S. Army battery with virtually the same weapons.

This was cause enough for concern, but the problem of shortages and makeshift solutions ran much deeper, permeating the whole garrison. Tiny as Wake Atoll is, it has twenty miles of shoreline, and even if enough personnel had been available to man all the machine guns, there was only one gun for every quarter mile of beachfront on the three islands.

Virtually every other section of the garrison was similarly shorthanded. On Devereux's staff, for example, Major George S. Potter Jr., an Annapolis graduate and one of the first artillerymen to complete heavy weapons training at Quantico, Virginia, served as executive officer—and also as adjutant, operations officer, intelligence officer, and supply officer. He was a virtual one-man staff.

Vital equipment of various kinds was simply not to be had. Only one three-inch battery had the full allowance of fire-control equipment. One had no height finder and had to get its altitude data by phone from another battery. Worse yet, the Navy and Army personnel sent to Wake just before the war started were without rifles, gas masks, or helmets—even the officers lacked sidearms—and the Marines had none to spare.

The semiautomatic Garand M-1 rifle had been adopted by the U.S. military in 1936 and put into production that same year, but its distribution had proceeded at a snail's pace. In late 1941, Wake's Marines still carried bolt-action 1903 Springfields. They also wore World War I vintage, British-style helmets.

Another Achilles' heel for the defenders was the antiquated communications system linking the widely scattered batteries and outposts with command posts on the three islands. The telephone lines were old and frayed in spots, and since there'd been no time or equipment to bury them, they were all run aboveground, where they could be easily cut or damaged. Many were strung along main roads and readily visible if enemy troops came ashore.

Except for a crude, unreliable walkie-talkie network, these phone lines were the defenders' only means of keeping their commanders informed of battlefield conditions.

By early November, it was painfully clear to Devereux that no matter how hard and long he drove his men, they couldn't hope to complete all the necessary fortifications in time. He worried constantly that an attack might come any day, any moment, and he could take little comfort from what his superiors had told him just before he left Pearl Harbor. When he asked what he and his men should do in case of a full-scale attack before defensive preparations were complete, he received a blunt, five-word reply from Colonel Harry Pickett, Admiral Kimmel's assistant operations officer:

"Do the best you can."

That was precisely what Devereux had done, but his Marines' picks and shovels weren't enough. To have any remote chance of finishing the most vital portions of the work before the end of the year, he needed help from the civilian contractors and their vast array of heavy equipment.

As senior line officer on Wake, Devereux was also island commander, but he had no jurisdiction over M-K employees, who answered solely to the contractors' general superintendent, Dan Teters. The civilians would come under Devereux's orders only in an emergency. He had no authority to pull civilian crews off their regular jobs on routine projects to build gun emplacements or other essential defense installations.

Devereux credited Teters and Commander Greey, who was supervising the work for the Navy, with giving the Marines "as much help as they could" without robbing their own projects of machines and manpower. If Teters wasn't using one of his bulldozers, he'd let the Marines borrow it for a couple of hours. He also lent Devereux's men some jackhammers to dig the battery emplacements at Toki Point on Peale Island and generally encouraged his contractors to be helpful.

Understandably, though, the civilians were primarily concerned with completing their own assigned tasks. This was a natural reaction, since it was what they were being paid to do, but it left the military garrison with so much construction work to do that it was impossible to carry out the intensive training that Devereux and his officers had planned. A sizable percentage of the Marines on Wake were recent recruits who had been in the Corps for only three or four months.

Complicating matters further, the Marines were frequently pressed into what Devereux called "the filling station business." Flights of B-17s were landing on Wake at regular intervals on their way to the Philippines (where most would be destroyed on the ground before they ever flew a combat mission), and since no provisions had been made to refuel them, the Marines inherited the job.

Tankers anchored offshore were equipped with automatic pumps to deliver their thousands of gallons of gasoline into storage tanks on Wake. But from that point on, the task of moving the fuel to where it was needed had to be done by hand. Marine work parties used small power pumps to empty the big tanks into fifty-gallon drums, then carted the heavy drums to widely scattered fuel dumps hidden in the brush to protect them against enemy attack.

Although a gasoline tanker truck was available, there was no way to fill it quickly enough to service the arriving B-17s and get them on their way on schedule. Instead, the Marines had to carry the heavy drums back to the airfield and pump their contents into the planes. At times, they were kept working in shifts for twenty-four straight hours to finish the task.

Each time a new ship arrived with supplies, it meant further interruptions. Marines were routinely pulled off their regular work details to serve as stevedores. Loading heavy equipment on lighters, unloading it on shore, then delivering it to where it was needed were tasks that could occupy dozens of men for several days.

Many of the Marines and civilians who labored on Wake during these last fleeting days of peace had been brought together there by the same basic set of circumstances—the floundering economy and persistent lack of jobs back home. Despite myriad federal pump-priming programs aimed at stimulating economic growth, the Great Depression had dragged on without much real letup through the late 1930s and into the 1940s. Small businesses, large industries, and the nation's farmers were still suffering, and employment prospects for young men just out of high school or college generally ranged from uninspiring to dismal. In countless youngsters, the long stretch of hard times had stirred up a restless wanderlust. They yearned for escape, adventure, and a fresh start—and they were more than willing to give up drab, familiar surroundings to go in search of them.

Fed up with school and unable to see any future for himself in the little farming community of Leesburg, Indiana, Walter Bowsher had made up his mind in 1932 to seek his fortune elsewhere.

"I ran off from home, and my dad went along with me," Bowsher recalled. "We hitched rides on freight trains and followed the harvests from May to November that year. When the last crop was in, we were in Oklahoma, and I decided to join the Army."

Bowsher was only sixteen, but he was toughened by hard work and as strong as any man, so when his ex-soldier father offered his encouragement, he lied about his age and joined up. After enlisting at Fort Sill, he was assigned to field artillery school, and he found Army life much to his liking. He got a paycheck every month, three square meals a day, and a place to live, which was more than he'd had before.

But when his three-year enlistment was up in 1935, Bowsher decided to give civilian life another try. He went to Iowa and worked for a year and a half, but then he got restless again. By this time, Hitler was on the move and the Japanese had invaded Manchuria. Bowsher could sense that war wasn't far away, and he felt the need to get back in the military. This time, he joined the Marines.

As the second half of the 1930s unfolded, Frank Gross was having similar experiences a few hundred miles away. The second-youngest of twelve children, he'd grown up on his parents' farm near DeWitt, Missouri, and worked there—first for his father, then for his older brother, who took over after his dad retired—from the time he was old enough to plow until he was sixteen. But then he got restless, dropped out of school, and decided he was tired of the same old surroundings, so he hitchhiked to Minnesota, then to North Dakota, paying his way by working in the wheat harvest. Then he hopped a freight train to Washington State.

In 1937, he hoboed down to California "just to look around" and saw the first Marines he'd ever laid eyes on. He also saw a Navy recruiting poster that said "Join the Navy and see the world," and that sounded pretty interesting, too. After Gross got back home, he kept thinking about it. One Saturday in December 1938, he went to Kansas City with every intention of becoming a sailor, but on his way to the Navy recruiting office, he ran into two Marines in their dress-blue tunics and red-striped trousers.

"You'll have to wait ninety days to ship out with the Navy, son," they told Gross, "but if you sign up with us, we can have you on your way in a week."

"Okay, why not?" Gross said. "It's better than hoeing that corn back on the farm." On January 5, 1939, a few days after his eighteenth birthday, he was on his way to boot camp.

Clifton A. Sanders, meanwhile, had followed the same path as the Depression-era "Okies" immortalized in John Steinbeck's *The Grapes of Wrath*. He fled his birthplace of Comanche, Oklahoma, and the state's notorious "Dust Bowl" of the late 1930s to head for California. He didn't have much luck finding a decent job there, either, so he joined the Marines in Bakersfield in October 1939.

The story was much the same for Glen Walden, a young Arkansan, except that he became a civilian bulldozer operator on Wake instead of a Marine. Walden was in a Civilian Conservation Corps (CCC) camp in Idaho that was about to be shut down when he heard that a construction company in Boise was looking for people to go to Wake Island. Walden was only nineteen, and the minimum age for workers sent to Wake was supposed to be twenty-one, but when M-K officials looked him over, they decided Walden was big enough for the job, so they hired him anyway.

The work was far from easy, but wages earned by Walden and the other 1,145 contractors on Wake in December 1941 were substantial for the period. Base salaries started at around $140 per month for unskilled laborers who would have been lucky to earn $10 to $15 per week in the States—if they could find a job. Skilled workmen could earn up to $500 per month, or two or three times the stateside average. Many workers also collected an additional $50 to $100 per month in overtime, plus bonuses for each month they stayed beyond the first ninety days. As a further incentive, en route to their new jobs, the men were treated to cruises aboard luxury passenger liners and Hawaiian vacations in posh hotels. On Wake, there was little to spend money on, so a man could build up a significant nest egg during a nine-to-twelve-month assignment.

Twenty-one-year-old civilian John Rogge had been out of high school and knocking around his small hometown of Weiser, Idaho, for about three years when he heard about the Wake job. On June 4, 1941, he went down to Boise to apply, got hired as an office clerk, and less than two weeks later was aboard the cruise liner S.S. *Lurline* bound for Hawaii. "They put up six of us guys in the bridal suite—the fanciest surroundings any of us had ever seen—and the food was wonderful," Rogge said. "We lived it up for another week or so in Honolulu before they loaded us on an old transport, the U.S.S. *Henderson,* for the trip to Wake. That brought us back down to earth again."

Civilian Chalas Loveland of Boise had also just turned twenty-one, and the draft board was breathing down his neck that spring. One way or another, he figured he was going to be shipping out soon, but as a canteen worker on Wake he'd be doing a job classified as vital to the nation's defense. Not only would it keep him out of the service, but it also paid a lot better than the Army. "A buck private's pay was $21 a month, and M-K offered me $130," Loveland said, "so it wasn't a hard choice for me. I'd probably have signed up even if I'd known the war was coming."

For many of the young Marine enlistees who found their way to the remote Pacific outpost, however, a patriotic spirit and an unabashed urge to "do something" for their country were additional major motivators. These often played as large a role as youthful adventurism in bringing them there.

Robert M. Hanna, a strikingly handsome young second lieutenant from Fort Worth, Texas, originally assigned to Wake as a machine gun officer, would emerge as one of its foremost heroes and eventually retire from the Marine Corps as a full colonel. But Hanna's first military experience had come as a high school cadet in the Reserve Officer Training Corps. By the time he enrolled at North Texas Agricultural College in the small town of Arlington, his sights were set on becoming a career officer; it simply felt like the "right thing to do." In 1932, he left school and joined the Army's 77th Field Artillery, but it took six years and a switch to the Marines before he won his commission in 1938.

Captain Bryghte Godbold, a willow-thin officer with a soft southern accent, a gentlemanly manner, and a degree in electrical engineering, followed a similarly indirect path to the Marine Corps and the role of strongpoint commander on Peale Island. He'd signed up for the Army ROTC at Auburn University, and after two years, he made up his mind to stay in the program and try for a commission. In 1936, he'd been one of the university's two highest-ranking ROTC graduates, a distinction that brought an offer of the second-lieutenant's bars he wanted. "The difference was," said Godbold, "the offer was from the Marines, not the Army."

Wiley Sloman had never been to college, but he also had no doubt that he wanted to serve. "I joined the Marine Reserve when I was fifteen," he said. "Everybody in the unit knew I wasn't old enough—the company clerk was my high school English teacher, and the first sergeant was my neighbor—but they kind of looked the other way and let me in. As young as I was, I was dead certain we were going to be in a war before long, but I always figured we'd be fighting the Nazis when it happened. I never once gave any thought to Japan."

Up until he went on active duty in the summer of 1939, Sloman had remained a typical small-town kid who never traveled far beyond the confines of Texas City. A trip to the Texas Centennial Exposition in Dallas in 1936 had been the longest trip of his life, and his greatest accomplishment had been graduating from high school as one of a class of thirty students.

But by then he'd learned a lot of things that weren't taught in the classroom, some of which would stand him in good stead in the Marines. His grandfather had been an expert woodworker, and Wiley had picked up a smattering of the craft during their long hours together. "Gramps" had also been a prodigious walker who'd set off on a ten-mile hike at the drop of a hat, and his grandson had learned to take long, purposeful strides by mimicking him. From the example of his father, who worked as a longshoreman, a truck driver, an oilfield roughneck, and just about anything else he could do to turn a dollar, Wiley had come to accept the necessity of physical labor and even appreciate its merits.

As a teenager, Sloman had run with a somewhat older crowd, and he was husky and muscular for his age. When he wasn't dragging two-by-sixes around a construction site or drilling with the Marine Reserves, he often worked after school on the Texas City docks, loading scrap iron aboard ships bound for Japan.

"We used to joke about the Japs shooting that stuff back at us," he said. "It turned out that was just what they did."

During the first week of November 1941, Devereux and the commanders of other budding island bases in the Pacific received a terse communiqué from Navy headquarters at Pearl Harbor: "International situation indicates that you should be on alert."

To Devereux, this warning meant it was time to curtail all nonessential construction. He wanted to turn the civilians' full and immediate attention to defensive fortifications—bunkers, magazines, artillery emplacements, bomb shelters, and protective revetments for the squadron of planes that was supposed to be coming to Wake.

Of course, he could do nothing without first clearing it with headquarters, so he fired a loaded question back to Pearl in a priority cable: "Does international situation indicate employment of contractors' men on defense installations which are far from complete?"

Devereux felt so certain of an immediate affirmative reply that he called a conference with Teters and Commander Greey to plan a full-scale refocusing of civilian efforts. Both men were completely cooperative, and together they began organizing work gangs and making lists of equipment that could be shifted to bomb shelters, aircraft revetments, and other defensive installations. However, they delayed actually transferring any civilian workers to defense projects until an official go-ahead was received from Pearl. Devereux and the others expected a quick response, but when the reply finally came two days later, it was negative. Nondefensive work was to continue according to schedule.

Disappointing as it was, the response was actually reassuring in a way. The message—and the delay in sending it—implied that the situation wasn't as volatile as the earlier communiqué had suggested. Still, Devereux remained sufficiently uneasy to order his Marines to set up more observation posts around the islands and have more rifle ammunition moved from Camp One out to the gun positions. He also made sure that the long days of fortification-building continued unabated within the limits imposed by headquarters.

Meanwhile, among the routine distractions faced by Devereux as island commander was the chore of playing official host to various dignitaries who showed up periodically aboard Pan Am's Clippers. On one occasion that hectic fall, the major was giving a high-ranking British diplomat and his wife a brief auto tour.

As they drove around the island, Devereux remarked: "We're trying to get ready as fast as we can."

"Yes," the British diplomat's wife replied, "it would be nice to have six more months, wouldn't it?"

Devereux wondered what the woman knew that he didn't. He waited for the diplomat to say something—anything that might provide a clue to just how tense the international situation was becoming—but there was only an ominous silence.

Ironically, one of these VIP visitors to Wake at this time was Japanese envoy Saburo Kurusu, who was on his way from Tokyo to Washington for last-ditch peace talks. The talks, of course, were a sham. A few days earlier, on November 3, Admiral Osami Nagano, chief of the Japanese navy's general staff, had approved a timetable for conquest in the Pacific, including the attack on Pearl Harbor.

Sergeant Walter Bowsher, who served as postmaster for Wake's garrison in addition to his regular job as an artilleryman on Peale, happened to be at the Pan Am dock when Kurusu's plane taxied up to it. As Kurusu came down the ramp, followed by his secretary, he asked Bowsher a pointed question.

"He wanted to know if they could look around," Bowsher recalled. "I figured that was the last thing we needed, and I said no, not unless they got permission from Major Devereux."

The sergeant's rebuff was apparently still fresh on Kurusu's mind when he was greeted by Devereux a short time later.

"I suppose you have come to tell me I can't leave the hotel," Kurusu said as soon as Devereux had saluted and introduced himself.

"No, sir, but you understand how these things are," the major told him. "None of the passengers may leave the vicinity of the hotel without special permission."

Over the next hour or so, Devereux and Kurusu shared several rounds of drinks at the hotel. Kurusu ordered scotch and water and insisted on paying, saying he had "ample funds" for such diversions.

"I am just going to Washington to see what I can do," he said at one point. "I hope I can straighten out affairs and avoid trouble."

Years later, Devereux would still wonder how much Kurusu knew about what lay just ahead.

"He may have known even as he said it that Japan was determined on war," Devereux mused. "He may have known as we sat with our highballs on Wake Island that the conferences in Washington were only diplomatic double-talk to get us off our guard."

By November 10, Kurusu and Japanese ambassador Kichisaburo Nomura were meeting with FDR and Secretary Hull at the White House, but the Japanese parliament had already taken steps that made war virtually inevitable. As the Associated Press reported on that date:

> In an atmosphere of gloom that perhaps was more suggestive than what actually was said, the Japanese parliament gave the impression Monday night that the empire was fatalistically resolved to go to war with the United States unless Washington made what would amount to utter capitulation in the Pacific.
>
> Japan's house of representatives heard...those "minimum"

peace requirements which the house of peers already had approved. These are that the United States quit helping China and drop its alleged participation with Britain, China and the Dutch East Indies in what Tokio claims is an "economic blockade" and "military encirclement." . . .

Nothing said in the house suggested that the government was going to be checked in any way, and barring the single possibility that it was a grandiose and terribly hazardous bluff, it appeared that the United States could not make friends with Japan short of getting out of the Far East.

This dispatch was prominently displayed on newspaper front pages all over the country nearly a month before the Pearl Harbor attack. It also mentioned the parliament's speedy approval of an "extraordinary" Japanese military budget and the fact that 50,000 more Japanese troops were moving into Indochina. The Japanese public was clearly being prepared for all-out war, but official Washington was described as "noncommittal," and Americans in general seemed strangely apathetic—almost as if they were deaf and blind to the furious storm boiling up in the Pacific.

This attitude was exemplified by a letter written about this time to PFC Verne L. Wallace, an artilleryman on Peale, by his girlfriend back in Pennsylvania: "As long as you have to be away, darling, I'm so very, very happy you're in the Pacific, where you won't be in danger if war comes."

Up to this point, Devereux had been in complete charge of all military operations on the atoll, but a crucial change was about to take place in the command structure at Wake.

On November 28, 1941, the seaplane tender U.S.S. *Wright* reached Wake after an eight-day cruise from Pearl. Aboard were more tons of supplies and the first contingent of sixty-four Navy bluejackets and eleven officers. Most were assigned to Wake's naval air station, although the station itself wasn't yet functional, but they included several hospital corpsmen and a medical officer, Lieutenant (jg) Gustave M. Kahn, who would be attached to Devereux's command.

Also arriving on the *Wright* were forty-seven mechanics and ground crewmen for a squadron of Marine aircraft that was expected shortly. They were accompanied by Second Lieutenant Robert J. "Strawberry" Conderman, who would assume pilot duties when the rest of the squadron arrived, and Major Walter Bayler, a communications specialist assigned to set up ground-to-air radio facilities on Wake before moving on to perform the same job on Midway. The Army had also sent a detail to Wake—five enlisted men commanded by Captain Harry S. Wilson—to install a separate communications system for Army planes passing through.

The *Wright* also brought equipment for Wake's own long-promised air squadron. Unfortunately, plans had been kept so secret that no one knew at this juncture whether the squadron designated for Wake would consist of patrol planes or fighters. A hitch developed when it was discovered that equipment for not one but two air squadrons—one fighter and one patrol—was aboard the ship.

Eventually, someone decided that a patrol squadron was better suited to Wake's needs, so the patrol equipment was unloaded and painfully lightered ashore. Then a clarifying message arrived from Pearl saying that Wake was getting the fighter squadron. This meant reloading all the unloaded equipment, then going through the unloading process all over again. For the *Wright*'s skipper, the resulting delay was an annoyance that turned into a godsend. If the ship had been able to depart on schedule, it would have been lying at anchor at Pearl Harbor on December 7.

But the most important "cargo" aboard the *Wright,* from the standpoint of Wake's military future, was Navy Commander Winfield Scott Cunningham, who would not only take charge of the new naval air station but also become the island's overall commander, replacing Devereux.

Few if any of the rank-and-file Marines who now fell under "Spiv" Cunningham's authority were even aware of the change. The new commander, a 1919 graduate of the U.S. Naval Academy whose career in naval aviation dated back to 1924, met with Devereux, Major Potter, and some of the other Marine officers, but he did no mingling with the troops. He promptly moved into one of three new VIP cottages that had been built near Camp Two and took over an office in one of the contractors' buildings. Both were across the lagoon from where the "grunts" were quartered, so Cunningham generally remained out of sight and out of mind—an anonymous, unfamiliar figure lurking in the background.

"None of us had any doubt about who our commander was," said Corporal Frank Gross. "It was obviously Devereux. We never saw Cunningham and probably wouldn't have recognized him if we did. As far as we were concerned, Devereux still called the shots."

In truth, nobody particularly wanted Cunningham as commander of a high-risk target like Wake. He got the job by sheer chance when the Navy officer originally picked for it was unavoidably delayed. Cunningham was sent as a short-term substitute, simply because he was the nearest qualified officer available and there was a sense of urgency about filling the position. Cunningham had first been assigned to Johnston Island, a much lower-profile outpost, which was never seriously threatened by the Japanese and where his command abilities would have been less severely tested.

Cunningham wasn't personally overjoyed about his new assignment, either. After a long stint of sea duty aboard the aircraft carriers U.S.S *Lexington* and *Yorktown,* followed by eighteen months as the *Wright*'s navigation officer, he'd been hoping for a stateside job. He was trained in aviation and was an experienced shipboard officer, but nothing in his background had prepared him for the tortuous command decisions that lay ahead.

By his own admission, Cunningham received his reassignment with the feeling that his tour of duty on Wake would be "uneventful." One of his top priorities upon his arrival was listening to the annual Army-Navy football game on Saturday, November 29 (which started early Sunday morning, November 30, Wake time). While the sailors who came with him lacked the most basic battlefield equipment, Cunningham had thought to bring along a shortwave radio especially to tune in the big game. He'd also brought his golf clubs, his "dress blues," and many other accessories and changes of clothes.

Among his first official chores was meeting with Devereux and some of his unit commanders and taking a cursory tour of defensive preparations. Afterward, Cunningham offered a grim assessment.

"It was not good," he said. "I could only hope for time and reinforcements."

Initially, the state of Wake's defenses wasn't the new commander's most pressing concern, however. His highest priority was speeding up work on the naval air station. He spent most of the morning of his first full day ashore driving around and looking over the roads and various work sites. After lunch, he devoted his attention to, as he put it, "the problems of construction, garbage disposal, maintenance of adequate water supplies, and the like." He also took a quick swim in the contractors' pool.

As dawn broke over Pearl Harbor on Friday, November 28, 1941, a flight of twelve brand-new Grumman F4F-3 Wildcats took off from the old Marine airfield called Ewa Mooring Mast seventeen miles from Pearl. After a brief stop at the naval air station on Ford Island, they headed west over the open sea toward a rendezvous with the aircraft carrier U.S.S. *Enterprise* and what they were told would be a short-term training exercise.

This type of mission made sense because none of the members of the newly organized Marine fighter squadron designated as VMF-211 had logged more than a few hours' flying time in the unfamiliar Wildcats. The stubby fighters themselves were so fresh from the factory that they hadn't yet been fitted with their .50-caliber machine guns and gun sights or sprayed with blue and gray camouflage paint. They were fast, rugged, maneuverable little planes with good firepower and the capability of carrying a hundred-pound bomb under each wing, but their range was relatively short, and they were poorly suited for patrol duty. They also had neither protective armor nor self-sealing gas tanks, two major hazards to the men who flew them. Another drawback of the F4F-3s was that their landing gear had to be raised and lowered with a hand crank inside the cockpit. Because of this, the planes were frequently seen to seesaw back and forth in midair after take-off as the pilot struggled to retract his landing gear.

Major Paul A. Putnam, the squadron's thirty-eight-year-old commander, was under top-secret orders not to reveal the truth about their mission to his aviators. The eleven of them had been told to bring along only their toothbrushes and a change of skivvies—a good indication that they'd be back at Pearl within twenty-four hours.

When they touched down and were jerked to a halt on the flight deck of the *Enterprise,* however, the pilots were met by grinning Navy flight crews who broke the news: "You guys are going to Wake Island."

The carrier plowed steadily westward through the Pacific swells, screened by Navy patrol planes and protected by three cruisers and nine destroyers operating under full war alert. The Wake-bound task force, commanded by Vice Admiral William F. "Bull" Halsey, had received its orders straight from Admiral Kimmel himself: to destroy any Japanese aircraft or surface vessels they encountered. Under no circumstances, Kimmel emphasized, could the Japanese be allowed to learn the purpose of their mission.

"How far do you want me to go?" Halsey had asked.

"Goddamn it," Kimmell told him, "use your common sense."

Halsey relished the order. "If anything gets in my way," he told Commander William Buracker, his operations officer, "we'll shoot first and argue afterward."

On the morning of December 4, at a point about 200 miles northeast of Wake, the *Enterprise* turned her bow into the wind, and the twelve Wildcats roared off the flight deck. Less than two hours later, escorted by a lone Navy PBY sent out from Wake to guide them in, they popped out of the clouds above the atoll in four three-plane V formations.

With Putnam in the lead and virtually every one of the 1,700 civilian and military personnel on Wake lined up along the runway cheering, each plane made a perfect landing and coasted to a stop. Even the bosun birds and peewees flocked around, looking curious.

Putnam, who had dropped out of Iowa State College to join the Marines as a private in 1923 and made second lieutenant just three years later, had won his wings as a Navy aviator in 1929. He'd flown numerous combat missions in Nicaragua in the early 1930s, won commendations from the secretary of the Navy, and piloted virtually every type of plane, from a Ford Trimotor to an F4F-3, but never in his life had he received such a royal reception as this.

As the onlookers cheered, the eleven other pilots took off their goggles, and stepped out of their snub-nosed little planes. At the controls of the Wildcat just behind Putnam's was Captain Henry T. Elrod of Thomasville, Georgia, the squadron's thirty-six-year-old executive officer and a Marine since 1927. The next plane in line was piloted by Captain Frank C. Tharin of Washington, D.C., flight officer of VMF-211 and Elrod's best friend. Tharin was closely followed by Captain Herbert Freuler of Berkeley, California, squadron ordnance and gunnery officer, who had been flying Marine aircraft since 1931.

Backing up these four well-seasoned veterans was a cadre of younger, less-experienced pilots untested in combat. First Lieutenant John F. Kinney of Endicott, Washington, had been a mechanic for Pan Am during his days in the Marine Reserves before completing flight training at Pensacola, Florida. In days to come, his mechanical expertise would prove as valuable to his mates as his feats in the air. First Lieutenant George A. Graves of Grosse Ile, Michigan, was the engineering officer for VMF-211 and a friend and ex-classmate of Kinney's at the Marine Officers Basic School in the fall of 1939. First Lieutenant David D. Kliewer of Wheaton, Illinois, had become a military pilot against the wishes of his pacifist family, and his real goal in life was to be a physician. Second Lieutenant Frank J. Holden of Tenafly, New Jersey, and Second Lieutenant Carl R. Davidson of Teaneck, New Jersey, the squadron's assistant gunnery officer, were another set of best friends who had gone through flight training together a few months earlier. Second Lieutenant Henry G. Webb of Oxford, North Carolina, was an able young flier who aspired to go to law school and become an attorney after the war.

Rounding out the squadron were two enlisted pilots, a fairly common breed in late 1941 among Marine aviation's shorthanded ranks. They were Sergeant William J. Hamilton of San Diego, California, an able aviator and skilled aircraft mechanic, and Sergeant Robert O. Arthur of Sacramento, California.

In light of the applause and obvious excitement generated by his squadron's arrival, Putnam may well have thought back to something he'd written the day before in a letter to a friend: "I feel a bit like the fatted calf being groomed for whatever it is that happens to fatted calves, but it surely is nice while it lasts, and the airplanes are pretty and sleek, too."

Lieutenant Kinney, meanwhile, had hardly climbed out of his cockpit before he found his mind occupied by more practical concerns. For one thing, he worried about the condition of the runway, which didn't have enough well-compacted surface to allow more than one plane to land or take off simultaneously. For another, there were no protective revetments ready for the planes. For yet another, there were no spare aircraft parts and not a single repair manual for the Grummans.

"The F4F-3s were the best and latest planes the Navy had available at the time," Kinney would later remember. "But our mechanics had never even seen one of these planes before, and our pilots had only about thirty hours in the Wildcats, which was barely enough to qualify. None of us had ever fired our machine guns or dropped a bomb from an F4F-3."

When Putnam saw that no work had been started on revetments—underground shelters carved out of the coral that could both protect and conceal the Grummans—he was as concerned as Kinney, if not more so. He angrily demanded that excavating for the shelters begin immediately, and when his complaints produced only a surveying crew, he really lost his temper. For the next hour, he abandoned his usually calm demeanor and used some of the most profanely explicit words his men had ever heard from him, but he succeeded in getting two bulldozer crews to work on the shelters. Then, slightly calmer, he ordered the Wildcats dispersed as much as possible until the revetments were ready for them.

At long last, Wake had its "air force," small and limited though it was, and it was soon apparent that VMF-211 would bear total responsibility for the atoll's aerial defense. On the morning of December 6, the twelve Navy PBYs that had come to Wake as air cover for the *Enterprise* task force left to perform the same function as the task force steamed toward Midway. From that point on, VMF-211 was on its own.

Putnam had already ordered daily four-plane dawn-to-dusk patrols by the Wildcats, but the F4F-3s were short-range attack aircraft and poorly suited for patrol work. They were designed to deliver swift, stinging blows to the enemy, not for scouting vast stretches of ocean in search of his planes and ships.

For months, there had been repeated indications and vague promises that one of the prized new radar units being deployed at strategic U.S. military installations was on its way to Wake. And of all the handicaps and shortcomings faced by Wake's defenders, the lack of radar may have been the most critical.

The Marines had to depend on human lookouts atop scattered observation stations and the two fifty-foot steel water towers, the highest structures on the island, to warn them of unfriendly aircraft. Their own eyes and ears were the only detection devices available, and they were woefully inadequate.

As the last large vessel to bring supplies and personnel to Wake, the *Wright* was the object of great anticipation. Surely the radar unit would be aboard, advance scuttlebutt said—only it wasn't. After the ship weighed anchor and headed back to Pearl, the atoll was alive with rumors and guesses about the cause of this latest disappointment. One often-repeated story was that, when the loading was almost done, there was room on the *Wright* for one more big piece of equipment, but there were two candidates for the space. "We heard it came down to a choice between a garbage truck and the radar unit," said Wiley Sloman, "and somebody decided we needed the garbage truck worse."

At the time, radar units weren't commonplace, and there was undoubtedly keen competition for the relatively few units available. There was also concern about the then top-secret devices falling into the hands of the enemy. Many members of the Wake garrison eventually came to believe that the Navy was hesitant to put radar on the atoll because of how vulnerable to capture it was. Those suspicions were never officially confirmed, but in retrospect they seem as plausible an explanation as any.

After a morning drill on Saturday, December 6—the first he'd conducted in weeks—Devereux finally gave his long-suffering work details the rest of the weekend off. Some of the men napped, caught up on their letter writing, or just loafed.

PFC Wiley Sloman spent the better part of an hour composing a long letter to a girl named Mildred back in Texas City, then dashed off a shorter one to his mother. "Sure would like to be home for some of those great cakes and pies you make every Christmas," he wrote, "but it looks like we'll be stuck out here for Lord knows how long."

Corporal Ralph Holewinski, a husky twenty-year-old from the farming country of central Michigan and one of Wake's biggest "bookworms," planned to spend his weekend reading. He picked up a couple of novels at Camp One's makeshift library just before noon, then stopped by the mess hall for lunch before heading back to his bunk to start on the first one. The meal was no worse than usual as far as Holewinski could tell—although it *was* a far cry from his mother's home cooking—but a couple of the other Marines at his table started complaining loudly about it to Mess Sergeant A. R. "Slim" Hughes.

"Listen, you jerks, you better enjoy this good chow while you can," yelled Hughes, a smallish man with a large voice. "This time next week you'll probably be eatin' rice and fish heads." Everybody at the table laughed.

PFC Artie Stocks of Battery L bought a case of beer and invited three civilian contractors, old friends who had grown up with him back in Utah, to share it with him. "There was no refrigeration available, and we had to drink it warm," Stocks said, "but it tasted pretty damn good anyway."

Others celebrated by splashing in the swimming pool, boating in the lagoon, or fishing from the reef. The outdoor movie theater was crowded with patrons, who contented themselves with nonalcoholic libations. Civilian canteen worker Chalas Loveland remembered making "at least five hundred" milk shakes for thirsty theatergoers that evening. A number of poker games broke out. The bar in the officers' club tent, where hard liquor as well as beer was served, did a brisk business. Cunningham played a few sets of tennis with a young ensign. He lost.

Even the hard-driving Devereux relaxed a little. He remembered feeling philosophical that Sunday evening about his battalion's state of preparedness: "If we had time to get ready, well and good. If we didn't, we'd have to make do with what we had. Meanwhile, there was no use fretting."

The next day was Monday, December 8, on Wake Island. But back at Pearl Harbor, on the opposite side of the international date line, it was Sunday, December 7. Wake's garrison had done all the getting ready it would be allowed to do.

*

*Lieutenant Robert J. Conderman of Marine
Fighter Squadron VMF-211 was mortally
wounded as he tried to reach his F4F-3
Grumman Wildcat during the first Japanese
raid on Wake on December 8, 1941.
(Courtesy National Museum of the Pacific War)*

"Those Aren't B-17s—
They're Japs!"

It was approaching 7:00 A.M. that Monday—breakfast time on Wake—and Army Staff Sergeant Ernest Rogers was hungry. He was also a little bored. He yawned and stretched, wishing the Marine who was supposed to drive him to the mess hall at Camp One would hurry up.

When he heard the driver's motorcycle approaching, Rogers stood up from his chair at one of the two radio receiving stations in the trailer where he worked. The trailer was about the size of a small mobile home, and it stood by itself in an out-of-the-way spot near the edge of the airfield. There was nothing else anywhere nearby except the truck containing the Army detachment's bulky radio transmitter, which was parked about 150 yards away.

At this moment, the portable Army radio unit was one of four receiving and transmitting stations on Wake. The one Major Bayler, the visiting Marine communications specialist, had set up for VMF-211 was some distance away but also on the fringe of the airport. The Navy radio station was near Camp Two, and Pan Am had its own radio facilities on Peale Island.

Rogers had joined the Army in July 1939 after he'd been laid off from his job as a telegraph operator for Western Union back in his native Virginia. He'd enjoyed being stationed in Hawaii, but Wake was a different kettle of fish. Since he'd been there, he and the other members of his Army

Air Corps communications team had spent most of their waking hours at the receivers in the trailer. Right now, Rogers was the only operator on duty, but his eight-hour shift was over, and he was due to be relieved by Sergeant James B. Rex, a passenger on the arriving motorcycle. The senior member of the team and the man who ran the Army station, Staff Sergeant Clifford Hotchkiss, was sleeping in the transmitter truck.

None of the three had been eager to volunteer for the job on Wake when they'd first been approached about it on October 25. But the four-dollar-a-day per diem they were offered during their stay in addition to their regular pay—with thirty days' worth paid in advance—had been enough to persuade Rogers and Rex to make the trip. Hotchkiss had cut an even better deal for himself. Along with the per diem, he'd been promised a promotion to master sergeant when he rejoined his regular unit.

They'd been on Wake since November 11, and their only job was to provide radio guidance for occasional flights of B-17s passing through on their way to the Philippines. It was a tedious assignment, and Captain Henry Wilson, their commanding officer, didn't make it any easier. Wilson was a nervous, middle-aged reservist in the Army Signal Corps who'd been a minor official with the U.S. Customs Service until he was called to active duty a few weeks ago, and his insecurity was obvious. The captain always seemed to be fretting or raising hell about something, and Hotchkiss frequently cussed him behind his back as a bumbler and a nuisance.

At least 95 percent of the time, the operators' duties consisted of sitting in the trailer, listening to the airwaves, and waiting while the hours slowly dragged by. There'd been no B-17s for several days now, and it was anybody's guess when there'd be more. The movements of the big bombers were one of the Army's most closely guarded secrets.

Rogers reached up to remove his headset, already thinking about the steaming bacon and pancakes in the mess hall at Camp One. Just then he heard the high-pitched *dit-dit-da-dit-dit* of an incoming message from Hawaii. Everything had to be sent and received by hand transmitter; the equipment had no voice capabilities.

The receivers, powered by a portable gas generator, were usually kept on the same frequency with Hickam Field, the nearest Army air base, which was right next door to Pearl Harbor. Most of the messages out of Hickam were in military code that could be translated only by Captain Wilson, so it struck Rogers as strange that this one was coming through loud and clear in plain Morse.

His first thought was: "Somebody's gonna be in trouble for this!"

He deciphered the transmission effortlessly, feeling a chill race up the back of his neck as he did:

> *S-O-S... S-O-S... Pearl Harbor is under attack by Jap dive bombers... This is the real thing... This is no drill...*

The message finished repeating itself just as Sergeant Rex stepped into the trailer. He stood there for a moment with a puzzled expression on his face, then came and looked over Rogers's shoulder. Before Rogers could finish typing out the words on his keyboard, the transmission was cut off, and the receiver went dead.

Rex read the message instantly and snatched up the telephone. There was no phone hookup to Camp One, but he had the presence of mind to ring Hotchkiss in the transmitter truck and wake him up. As the detail's ranking noncom, he'd have a better idea of what to do.

"I can't believe it's for real," Hotchkiss said groggily, "but tell Rogers to get the message over to Wilson on the double."

Rogers jerked the paper out of the machine and ran outside. As he climbed into the motorcycle's sidecar, his heart was pounding, and his appetite was suddenly gone.

If his driver had shown up thirty seconds earlier, Rogers thought, he would have already been out the door and on his way to breakfast when the message came in, and it might have gone unheard.

"Step on it," he snapped. "I'm in a rush." He wondered if he should tell the Marine about the message, then quickly decided not to. There'd been several false alarms recently, and Rogers didn't want to set off another one.

The Marine revved the motor. "Okay, okay," he said. "Christ, you act like you haven't had anything to eat in a week."

"No, it's not that," Rogers said. "I've got to see Captain Wilson. Let's go."

The cycle lurched forward down the narrow coral road.

At approximately that same moment, Commander Cunningham was finishing his coffee in the dining hall at Camp Two on the other side of the lagoon. As he ate breakfast, he'd watched the Pan Am Clipper take off on its flight to Guam, then spent a few minutes glancing over a mimeographed sheet of European war news gleaned from overnight radio broadcasts out of Hawaii.

As he stepped outside into the warm, overcast morning and started toward his pickup truck, Cunningham saw someone running toward him. Although Cunningham didn't know the man's name, it was Radioman Third Class John B. Anderson, an operator from the Navy radio shack down the road. The guy waved his arms and shouted something that Cunningham couldn't make out over the ceaseless roar of the surf.

Anderson's face was flushed, and he was panting hard. He stumbled and almost fell, then caught himself. Cunningham grasped the crumpled sheet of paper the radioman shoved toward him and read the four words written there:

"Pearl Harbor under attack."

"It just came in," Anderson said, fighting for breath. "The Pearl operator kept saying 'This is no drill, this is no drill.'"

As an always-hungry country boy from rural Alabama, PFC Richard Gilbert made a special point of getting to the Camp One mess hall early that Monday morning. One of the cooks had given him the word the day before that they'd be serving his favorite breakfast—hotcakes. The young Marine had been licking his chops in anticipation ever since.

"It's funny the things that stick in your mind," Gilbert said decades later, "but the thing I remember most about that day was those hotcakes. Man, they were good. I ate eleven of the doggone things—big ones that nearly covered the plate—and I loved every bite. I still feel like I was lucky to have all the hotcakes I could hold that morning. Lots of other guys didn't get any breakfast at all."

Barely eighteen years old, Gilbert may have been the youngest Marine on Wake, and by his own description, he'd been "the happiest boy in the whole country" the day his parents signed to let him enlist early in April 1941. He'd been sick of farming for fifty cents a day, and the $21-a-month salary of a Marine private—plus all his food and clothes—had looked almost too good to be true.

As he rose heavily from the table, Gilbert heard the sound of a bugle playing something he couldn't identify, and he hurried outside into a sea of confusion. Some men scurried around, scooping up their gear. Others went on with their chores, and still others stood around looking puzzled and uncertain.

Minutes later, still comfortably full but slightly stunned, Gilbert found himself bouncing along in the back of a truck bound for his post on the range finder of one of the five-inch guns at Peacock Point down on Wake's easternmost tip. He still wasn't sure what was going on, but somebody said the war had started.

Major Devereux was shaving when Captain Wilson burst into his tent without bothering to knock and handed him the piece of paper Sergeant Rogers had thrust into his hands just moments ago.

Devereux read the message without comment. He frowned as he swiped at the lather on his face with a towel and grabbed the phone. He got no answer at Cunningham's office, so he rang the Navy radio station.

"Have you received a priority message from Pearl Harbor?" he asked.

"Yes, sir," the radioman said. "It's being decoded now."

Devereux needed no further verification. He ran for his office about fifty yards away, yelling as he passed the guard tent for Field Music First Class Alvin Waronker, the battalion bugler.

In the office, First Sergeant Paul Agar was already at his desk. He opened his mouth to say good morning, but the major cut him off.

"It's started," Devereux said. "The Japs have attacked Pearl Harbor."

Agar gaped in disbelief. "I'll be goddamned," he whispered.

Waronker ran in. "Sound the call to arms," Devereux ordered.

The major followed the bugler outside and watched as Waronker nervously blew the first wavering, off-key notes. As everyone in the garrison knew, Waronker wasn't much of a bugler, and what he was blowing didn't sound much like general quarters.

Devereux fumed as many of his men took their time finishing what they were doing. It also didn't help that they'd had their first general quarters drill in six weeks just two days before. He could tell that the men thought it was just another "dummy run." Most of them went right on laughing and skylarking as they collected their gear. When the trucks began rolling up to take them to their gun positions, some of them started off without the rifle ammunition they'd been issued a few days earlier for just such an emergency.

"This is no drill!" Devereux thundered. "This is no drill! Pass the word!"

Some of the men gawked back at him for a second before it finally sank in. Then they all started scrambling at once—trying to grab everything they could get their hands on, stumbling over each other, and dashing headlong for the trucks.

In the space of a minute or two, the word spread across Camp One, triggering pandemonium. The strident shouts of platoon sergeants rang above the sound of the surf: "This is no drill! This is no damned drill!"

The scene reminded Wiley Sloman of something out of the Keystone Kops. The difference was, it was really happening, and he was right square in the middle of it.

"Poor Waronker was undoubtedly the worst bugler in the Marine Corps, and you could never be sure what the hell he was playing," Sloman recalled. "I heard the bugle while I was still eating breakfast, and I rolled a pancake around a sausage, grabbed three bandoliers of ammo, and ran for my tent. But by the time I got there, old Music must've got confused, because I swear he started playing fire call. Sergeant Henry Bedell thought so, too, and he yelled, 'Get your buckets.'"

Sloman ran back inside the tent to obey the order from Bedell, a crusty twenty-year veteran with a voice like a buzzsaw hitting a ten-penny nail, and came back out with the bucket in one hand and his rifle in the other. But in the confusion, he went off and left his hard hat behind. He didn't realize he didn't have the helmet until he was halfway to his battle station on Wilkes Island, and he never got a chance to go back to Camp One. "If I'd thought about it," he said, "I probably could've picked up another helmet somewhere, but I just didn't."

Despite the chaos, most members of Wake's garrison were at their assigned battle stations less than forty-five minutes after Captain Wilson had burst into Devereux's tent. By 8:00 A.M., field commanders at scattered defensive outposts were phoning in to report that they were "manned and ready." The only notable exceptions were Sloman and the other Marines assigned to Wilkes, who had to be ferried across the channel to their posts in small groups. The tricky currents acted up as usual, which added to the delay, but by around 8:45 A.M., every Marine on the three islands was where he was supposed to be.

Devereux took only small comfort in this, however. Hundreds of loose ends were still dangling, and there was next to no time left to get them tied up. The major's makeshift office was swamped with people asking urgent questions and hunting solutions for crucial problems—and they all wanted answers *right now.*

Obviously there weren't nearly enough bomb shelters and supply caches to go around. There was only the most rudimentary plan for supplying all the far-flung outposts with food, water, and additional ammo. Some of the batteries still weren't fully sandbagged. Communications had to be checked and alternate lines laid. Then there were the Navy and Army personnel, who had no weapons of any kind, no gas masks, no helmets.

In the midst of all this, Cunningham rushed into Devereux's office. The island commander seemed as stunned and disbelieving as everyone else. As Cunningham later described, half of his mind kept telling him it couldn't be true while the other half kept assuring him it was.

"I see you already know," he told Devereux. "Anything I can do?"

"I don't know of anything right now," Devereux said.

"My command post will be at Camp Two," Cunningham advised.

"Okay," Devereux replied. "I'm moving my CP into the brush as soon as we can set up a switchboard."

Cunningham ran out again. From his own office, he'd already alerted

VMF-211's Major Putnam and approved Putnam's plan to get four of his Wildcats into the air immediately. Putnam had the other planes dispersed as well as he could, but they were sitting in the open on the parking area of the airfield less than fifty yards apart. They were all crowded onto about three-quarters of an acre because there wasn't enough cleared space to separate them any more.

Cunningham had also called the Pan Am manager, John Cooke, and urged him to order the Guam-bound Clipper that had left minutes earlier to return to Wake. If it continued on toward Guam, it would be flying into the teeth of Japanese forces in the Marianas.

As Cunningham hung up the phone, CPNAB construction superintendent Dan Teters threw open the office door. It was the first time they'd met face to face.

"I'm Dan Teters," the husky Irishman said. "What can I do to help?"

Cunningham, Teters, and Lieutenant Commander Elmer Greey, the second-highest-ranking Navy officer on Wake, quickly put their heads together. More than 150 civilians, some of them military veterans like Teters himself, had been training voluntarily to work and fight alongside the Marines in case of emergency. Now Teters offered to round up all these volunteers and put them at Devereux's disposal.

Incredibly, though, given the circumstances, Cunningham seemed unable to shake free of peacetime priorities that no longer mattered. No one had yet rescinded the orders of Cunningham's immediate superior, Admiral Claude Bloch, that nothing be allowed to interfere with work on the naval air station, so Cunningham hesitated.

Finally, he agreed to let Teters go ahead and get the trained volunteers together, but he warned Teters to handle it quietly so the other civilians wouldn't find out. Cunningham's decision meant that almost 1,000 contractors would be left "undisturbed" by news of the Pearl Harbor attack and remain at work as if nothing had happened.

Blissfully ignorant, civilian Glenn Newell and his brother, Emmett, went on to their assigned projects just as if it were any other day. After growing up on a cattle ranch north of Boise, the two Idaho natives had gone into different trades—Glenn as a welder and Emmett as a carpenter. Emmett had signed up first for duty on Wake, then talked Glenn into coming along. On December 8, Glenn was with a crew laying concrete pipe for a sewer line on Peale, and Emmett was working not far away on one of the new buildings for the naval air station.

Cunningham believed that the normal dispersal provided by the civilians' jobs was sufficient protection for the time being. His decision not to make them aware of the situation was made hurriedly and without much time to weigh the pros and cons. He was clearly counting on the patrols by VMF-211's four Wildcats to provide enough advance warning of approaching peril to allow the workers to be alerted and gotten to cover.

It was a disastrous miscalculation.

The island commander then jumped in his pickup and spent the next hour or so driving around Wake proper to see for himself that the airport and various defenses were in as high a state of readiness as possible.

At 8:00 A.M., Field Music Waronker stood in front of the flagpole at Camp One and played Morning Colors as the Stars and Stripes were raised above the camp—a daily ritual at Marine installations around the globe. By this time, most of the Marines were either at their posts or on their way, and Waronker's audience was small.

Those on hand, however, were treated to something they'd never witnessed before. Waronker's inability to play Colors right was a battalion joke. But on this first morning of a sudden new war, the "worst bugler in the Marine Corps" played the clear, crisp notes with flawless perfection and stirred the emotions of everyone who heard them. In Devereux's words: "It made a man's throat tighten to hear it." It was also the only time it ever happened.

At the Army radio station, an uneasy Sergeant Rex was fidgeting impatiently when Captain Wilson and Sergeant Rogers drove up. Rex let out a sigh of relief when he saw them. He had a suggestion that wouldn't keep, and he blurted it out the moment Wilson entered the trailer.

"I'm afraid our transmitter's too exposed here so close to the airfield, sir," Rex said. "I think we ought to move the truck someplace else."

Wilson thought about it for a minute. "Where'd you have in mind?"

"Someplace out in the brush where it can't be seen from the air, sir."

Wilson nodded. "You and Rogers go to it," he said.

The idea was simple—one that no officer in a combat zone would have had to think about twice later in the war. But if Rex hadn't mentioned it, the story of Wake's defense might well have remained unknown to the folks back home until the war was over. "If we hadn't moved the equipment when we did," Rogers said, "we wouldn't have had anything left to move by that afternoon."

Busy as they were that morning, only a handful of the men on Wake were prepared, either physically or psychologically, for what was about to descend on them. In spite of all the reports of a raid on Pearl Harbor, there were still pervasive feelings of unreality—and skepticism—among the Marines.

"This has to be a big foul-up," complained Lieutenant Clarence Barninger, fiery commander of the five-inch battery on Peacock Point, as he studied the empty ocean through a scope. "Those bastards haven't got the guts to attack us."

Except for a handful of veterans with previous combat experience, no one on Wake—military or civilian—had ever been under enemy fire, much less on the receiving end of a bombing raid. Most had no concept of the awesome destructive power wielded by modern military aircraft.

At the airfield, Major Putnam wrestled with a tormenting quandary: Moving his planes out of the airstrip's small regular parking area meant pushing each 5,200-pound Grumman over rough ground and running a high risk of damage. Since there were no spare parts, damaged planes were, in essence, lost planes, which made moving them a bad option.

On the other hand, Putnam had seen with his own eyes, as he broke through the clouds above the airport that morning at the end of a forty-five-minute patrol, just what tempting targets his planes on the ground really were. Leaving them there was begging for trouble.

It was a damned-if-you-do, damned-if-you-don't situation, but as Putnam saw it as squadron commander, he had only two distasteful and dangerous options: He could either let the planes stay where they were for now, or he could take a chance on moving them to safer ground and damaging them in the process.

Apparently, Putnam gave little thought to a third choice, which seems, in retrospect, too obvious to overlook—namely, putting more of the Wildcats in the air. This could have offered at least a short-term solution, but instead, with held breath and crossed fingers, he counted on the protective revetments that had been under construction for several days being completed within the next little while. The men working on the revetments estimated they'd have them ready to start receiving planes no later than 2:00 P.M. Other men were digging foxholes and bomb shelters along the perimeter of the airport. They were also due to be ready by early afternoon.

It was about 11:00 A.M. now. That meant if fate would give them just three more hours of grace, most of the squadron's planes and personnel would have a measure of protection. They wouldn't be totally out of harm's way, but at least they'd have better odds of surviving an attack. Meanwhile, Putnam kept four of the F4F-3s in the air, kept another four fueled up, loaded with bombs and ammo, and in position to take off—and prayed for a little extra time.

Right now, Captain Henry Elrod was leading the four-plane patrol mission, and Second Lieutenants Kinney and Davidson and Tech Sergeant Hamilton, one of the squadron's two enlisted pilots, were flying with him. Once they reached an altitude of 13,000 feet, however, Elrod divided the patrol into two sections. Kinney and Hamilton turned southwest, toward the Japanese-held Marshall Islands some 600 miles distant, while Elrod and Davidson flew north.

Putnam saw the Marshalls as the likeliest source for land-based enemy bombers targeting Wake. But because none of the Wildcats was equipped with homing devices, Kinney made the decision to limit the range of the southward patrol to no more than sixty miles. That wouldn't leave much time to warn the garrison, but it seemed the only intelligent thing to do.

One of Kinney's major concerns was making sure that he and Hamilton could find their way back home, so they maintained constant visual contact with each other. For the most part, they maintained radio silence, hoping to avoid being overheard by any enemy ships or planes in the area.

When a thick bank of clouds parted momentarily, they suddenly spotted two V formations of strange planes 10,000 feet below them. At the same time, they discovered that their radios weren't working.

By this time, the Japanese planes—part of a squadron of twenty-seven twin-engine, twin-tailed Mitsubishi "Nells" from the Chitose Air Group of Japan's 24th Air Flotilla—were three miles west of Wake. Seconds later, Kinney and Hamilton spotted columns of greasy, black smoke rising ominously through the clouds.

This was all the confirmation Kinney and Hamilton needed. They cleared their guns and streaked after the Japanese planes now retiring rapidly in the distance, but the attackers had too big a lead and the American pilots had to break off their pursuit.

By then, even if their radios hadn't malfunctioned, it was too late. At the airfield below, the worst had already happened.

It was a few minutes before noon. At the Pan Am hotel on Peale, passengers from the recently returned Clipper were having lunch and speculating in grim tones about the damage at Pearl Harbor.

The Clipper's pilot, a Navy reserve officer named John Hamilton, was at the pier, supervising the unloading of cargo and getting set to take off within the next few minutes on a reconnaissance mission requested by Commander Cunningham.

Cunningham himself was in his office, still filled with what he later described as "a strange sense of unreality" as he mulled over such ideas for improving Wake's defenses as mining the airstrip and mooring a dynamite-laden barge in Wilkes Channel to prevent enemy landings by plane or small boat.

Somewhere to the south, he heard an explosion. His first thought was an accident of some sort. Then he heard another blast, and another, and another.

He glanced at his watch. It was nearly noon. He jumped up and ran to the large drafting room just outside his office.

At that instant, machine gun bullets ripped through the ceiling above

Cunningham's head. He saw a civilian worker dive under a nearby desk. Cunningham did likewise.

All across the three islands, from Toki Point on the westernmost tip of Peale to Peacock Point at the eastern extremity of Wake proper, men stared at the skies and felt the ground shake under their feet. Yet most were gripped by the same inability to comprehend the horrifying realities unfolding before them.

"I'll never forget it as long as I live," said Frank Gross. "I was standing there by one of the machine guns talking to Lieutenant Hanna when I looked up and saw all these planes come falling out of the clouds right above us."

The planes came in fast and very low. Gross pointed at them and wondered aloud: "What are they, B-17s?"

"B-17s, my ass!" somebody yelled a few feet away. "Those aren't B-17s—they're Japs!"

Then Gross saw the first of the bombs hit the airfield.

Not far away, at Battery E on Peacock Point, Lieutenant William W. "Wally" Lewis, the three-inch antiaircraft battery's coolly professional commander, was on the phone with Devereux when the first formation of bombers zoomed over the beach.

"Major, there's a squadron of planes coming in from the south," Lewis said. "Are they friendly?"

Just then someone nearby said: "Hey, they're dropping their wheels."

"Those are bombs!" yelled Corporal Robert Haidinger, in charge of the battery's number-four gun. "Open fire!"

Chicago-born Haidinger, who had sailed around the world on merchant ships before joining the Marines, instantly showed why he was known as a self-starter among his mates. He ran for the gun as hard as he could go, waving and shouting for his three crewmen hidden in some nearby brush. Unwilling to wait for the others, he started jamming shells into the breech, then fired two or three rounds from the three-incher by himself without aiming. None came anywhere near the attacking planes, of course.

Nearby, several Marines blazed away at the bombers with their rifles—an equally futile gesture.

Roughly a mile to the west, in the brush near the airfield's main runway, Sergeant Ernie Rogers heard the shriek of diving aircraft and looked up from cleaning gelatinous Cosmoline off the rifle a Marine had handed him earlier. Above the roof of the receiver trailer, he saw planes—lots of them. He immediately noticed their peculiar shape, but the idea that they were Japanese never entered his mind.

"Man," he told himself, "I never saw American planes with twin tails like that. They must be new."

A split-second later, Rogers spotted the fiery red circles on the undersides of their wings. He also saw dark objects falling from the planes toward the ground. *Japs!* he thought. *Bombs!* He threw himself into the brush as the first blasts showered the trailer with dust and chunks of coral.

Major Bayler, the Marine radio specialist, was about to eat lunch in the squadron tent on the parking apron at the edge of the airfield. With him were Putnam and five of the other pilots from VMF-211—Captain Tharin and Lieutenants Graves, Holden, Conderman, and Webb. There were nine or ten of them altogether, including several noncoms, lounging under the tent fly, waiting for some sandwiches to be delivered, when they heard what Bayler called "a deep droning from the sky."

They piled outside and saw two V formations of large aircraft streaking in at low altitude from the south. In the space of a breath or two, the planes were right on top of them, and like so many others on Wake that fateful noon, Bayler and his lunch mates were slow to recognize their peril.

"Those must be our B-17s," somebody remarked matter-of-factly.

But one of the pilots in the group knew better. "Hell, those aren't our planes," he yelped. "They're Japs!"

It was precisely 11:58 A.M.

Bayler, a Harvard-educated Californian, had the exact time permanently branded on his brain because he'd just glanced at his watch a second earlier. He catapulted out of the tent and ran for all he was worth. It was about 200 feet from the tent to the edge of the woods and the nearest cover of any kind. Bayler made it. He plunged headlong into the undergrowth, hugged a small tree, and pressed his face to the earth as hundred-pound fragmentation bombs shook the ground.

Frank Holden and "Spider" Webb, who were only a second or two behind Bayler, weren't so lucky. A burst of machine gun fire riddled Holden's body, killing him instantly and ripping open his parachute. He fell on his back in a widening pool of his own blood. A slug from the same burst caught Webb in the belly, and chunks of shrapnel ripped him from head to foot. One of the fragments tore off his left boot and three of his toes. Amazingly, though, he was still alive.

Staff Sergeant Walter T. "Tom" Kennedy of Orange Cove, California, had first joined the Marines in 1934 because he was a pretty good trumpeter and aspired to play in the Marine Band. He didn't make it, and after a four-year hitch as a bugler, he left the Corps but soon reenlisted and went to school to become an aviation radioman. In November 1941, he'd been transferred from a dive bomber squadron in San Diego and sent to Wake for what he was told would be only a "six-week maneuver."

On the morning of December 8, Kennedy had driven Major Bayler to the airfield from Camp One, then spent the next little while setting up a loop antenna as a homing device for the fighter squadron. But he was in the tent with the others waiting for food when bedlam broke out.

"I remember a guy pulling back the tent flap, and the planes were right there," Kennedy said. "I swear some of 'em weren't over eight or nine hundred feet off the ground, and we had maybe three or four seconds before the first bombs went off."

Kennedy made a mad dash for the bushes, and the whole place started exploding. Some of the planes on the ground were already ablaze as he ran past them. He heard something spattering the ground around him and thought for a second it was raining. Then he realized the sound was actually machine gun bullets.

Just as he dove into the brush, one of the "raindrops" found him, and he felt a white-hot pain knife through his arm. Moments later, when he tried to stand up, he discovered that a jagged hunk of shrapnel had buried itself in his leg a few inches above the ankle. He fell back down again.

Captain Herb Freuler saw the planes swooping down as he stood in front of the VMF-211 ordnance tent. He threw himself into a shallow hole in the ground nearby just as a bomb hit only yards away, but two enlisted men who'd been with him seconds before were slower to find cover. Both were blown to pieces by the blast.

Two of the other pilots from the squadron tent darted through machine gun bullets in a valiant effort to reach their planes. George Graves had just climbed into the cockpit of his Wildcat when a bomb landed a few feet away, setting his plane on fire and hurling his lifeless body underneath it. Moments later, the plane's fuel tank exploded, engulfing Graves's corpse in flames.

"Strawberry" Conderman, a friendly, freckled redhead just two years out of the University of North Carolina, was only a few steps from his Grumman when machine gun bullets cut his legs out from under him. As he sprawled on the tarmac, another bullet slammed through his neck. His F4F-3 also caught fire, and the flames spread quickly to nearby tents and equipment as the mortally wounded pilot watched helplessly.

The scene before Conderman's dying eyes was like something out of the deepest reaches of hell. The whole airfield seemed to be on fire. One of the raiders' first targets was the main VMF-211 fuel dump, where two 25,000-gallon gasoline storage tanks and hundreds of 55-gallon drums of additional fuel were concentrated beside the runway. The dump erupted into a giant fireball that sent a plume of black smoke hundreds of feet into the sky.

All eight of the Wildcats on the ground were destroyed or heavily damaged. Seven planes were blazing furiously, and the eighth was a mass of bullet holes. Some of the ground crewmen who were loading the planes with bombs and ammo had foolishly taken cover under them, and their bodies now littered the tarmac.

Dead and wounded men were strewn everywhere. Gasoline drums popped like firecrackers. On the burning planes, belts of .50-caliber tracer bullets exploded and sprayed themselves in crazed, whining volleys. Now and then, one of the hundred-pound bombs racked under the wings of the ruined Wildcats went off with an ear-splitting roar. A flood of flaming gasoline from the fuel dump spread a wall of fire across the parking area, and a brisk south wind drove it toward a dozen trapped and wounded men.

Two Marines, one of them badly hurt himself, tried to pull Conderman out of the path of the fire.

"Let me go," he told them. He tried to point to the others who lay around him. "Take care of them."

As the bombers flew away from the airfield and on to other targets, Bayler emerged from the woods, shaken and covered with coral dust but unhurt. He saw Putnam standing dazed on the runway some distance away. The squadron CO was bleeding from a wound near his left shoulder blade and clearly in a state of shock. To Bayler, he looked like "a man walking aimlessly in his sleep."

Two bodies were crumpled just a few feet from the brush where Bayler had taken refuge. They were beyond help, so he moved on to where Lieutenant Webb was lying. Webb was covered with blood from shrapnel wounds, but he was conscious as Bayler knelt beside him.

A tall, gangling Marine private appeared and helped Bayler fashion a crude litter from a piece of burlap. When they put Webb on the litter and started to pick him up, the wounded pilot lifted his left leg slightly and stared at the remains of his boot and the place where his toes had been.

"Just look at that damned foot," he said disgustedly.

Eighteen of the bombers in this first attack concentrated their fury on the airfield. When they finished their initial bombing runs, virtually the only thing left intact was the runway itself. Clearly the enemy had plans to use it later for its own aircraft. Practically everything along the runway's perimeters was obliterated.

The raid was a textbook exercise in precision bombing and strafing. It disproved—once and for all and in spades—the popular myths that Japanese pilots were mediocre fliers and that Japanese gunners and bombardiers were inferior marksmen.

After expending their bombs, half of the attacking Nells—nine planes—returned for another strafing run. Their human toll might have risen still higher if not for the pall of black smoke that now hung over the field, obscuring their targets.

The smoke probably saved the lives of several gutsy Marines who ran into the flames and carnage to help the wounded. Corporal Robert E. Lee Page and Sergeant Andy Paskiewicz had been working together when the raid started, and fragments from one of the first bombs had shattered Paskiewicz's right leg. Page dragged the sergeant, dazed and losing blood from several other wounds, out of the path of the spreading flames, then went back for another critically injured sergeant whose leg was hanging by a thread.

As Page dragged the second man to a safer area, he was amazed to see Paskiewicz, a twenty-year veteran of the Corps, crawling back toward the inferno to help other wounded and dying men. Page dragged Paskiewicz back a second time, but the hardheaded old Marine refused to stay put.

Paskiewicz dug in a heap of wreckage until he found a charred stick he could use for a crutch. Then he stumbled along from one wounded man to another, doing his best to give them first aid.

Bullets impacting all around him, Page doggedly continued his rescue efforts in heat as intense as a blowtorch. Often he had to press his face to the ground to find enough oxygen to breathe. Again and again, his shirt and pants caught fire; he had to beat the flames out with his cap. By the time he finished his lifesaving work, Page's eyebrows and hair were singed off, most of his clothes were burned completely away, and his body was covered with blisters.

Sergeant Robert Bourquin, a VMF-211 ground crewman from Oregon, was a mile or so away at the central fuel dump when the raid started, and the departing Nells flew directly over him, so close that he could look straight up into their open bomb bays. He raced back to the field on foot to confront a sea of flames and a dying friend.

"It was the shock of my life," Bourquin said. "My old tentmate, Sergeant Bob Edwards, was still alive when I got to him, and the only thing I could think about was getting him to the hospital. A civilian came along in a truck, and I commandeered it. The guy was determined to keep going, and I had to take my pistol to him to get him to stop. It didn't matter much, anyway, I guess. I think Bob was dead by the time we got him there."

VMF-211 was decimated by the attack. Of fifty-five personnel on the ground when the raiders struck, only twenty-one escaped unscathed. Edwards was among twenty-three men either killed outright or mortally wounded—Lieutenant Conderman remained conscious for most of the day, but he died that night—and eleven others suffered disabling injuries.

All told, the aviation unit's casualty rate was over 60 percent, including four of its aviators. This didn't count lesser wounds to three other pilots—Putnam, Captain Frank Tharin, and Sergeant Bob Arthur—all of whom managed to keep flying.

Bad as it was, the battering of the fighter squadron was only part of the story. While the horror at the airfield was unfolding, the other Nells rained bombs and machine gun fire on the rest of Wake proper and on Peale and Wilkes.

Incendiary bullets ripped through Camp One, destroying the mess hall, the officers' club, and many of the tents. Fortunately, though, the camp was mostly vacant at the time, and there were no casualties.

At Camp Two, however, it was a different story. A large group of civilian workers had gathered there for lunch, making a tempting target. Several dozen were killed or maimed as the raiders poured machine gun fire into the new barracks and other structures.

On Peale, a bomb incinerated the Pan Am Inn and killed ten of the airline's Chamorro employees. Others escaped only by jumping into the foundation hole of a building under construction. The budding naval air station was also hit, and the docked Clipper in the lagoon was punctured by scores of bullets but wasn't seriously damaged.

Just before noon, civilian Glenn Newell heard machine gun fire and jumped out of the pit where he was working. Just as he crawled under a small shrub, a bomb hit the hotel about 300 feet away, and another went off almost simultaneously on Newell's other side, covering him with dirt. Wondering where his brother, Emmett, was, he started running for the side of one of the buildings under construction, but all he could see was "boards and rocks and debris flying everywhere."

As the raiders turned back south, they made one last pass over Wilkes.

They were out of bombs by now, but they still had plenty of bullets for a final strafing run. They killed Navy bluejackets Thomas Kilcoyne and Richard Jacobs and civilian Johnny Hall—all caught out in the open as the planes streaked across the channel between Wake and Wilkes.

Then, as the raiders roared low over the beach on Wilkes, one of the most tempting targets to appear in their gun sights was Wiley Sloman.

Sloman, Battery L's jack-of-all-building-trades, had been putting the finishing touches on a special new foxhole he'd just dug for Lieutenant John McAlister, his battery commander. The hardest part of the job was done now, and Sloman was neatly stacking sandbags around the top of his creation when he heard a guy on a nearby lookout tower yell, "They're bombing the airport! They're bombing the airport!"

Sloman had heard the faint sound of explosions, but he'd thought it was the contractors doing some more dynamiting down by the new channel. He shoved a final sandbag in place, clambered out of the hole, and stood up—in time to see a sky full of Japanese bombers heading straight at him.

They zoomed low over Sloman's battery, their machine guns kicking up coral splinters. They were so close, he thought he could have hit one of the red balls on the undersides of their wings with a baseball. Sloman saw the puffs of black smoke from one of the three-inch antiaircraft batteries blossoming against the gray clouds, but none of them came close to the attacking planes. The ack-ack crews might as well have been throwing baseballs themselves.

Like all but one or two of his battery mates, Sloman had never been under fire before. He quickly showed his inexperience—and almost died for it. Instead of jumping back in the hole he'd just dug, Sloman broke and ran for his own foxhole, where he'd left his rifle. "It was a silly thing to do," he admitted, "and that damn hole turned out to be a lot further away than I thought it was."

As nearly as he could calculate, the distance was about forty yards. It was the longest forty yards of Sloman's life. The bullets were hitting right at his heels every step of the way, and he couldn't see how they kept missing him. For a split second, the image of his marathon-walking grandfather flashed through his mind. He could almost hear Grandpa's voice in his ear: *Come on, damn it! Take longer strides!*

Then, when he finally reached his goal, Sloman found three other Marines already jammed into the one-man shelter, leaving no room for him. In desperation, he leaped behind a coral boulder and huddled there facedown until the firing stopped.

Sloman noticed streaks of blood on his arms and legs and felt his skin "stinging like hell." For a moment, he thought he'd been hit. Then he realized he'd just been nicked in a dozen places by razor-sharp fragments of flying coral.

"Stupid greenhorn," he muttered to himself, shaking and panting as he watched the planes disappear over the ocean.

A hundred or so yards away, Corporal John Johnson was in a much better protected spot than Sloman, and he also had something to shoot back with.

Sitting in the firing mount of his .50-caliber machine gun on the south beach of Wilkes, Johnson had also heard the explosions at the airport. Because of the tall brush between his position and the airfield, he couldn't see what was happening, but he recognized the sounds almost immediately as bombs.

Then he saw the bombers—nine of them that had banked around for another run at the airfield and now zoomed toward him out of the north. When he heard one of the machine guns north of him open fire, he swung his own gun around and lined up the lead bomber in his sights.

"I figured the pilot of the first plane was the flight leader, so I concentrated on him," Johnson said. "As he passed over us and headed out to sea, I saw smoke coming out of one of his engines, but he stayed in formation and kept on going."

Johnson swore under his breath. He'd really wanted a piece of that guy, and he felt cheated and mad at himself.

At least he'd hit *something*, though—which was more than most of the awed, inexperienced Marine gunners could say that first day. As nearly as can be determined, no more than three or four of the attacking planes were hit, and none was seriously damaged. All twenty-seven raiders returned safely to their base.

As they streaked away from the scenes of death and devastation they'd left on Wake, a Japanese observer aboard one of the planes could see pilots grinning broadly in their cockpits. All the planes, even those with a few bullet holes, waggled their wings at each other—their way of shouting "Banzai!"

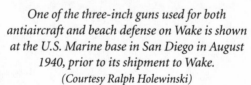

*One of the three-inch guns used for both
antiaircraft and beach defense on Wake is shown
at the U.S. Marine base in San Diego in August
1940, prior to its shipment to Wake.*
(Courtesy Ralph Holewinski)

⋆ 5 ⋆

Picking Up the Pieces

Within twelve minutes or less after the first bomb fell, it was all over. The Japanese planes were gone.

In the time it took to hard-boil an egg, the attackers had painted an awesome panorama of destruction across Wake Atoll. Many of the visible structures built since 1935 lay in ruins. Much of what hundreds of Marines and civilian contractors had labored for months to assemble had been laid to waste in one ruthlessly efficient, superbly executed stroke.

At the airfield, gasoline drums still exploded in the searing heat, and fires continued to rage far into the afternoon. It would be more than three hours before the parking area, where the ruined Wildcats lay like scorched and slaughtered pigeons, cooled enough for anyone to examine what was left of them.

Seven of the eight F4F-3s that had been on the ground were little more than charred piles of scrap. Only the eighth offered a remote possibility of salvage. To make matters worse, as the four Wildcats on patrol returned to the field about 12:30 P.M., the one piloted by Captain Elrod hit some debris that had been blown onto the runway, bending its prop and damaging its engine mounts. That left VMF-211 with exactly three flyable planes.

The scene that confronted the returning fliers was a nightmare in broad daylight. Even before he landed, Lieutenant Kinney sensed the enormity of the damage and was already gripped by the worst case of nerves he'd ever had. His feet were shaking so hard that he could hardly keep them on the rudders of his plane.

Every tent and building around the airfield was gone. So were all the squadron's maintenance equipment and the air-to-ground radio unit set up by Major Bayler. Except for Sergeant Earl Hannum, hospitalized with dysentery, every mechanic in the squadron was either dead or wounded. As the magnitude of what had happened slowly sank in, some men who'd braved bursting bombs and incendiary bullets without flinching a few minutes earlier succumbed to fear, shock, and feelings of helplessness.

No man on Wake had a more gut-wrenching job that day than PFC Joseph E. "Ed" Borne, a truck driver from the Marine motor pool, who was dispatched to the airfield with a dump truck to pick up the dead and take them to a cold-storage reefer at Camp Two until burial could be arranged.

Borne had driven to the airfield just before the raid with orders from Gunner John Hamas to distribute gas masks to members of the aviation unit. Hamas, a Czech-born professional soldier, had fought on both sides in World War I, first for the Austro-Hungarian army, then on the Allied side for the Czechs. He'd immigrated to the States in the early 1920s and immediately joined the Marines, winning the Navy Cross for valor in Nicaragua. Now he was a kind of father figure to the youngsters on Wake, and Borne knew that if anybody on the atoll understood the value of a gas mask, it was Hamas. Borne's reception by VMF-211 had been less than cordial, however.

"Everything at the airfield was screwed up and in disarray, and everybody was pissed off because they didn't have what they needed," Borne recalled. "They were all so mad that when I asked 'em where they wanted me to put the gas masks, they said, 'Shove 'em up your ass.' I left the masks anyway, and I'd just made it to Toki Point at the far end of Peale Island when the bombs started falling."

When the raid ended, Borne was ordered by Mess Sergeant A. R. "Slim" Hughes to take his truck back to the airfield to "pick up the stiffs."

"I'd never seen anything like it, and I hope to God I never do again," said Borne, a native Louisianan who had witnessed his share of unsavory sights while growing up on the New Orleans waterfront. "There were dismembered bodies everywhere, and you could smell human flesh burning."

Some of the bodies had been reduced to loose piles of severed limbs and mangled organs that defied efforts to pick them up, and the charred corpse of Lieutenant Graves broke into pieces when it was lifted. "The plane was still hot to touch, and when the body cracked open, some kind of horrible-smelling steam came out of it," Borne said. "I just couldn't take it at first. It made me so sick I thought I'd never stop throwing up. I felt so bad that I left and went back to the garage, but Hughes made me turn right around again."

On his second try, Borne got help from a small detail of Navy bluejackets and a few civilians. Together, they managed to fill the truck with remains, and Borne hauled them away to the reefer. A day later, when the makeshift morgue was hit during another bombing raid, Borne would be pressed into service to move the same bodies a second time.

Meanwhile, the wounded were loaded onto another truck and driven to the civilian hospital at Camp Two. There Lieutenant Gustave Kahn, a recent graduate of the University of Texas Medical School at Galveston and the only military physician on Wake, along with Dr. Lawton E. Shank, a small-town surgeon from Indiana employed by the contractors, would work nonstop on the casualties until dawn the next day. Assisted by eight Navy corpsmen and several civilian male nurses, they dealt with the most critical cases first, then worked their way down to the less seriously injured.

It was after eleven o'clock that night when an exhausted Dr. Kahn finally got a chance to look at Seaman First Class James Darden, a North Carolinian bluejacket assigned to the staff of the naval air station. Darden had a gaping hole in his left thigh—a souvenir from a fragmentation bomb at the airport.

By then the medics were out of antiseptic, anesthesia, sutures, and almost everything else. Kahn had nothing but table salt dissolved in hot water to disinfect Darden's mangled leg as he swabbed leaves, twigs, sand, and chunks of coral out of the wound and nothing but cotton twine with which to reattach the severed muscles and tendons.

"This is going to hurt, Darden," Kahn said.

He was right. The salt solution burned like liquid fire, and it was all Darden could do to keep from screaming each time Kahn applied it. But even in his agony, the sailor kept reminding himself that the pain was better than gangrene.

Three pilots who were among the "walking wounded"—Major Putnam, Captain Tharin, and Sergeant Arthur—opted for first aid at the airfield and stayed on duty. No man who could still move around on his own could be spared, Putnam told the remnants of his unit. There was too much to do, and far too few hands to do it.

One of Putnam's first and most crucial moves was to name a new engineering officer to replace Lieutenant Graves. VMF-211 still had three unblemished Wildcats, a fourth in need of repair, and another that might—with enough patchwork and prayer—be coaxed to fly again. But it would take someone with tireless energy and plenty of mechanical skill to keep Wake's tiny air force in action.

Putnam turned to Lieutenant Kinney, whose lengthy experience as a civilian aviator and mechanic prior to joining the Marines gave him all the necessary qualifications.

"Kinney," he said, "you're now the squadron engineering officer. We have four planes left. If you can keep them flying, I'll see that you get a medal as big as a pie."

"Okay, sir," Kinney replied with a tight smile, "but only if it's delivered in San Francisco."

Sergeant Hamilton was appointed to assist Kinney, and he went immediately to Camp Two to scrounge among Navy stores there for tools and potentially usable airplane parts. As soon as the wrecked planes cooled sufficiently, they were also examined for salvageable parts that might be used to get the two damaged fighters up and running. Over the next two weeks, Kinney and Hamilton would perform one small miracle after another to keep VMF-211 in the air.

The squadron couldn't afford any more surprises, so the three undamaged Wildcats were quickly sent back aloft, both to keep an eye out for Japanese planes or ships and simply to keep them off the ground. Every available man worked to finish the foxholes and bomb shelters that had been started around the field before the raid. Construction also moved ahead at full speed on the uncompleted revetments for the surviving planes, plus an underground service shelter that could be blacked out for nighttime repairs.

Putnam ordered dynamite charges placed at 150-foot intervals along the runway to prevent any Japanese airborne invasion attempt. Deep furrows were bulldozed in the areas surrounding the field so that enemy planes couldn't land there, and tractors and other pieces of heavy equipment were brought to the field to barricade the runway at night, after the last F4F-3s returned from patrol.

The Japanese would like nothing better than to finish off VMF-211 once and for all, Putnam knew. But as he looked into the faces of his remaining men, he could tell the feeling was mutual. They were itching to even the score and ready to do whatever they had to do to get another crack at the enemy.

From all indications, they wouldn't have to wait long for their chance, but the big question was "When?"

Clearly, the Japanese bombers had come from a land base in the Marshalls. Wake was too far from Hawaii to be hit by the same planes that had raided Pearl, they reasoned. By figuring the distance enemy planes had to travel from the Marshalls—about 600 nautical miles—and their likely speed, Putnam's squadron could project the time of the next Japanese attack with a fair degree of accuracy.

According to their best estimate, they could expect to have another date with Nell about noon tomorrow.

From one end of Wake to the other, men in gun pits, foxholes, and dugouts were asking themselves similar questions about the enemy's next move. Their conclusions were based on less precise information than Putnam and Kinney had at their disposal, but they boiled down to the same thing: The enemy wanted Wake, and they wanted every American on it dead. They'd be back—and likely very soon.

Almost as unnerving as the actual loss of men and material was the dawning realization that the garrison's ordeal had scarcely begun. Without radar or listening devices of any kind, what was to keep the Japanese from repeating their success tomorrow and the next day and the day after that? Obviously the first raid was only a curtain-raiser. The Japanese would come back again and again until they assumed the defenders were helpless. Then they'd send their ships and landing parties in for the kill.

It was especially disheartening to Devereux that the beating had been administered without retaliation, despite the fact that every man in the battalion had been at his post and supposedly prepared for an attack. It was "cold comfort," he said, to realize that his guns had all been manned and ready, and that the garrison had still been caught by surprise. With radar, Major Putnam's whole squadron would have been airborne to greet the Japanese bombers, instead of having most of its planes sitting helpless on the ground.

"Whatever might have happened if we'd had our radar, the simple fact remained that we'd lost the first round of the battle for Wake Island," Devereux concluded. "The enemy had hit us a staggering blow and escaped almost scot-free."

So the big question now was: Would the same thing happen the second time around?

For the most part, Camp One had been reduced to mounds of shredded canvas, but in a practical sense, its uninhabitable condition made little difference. Its Marines were now securely dug in around their battle stations and had no desire to go back to their vulnerable tents.

The new barracks and other structures at Camp Two had merely been strafed, not bombed, so damage was fairly light, but they made too tempting a target to escape the enemy's attention for long.

At the Pan Am compound on Peale, however, the damage was mind-boggling. The airline's radio station, machine shop, and hotel were in total ruins, and some of its fuel storage tanks had blown up. The Clipper in the lagoon was riddled by bullets, but the enemy gunners had somehow missed its vital parts and it was still fit to fly. All its passengers had also miraculously escaped serious injury.

Any thought of using the Clipper for a reconnaisance mission was now forgotten. The only sensible thing left to do was get the big flying boat and however many noncombatants could be squeezed aboard out of the war zone as soon as possible. The problem was that the number of people needing to be evacuated far exceeded the Clipper's normal capacity. John Hamilton, the Clipper's pilot, hoped to get airborne with sixty people on board a plane that usually carried less than a third that many on its trans-Pacific hops.

After all nonessential cargo was dumped, including the outgoing mail, all twenty-seven of Pan Am's American employees, including two with minor wounds, piled onto the big flying boat, along with the regular passengers. Two dozen Chamorros, dark-skinned natives of Guam who also worked for the airline, weren't allowed aboard, however. When a pair tried to stow away, they were promptly ejected.

"I knew the plane had limited space," Commander Cunningham said later, "but it seemed to me an unfortunate time to draw the color line."

About 1:30 P.M., Hamilton started trying to take off. Twice, however, he had to cut the engines and abort at the last moment to keep from slamming into the opposite shore of the lagoon. Finally, on the third attempt, the overloaded Clipper rose unsteadily from the water. It barely cleared the trees on the southern leg of Wake proper and remained at a precariously low altitude as it headed northeast toward Midway and safety.

Left behind were two passengers who somehow failed to get word the Clipper was leaving. One was August Ramquist, a Pan Am mechanic, who missed the flight while he was helping transport wounded Chamorros to the hospital. The other was Herman Hevenor, a representative of the Bureau of the Budget in Washington, who was checking out the construction on Wake to make sure America's taxpayers were getting their money's worth.

Fortunately, there was some positive news mixed in with the bad. In spite of massive losses to the islands' fuel supply, there was still plenty of gasoline in six widely scattered dumps concealed in the brush. Some 600,000 gallons of fresh water were stored in underground reservoirs— enough to meet the garrison's drinking and cooking demands for months, even if the seawater desalinization plants were destroyed. Enough ammunition for an extended siege had been stockpiled in bombproof magazines.

A six-month supply of food was also on hand, but getting it to the hungry men dispersed over the three islands posed a major logistical problem, especially since few Marines could be spared for mess duty. CPNAB superintendent Dan Teters came to the rescue, taking personal charge of the feeding operation and using civilian manpower and equipment to prepare and distribute rations twice a day to all personnel.

The best news of all on the afternoon of December 8 was that Wake's Marine Defense Battalion and its painstakingly constructed network of antiaircraft emplacements, shore batteries, and machine gun pits had come through the first attack virtually unscathed. Not a single member of Devereux's force had been killed, and except for a few minor scratches, nobody was hurt.

The major knew, however, that the only reason for this bit of good luck was the enemy hunters' preoccupation with different game on this first day. The attackers were almost certain to concentrate on the defense battalion and its artillery the next time around. The Marines' five-inch guns were well entrenched and camouflaged, but the three-inch antiaircraft batteries were easier for the attackers to spot, especially when the guns were in action, and therefore more vulnerable. There were still more foxholes and shelters to be dug for the gun crews, and others to be deepened. There were damaged sandbags and old camouflage foliage to be replaced. There were food, water, and ammunition caches to be built and stocked in scattered locations around the three islands. Sanitary field facilities were now a matter of major importance, so slit trenches had to be dug and covered latrines built. Otherwise, a dysentery outbreak could fell men as ruthlessly as Japanese bullets. It added up to dirty round-the-clock labor.

To bolster the garrison's defensive capabilities, Devereux also moved quickly to assign all clerks, cooks, and other personnel without a primary combat post—seventy-three men in all—to a new mobile reserve force. Picked to command it was Second Lieutenant Arthur Poindexter, a young Kansan whose amiable exterior concealed a fierce will to win at anything he undertook. To give the force extra firepower, four machine guns were mounted on the bed of a truck so that they and the experienced gunners manning them could be rushed anywhere they might be needed.

As tired as they were, the Marines would have a hard time sleeping in their foxholes that night. Field commanders had ordered their machine guns manned constantly, and every battery maintained a high state of alert. Beach patrols kept watch all along the shore. Even the men who drifted into a fitful slumber while they weren't on watch tended to jerk awake every few minutes. Many of them just kept digging in foxholes and shelters that never seemed quite deep enough.

Along with his men, Devereux also moved under cover, setting up a makeshift command post in a dank dugout well hidden in the brush.

In the midst of all this, Commander Cunningham was still finding it difficult to shake free of peacetime procedures and priorities that no longer mattered and focus on the most urgent of wartime needs. Although the island commander allowed some Navy personnel to be shifted to defensive duties, he refused to reassign a number of others designated as staff for the naval air station.

For reasons best known to Cunningham himself, he also insisted that construction work continue on the air station, although the odds of it being completed, or even surviving the future Japanese raids that were sure to come, were next to nil.

Because of a single raid, Cunningham reasoned, it couldn't be assumed that all work on the naval air station should come to a standstill. On the contrary, to his way of thinking, the urgency of the construction job was even more pressing now than before. Only when it was impossible to carry on normal construction operations should the work be discontinued, he insisted.

The majority of those on Wake would doubtless have said that that time had already arrived. In light of the day's disaster, continuing to expend manpower and materials on an unprotected construction project was the equivalent of trying to build a snowman in a hot oven.

This doesn't mean, however, that Cunningham wasn't doing anything worthwhile. He sent three mechanics from the seaplane base to the airfield to help Lieutenant Kinney and Sergeant Hamilton with the Wildcats. He also dispatched eighteen bluejackets to join Lieutenant Poindexter's mobile reserve.

That afternoon, Cunningham sent an urgent radio message to Pearl Harbor detailing the attack on Wake, the loss of the eight Wildcats, the twenty-five men killed, the thirty wounded. Soon afterward, he remembered to contact the U.S. submarines *Triton* and *Tambor,* which were operating off Wake. They'd both been submerged all day and out of radio contact. When Cunningham realized that they had no knowledge of the attack on Wake, or even of the outbreak of war, he gave his radioman, Ensign Bernard Lauff, a message telling the subs' skippers what had happened and directing them to stay on the alert for enemy ships.

Not long after that, an eight-word transmission came back from Fourteenth Naval District headquarters at Pearl:

EXECUTE UNRESTRICTED SUBMARINE AND AIR WARFARE
AGAINST JAPAN

Cunningham didn't know whether to laugh or cry. The battered, bomb-blasted defenders of Wake finally had official permission to fight back.

Meanwhile there was the pressing problem of unmanned batteries and machine guns around the islands. These armaments could exact a heavy price from future attackers, possibly even spell the difference between survival and annihilation for the defenders—but only if enough men could be found to put them into action.

Even if Cunningham had approved the use of every available man, Wake's military personnel couldn't begin to meet all these needs by themselves. Fortunately, they had a strong, resourceful ally that the Japanese may not have reckoned on—a small army of civilian contractors, ranging from fuzzy-cheeked teenagers to gray-haired grandfathers.

To be sure, not all of the CPNAB workers took part in this sacrificial volunteer effort. Many of them vanished into the brush within minutes after that first air raid, taking such food and other supplies as they could carry, and hid out there for the duration of the battle. They not only refused to expose themselves to combat but also refused to do any kind of work. Given the fact that few of them had been forewarned of the impending danger, that almost nothing was done to protect them from the initial attack, and that a disproportionate number of the dead and wounded were civilians, it's hard to fault those who followed this course.

The Marines were conditioned to react differently. A few of them had fought in World War I, and a sizable number had seen service in Nicaragua, but even the greenest recruit had been schooled from his first day of boot camp to regard war as his trade. Their attitude was that fighting—and killing or being killed if necessary—was just part of the job. Since the civilians lacked this psychological conditioning, it's easy to understand why many of them tried to hide from danger. But this same lack only made those who joined the fight more deserving of admiration.

All told, an estimated 300 to 400 civilians chose to become a powerful auxiliary force in the atoll's defense. They supplied ammunition to numerous machine guns and batteries. They delivered food and water. They stood watch in relief of bone-tired Marines. They filled sandbags, operated heavy equipment, helped bury the dead and tend the wounded. One of their greatest contributions was repeatedly helping to move the three-inch antiaircraft batteries to keep the Japanese bombers from being able to zero in on their locations and destroy them.

"On the evening after the first raid, about two hundred of us met with Dan Teters," Idahoan Glenn Newell recalled. "He told us, 'We're gonna work with the Marines, and when the Japs come back, we're gonna shove the shaft right to 'em.' They gave my brother a truck and put him to hauling sandbags. I helped move the big guns at night and carried ammo."

"We called ourselves the 'dirty dozen,'" said Chalas Loveland of his group of civilian volunteers. "We went wherever we were needed and worked around the clock. One night when there were no guns to be moved, we hauled a bunch of thirty-foot steel H-beams to build a big underground shelter on Peale."

"That first night, the Marines gave us the impression we were pretty much on our own," said civilian Ed Doyle, who had come to Wake to do concrete work for a new submarine base, then sent such glowing letters home to his brother, Bob, that he signed up with M-K, too. "Bob and I wanted to get the hell out of there, but there was no place to go. Then they told us we were all needed, and I think most of the civilians responded. They gave me a truck and told me to be available day or night. I hauled men, food, ammunition, and just about anything else that could be hauled."

More than a few of the civilians actually took up arms and fought as full-fledged soldiers.

No survivor of Wake knows the importance of the civilians' contribution better than Sergeant Walter Bowsher, and none worked harder to develop it. Through a unique set of circumstances, the veteran artilleryman was handed the job of recruiting, training, and commanding the only all-civilian gun crew on the atoll. Without these civilian volunteers, who worked for Bowsher on a previously unmanned antiaircraft gun on Peale Island, the three-incher would never have fired a single shot at the enemy.

Bowsher was in sick bay with a bad knee on the morning of December 8 when he got word about the raid on Pearl Harbor. The knee was painful and swollen with what had been diagnosed as a thrombosis or blood clot, and Bowsher had been warned to keep off the leg and stay in bed.

He fidgeted for a while, then sat up. *I'm not lying here on my fanny and waiting to get shot,* the onetime Indiana farmboy told himself. *If the Japs are going to shoot me, I'd rather be on my feet when it happens.*

Bowsher grabbed his crutches and a bandolier of ammo and hobbled to his battle station at Battery D, the antiaircraft emplacement on the north shore of Peale. One of the first people he ran into was Captain Godbold, the island's strongpoint commander.

"You shouldn't be out here with that leg of yours," Godbold said. "You need to head back to the hospital."

"I just don't feel right there, sir," Bowsher said. "I feel like I need to be doing something."

Godbold frowned, and Bowsher was sure he was about to be banished to sick bay again, but after a few seconds, the captain relented. He sent Bowsher to a nearby ammunition magazine instead, where he could sit down at least part of the time while he sorted and distributed ammo.

During the first raid, Bowsher stayed in the magazine, obviously one of the safest places on the atoll, but the sound of bursting bombs and the staccato crack of the battery's three-inchers set his adrenaline to pumping furiously. That night, physically exhausted and emotionally drained, he fell asleep on a stack of three-inch shells.

Bowsher never knew exactly how it happened, but when he woke up the next morning, the swelling had gone down in his leg. A corpsman looked at it and speculated that all the excitement of the past twenty-four hours had somehow caused the clot to break up. He told Bowsher it was okay to walk on it but just to take it easy.

Now that he was mobile again, Bowsher was ready to return to his regular post on the battery, but Godbold had a more important assignment for him.

"As you know, there's no crew for our number-three gun," Godbold said. "Since you're one of our more experienced hands, why don't you see if you can get enough civilians together to man the gun. Otherwise, it's just going to sit there useless."

It was a tall order. If you went by the book, it took a minimum of fourteen men to operate a three-inch gun, but when Bowsher started his search, he got lucky almost immediately. Somebody steered him to Amos White of Rahway, New Jersey, an Army veteran who'd trained on three-inch antiaircraft guns with the U.S. Coast Artillery. It was only a start but a promising one.

Over the next few hours, Bowsher interviewed about thirty civilians in all, and White was the only one he found with any real artillery experience. So Bowsher started concentrating on men who'd been in ROTC or National Guard units, or even in the National Rifle Association. At least, he figured, they knew a little something about weapons—enough to have a healthy fear of them, if nothing else.

Before the day was over, the sergeant had found his fourteen men, and they were an intriguing cross section of the workers brought to Wake by CPNAB. At one end of the spectrum was seventy-two-year-old George Lawback of Milton, Georgia. Lawback's age didn't allow him to operate the gun in battle, but he was so determined to help that Bowsher let him handle general maintenance. At the other end was twenty-two-year-old Eldon Hargis of Roseburg, Oregon, who became a shell passer.

Because of his National Guard experience, Elmo "Doc" Robinett of Milton, Oregon, was named assistant gun captain and fuse setter. Don Ludington, a sheet metal foreman from McCall, Idaho, who was experienced with small arms and machinery, was assigned to operate the azimuth, an instrument for measuring horizontal direction. Earl "Shorty" Row of Jasonville, Indiana, was designated as a fuse cutter, partly because he'd developed an interest in soldiering as a high school student at a military summer camp.

Other members of the crew included Harold Cleft of Nampha, Idaho, number one loader; Arthur Griffith of Fairfield, Idaho, hot shellman; Harvey Burdett of Oakland, Oregon, ammo handler; Darwin Miners of Spokane, Washington, breech operator; William Myrdock of Elco, Nevada, shell passer; Marshall Talbot of Los Angeles, California, elevation operator; and H. Floyd Turner of Platsburg, California, shell passer.

Ludington, the only surviving member of the all-civilian crew as this book was written, had volunteered for three-inch duty even before the war started and had taken part in several practice runs with the battery. "We didn't actually fire," he said, "but we went through all the motions. Everything changed, though, when people were actually dropping bombs at you. Each one of them looked like it was going to hit you right on the nose." Ludington, who was twenty-five at the time, was left shaken but fighting mad by the first bombing, and he jumped at the chance Bowsher offered to strike back at the Japanese.

During twelve hours of nonstop orientation, Bowsher met with each member of his new crew individually, patiently explaining their specific duties. He also put the men through an intensive three-hour crash course in operating the gun as a unit.

"They had some trouble concentrating at first," Bowsher said. "They kept wanting to stop every time they fired a round and look up to see where it went, but after a few days they managed to break themselves of that habit, and they did just fine. They were willing and worked hard, and before long, their gun was making about as good a showing as the others in the battery."

It wouldn't take long for the only all-civilian gun crew on Wake to put its rudimentary training to its first major test.

Tuesday, December 9, dawned bright and clear. General quarters sounded at 5:00 A.M., and red-eyed Marines crawled out of their foxholes to find food and hot coffee being distributed by Teters's contractors. They gulped down their breakfast and hurried to their battle stations.

Devereux declared a Condition One Alert, meaning that all field telephones, batteries, machine guns, and lookout posts across Wake were to be manned constantly. At the airfield, after working all night to repair the Wildcat damaged in the raid, Kinney and Hamilton now reported it ready to fly and turned their attention to the fighter with the bent prop. At 5:45 A.M., two planes took off on morning patrol. The two operable planes left on the ground were out of sight in protective revetments.

About an hour later, after the F4F-3s made certain no Japanese ships had slipped into the area overnight, Devereux downgraded the alert status to Condition Two, which required only half the guns to be kept fully manned. It wasn't that the threat of attack had eased—on the contrary, the danger stood to increase as the morning wore on—but Condition Two allowed many of the Marines to get back to work on numerous unfinished defensive preparations. One of the biggest of these involved filling 500 sandbags and placing them around the antiaircraft batteries on Wilkes.

In the antiaircraft emplacements, gun crews debated among themselves over whether the next raid would come from the same low altitudes as the first one or from a higher elevation. Lieutenant Wally Lewis, commanding Battery E on Peacock Point, had been among the first to spot yesterday's attackers—and also among the first to see how ineffective his battery was against the fast-moving Nells at 1,500 feet or less. Nevertheless, he was outspokenly predicting a high-altitude raid today.

"We didn't hit a damn thing, but we put up a lot of rounds yesterday," Lewis said. "That's going to make the Japs feel safer up high today. They won't be safer, though, they'll just think they are."

This time, the surprise belonged to VMF-211.

As noon approached, all four of the depleted squadron's usable fighters were aloft and scouring the clear skies for enemy planes. Flying well south of Wake were Sergeant Hamilton, who'd been up all night patching bullet holes in the wounded Wildcat but still insisted on taking his turn on mid-day patrol, and Lieutenant Dave Kliewer.

At about 11:30 A.M., the two pilots spotted a chillingly familiar sight—twenty-seven twin-tailed Nells in three tight Vs headed straight for Peacock Point at 13,000 feet.

In a lookout tower on the ground, meanwhile, Gunner Harold C. Borth also saw the bombers approaching and shouted a warning into his phone. Immediately, the only effective air raid signal that the garrison had been able to come up with—three shots fired in rapid succession from a rifle or sidearm—echoed and reechoed across the atoll. Gun crews began tracking the incoming planes, and everybody else scrambled for shelter.

Hamilton and Kliewer pushed their F4F-3s into a screaming dive and fell on the nearest nine-plane V with their .50-caliber machine guns blazing, attempting to break up the formation. The bombers held steady on course, and their gunners returned a heavy fire, but the Wildcats wheeled around for a second pass, then a third.

One of the enemy planes started to wobble, and the Marine fliers smelled blood. Hamilton closed in for the kill, pouring a hail of bullets into the faltering Nell. It was already in flames when Kliewer finished it off.

By now, the rest of the enemy planes were almost over Peacock Point, and black puffs of ack-ack dotted the sky. The Grummans radioed the batteries below that the raiders had dropped down to 11,000 feet. Then they pulled back to avoid the friendly fire and watched as the blazing Japanese bomber spun into the sea.

Wake's defenders had scored their first official "kill"—and they weren't done for the day by any means.

Lieutenant Lewis's three-inchers filled the air around the attackers with flak, getting off close to a hundred rounds in a single minute, and another Nell spurted smoke and fell out of formation. Sergeant Charles Holmes, supervising Battery E's director crew, grinned when he saw the hit and the general effectiveness of the battery's fire.

Despite the heavy antiaircraft barrage, most of the attackers stayed on course, laying a line of bombs across the base of Wake proper, from Peacock Point to the lagoon, and forcing the gun crews to stop firing and duck for cover. The bombs came perilously close to the three-inch battery on Peacock, close enough to shower it and the surrounding foxholes with coral dust and debris.

Many of the bombs were "screamers" that made an eerie whistling sound as they fell. A couple of hundred yards from Holmes's position, his friend and fellow Texan, PFC Jesse Nowlin, cowered in a foxhole near Battery A, the five-inch emplacement on Peacock, and tried to avoid looking up. Each bomb, he said, seemed to be aimed "directly at my belly button."

Nowlin, Holmes, and most of their battery mates came through the attack with nothing worse than concussions, but Private John Katchak wasn't so fortunate. A bomb exploded within about six feet of the nineteen-year-old rookie crewman on Battery A, blowing his body to pieces and turning his foxhole into his grave. As soon as it was safe to come out, Katchak's comrades built up a small mound of coral chunks over his body, mumbled a quick prayer, and left his remains where they lay. He was the first member of Wake's Marine Defense Battalion killed in action.

From Peacock, the planes swept north and west over Wake proper, wasting some of their bombs along the north side of the airfield, where there was nothing to hit but empty scrub. But they scored a direct hit on a gasoline truck carrying three Marines, whose bodies were found ten days later.

Then the raiders crossed the lagoon and loosed their full fury on Camp Two. After escaping with only a strafing in the first raid, virtually every modern wooden building in the camp was heavily damaged. The barracks where the civilians had lived, the quarters housing the naval air station personnel, storehouses, machine shops, and a huge garage filled with vehicles were largely reduced to splinters.

Worse yet, despite a directive from Cunningham that civilians should stay dispersed, many contractors had drifted back to their comfortable barracks after a night of roughing it in the open. Scores were concentrated in the camp, apparently unaware of the danger, as the enemy bombers roared over. More than thirty were killed outright or mortally wounded, and about twenty others were injured.

Dan Teters and another man barely escaped the Camp Two carnage by hiding in a storage vault and slamming the heavy steel door shut behind them. Seconds later, a bomb blast bent the door so severely that they couldn't open it, trapping the pair inside and threatening them with suffocation until help arrived to free them.

The raiders moved on to inflict heavy damage on Peale Island, where their closely patterned bombs pounded the unfinished naval air station, demolished the Navy radio station, battered a large warehouse crammed with $1 million worth of materials, and destroyed what remained of the Pan Am hotel.

But for Wake's defenders, the enemy's most heartless and unforgivable act that second day was deliberately targeting the hospital at Camp Two.

The T-shaped wooden structure had a large red cross clearly painted across its roof, but the Japanese bombardiers either didn't see it or didn't care. Inside, dozens of wounded men lay helpless, unable to move, much less save themselves. Many were unconscious or dazed by pain or medication, but others could clearly hear the sound of the bombs getting closer and closer.

Near Devereux's command post on the other side of the lagoon, Marines watched in horror as the bombers closed in on the hospital. When they realized where the enemy bombs were heading, they could only shut their eyes and curse.

Sergeant Tom Kennedy of VMF-211, whose arm and leg wounds were painful but not nearly as serious as those of many others in his ward, heard the first explosions. After yesterday, there was no doubt in his mind that they were bombs, but he wasn't really worried.

"Just take it easy," he reassured the Marine on the bed next to him. "They won't bother us here. They know this is a hospital."

Just then, a stream of machine gun bullets gouged holes in the ceiling above his head. Kennedy couldn't get up but he squirmed down as close to the foot of the bed as he could, hoping it was far enough to get him out of the line of fire.

A few feet away, Dr. Kahn dove under a bed and pulled a foot locker down on top of it for protection as another burst of machine gun fire plowed up the floor inches away. The bullets shredded a pair of shoes at the edge of the bed, and one ricocheting slug pierced Kahn's pants leg but somehow didn't break his skin.

A moment later, a half-dozen bombs struck one wing of the hospital almost simultaneously, turning it into a roaring inferno. Kennedy could hear wounded men screaming.

Navy Commander Campbell Keene, a balding, affable Navy aviator who was in charge of Wake's budding seaplane base, and Yeoman Glenn Tripp, who had started the week as Cunningham's office assistant, ran through the blazing shambles, shouting for everyone who was able to get out before the fire reached them. Several wounded civilians took them at their word and ran outside, taking cover under a tractor. In the next second, another bomb hit the tractor, and it and the men under it disappeared.

Keene pulled Kennedy off the bed and tried to get him to walk, but Kennedy was too weak and in too much pain. As big and husky as Keene was, it took the help of another man to move the wounded sergeant outside and steer him to a nearby building that hadn't been hit. Another patient, Seaman First Class William Manning, hit three times by machine gun fire on December 8 as he arrived at the airfield with a truckload of bluejackets, had suffered seven fresh wounds from bomb fragments. Manning was bleeding profusely, but he managed to drag himself out of the burning hospital.

Meanwhile, Tripp ran straight to the cot where severely wounded pilot "Spider" Webb lay helpless and unconscious. He scooped Webb up and struggled with him through leaping flames toward the nearest exit.

The hospital was blazing like a torch when Ed Borne showed up in his truck. Borne had been nicked in the leg moments earlier by a piece of shrapnel, but when he saw Dr. Kahn trying to drag a bedsheet filled with medical supplies out of the building, he ran over to help.

"What do you want me to do, Doc?" Borne asked.

"Just grab anything you can get," Kahn panted. "Otherwise, we're going to lose it all."

Borne forced his way inside, shielding his face from the intense heat with his arms. He ripped the sheets from the nearest bed and dumped part of the contents of a supply cabinet on them. Then he wrapped the sheet around them and pulled it toward the door.

When he got outside, Kahn helped him get the stuff to a safe area, and Borne turned back toward the hospital.

"You better not go back in," Kahn yelled. "The whole thing's about to go up."

"I can make it one more time," Borne said.

Back inside, flames were leaping everywhere, and the heat was almost unbearable, but Borne spotted another storage unit filled with large glass bottles. He struggled forward for a closer look and saw that they were quarts of clear liquid.

"The labels said 'vodka,' and I started grabbing them," Borne recalled many years later. "I got a whole armload, as many as I could carry, and I ran like hell."

He found Kahn waiting nervously for him outside. The young Navy doctor from Amarillo, Texas, was haggard, unshaven, and near collapse from stress and lack of sleep, but when he saw the bottles, his soot-streaked face brightened slightly.

"Hey, hand me one of those," he said.

Kahn broke open a quart of the vodka, offered it to Borne, and they both had a long, unceremonious snort from Wake's last surviving stock of medicinal alcohol.

"I feel like kissing you, Borne," Kahn said.

It was a rare moment of levity in the middle of a holocaust. Behind them, in the ruins of the hospital, the attack had taken a heavy toll among the wounded. At least three injured Marines and four or five civilians were killed, and Seaman Manning was among several others who suffered new wounds.

As the Japanese bombers streaked north over Peale, Captain Godbold's Battery D on Toki Point threw everything it could at them. The battery's three guns—including the one manned entirely by Sergeant Bowsher's civilians—fired more than a hundred rounds before the planes moved out of range.

Godbold counted five of the Nells trailing smoke as they turned back to the south. While it was still in sight, one of the planes exploded and fell in fiery fragments into the ocean. "The other damaged Japs were smoking so badly," Devereux said, "that our aviation men calculated they'd never get home."

Even if that was only wishful thinking, the attackers had, at least, paid a price this time. But once more, the enemy had dealt Wake's defenders a much more devastating blow than anything they'd received in return.

Now it was time to collect the bodies of the freshly slaughtered. Time to try to take care of the wounded with almost no medical supplies and nothing resembling a proper hospital. Time to pick up the pieces again.

It was also time to accept the undeniable certainty that tomorrow would bring more of the same—if not something even worse.

*Major James P. S. Devereux, commander
of the Wake detachment of the First
Marine Defense Battalion, directed the
artillery barrage that sank one major
Japanese ship, heavily damaged several
others, and repelled a Japanese invasion
attempt on December 11, 1941.*
(Marine Corps Historical Center)

☆ 6 ☆

The Spider and the Fly

With three-fourths of the conventional buildings on Wake reduced to piles of rubble, four large powder magazines just east of the airfield now assumed paramount importance for the atoll's defenders. The fact that they were built partially underground with igloo-style domed roofs of reinforced concrete made them the safest structures on the islands. Each magazine measured about forty by twenty feet, with a fifteen-foot ceiling and the additional protection of several feet of dirt piled on top.

This was called "elephant-back" construction because that's what the finished exterior structure looked like. More of the same type magazines were planned on both Wake proper and Wilkes, but only these four were anywhere near complete when the Japanese attacked.

Soon after the second enemy air raid, the garrison tackled the task of moving all surviving patients and the small stores of supplies and equipment salvaged from the bombed-out hospital at Camp Two into two of the magazines. The one farthest to the north was designated for civilian wounded and supervised by Dr. Shank; the one farthest south housed Marine and Navy casualties, with Dr. Kahn in charge.

There was room for twenty-one beds inside each hospital magazine. Small generators provided electric power, and their sunken construction allowed them to remain lighted all night without interfering with the enforced islandwide blackout. By now it was clear that structural steel and concrete were far more reliable protection for the American wounded than a Red Cross symbol on a roof.

Commander Cunningham ordered the Army radio unit's portable equipment—now the atoll's sole remaining means of sending and receiving messages to and from the outside world—installed in one of the remaining two magazines. Cunningham also relocated his command post to the same magazine, although he continued to sleep in his VIP cottage near what was left of Camp Two.

For his own separate command post, Devereux chose a spot at the edge of Wake's south beach, where he had an eight-foot-deep dugout scooped out of the coral, roofed with heavy timbers, and then covered with a layer of coral and sand several feet thick. Its roof afforded a good view of the sea, but it was in a much more vulnerable location, and within a few days, Devereux would relocate his CP to the fourth magazine.

These moves enabled Wake's command staff to withstand virtually anything that enemy ships or aircraft might throw its way. Unfortunately, they did nothing to ensure that Cunningham and Devereux could maintain effective contact with their widely scattered defensive outposts if the enemy landed ground forces on the islands.

Another crucial concern was keeping the antiaircraft guns and shore batteries functioning at peak capacity. So far, the gun emplacements had fared surprisingly well, but the second raid had created a number of problems. One of Lieutenant Lewis's three-inch AA guns had been damaged in the attack on Peacock Point, so Devereux ordered Gunner Clarence McKinstry to gather a crew to move the damaged gun to Wilkes Island, then bring back one of the guns from the unmanned three-inch battery there to replace it.

McKinstry's rugged good looks were a prototype of the "rough-and-ready" Marine image. Back in the days before he'd decided to let his red beard grow long, he'd been featured in a series of shaving-cream ads in national magazines. "Big Mack" was every bit as tough as he looked, but like his tentmate, Gunner John Hamas, he had a soft spot a yard wide where his men were concerned.

After dark that evening, Devereux also had Lewis's battery moved more than five hundred yards to a new position farther inland. It was a grueling, hours-long ordeal for the gun crew—the first of many all-night moving chores faced by the crews in coming days to keep the enemy guessing about the AA guns' location. Each of the three effective guns in Lewis's battery weighed eight tons, and each had to be jacked up and mounted on a "bogie," a removable truck consisting of an axle and two big wheels with pneumatic tires, then rolled to the new location.

But that wasn't all. Protective sandbags had to be filled and placed around the new position. Ammunition had to be hauled and stored in dumps within easy handling distance of the guns. The new position also had to be camouflaged, and, as a final creative touch, dummy guns made from wooden timbers were erected in the old position so that it appeared unchanged from the air.

It was a man-killer of a job—one the Marines didn't finish until five o'clock the next morning. Wake's three-inch gun crews had to keep playing an arduous game of cat and mouse throughout the siege. Otherwise, they'd soon forfeit their ability to strike back at their tormentors.

Devereux later took some criticism for moving his antiaircraft guns farther from the beach. His order admittedly ran counter to the established theory that AA batteries should be positioned to strike attacking planes while they were still as far from their bombing targets as possible. But Devereux had a lot more than theoretical problems to deal with. There was convincing evidence that the enemy had spotted Lewis's position. Not only had the Japanese planes damaged one of his guns, but one plane had broken formation during the raid and circled over the battery, probably taking photographs to guide the next wave of attackers. There was no way to replace the three-inchers if they were knocked out, and without them, the enemy would be able to bomb the islands almost at will.

The next day, December 10, the Japanese bombers came calling a bit earlier than usual. It was only 10:45 A.M. when they made their third appearance over Wake.

Most observers placed the number of Nells at eighteen this time, divided into two nine-plane V formations, but others claimed to count as many as twenty-seven planes. They came in high at 18,000 feet, one section of them heading straight for the old antiaircraft position on Peacock Point. Within seconds, it became painfully obvious that only Devereux's stubborn sixth sense and his men's sweat and sleeplessness had saved the battery from disaster.

From his strongpoint on Peacock, Lieutenant Clarence Barninger described the scene in terms that any bowler could appreciate: "The Japs rolled right down the alley that had Lewis's old position for its number-one pin."

The old position was soon pocked with bomb craters, and direct hits splintered two of the dummy guns. The run showed with stunning clarity the enemy's ability to "do excellent bombing," as Barninger bitterly conceded.

Even in its new position, the AA battery had a close call and quite a scare. One bomb hit among a hundred three-inch shells in a new ammo dump nearby, touching off a rapid-fire chain of explosions that shook the ground and filled the position with smoke and dust. "That day I kissed the old sandbags," said an appreciative Sergeant Charlie Holmes.

The Japanese saved the very worst of their fury that morning, however, for Wiley Sloman's Battery L on Wilkes.

Enemy bombs pounded Battery L saturation style, destroying both scopes on one of its two five-inch guns. They also disabled one of the three-inch AA guns nearby and wrecked a searchlight and the truck it was mounted on. By this time, Sloman was huddled as far down as he could get in what he called his "fancy foxhole," which was not only extra deep but carved back under a cover of scrub brush. "I was in pretty good shape," he said, "but when the bombs hit, they stripped every leaf off the bushes and picked me up and shook me like a rag doll."

Fate was still watching out for Sloman, however. No more than eighty feet away, several of his battery mates in shallow foxholes were literally blown out of the ground by the impact of the blasts.

One of them, Corporal Paul Tokryman, was hurled into the air and mortally wounded, his body torn apart by bomb fragments. Quiet, slightly built PFC Herbert Byrne, another crewman on Battery L, was sent sailing, then flung back to earth bleeding from multiple shrapnel wounds, but he managed to survive.

PFC Jack Skaggs, an Oklahoman just four weeks past his nineteenth birthday, narrowly avoided a similar fate. Skaggs was sharing a large dugout with Private Dempsey Smith, a nervous, sandy-haired eighteen-year-old, and like Sloman, the two of them had spent all their spare time for the past couple of days digging in as deep as possible. But Skaggs was in a smaller foxhole when he saw the Japanese bombers coming, and he made a wild dash for the bigger one.

He was about halfway there when the first bomb went off about a hundred yards behind him. Skaggs hit the deck out on the open beach and cowered there, holding his breath and praying as a line of explosions drew steadily closer. He expected the next bomb to hit him "square in the back of the head," but the planes pulled out of their run in the nick of time.

Almost simultaneously, another bomb hit an underground pit filled with 3,000 cases of dynamite cached there by the contractors for work on the new Wilkes Channel. There were 125 tons of it, and it all went up in one thunderous cataclysm, leaving a crater the size of a small lake. "It felt like the whole island came up about two feet out of the water and then slammed back down again," Sloman said.

The dynamite blast, coupled with the bombs, blew away everything in sight for more than a hundred yards in all directions. "I don't know how I kept from getting beat to pieces by all the stuff that was flying around," said Skaggs, "but somehow it missed me."

At the same time, nine of the bombers made two passes at Peale, but their effect was far less spectacular and the damage was negligible. Although the power plant on Peale's antiaircraft battery failed, Captain Godbold's gun crews threw up a firestorm of flak that sent one enemy plane reeling away smoking and kept the others too high to bomb the Americans with accuracy. Most of their bombs fell harmlessly into the lagoon or onto the reef off Toki Point, but two Marines were wounded when one struck near a machine gun pit.

All four operable Wildcats were also in the air, tearing repeatedly into the enemy formations. Captain Henry Elrod, who picked up the nickname "Hammering Hank" that day, was credited with two kills before the attackers headed back to their base.

Overall, the losses in this raid were the lightest yet. The damaged five-inch gun at Battery L on Wilkes was quickly repaired, although only one spare scope was available to replace the two that had been ruined. Within an hour or two, the big gun was again ready for action.

The battle for Wake was about to enter a totally new—and even more dangerous—phase. The men of Battery L didn't know it as they worked to repair their gun that afternoon, but the next morning they would find a special place in Marine lore.

Before sunrise on December 11, Devereux and his artillerymen would temporarily set aside their cat-and-mouse tactics to play another desperate, white-knuckle game of chance.

This one could aptly be called "the spider and the fly."

Late on the night of December 10, lookouts scattered around Wake started noticing some sort of mysterious movements far out at sea to the southeast. They rubbed their sleep-starved eyes, straining to tell if the movements were real or merely optical illusions brought on by exhaustion and three days of forced wakefulness. The night sky was clear—something of a rarity in itself—with only a few scattered clouds and a half-moon shining down. As midnight came and went, the number of sightings increased.

"I seemed to see something way out in the distance," said Jack Skaggs, who stared at the southeastern horizon from the beach on Wilkes Island. "Sometimes it looked like the faint outline of ships, but it was hard to decide."

Was it ships or phantoms? And if it *was* ships, were they friend or foe?

To many Marines, the suggestion that ships might be approaching wasn't necessarily a cause for alarm. It was fairly common knowledge that both U.S. and Dutch submarines were operating in the vicinity, and the optimists among Wake's weary defenders were convinced that a large

American task force was on its way from Pearl with reinforcements. On the other hand, everyone knew an enemy invasion was a growing possibility, and most of the defense battalion's officers were convinced that a Japanese landing attempt was imminent—a matter of "when," not "if."

At about 2:45 A.M. on December 11, Captain Wesley Platt, the strong-point commander on Wilkes, stood outside his bunker not far from Skaggs's position and squinted through his binoculars at the barely visible horizon. For a long moment, he stood very still, frowning. Then he swore softly under his breath and turned quickly back toward the phone in his dugout.

Meanwhile, across the channel on Wake proper, Marine lookouts were alternately staring seaward and arguing with each other about what they were seeing. Some were certain they saw movements at sea. Others didn't think so. After a while, one of them cranked his field telephone and rang Corporal Robert M. Brown, a skilled typist who had been working as Major Devereux's clerk and was now pressed into service as the "phone man" at the major's command post.

"Something seems to be moving out on the water," the caller told Brown. "I think maybe we saw a faint light blinking out there, too." Within seconds, the man was repeating his message to Devereux.

Almost simultaneously, Platt called in. "Sure looks like some ships out there to the south, sir," he said.

"Yeah, I'm getting some other reports about movements at sea," Devereux said. "I'm going out to take a look for myself."

Platt was a tough, seasoned leader whose tenacity and fearlessness would make him a legend among the Marines he commanded in the days ahead, but he was also recognized as a rare breed of officer—one who would strip down to his T-shirt and help tackle the dirtiest, toughest job right alongside his men. Devereux had known Platt for a long time, and he knew that no one on Wake was less likely to jump to hasty conclusions or be panicked into seeing things that weren't there than Wesley Platt. But Devereux wanted to be absolutely sure what was coming their way before he alerted the garrison.

A few minutes later, Devereux and Brown trotted up to a searchlight position beside a fifty-foot lookout tower on the south beach of Wake near the Wilkes Channel, where another group of Marines had reported suspicious activity on the ocean to the south.

"There were six of us at the position, taking turns on the watch," said Ed Borne, who was assigned to the searchlight truck that night. "Some of the men had been there for three solid days, ever since the first alarm sounded. We were all tired, but we didn't have any doubt about what we'd seen. I told Devereux we'd sighted ships out there, and I handed him a pair of binoculars."

As Devereux later recalled the moment: "I studied the sea through the night glasses, powerful binoculars with a wide field of vision. If anything had come close to shore, it had moved out again. The sea seemed empty, but then—"

The major froze with the glasses against his cheeks. Several miles away on the horizon, he was able to make out a number of blurred shapes that were just a half-shade darker than the surrounding waves and sky. They were unmistakably ships.

"Well," he said quietly, "there they are."

There were a dozen or more of them, as nearly as Devereux could tell, and since he knew there was no U.S. task force of that size anywhere in the vicinity, there was only one inescapable conclusion: A Japanese invasion fleet was bearing down on Wake Island. By daybreak, enemy troops would be storming ashore—unless the Marines could find a way to stop them.

In all likelihood, the first hostile ship spotted by Wake's defenders had been a Japanese destroyer deployed as a picket some ten miles in advance of the main convoy. The ship had approached within sighting distance of the atoll sometime before midnight on December 10 and had been tracked for over an hour by the submerged U.S. submarine *Triton*.

At 12:17 A.M. on December 11, believing the destroyer might have discovered the sub's presence, the *Triton*'s skipper, Lieutenant Commander W. A. Lent, unleashed four torpedoes from her stern tubes at the enemy craft. They were the first torpedoes fired under combat conditions by an American sub in the Pacific war. *Triton* crewmen reported hearing a dull explosion, indicating that at least one torpedo hit its mark, and soon afterward, the destroyer's propeller noises ceased. However, the destroyer apparently left the area without ever being aware of the sub, much less the torpedoes fired at it. Some time later, the rest of the invasion armada passed unnoticed by the *Triton,* and since Lent was unable to use his radio without surfacing, no report of the encounter with the destroyer reached Wake for more than twelve hours.

The dim shapes in Devereux's night glasses were a flotilla of fifteen warships drawn from Japan's Fourth Fleet and commanded by Rear Admiral Sadamichi Kajioka. Listed on the Imperial Japanese Navy's battle plan simply as "Wake Invasion Force," the armada was led by the light cruiser *Yubari,* which Kajioka had designated as his flagship. It also included two other light cruisers, the *Tatsuta* and *Tenryu;* six destroyers, the *Mutsuki, Kisaragi, Yayoi, Mochizuki, Oite,* and *Hayate;* two destroyers reconfigured as troop transports and renamed *Patrol Boats No. 32* and *33;* and two armed merchantmen, the *Kongo Maru* and *Kinryu Maru.*

The invasion force was also supported by two Japanese submarines, which had ranged seventy-five miles ahead of the surface ships to scout the area around Wake for American PT boats, of which Kajioka was very wary.

The 3,587-ton *Yubari* was one of Japan's older cruisers, launched in 1923, but she mounted six 5.5-inch guns, and the other two cruisers carried four 5.5-inch guns apiece. Coupled with the destroyers' 4.7-inch guns, this gave the Japanese force an overwhelming edge in firepower, plus the ability to stand out of range of Wake's shore batteries and hammer the atoll at will.

At about the same hour on December 8 that the first squadron of Japanese bombers had taken off for Wake, Admiral Kajioka's task force steamed out of Ruotta Anchorage at Kwajalein bound for the same destination. But despite his countrymen's resounding successes at Pearl Harbor and points across the Pacific, Vice Admiral Shigeyoshi Inoue, commander of Japan's Fourth Fleet, ordered Kajioka to use extreme caution. Instead of heading directly for its target, the Wake Invasion Force made an exaggerated feint to the west to disguise its intent, then turned back to the northeast on a course that would bring it to Wake in about three days.

Even that was too soon to suit Inoue. He would have much preferred to continue the bombing raids for another week before trying a landing, but Tokyo was adamant. Admiral Isoroku Yamamoto, commander in chief of the Combined Fleet and the author of Japan's grand strategy in the Pacific, refused to alter his timetable for conquest. The invasion of Wake would take place as scheduled on December 11.

Inoue's misgivings were well founded, however, even if they were based in part on bad information. He knew that Wake was much better defended and more strongly fortified than the other island outposts his forces were charged with capturing—Guam, British-controlled Makin and Tarawa, and the Australian outpost of Rabaul. But Inoue's intelligence reports had, in essence, erroneously transposed the number of military and civilian personnel on Wake. The reports set the Marine garrison's strength at 1,000 men, more than twice its actual size, and the number of construction workers at just 600.

This misinformation caused Inoue further concern, but the fall of Guam on December 10 after only token resistance may have reassured him. The task force assembled to subdue Guam's 424 Marines and 300 or so native militiamen was spearheaded by four heavy cruisers and an invasion force of nearly 6,000 men. It was clearly excessive—akin to using a steamroller to squash a cockroach—and Guam surrendered so quickly that the cruisers never had an opportunity to fire their eight-inch guns. Maybe Wake would be taken with equal ease.

Kajioka was further relieved when a rain squall descended on his armada about a hundred miles south of Wake. The foul weather buffeted his ships, but it also lessened any remaining chance of encountering a sizable U.S. naval force, and it was now apparent that no American PT boats were in the area.

As Wake's dark, silent form appeared on the horizon with no signs of life, Kajioka's chief remaining worry was the small size of his landing force. Partly as a result of the nonbattle for Guam and partly because of reports of heavy damage to Wake's fortifications by Japanese bomber pilots, Inoue had allotted Kajioka a landing force of just 450 men. A third of them would go ashore on Wilkes, and the rest would hit the south beach of

Wake proper. If more assault troops were required, Kajioka planned to run his six destroyers aground and use their crews to reinforce the landing force.

From the lookout station on the beach, Devereux raced back to his command post and ordered his field commanders to prepare their units for battle. All outposts were told by phone to stay on the highest level of alert, keep quiet, and maintain blackout conditions. This time, Devereux wanted no blaring bugles to warn the Japanese that the Marines were aware of their approach.

When all posts were manned and ready and every usable gun primed and loaded, Devereux issued a blanket order to all hands: "Hold your fire until I give the word."

Only then did he take a moment to phone Commander Cunningham and apprise him of the situation.

"A convoy of enemy ships is off our south shore and standing in for an attack," Devereux said.

Cunningham's response was hesitant, uncertain. "Are you sure?"

"I've seen them myself," Devereux said tersely. Then the major briefly outlined his plan of action to the island commander: The ships were still too far away and it was still too dark to determine their size and number. All gun crews had been instructed to remain at the ready but hold their fire until further notice in hopes that the Japanese could be lured into range of the Marines' five-inchers. It was a simple plan, and there were no guarantees that it would work, but it was all they had.

"It seemed to me that our one slim chance was to draw the enemy close enough for our five-inch guns to hit him crippling blows at the start of the attack," Devereux said.

For what it was worth, Cunningham seemed to approve the strategy. "All right," he said. "I'll be over."

Next Devereux called the airfield and asked Major Putnam how many planes he had that were fit to fly. The answer: "Four."

"And when will it be light enough to send them up?" Devereux asked.

"A half hour or so before daylight," Putnam said. "That's the earliest we could attack effectively."

"You'll have plenty of opportunities for action, Paul," Devereux said. "But don't take off until I open fire. I'm trying to draw them in, and the planes could give the show away."

"Okay," Putnam said. "Good luck."

As Devereux hung up the phone, a wave of uneasiness passed through him. What if a Japanese aircraft carrier was lurking somewhere out there in the darkness? If it were, what kind of air cover would the enemy send to support the invasion that was surely coming? And what could four lonely little Grummans do to counter them?

"Well," he told himself grimly, "we'll see."

Across the channel on Wilkes Island, Captain Platt's call to general quarters had reached everyone except Corporal John Johnson's .30-caliber machine gun section. Johnson had gone off watch for a four-hour break at midnight, and when he got up at 4:00 A.M. to return to his gun, he was blissfully unaware that an enemy invasion force lay only about 12,000 yards offshore.

The night before, Johnson's squad of one other Marine, PFC Marvin McCalla, and six civilians had moved their two guns from their original positions to other points near Kuku Point, where Johnson's gun could cover the south beach of Wilkes and McCalla's could cover the lagoon. Other Marines often teased McCalla for his deep—and some thought radical—religious convictions, but Johnson had served in the same outfit with McCalla since artillery training in San Diego, and he trusted the quiet twenty-year-old from Alton, Illinois, implicitly.

They'd set up the guns about 150 yards apart and within about 25 yards of the water's edge behind barriers of sandbags stacked four high. These preparations were clearly in anticipation of a possible enemy landing. Yet the machine gun crew still held out hope that it would never happen and clung to the reassuring rumor that a relief force was on its way from Pearl to rescue them.

Shivering in the early-morning chill, Johnson groped for his binoculars and took a routine look out over the Pacific, moving the glasses slowly from east to west along the southern horizon. When he noticed a brief, far-away flicker of light, he stopped his sweep and stared at the spot where the light had been.

"Must've been a flash of lightning," Johnson told himself. But then he saw a series of other, smaller lights blinking. They were just barely visible above the line where the sky and sea came together, but there was a pattern to them—like ships signaling each other.

Oddly enough, considering their preparations of the previous evening, Johnson's first reaction was pure elation. When he realized that ships were nearby, excitement surged through him, and he felt like cheering.

"It's our reinforcements," he whispered jubilantly. "Our reinforcements are here." His mind raced on. "Hey, maybe I'll be home for Christmas. Maybe I'll even be home for my birthday on December 23. It's about time I got a break. I haven't had a leave in almost two years."

Johnson snatched up his headset to report his sighting to Platt, but before he could say anything, he overheard an urgent exchange between the captain and Major Devereux. Their words sent his high hopes crashing into a pit of gloom.

"...ships could be American, though, couldn't they?" Platt was asking. "Or maybe Dutch or Australian?"

"We can't rule that out yet," Devereux replied, "but the odds are ten to one they're Japs, so unless they do something to prove otherwise, consider them hostile. Be sure your guns are manned and ready, but don't fire until I tell you."

When the conversation ended, a crestfallen and increasingly apprehensive Johnson identified himself to Platt and asked for help.

"Our two .30s are ready to go, sir," he said, "but McCalla and I are the only ones with rifles over here. Any chance we could get some weapons for the civilians?"

"Sorry, son," Platt said. "I've got no weapons to give you. I'll send over a couple boxes of hand grenades. That's the best I can do."

Johnson hung up the phone and went to rouse McCalla and the others.

When the grenades showed up, they broke open one box of them, and he and McCalla gave the civilians a quick briefing on how to use the "pineapples."

Then Johnson eased himself into position behind his machine gun, gazed grimly out to sea, and waited—like everyone else on Wake. In the semidarkness, his watch showed 4:17 A.M. It was hard to believe that, less than seventeen minutes ago, he'd been happy as a lark.

Carrying a phone on an extension line, Devereux walked back outside to watch the approaching Japanese convoy through his glasses. The sky was a little lighter now, and although the enemy was still well off to the south, the ships were closing fast. As Devereux stood beside his dugout, he saw Cunningham drive down toward the beach in his pickup and also observe the incoming ships. On his way back, Cunningham braked to a stop a few yards away.

"What's our situation?" he shouted above the omnipresent sound of the surf.

"All positions are manned and ready," Devereux called back. "All we can do now is wait."

Cunningham nodded and drove back to his command post. Devereux resumed his vigil.

By 5:00 A.M., the ships had moved in close to shore, and the sky was light enough to make out the composition of the enemy armada. To Devereux's relief, there was apparently no carrier with the task force, but the rest of what he saw was less than encouraging.

He could make out two light cruisers, six destroyers, two transports, and four smaller vessels that he guessed were probably gunboats. Some other observers reported sighting several additional ships, including more cruisers and destroyers. At any rate, in Devereux's view, the task force contained everything the Japanese needed to take Wake—and then some.

The cruisers alone carried far more firepower than the Marines' three five-inch batteries combined, which meant they could stand off at a safe range and pound the atoll to pulp. Then they could send in hundreds, maybe thousands, of fresh troops from their transports to mop up any remnants of American forces that might be left.

Devereux picked up the phone again and sternly repeated his orders to every gun commander: "Under no circumstances are you to fire until I give the word."

The blinking lights seen by Corporal John Johnson and other Marines along Wake's southern coast were likely caused by an abortive attempt to transfer the Japanese invasion force from the transports to landing barges while they were still several miles out to sea.

Like many another experienced seafarer before him, Admiral Kajioka had deduced that the fierce tides and pounding surf along Wake's northern coast would make a landing there impossible. This left him with only one real option: to send his troops ashore on the south coast of Wake where the Americans were expecting any invasion attempt and where their beach defenses were strongest.

Fourth Fleet intelligence reports assured Kajioka that most, if not all, the Marines' coastal batteries had been silenced and its fighter squadron virtually eliminated. But the task force commander decided to disembark his assault troops while the operation was well out of range of any still-functioning U.S. artillery and send the landing barges in under cover of darkness.

The problem, however, was getting the men into the barges in the first place. Kajioka expected this to be a routine procedure, but he failed to consider the high winds and heavy swells that churned up the sea, tossed the barges around like corks, and turned the whole affair into a nightmare.

When the debarkation attempt began around 3:00 A.M., many of the flat-bottomed barges capsized the moment they hit the water. Some of the troops were hurled into the sea and had to be fished out again. Over the course of an hour, it became obvious that launching the invasion under these conditions would be nothing short of suicidal. Meanwhile, Kajioka and the frustrated captains of his transports spent that hour flashing signals back and forth to each other.

Kajioka finally gave up on his original scenario, electing to move the debarkation to calmer waters closer to shore. He lined up his flotilla in a column, with his flagship *Yubari* leading the way, followed by the other two cruisers, then the six destroyers. The warships would use their big guns to "soften up" Wake's remaining fortifications, then form a screen for the transports and troop-carrying patrol boats while the assault force was transferred into the barges.

If the intelligence reports had been accurate, Kajioka's revised plan might have worked well enough. But the reports were wrong, and because of the fiasco with the landing barges, the invasion force had forfeited both the element of surprise and the chance to make its landing before full daylight.

By 5:00 A.M., the *Yubari* had closed to within 8,000 yards of Wake's south beaches, with the rest of the armada lying somewhat farther out. The helmsman turned the cruiser broadside to the shore and started a new course, running at a rather leisurely speed parallel to the island.

While still proceeding with caution, Kajioka now made the lethal mistake of underestimating his foe's defensive capabilities. The admiral was growing more convinced by the minute that the Wake operation would prove to be a mere "cake walk," just as one of the officers of the Special Naval Landing Force had predicted.

Surely the American batteries would be firing by now if any of them were still able to fire, Kajioka thought. Surely any remaining airworthy American planes would already be overhead and ready to attack. Perhaps it was true that Wake was nothing more than another Guam, after all.

Through his binoculars, Kajioka studied the dark, low-lying landmass before him. From one end of the atoll to the other, he detected no evidence of human activity. Not a single speck of light. No movement of any kind. It was as if everyone on the island were still sound asleep, or hiding like rats in their holes. It was even conceivable that most of the defenders were dead.

Kajioka ordered his gun crews into action and alerted the other two cruisers and three of his destroyers to follow suit. Maybe an artillery barrage would wake the Americans up and wring some kind of response out of them.

At 5:30 A.M., now about 6,500 yards offshore, the *Yubari* shuddered in the water as all six of her 5.5-inch guns opened fire.

For forty-five minutes before the first enemy shell bursts hit the island, Lieutenant Clarence Barninger's Battery A on Peacock Point had been tracking the lead Japanese cruiser. Earlier, guessing correctly that the higher ground behind his position would keep the attackers from seeing the battery in the faint early light, Barninger had impatiently ordered the camouflage removed from around his guns. Now the two five-inchers were primed and loaded, and the gunners' sweaty hands were tight on their lanyards, ready to fire at an instant's notice.

The guns' long barrels swung slowly to the right, moving in time with the cruiser's westward passage. They followed her relentlessly as she steamed the length of the island, then reversed her course. The cruiser continued firing at intervals as she went on her unhurried way, and each run she made along Wake's southern coast brought her closer in to shore.

Farther out, the other two cruisers also opened fire. High-velocity shells exploded along the beach and near the abandoned remains of Camp One. A pair of diesel storage tanks erupted in bright orange flame, and black smoke billowed skyward. Most of the Japanese salvoes fell harmlessly in the sea or the lagoon, and the physical damage from the barrage was minimal. Nevertheless, the psychological impact was demoralizing to many Marines who hugged the dirt and listened helplessly to the *crump-crump-crump* of bursting shells.

At Battery L on Wilkes, no sandbags protected Lieutenant McAlister's gun crews, and Wiley Sloman was shielded only by a small shedlike structure about sixty feet from the battery itself as he manned the range finder for one of the guns. Sloman saw no reason to worry because the gunners on the Japanese ships didn't show much skill as marksmen. Not once did Sloman see a shell hit land. Everything the enemy fired toward Battery L landed somewhere out in the water.

A number of Sloman's battery mates were considerably more apprehensive, however. PFC Henry Chapman had been in the First Defense Battalion ever since February 1941 and had served on both Johnston Island and

Palmyra before coming to Wake, but he'd never been under hostile fire before. Now he felt himself shaking, and he knew he was scared to death.

As he crouched a few yards from Chapman and stared seaward, Corporal Bernard Richardson could almost envision what was about to happen. An aspiring novelist who had spent most of his free time before the war working on a book about the Depression, Richardson didn't like the way the plot of this story was shaping up. He'd already seen his 150,000-word manuscript blown to confetti when his tent at Camp One was hit in the first air raid, and now the defenders of Wake seemed to be surrounded.

Richardson heard one of his young battery mates swearing in a state of near panic that he could count sixty-four ships in the Japanese flotilla—more than four times as many as there actually were.

No fear was evident, though, among the more experienced Marines and their battery commanders. As hysteria gripped some of the men in Battery L, Platoon Sergeant William Beck drew his .45 and threatened to shoot anyone who tried to leave his post.

Among the field officers, the prevailing emotions were anger, impatience, and near defiance at Devereux's continued hesitation to return the Japanese fire.

"What does that sawed-off son of a bitch think he's doing?" McAlister fumed at one point. "Is he gonna let 'em walk right up on the beach? What the hell's he waiting for?"

Battery L's PFC Artie Stocks kept quiet, but he sympathized with McAlister and the other guys who were mouthing off at Devereux. The gun crew had never faced a situation like this before, but they were well trained with plenty of practice. By this time, they could practically see the whites of the enemy's eyes on those ships, and Stocks knew he was as ready for the real thing as he'd ever be.

Meanwhile, Lieutenant Barninger, whose battery was now also within almost point-blank range of the enemy ships, could hardly contain himself. PFC Jesse Nowlin, who was standing at Barninger's elbow, listened to his battery commander "frothing and blowing smoke" as he argued by phone with Devereux. Barninger and McAlister kept the command post phone ringing incessantly, begging for permission to open fire. But Corporal Brown, who was fielding the calls, just kept repeating the same response over and over, like a broken record:

"Hold your fire until the major gives the word."

It was almost 6:00 A.M. As the Japanese ships drew steadily nearer and more brazen in their approach, even Major Potter, Devereux's executive officer and commander of the battalion's five-inch group, openly challenged his boss's strategy.

Potter feared the Marines were missing their chance, and he pleaded loudly with Devereux to order the atoll's searchlights turned on and its guns to start firing.

But Devereux continued to stand impassively on the roof of his command post. His reply was a clipped "Not yet."

For Sloman, the waiting was compounded by an intense feeling of being alone and isolated from his mates. He was too far away from the rest of the gun crew to hear guys cursing and calling Devereux a "dumb little bastard," but he might have joined the chorus if he had. His nerves were raw, and he was holding his breath.

It was much more than mere obstinacy that motivated Devereux to oppose most of the officers in his command and stand fast against a fury that sometimes verged on mutiny. Devereux knew there would be no second chances. Only two of the three five-inch batteries on Wake were positioned to bear on the course the Japanese were following. Only Barninger's two guns on Peacock Point and McAlister's pair on Wilkes could be effective against the invasion fleet, which was beyond reach of Lieutenant Kessler's battery on Peale. Both Barninger's and McAlister's batteries were partly crippled by lack of fire-control equipment, which had been destroyed in the enemy raids. Barninger had no range finder; McAlister had to guess both range and deflection. It was a situation that called for the closest possible calculations and the fewest possible missed shots.

As the man handling Devereux's phone calls, Corporal Brown repeatedly had to clean up the language in the messages he relayed to his commander. By 6:00 A.M., McAlister and Barninger were calling Devereux "every kind of son of a bitch" and asking Corporal Brown if the major had "lost his goddamn mind."

Each time Brown passed along a sanitized version of their tirades, Devereux's response was invariably and unflappably the same.

"Just repeat the order," he said with a serenity that amazed those who heard him. "Nobody fires until I give the word."

The cruiser *Yubari* was now a mere 4,500 yards from Battery A on Peacock Point—practically sitting in Barninger's lap—and a particularly aggressive Japanese destroyer, the *Hayate,* had closed to within about the same distance of Battery L on Wilkes. Roughly a mile farther out—and also within range of the shore batteries—enemy troop ships were again preparing to disembark their landing parties.

By now, Kajioka had assumed the role of unsuspecting fly venturing ever deeper into an unseen web of peril. He had no remaining doubt that the bombers had destroyed or disabled all of Wake's batteries. Obviously, the Americans had no effective means of striking back at his ships, he told himself confidently, so the invasion could proceed without further delay.

At 6:10 A.M., Devereux calmly ordered his poised spider to strike: "Commence firing."

This is one of several editorial cartoons celebrating the Marines' stand at Wake Island that appeared in many U.S. newspapers in late 1941 and early 1942.
(National Archives)

A Bloodied Foe—
and Pure Elation

Battery A's two guns exploded instantly in response to Devereux's order, but their first salvo went high, hurling up twin geysers of water well beyond the *Yubari*. The cruiser immediately wheeled and tried to run for it, but as she zigzagged wildly toward the open sea, all six of her powerful guns swung astern and blazed in reply.

The first muzzle flashes had betrayed Battery A's position, and the Japanese shells came perilously close. One blast hit within fifty yards, and a few fragments ripped into the roof of the command post. They narrowly missed Lieutenant Barninger, who was visually directing his gunners from the top of his command post because they had no mechanical fire-control equipment. Although Barninger wasn't scratched, PFC Sylvester Gregouire, a shellman on Gun No. 1, was less fortunate. A piece of shrapnel gouged a silver dollar–size hole in his thigh, but the Bible-reading ex–Louisiana farmboy bit his lip, muttered a prayer, and kept on working.

"Lower your range five hundred yards," Barninger yelled as dirt from the blast pelted down around him.

The Marines' second salvo missed again, this time falling short. The next two shells straddled the cruiser, still leaving her unscathed. Since the battery was firing armor-piercing shells that didn't explode on contact with water, the only way to tell where errant shells were hitting was to watch for splashes, which were a lot harder to see than explosions.

"Damn it," Barninger swore, "let's get that son of a bitch." He strained his eyes through his binoculars and corrected the range again.

The *Yubari* was 5,700 yards out and still fleeing as fast as she could go when Barninger's gunners caught her. Both shells from the salvo hit the cruiser almost simultaneously and squarely amidships, tearing gaping holes in her side just above the waterline.

Smoke and steam gushed from the holes, and the cruiser sagged in the water, rapidly losing speed but trying desperately to limp away. But now that Barninger's crew had the range, they continued to pound the Japanese flagship. At 7,000 yards, they hit her twice more, in almost exactly the same locations.

As Devereux described the scene from the roof of his own command post: "She veered crazily. The smoke and steam poured more thickly from her side. The crippled ship tried vainly to turn into the smoke, to hide in the cloud spilled from her own wounds."

A destroyer rushed in, trying to lay a smoke screen between the *Yubari* and the shore, but the smaller craft took a punishing hit on the forecastle for her trouble. Then the would-be rescuer quickly turned tail and abandoned the cruiser.

"It was a lucky shot on the destroyer," Barninger told his men, "but we'll take it." He was determined to sink the struggling *Yubari,* and before she disappeared behind a curtain of her own black smoke, his gunners scored a fifth major hit, wrecking the cruiser's forward turret and silencing its guns. If a group of civilian shell handlers hadn't inadvertently brought up a load of harmless practice shells instead of more armor-piercing ammo, Barninger might have gotten his wish and sent the enemy flagship to the bottom.

After tracking his prey relentlessly for three-quarters of an hour before ever firing a round, the fiery young battery commander was hell-bent on finishing the job. Even after losing sight of the quarry, he refused to give up, elevating his guns at an extreme angle and continuing to fire in her direction. At a range of 12,000 yards, however, the recoil from the elevated five-inchers was too great. It kicked the guns back against the coral boulders that secured their platforms, and Barninger had to let the battered cruiser drag herself away.

The last Barninger saw of the *Yubari,* she was beyond his range, still spewing smoke and steam and lying dead in the water.

At long last, however, the "five-inch guys" on Peacock Point had been able to inflict ugly, gratifying wounds on an enemy that had always been out of reach before. They were amazed at what they'd done, and all the tensions and frustrations of the past few days gave way to jubilant shouts, raised fists, and backslapping glee.

While the men of Battery A had every right to celebrate, the honor of sinking the first major Japanese fighting ship of World War II belonged to Lieutenant McAlister's Battery L on Wilkes. There, even as Battery A was ravaging the *Yubari,* Wiley Sloman and his comrades were raining death blows on the destroyer *Hayate.*

"We were all wound as tight as a coiled spring while we waited for Devereux to give us the go-ahead and watched those ships coming closer and closer," Sloman said. "But once we got the order to fire, it was all routine, just like training camp. It just became automatic."

McAlister was worse off than Barninger when it came to the desperate guessing game he had to play in determining range and deflection. His battery was doubly handicapped in that it had only one of two scopes and no automatic fire-control equipment. Consequently, the first two salvoes disturbed nothing but seawater—but on their third try, Battery L's gunners hit the jackpot.

Sloman was hooked up by phone to Lieutenant McAlister in the command tower and relaying McAlister's corrections, based on what he could see visually, to the man operating the battery's range-keeping instrument. The tower, which Sloman had built himself, stood about a hundred feet behind the gun and about eighteen feet high, resembling a windmill with no blades. Because of the unwieldy range-finding setup, Sloman wasn't surprised by the early misses, but he was pretty sure their aim would get better. When a good five-inch gun crew got into a rhythm, it could fire about one round every six to ten seconds, and Sloman knew Battery L's crew was good. He also knew that, to a man, they were itching to kick the hell out of somebody.

Captain Platt had come out with his binoculars to help keep track of the splashes when the shells struck water. He watched the *Hayate* turn broadside toward the beach just 4,500 yards away, so close that he could practically count the rivets in her hull. He saw Japanese sailors scurrying around on deck and their six 4.7-inch guns swinging directly at him. Platt's heart was racing, but his voice was even, almost expressionless, as he spoke to McAlister on the phone.

"You're over, Johnny Mac," he said quietly after the first salvo went long.

"You're under, Johnny Mac," he said in the same tone after the second salvo went short.

But when the third salvo struck home, Platt let out a howl that McAlister probably could've heard without a telephone: "You're in, Johnny Mac! You're in! Oh, hell, he's gone! Let's get another one!"

It happened with a suddenness that stunned the onlookers. The doomed *Hayate* went up like a Roman candle, creating a sight and sensation that defied description—the most incredible sight that any of them had ever seen. Sloman guessed that the shell must have hit the destroyer's fuel tanks and ammo magazines at the same exact moment. Everything blew up at once, and the ship broke completely in half. It sank almost instantly. In a minute or two, it was gone. It seemed impossible that anyone on board could have gotten off alive.

To PFC Artie Stocks, the first shellman on Gun No. 2, who seconds earlier had rammed home one of the lethal rounds, it looked as if the whole ship came up fifty feet out of the water, then dove straight down. It was the prettiest sight he'd ever seen, and he felt like reaching over and kissing that gun. Up until then, he hadn't had any idea what it could do.

There were no survivors among the *Hayate*'s 167-man crew. If any of them weren't incinerated instantly in the blast, they were sucked under as the ship plunged to the floor of the Pacific. When the Marines in Battery L saw the destroyer explode and vanish beneath the waves, many went wild with excitement and promptly forgot about the other targets that were well within their range.

They jumped up and down, screamed themselves hoarse, and congratulated each other until gravel-throated Platoon Sergeant Henry Bedell put an end to the celebration. Bedell raised his own voice and jolted them back to reality in a tone more menacing than the one that had caused Wiley Sloman to leave his helmet behind on the first morning of the war.

"Knock it off, you bastards, and get back on the guns," the veteran thundered. "Whaddaya think this is, a damn ball game?"

In the days that followed, men would joke that the real reason the enemy ships took off so fast was because they thought Bedell was yelling at them instead of the guys in the battery. But at the moment, no Marine within earshot dared to laugh. "When Bedell chewed your butt out, you knew it had been chewed," said Stocks. "He knew those guns to a T, and we knew enough to do what he said."

After the men of Battery L got their elation under control, they unleashed a savage barrage against the rest of the would-be invaders. Shifting their attention to a second destroyer, the *Oite,* McAlister and his gunners hit home with at least two rounds as the enemy ship fled toward the west. The Japanese later admitted to suffering nineteen casualties aboard the *Oite* before she was able to hide behind a smoke screen and move out of range.

Battery L also scored a hit on the transport *Kongo Maru* and blasted the aft turret on one of the other light cruisers, either the *Tatsuta* or the *Tenryu,* which wheeled away trailing smoke.

Observing from 10,000 yards away on Wilkes, Gunner Clarence McKinstry reported seeing Japanese troops being taken off the floundering transport by a destroyer. McKinstry described the transport as badly hit and said he believed it exploded and sank, although this was never confirmed.

The damage inflicted by Battery L might have been even greater if its gun crews hadn't run out of ammunition a couple of times and had to cease fire for several minutes while Marines and civilian volunteers brought more up from the nearest magazine. Even with the delays, McAlister's gunners got off a total of 120 rounds in about forty-five minutes, and before they ran out of targets, their shells had hit nearly half the surface ships in the enemy armada.

With the Japanese task force scattering helter-skelter in all directions, Battery B's five-inchers on Toki Point at the tip of Peale were finally able to join the fight. Lieutenant Woodrow Kessler and his men could do nothing but bide their time—and none too patiently—for fifteen minutes after the first American salvoes. But now three enemy destroyers—the *Yayoi, Mutsuki,* and *Kisaragi*—fled blindly to the northwest and blundered into their range.

Like the other two batteries before them, Kessler's gunners overshot their initial target, in this case the lead destroyer *Yayoi,* when they opened fire from 10,000 yards. Their first two shells came nowhere near the ship, but the muzzle blast from the salvo disabled the battery's 1911-vintage range finder, which lay directly in their line of fire. Kessler had personally scrounged the old range finder out of a shed at Pearl Harbor after hearing that Palmyra and Johnston Island were getting all the First Defense Battalion's allotment of range-finding equipment. The enterprising New Englander, who thrived on efficiency and organization, cursed when he saw what had happened.

But that was only the beginning. For the next few minutes, everything imaginable seemed to go awry for Battery B. Not only did the destroyers now have the battery's position spotted and begin to return fire with disturbing accuracy, but mechanical problems also just kept proliferating.

The same concussion that had knocked out the range finder also blew apart a makeshift sleeping billet that crew members had set up in front of the gun emplacement. It sent clouds of feathers from ripped-up pillows swirling through the air, further adding to the confusion. With no range finder, the gunners had to rely on estimates, and their next three salvoes were as ineffective as the first.

Then a plug blew out of a recoil cylinder on the battery's No. 2 Gun, putting it out of action and slightly injuring Corporal Arthur Terry, the gun's captain, who was struck in the belly by the flying plug. Terry doubled up momentarily, clutching a four-inch-long knot that looked like a hernia, but after a moment the wiry Texan waved medics away, hobbled over to the remaining five-incher, and pitched in to help increase its rate of fire.

The shells weighed fifty pounds apiece, and even with just one gun firing, keeping them coming was no easy job. PFC Jack Hearn, a first shellman on Battery B, was known as a "little shrimp" among his buddies, but he was conditioned to heavy work from loading and unloading hundred-pound sacks of livestock feed at the fifty-cent-a-day job he'd held before joining the Marines. Between them, Hearn and his friend and fellow shell-man, PFC Willie Tate, a little Cajun from south Louisiana, moved thousands of pounds of ammo that morning without breaking stride.

An enemy shell also severed the phone lines between Kessler's command tower and the battery, forcing him to send runners to deliver fire-control data to the men operating the gun. Meanwhile, the gunners aboard the Japanese destroyers were adding immeasurably to Battery B's problems. Initially, most of their shells fell harmlessly in the lagoon, but their aim steadily improved. Probably the only thing that saved the Marines from massive casualties was the fact that all the enemy guns were set to fire in a flat trajectory. This caused many rounds that came perilously close to Battery B's low-lying position to sail well beyond their intended targets before exploding.

Kessler noticed that the enemy's first shells burst in greenish-yellow acid blobs in the lagoon directly in front of the battery. Then the shells started flying over the battery position and landing on the north beach. Even when the Japanese gunners finally split the distance and got the battery squarely in the middle of their pattern, their fire was ineffective. It was unbelievable to see shell after shell burst around the battery position but cause no casualties or significant damage.

One enemy shell actually streaked directly between two rows of ammunition handlers before exploding harmlessly far beyond them. A few feet one way or the other and it could easily have wiped out half the men in the battery. As it was, not a single Marine was seriously hurt during more than five minutes of intensive shelling by the destroyers, but several—including Kessler—were hit by flying coral fragments and other debris.

"Your face is all bloody, sir," one of Kessler's men told him. "Are you okay?"

Kessler touched his nose and was shocked when his fingers came away covered with blood. "Yeah, I'm all right. It's just a scratch," he said, dabbing at his nose with a wet rag. "Hey, medic, give me a couple of Band-Aids over here."

In spite of everything, the men of Battery B hung tough. They kept firing their lone remaining gun, and on their tenth try, their stubborn patience was rewarded. Their victim was the *Yayoi*, the target that Kessler had concentrated on from the beginning. A shell blasted the ship's stern, inflicting eighteen casualties by the enemy's own count and setting off a raging fire.

"We got a couple of good hits on the destroyer, and you could see it burning and smoking as it ran away," said Hearn.

Hearn and his mates then turned their gun on the *Mutsuki*, the next nearest destroyer, and hit it, too, before it and the *Kisaragi* laid down a smoke screen and followed the stricken *Yayoi* out of range.

By 7:10 A.M., with Admiral Kajioka's plans thwarted, his attack shattered, and his ships in full retreat back toward Kwajalein, Major Devereux ordered a cease-fire. But although the remnants of the Wake Invasion Force were now out of reach of the American shore batteries, they were, in fact, far from safe—and their ordeal was far from over.

Before Wake's Marines finished with their adversaries that morning, the enemy had a second nasty surprise in store. The reeling Japanese armada was about an hour's sail southwest of the atoll when the planes of VMF-211 swooped down on them out of the clouds.

Over the next hour or so, the four little Grumman Wildcats must have seemed like five times that many to the men on the ships below. Spread out across miles of empty ocean and totally without air cover, the flotilla was an irresistible target for a handful of American fliers who thirsted mightily for revenge.

Major Putnam had picked his three most trusted, experienced pilots— Captains Henry Elrod, Herb Freuler, and Frank Tharin—to accompany him. The four Grummans had taken off as soon as the shore batteries had opened up, fully expecting to encounter a supporting formation of enemy planes and pleasantly surprised when none appeared. Each plane carried two hundred-pound bombs under its wings and all the belted .50-caliber machine gun ammo its wing guns would hold.

It seemed only logical that an invasion force of this size should merit at least limited aerial support, possibly fighters from a carrier operating somewhere over the horizon, or even a flight of land-based bombers to complement and compound the naval barrage. Thus, the first responsibility for the F4F-3s was to scout the areas on all sides of Wake for enemy planes and engage any they found.

Three of the planes took off without incident, but the fourth had starter trouble—a frequent problem—and was delayed about fifteen minutes. Then the four-plane patrol rendezvoused above Toki Point, climbed to 20,000 feet, and scoured the skies in all directions. They found nothing at all.

By the time they got back above Wake, they could see the Japanese task force withdrawing. It was already about fifteen miles southwest of the atoll and steaming for Kwajalein as fast as the perilous condition of its flagship allowed.

Based on their intelligence reports, the fleeing Japanese were prepared for some relatively minor harassment from the air. Yet it hardly seems possible that they could have expected the havoc the Grummans would wreak on them over the next hour or more. The enemy ships threw up heavy flak as the Wildcats repeatedly roared down, and all four planes were hit by machine gun fire.

The method devised by Captain Freuler for hooking bombs under the Grummans' wings gave them something more powerful than strafing fire with which to attack the enemy, but the planes still had severe limitations. Each F4F-3 could carry only two hundred-pound bombs at a time, so they had to shuttle back and forth, reloading after each bombing run. As the enemy fleet scattered over a wide stretch of ocean, each trip back to the airfield took longer, and relocating the targets grew more difficult. The Japanese gunners dotted all the Wildcats with holes.

One of the biggest problems for the little planes—as well as for military leaders who later sought an accurate assessment of the damage done that day by VMF-211—was having so many targets to choose from. In their zeal to deliver the maximum amount of punishment to whichever enemy ship they spotted first, it was often difficult for the pilots, diving at speeds up to 485 miles per hour, to tell if they were unloading their goods on a cruiser, a destroyer, or a transport.

In all, each of the four Wildcats flew ten sorties that morning, dropping a combined total of twenty bombs and firing more than 20,000 rounds through their machine guns. Midway during their sequence of attacks and returns to base for rearming, Putnam and Tharin were relieved by Lieutenant John Kinney and Sergeant William Hamilton, raising to six the number of pilots taking part in the action.

Early in the attack, the cruisers *Tenryu* and *Tatsuta* were both bombed and strafed, most likely by Elrod and Tharin. The *Tenryu*'s torpedo battery was knocked out, and the *Tatsuta*'s radio shack was destroyed. Meanwhile, Freuler planted a bomb on the stern of the transport *Kongo Maru*, touching off a gasoline fire that spread across the topside of the ship and into her hold.

Back at the central command post on Wake, Major Walter Bayler was among those monitoring the jubilant radio exchanges between two best friends, "Hammering Hank" Elrod and "Duke" Tharin, as they converged on the destroyer *Kisaragi*, mistakenly thinking they'd found the crippled cruiser *Yubari*.

"Hey, Duke, see that big fat son of a bitch straight ahead?" he heard Elrod ask Tharin.

"I see him," Tharin replied. "Let's get him!"

The voices stopped as the two planes went into a power dive. Then Bayler heard the sharp rattle of machine guns, followed by a shout from Elrod:

"You hit him, Duke. You hit him with your second. Look at the smoke!"

"You didn't do so bad yourself," Tharin replied matter-of-factly. "Your first one rattled his rivets."

Elrod and Tharin made two bomb runs apiece against the *Kisaragi*, and each dropped four bombs in her direction. Although their glib comments indicated that each thought the other had scored a direct hit, probably only one bomb actually found its target. That was enough, however. Although neither pilot realized it at the time, they left the destroyer mortally wounded.

Aboard the real *Yubari*, meanwhile, a Japanese news correspondent named Akira Ando heard a low-pitched roar and looked up to see Putnam's diving Wildcat coming at him out of the sun. The ship was already listing and barely able to proceed, and her only aerial defenses consisted of one lightweight antiaircraft gun and two machine guns. She was ripe for the kill, and Putnam did his best to put her under, showering the ship's bridge with bullets.

But the beleaguered flagship, which bore a disgraced Admiral Kajioka back to face the wrath of his superiors, refused to die. Despite claims to the contrary by Devereux and others that persisted until well after the war, none of the three cruisers in the Wake Invasion Force was sunk. All three made it home to Kwajalein, where they were hurriedly patched up and returned to the fight. The *Yubari* was unquestionably the most severely damaged of the three, but she remained afloat until April 27, 1944, when she was lost in the Battle of the Philippine Sea.

Actually, the biggest blow struck that day by VMF-211 was the bomb dropped by "Hammering Hank" Elrod on the *Kisaragi*.

The destroyer's bizarre fate began when the bomb penetrated her innards and ignited a fire belowdecks. The ship came to a full stop while crewmen fought the blaze for close to half an hour, apparently containing it enough to allow the *Kisaragi* to continue on its way again, although at a mere crawl.

Then, around 8:00 A.M., the flames reached what was later identified as a large stockpile of depth charges in one of the ship's magazines. At that precise moment, Kinney caught sight of the smoke trailing from the burning vessel and nosed his Wildcat down toward it. He could see it had been set afire by an earlier attack, and he couldn't wait to finish it off. He was just starting his first-ever bombing run in an F4F-3 when an amazing thing happened: The *Kisaragi* exploded into a giant fireball before he could attack.

Kinney felt sharply conflicting emotions when he saw the blast. In one way, the exploding ship was a welcome sight, but he also felt a twinge of regret that he hadn't had a chance to sink it himself.

When he located another destroyer, Kinney shook off his misgivings. He was worried that he'd had no opportunity to practice dropping bombs from a Wildcat before the war started, but he lost no time in testing his ability on this new target. He released his two bombs with what he thought was perfect timing and positioning, but all he got for his effort was another disappointment. Both bombs were near misses, and since he had nothing else to drop, he shook his head and headed back to Wake.

By this time, Elrod and Freuler were contending with far more serious problems than a "big one that got away." It was now a few minutes after 8:00, and both fliers had been aloft constantly, except for rearming stops, for two solid hours. Each time they attacked at hedge-hopping altitudes, their shot-up planes collected more bullet holes from enemy antiaircraft guns.

Their two F4F-3s were beginning to resemble flying sieves, and some of the holes were in vital spots. As Elrod made a final pass at an enemy ship, a burst of machine gun fire tore through the nose of his plane, ripping open an oil line.

It was almost thirty miles back to Wake, but with gushing oil spattering his windshield and his engine coughing and starting to lock up, Elrod made a frantic dash for it. He was determined to reach the airfield, but he was losing altitude fast—too fast—and he had to settle for the beach instead. From atop his command post, Devereux and numerous others watched the approaching speck in the sky grow larger, and lower, by the second.

The last flight of Wildcat No. 11 ended in a crash landing on the boulder-studded south beach of Wake. Devereux and Putnam were among the first to reach the wrecked Grumman, and they were expecting the worst. To their amazement, they saw Elrod climbing out of the cockpit unhurt, but the farthest thing from the pilot's mind was his own miraculous escape. His only concern was his Wildcat, which was a total loss. Those who rushed to his aid heard him apologize again and again for not being able to save it.

"Honest to God," said Hammering Hank with tears in his eyes, "I'm sorry as hell about the plane."

Freuler, piloting Wildcat No. 8, the patchwork plane that Kinney and Hamilton had resurrected from the "Grumman graveyard" at the airfield after the first enemy raid, fared only slightly better than Elrod—but he, too, made it home.

As he banked away from a final pass at the burning *Kongo Maru*, a stream of tracer bullets struck his engine, piercing the oil cooler and one of the cylinders. Freuler knew instantly that he was in trouble—in fact, engine damage this severe would have forced many a pilot to ditch in the sea—but he held his breath and made a beeline for Wake.

Although his engine breathed its last shortly before Freuler reached the field, the plane coasted to a perfect dead-stick landing squarely in the middle of the runway. It was another miracle finish.

Structurally, the banged-up Wildcat was still sound enough to fly, but its engine was a total loss. Since the nearest replacement was 2,000 miles away, this meant that old No. 8 had completed its last mission.

As the aerial action wound down that morning, one of the remaining Wildcats made two strafing runs against *Patrol Boat No. 33*, a converted destroyer carrying the troops who were to have landed on Wake. A half-dozen Japanese sailors were killed or wounded.

The pilots of VMF-211 had exacted a heavy toll on the thwarted invasion fleet. Official enemy sources, which often downplayed or concealed Japanese losses, would credit the four Wildcats with sinking the *Kisaragi* and damaging two cruisers and a transport. Considering that the entire crew of 167 men went down with the destroyer, the number of casualties caused by the aerial attacks on the enemy flotilla on December 11 probably exceeded 300.

Now the squadron was just two planes away from being out of business, and it wasn't even noon. Before the aviation unit had a chance to rest—much less do any celebrating—those last two Grummans had another big job in store.

In fact, the two serviceable planes were back in the air almost immediately for the regular midday patrol, and they hadn't been airborne for much more than fifteen minutes when their pilots, Lieutenants Kinney and Davidson, got another crack at the enemy. It was almost exactly 10:00 A.M. when they spotted a formation of land-based bombers approaching from the east at 18,000 feet.

By some accounts, there were as many as thirty enemy planes in that midmorning raid, but according to Kinney, who was right in the middle of the attackers, there were only seventeen, and they split into two groups as they approached. While Davidson chased after the nine planes heading southwest, Kinney stayed well above the other eight until they passed over

Wake's antiaircraft batteries, then attacked head-on from out of the sun. The bomber crews were apparently too intent on strafing targets on the ground to see him, and the lone Wildcat was able to surprise them. After an unsuccessful first pass, Kinney turned back for another try.

Kinney's second pass was from down sun, and this time he spotted gasoline pouring from the bomber he was tailing. He knew he'd scored a hit, but he had no time to congratulate himself, for just then, an enemy bullet plowed through the Plexiglas in front of him and lodged in the left lens of his flight goggles. Amazed that he was unhurt, Kinney counted only seven bombers still in the formation after his third pass and assumed the one leaking fuel had had to ditch.

Davidson's slashing attack on the other nine bombers was even more productive. He sent a pair of them spinning into the sea and was credited with two kills. Kinney's target was listed as a "probable."

The teams manning the three-inch batteries on Peale and Wake proper filled the air with over 200 rounds of antiaircraft fire, setting one bomber ablaze and cheering as it crashed into the ocean off Wilkes. Three other enemy planes were trailing smoke as they lumbered away.

It was a fitting way to cap off the best day American forces had had in the young war: three bombers definitely downed and four others last seen in deep trouble.

That afternoon, the Marines went back to their regular chores, but the routine wasn't the same as before. The work didn't seem nearly as hard and daunting. The tension, fear, fatigue, and hopelessness of the past few days were momentarily forgotten. The men's spirits were high, their bodies temporarily revitalized. It was more than mere relief; it was pride. They felt truly good about themselves for the first time—and they knew they had every right to feel that way.

Wiley Sloman had never experienced such elation, and the feeling was contagious. Sloman and other Battery L crew members slapped each other on the backs and howled with laughter. They were ready to take on anything. Artie Stocks felt as if he could lick a whole battalion of Japanese by himself.

Corporal Brown, who'd fielded so many angry, profane phone calls from Devereux's battery commanders early that morning, pretty well summed up everyone's feelings as the enormity of what Wake's Marines had done gradually dawned on them.

"Well," he remarked to his boss in a classic understatement, "it's been quite a day, hasn't it, Major?"

Indeed, it had.

Lieutenant David D. Kliewer, a minister's son, was so deeply religious that some of his fellow officers doubted his ability to kill the enemy when the chips were down. But Kliewer sank the first full-size Japanese submarine of the war with bombs from his Grumman Wildcat, led the perilous mission to dynamite Wake's airstrip, and won the Bronze Star for gallantry.
(Marine Corps Historical Center)

★ 8 ★

"Send Us More Japs!"

In a purely physical sense, the magnitude of the American victory and the embarrassing one-sidedness of the Japanese defeat are hard to exaggerate. The irreparable damage to the two Wildcats was by far the most serious blow to Wake's defenders. The only other material loss was a diesel storage tank set afire by the naval bombardment. Not a single defender, either military or civilian, was killed in the engagement. Four Marines were slightly injured.

On the other side, reliable estimates place Japanese casualties on December 11 between 700 and 800 men, the vast majority of them killed. Without question, two enemy destroyers were sunk with all hands. In addition, despite considerable confusion and some claims by Marine officers that were never substantiated, at least five other enemy ships—three cruisers, a transport, and a troop-carrying converted destroyer—suffered significant casualties and damage. Evidence suggests that two other ships, probably another destroyer and a gunboat, were also hit, but the damage was relatively minor.

In an effort to save face, Japanese officers falsified reports about the retreat from Wake, blaming it on weather-related problems alone. They implied that Kajioka's force had made an orderly, well-thought-out withdrawal on the afternoon of December 11 after deciding that "further plans" were necessary. Kajioka himself blamed the failure of the invasion on two factors that were, ostensibly, beyond his control: the four U.S. fighters and bad weather.

It wasn't Kajioka's fault, of course, that no air cover was provided for his task force. But no amount of excuses or cover-ups could conceal the fact that the Japanese commander committed grave tactical blunders in every phase of the aborted invasion attempt and panicked withdrawal. He squandered his tremendous advantage in firepower, which would have allowed his three cruisers to pound Wake's defensive positions at will from 16,000 yards out while leaving the defenders powerless to retaliate.

Once Kajioka realized his first mistake, his frantic and disorganized flight exposed his force to further grief. He clearly showed that the only thing on his mind was getting away from Wake Island and out of danger as fast as possible. After the first Marine salvo, his only responding fire came as he was in full retreat, and he never sought to retake the offensive by withdrawing out of the defenders' range and resuming his barrage.

As the enemy force ran for home, Kajioka allowed his ships to scatter out over a wide area of ocean, instead of keeping them bunched closely together in groups, where their concentrated antiaircraft fire would have been more effective. This basically left each enemy vessel completely on its own when Major Putnam's Wildcats attacked, and the Japanese vessels were dangerously short of antiaircraft guns. Aerial defenses on the flagship *Yubari* consisted of just two machine guns and one 3.1-inch antiaircraft gun. Kajioka had every reason to expect at least a limited threat from the air—his own submarines confirmed the presence of operable fighters on Wake—but he did nothing to prepare for it.

Kajioka wasn't the only one at fault. His immediate superior, Vice Admiral Shigeyoshi Inoue, commanding the Japanese Fourth Fleet, was a strong proponent of naval air power who argued outspokenly that battleships and the strategy that relied on them for control of the seas were obsolete. Yet he sent Kajioka to invade Wake with no air support and a hastily assembled armada of older, undergunned ships. No fighting vessel in the Japanese flotilla was less than fifteen years old.

Even greater and more far-reaching than their physical triumph was the vast psychological impact of what the little band of Americans on Wake had done. Today, it's inevitably the surprise attack on Pearl that Americans identify with the start of World War II, but in the dark days of late 1941, it was the struggle for tiny Wake Island that inspired the American people and bolstered their patriotic spirit. "Wake Up!" became a rallying cry for the nation.

As an editorial writer for the *Washington Post* was moved to note, Wake represented "one of those gallant stands such as led Texans 105 years ago to cry, 'Remember the Alamo!' "

Pearl Harbor angered Americans and helped galvanize them for the all-out effort it took to win the war, but it was still the most resounding, crushing U.S. military defeat of the twentieth century. Wake Island, on the other hand, represented a great moral victory. It demonstrated the courage, resolve, and resourcefulness of America's fighting men. It showed a demoralized public that we *could* fight back, that we *could* inflict serious pain and suffering on the enemy—and "make the bastards pay."

On the evening of December 9, 1941, fearful Americans had huddled around their radios to hear President Roosevelt tell them what they already knew—to that point, the war news had "all been bad." But three days later, the public got its first real piece of good news when initial reports reached the mainland of how Wake's defenders had stood off massive air and sea assaults and inflicted staggering losses to the enemy. Wake's heroic stand offered the first encouraging sign that the Japanese juggernaut was less than invincible.

In coming days, Wake would make the front page almost daily in news-papers across the country. The reports were inevitably short on detail and often lacking in accuracy as well, but they were long on patriotic prose, as the following Associated Press dispatch illustrates:

WASHINGTON, December 19 (AP)—Wake Island's indomitable little garrison of United States Marines still clung tenaciously to their scarred and battered atoll Friday night after beating off two more Japanese onslaughts.

Few chapters of the present war have so electrified the nation
as the picture of the stubborn little Marine garrison at Wake un-
conquerably fighting off a series of enemy attacks, and even sinking enemy warships off their shores.

"They have held the fort and kept Old Glory flying," said *The New York
Times* in praising the gallant stand by Wake's defenders and calling it "the
major event in the war thus far."

In his press conference on December 12, FDR also praised the Wake Islanders. "As far as we know, Wake is still holding out," said the President,
"and it is doing a perfectly magnificent job."

Japan's top military leaders could dismiss the pummeling their forces
had taken at Wake as merely a minor glitch in their overall plan of conquest, but it gave their rank-and-file officers pause—and their first reason
to question their own cocky self-assurance.

Despite his postwar claims to the contrary, Commander Cunningham
apparently played only an obscure background role in the action of December 11. While the Marine artillery was blazing away at the enemy ships,
Cunningham was deep in his bunker, which was an appropriate spot for
the island's commander and senior officer at such a time. As nearly as can
be determined, all the actual orders during the engagement were issued by
Devereux, and Cunningham was kept informed only by way of a courtesy
phone call from Marine Gunner John Hamas.

According to Cunningham's recollection, the conversation went like
this:

> **Hamas:** "Lieutenant McAlister reports a destroyer, range four-six-
> hundred, off Kuku Point. Lieutenant Barninger has ships in his
> sights off Peacock. Major Devereux ordered me to notify you."
> **Cunningham:** "What are we waiting for, John? Cut loose at them."

Cunningham placed the time of Hamas's call at 6:15 A.M., which would
have been five minutes after Devereux said he gave the order to commence

firing. The commander's watch may have been fast, of course. But Cunningham's brief description of the ensuing forty-five-minute artillery action in his 1961 book, *Wake Island Command,* is hardly that of someone in the thick of that action—much less the man directing it. His account of one of the most dramatic episodes of World War II takes up just slightly more than one page and provides only a cursory overview of what went on. Its lack of detail and emotion suggests that Cunningham was simply "out of the loop" when it came to either direct knowledge or personal involvement.

Nevertheless, no one on Wake was more eager than Cunningham to get word of the enemy's crushing defeat and withdrawal to his superiors at Pearl Harbor. Within a few minutes after VMF-211 had flown its last sorties against the Japanese flotilla, Cunningham ordered Captain Wilson's five-man Army radio team to put up their tall antenna outside his command post. Even at the risk of exposing the location of the island's only remaining radio station to observant Japanese airmen, Cunningham wanted to make sure the Navy brass at Pearl got a full report on the good news from Wake. In the commander's own words, composing and sending that victory message was "the proudest task of my Navy career."

The message went out around 8:45 A.M., and within minutes, gratifying replies were received from Admirals Kimmel and Bloch. News of the victory brought a response from Pearl Harbor that was as reassuring as anything Cunningham could have imagined, except for a promise of reinforcements. The admirals commended the Wake Islanders for performing their duties in keeping with "the highest traditions of the Naval Service."

It was Cunningham's finest hour. Ironically, it was also the last time that his status as island commander would be recognized—much less honored—by his bosses at CinCPac, headquarters of the Pacific Fleet. At this juncture, Admiral Kimmel was only hours away from being relieved of his command, and in the shake-up that followed, Cunningham's very existence seems to have been forgotten.

Otherwise, except for the rare chance that the messages offered to celebrate a U.S. military success and congratulate those responsible, it's doubtful that anyone noticed anything particularly unusual about the exchange of radio transmissions between Pearl and Wake that morning. But in one respect, the communications between the isolated atoll and the outside world were noteworthy and fraught with unexpected consequences.

As Cunningham's original message went through the process of being written, put into code, transmitted, then decoded and typed out at the receiving end, four historic little words somehow found their way into it. To this day, no one knows for sure how it happened or who did the actual deed—or, if they do, they won't admit it. Chances are, Cunningham had nothing whatever to do with the four words, but since they cropped up in a message sent by the island commander, he would get most of the credit— or blame—for them being there.

Wartime coding procedures called for padding out military messages with extraneous, basically meaningless words at the beginning and the end of the message itself. Usually this padding was pure gibberish, but in the case of Cunningham's report to Pearl, that wasn't quite true.

When the dispatch was transmitted by a decoder, it was prefaced by the following string of seemingly disconnected words:

SEND US STOP NOW IS THE TIME FOR ALL GOOD MEN TO COME TO THE AID OF THEIR PARTY CUNNINGHAM MORE JAPS...

If all but the first two words and last two words of the padding was discarded and the four remaining words hooked together, they formed a provocative message—one that was about to become the basis for perhaps the greatest propaganda hoax of the war:

SEND US MORE JAPS.

When word of the alleged message got back to Cunningham, by way of radio broadcasts picked up by shortwave receivers on Wake, the commander was aghast. "I had sent no such message," he said, "and since the release of dispatches was at all times under my direct control, I dismissed the story as a reporter's dream."

Years later, Cunningham claimed to have learned that two of his decoders, Ensigns George "Bucky" Henshaw and Bernard J. Lauff, had included the words as sort of a private joke between themselves, not expecting the padding to be filed with the text of the message.

However it happened, the decoders doubtless had no idea of the nationwide sensation their attempt at levity was about to cause back home. Someone in Hawaii with keen public relations instincts and a notable lack of veracity seized on the words and used them to create a legend. Through the invisible, complex pathways of commercial radio, the phrase reached a huge chunk of the American public, and the myth was readily accepted as a "true story" illustrating the toughness of Wake's defenders.

A few days later, those same defenders were shocked and angered when some of them picked up stateside radio announcements via shortwave crediting them with this classic expression of defiance and bravado.

In barbershops, lunch counters, commuter trains, and taverns from coast to coast, the story was repeated countless times. Asked by Pearl Harbor if they needed anything, the Marines on Wake were alleged to have replied: "Yes, send us more Japs!"

"Maybe it was a good recruiting tool," said machine gunner Frank Gross, "but any of us on Wake would've had to be stupid as hell to say something like that."

Wake's defenders needed more of many things—more rifles and small-arms ammunition, more medicine, more fighter planes and spare parts, more range finders and fire-control equipment for their batteries, and, most of all, more men. But more Japanese were definitely not on the most-wanted list of a tiny, beleaguered garrison crouching alone on the very doorstep of the Japanese Empire.

The defenders took fierce pride in what they'd done, but few of them harbored any false hope that the siege of Wake had been broken. At this point, most of the men still believed that the garrison would soon be reinforced. But their optimism was tempered when they remembered an old Marine Corps axiom that many of them had first heard in boot camp: "Maybe you oughta get more, and maybe you will get more, but all you can depend on gettin' is what you already got."

As the afternoon of December 11 wore on, any remnants of a celebratory mood quickly faded, and as the sun went down, it gave way to a somber ritual. It was time for Wake's garrison to bury its dead, most of whom had been killed in the first air raid. Since then, every minute had been occupied with essential defensive work, leaving no time or personnel available for a burial detail. Building bomb shelters for the living had been more crucial than digging graves, and even now the burials were carried out in darkness to conceal the extent of American losses.

Most of the men on Wake were busy with the never-ending chore of shoring up their defenses and protecting their armaments. On this particular evening, many were faced with the massive assignment of moving Captain Godbold's Battery D from one side of Peale Island to the other. Devereux had ordered the move after the battery's old position on Toki Point was heavily targeted in that morning's air raid. Devereux knew the Japanese had the position pinpointed, meaning that his best-equipped antiaircraft battery was in imminent danger of being knocked out if it stayed there. Moving the three-inch guns and all their attendant equipment was a monster job, but it had to be done. Dan Teters sent nearly 300 civilian volunteers to help, and they and the Marines worked until 4:45 the next morning to finish it.

These pressing other needs left only a limited number of personnel available for burial duties, but most of the bodies had been stored for more than three days in a refrigerated reefer at Camp Two, and the grim task at hand couldn't be postponed any longer. It was time to pay those who hadn't been buried where they fell a final tribute and give them as decent a burial as possible.

The bodies were wrapped in sheets, loaded into trucks, and taken to a site just off the road near Camp Two. There they were placed side by side in a common grave, civilian and military alike. There were more than seventy of them in all, including twenty-six officers and men from the fighter squadron, two sailors, three men from the First Marine Defense Battalion, and about forty civilians. A dragline dug a long trench into the coral, and a few onlookers stood silently as the bodies were laid into it. Moments later, a bulldozer filled in the grave.

The garrison had no military chaplain, but one of the contractors, John O'Neal of Worland, Wyoming, was a Mormon lay preacher, and he said a short prayer. The small group in attendance also included Cunningham,

Devereux, Teters, the father of one of the dead civilians, and four Marine riflemen, who fired volleys from their Springfields into the air to conclude the service.

The funeral ceremony left Cunningham in low spirits. It had marked the grim ending to an otherwise triumphant and uplifting day. While the island commander tried to stifle his feelings of depression, it was hard to recapture the confidence and thrill of victory he'd felt a few hours earlier.

In this mood, Cunningham ordered that no additional mass burials be held on Wake. From then on, the dead would be buried where they fell or in the closest practical space. One man, nineteen-year-old Private John Katchak, had already been buried in his own foxhole, where he'd been killed by a bomb. His comrades had simply piled a mound of dirt and coral over the spot, said a quick prayer, and left the young Pennsylvanian's remains undisturbed.

Lieutenant Barninger, Katchak's battery commander, wasn't known as a sentimental person, but he noted in his journal how it felt to have one of his men buried so close to where the dead man's battery mates spent their days and nights. "His grave in the middle of the battery position serves as a continuous reminder of the task before us and a source of inspiration to us all," Barninger wrote.

Cunningham was still brooding as he trudged back toward the cottage near Camp Two where he continued to sleep despite the risk of a night attack. He saw someone running toward him out of the gathering dusk and shouting something he couldn't hear. It was almost like an eerie replay of the morning of the Pearl Harbor raid, when a breathless radio operator had rushed up to tell him the war had started. This time, however, the news was good—so good that it buoyed the commander's sagging spirits instantly.

As Cunningham recalled the event on that evening of December 11, the messenger was shouting that Lieutenant Kliewer had sunk a Japanese sub. But others who were present at the airfield immediately after the mission—including Kliewer himself—set the time of the sinking as the evening of the following day, December 12. Regardless of the disagreement about the exact date, the facts remain the same: On one or the other of those evenings, Kliewer scored a major victory for Wake's defenders.

For a Marine fighter pilot, Second Lieutenant Dave Kliewer was anything but typical. Where his squadron mates tended to be brash and demonstrative, Kliewer was quiet, reserved, and introspective—almost shy. Only twenty-four years old, he was from a deeply religious family, many of whom believed the taking of human life was a mortal sin, regardless of the circumstances. Because of this, there was talk among the other junior officers that Kliewer had a "personal problem" when it came to combat. Some said it might prove to be a serious liability when the chips were down.

Religious or not, the tall, thin youngster from downstate Illinois had already shown his willingness and ability to fight. He'd been officially awarded an "assist" early on by Major Putnam for helping score the fighter squadron's first confirmed kill of an enemy bomber. Still, there was a lingering doubt in some minds about whether Kliewer had the mental toughness it took to show an enemy no mercy.

On a late afternoon in December 1941, the baby-faced lieutenant answered that question once and for all.

At about 4:00 P.M., Kliewer climbed into one of the fighter squadron's two remaining battle-scarred Wildcats and started trying to crank it up for the regular evening patrol. As often happened, the plane was sluggish about starting, and it took fifteen minutes or so to get it off the ground. Once airborne, Kliewer climbed to 10,000 feet and flew due south, the direction of most incoming enemy traffic.

He was approximately twenty-five miles southwest of Wake, bearing 225 degrees and scanning the infinite expanses of ocean when Kliewer saw a fully surfaced submarine far below, its dull gray hull clearly outlined against the blue Pacific. The sub was barely moving, and it gave no indication that anyone aboard had detected Kliewer's presence. It couldn't have presented a more inviting target, and the young aviator felt his pulse quicken in anticipation. The question was, was it friendly or Japanese?

Kliewer's mind was racing as he maneuvered his plane into a position west of the potential target to get the lowering sun behind him. He knew that the U.S. submarines *Triton* and *Tambor* were operating in the general vicinity, and he had no intention of attacking one of them by mistake. But he also knew that both American subs were under strict orders not to surface in broad daylight, so it seemed unlikely that the vessel below was one of them.

The lieutenant drew a deep breath and dropped his Grumman into a steep descent, straining his eyes for identifying markings as he zoomed toward the sub from directly out of the sun. He figured he'd have time for just one pass before the sub's crew tried to crash-dive below the waves. He'd have to take his best shot the first time. He probably wouldn't get a second chance.

The ocean rushed upward as the plane plummeted down. The sub's slender shape grew larger and larger in Kliewer's smarting eyes until he could see that the hatches were open and members of the crew were moving around on deck. He was convinced that no U.S. submarine would expose itself in such a way in broad daylight, but he was looking for absolute proof that this was an enemy sub.

Kliewer was below 1,000 feet and streaking toward the sub broadside when he finally spotted what he was looking for—some Japanese lettering clearly visible on the conning tower. An instant later, he opened fire from point-blank range with his .50-caliber wing guns, but he waited until the last possible second to release his two hundred-pound bombs. He was virtually on top of the sub when he let them go—so close that heat and shrapnel from the blasts scorched the underside of his plane and poked holes in its wings and tail section.

According to Kliewer's report, neither bomb hit the sub directly, but both landed within a few feet of it. When he pulled out of his dive and veered to the right to look back at his target, he caught a fleeting glimpse of the vessel going down. Then it was gone. To Kliewer, it seemed impossible that the sub could have submerged that quickly under its own power, and he had no doubt that he'd sunk it.

Somewhat shaken and now out of ammunition, the young lieutenant flew back to Wake, where he reported the apparent sinking to Major Putnam. The squadron commander jumped into the other Wildcat and, following Kliewer's directions, flew to the site to see if he could locate any trace of the sub.

What he found was a large oil slick. This discovery led Putnam to credit Kliewer with sinking Wake's third major Japanese warship with no survivors.

In addition to the telltale oil slick, Kliewer's claim is supported by other substantial evidence. A few days later, an enemy report contained the unlikely allegation that two Japanese subs had accidentally collided in the open sea near Wake and immediately sunk. This may have been a face-saving cover-up for what actually happened. In all probability, many authorities have concluded, one of these subs, identified as *RO-66*, was the one sunk by Kliewer.

At the moment, however, the Wake Islanders welcomed the news of Kliewer's amazing feat as it spread from the airfield across the atoll. It spurred another wave of excitement that lifted flagging spirits. It gave tired men in foxholes and gun pits one final reason to cheer before the tense realities of a long, grinding siege settled over them.

*Sergeant Walter Bowsher, who directed
the only all-civilian gun crew on Wake, is
shown during a rest stop at Pearl Harbor
following his release from a Japanese
prison camp.*
(Courtesy Walter Bowsher)

★ 9 ★

Waiting, Watching,

and Sweating

When Friday, December 12, dawned on Wake Island, it marked the beginning of a new phase in the fight for the atoll. It was a subtle shift, unnoticed at the time by Wake's defenders, but it would vastly alter the psychology of their struggle. The blistering battle of the previous day now gave way to a prolonged siege characterized by days of tedium but punctuated by moments of terror. It would drag on for more than ten days and soon make the exhilaration of December 11 just a distant memory. In its place came a hazy, indistinct period when, in Major Devereux's words, "time stood still."

Every day brought more of the same: another dose of work that never got finished, exhaustion that never eased, a routine that never varied, and waiting that never ended. Desperation and boredom mingled and fused together to create a depressing, predictable sameness. The men worked and waited and watched. Inevitably the enemy planes appeared to drop their daily allotment of bombs. Then, once the planes were gone, Marines, sailors, and civilians hurriedly made whatever repairs could be made, and the waiting started all over again. Even tension and danger grew monotonous.

Shortly before first light on the morning of December 12, the bone-tired men of Battery D finally finished moving their three-inch guns to a new location on Peale. It was a brutal task, complicated by the fact that virtually every sandbag surrounding the old position had been shredded by bomb fragments and machine gun fire and couldn't be moved. The garrison was now running out of material for making sandbags, and Cunningham had put in an urgent request for three hundred empty bags in the event that Wake was ever resupplied. Meanwhile, the new gun emplacements had to be protected by bags of cement and wooden cartridge boxes filled with sand. The move took the whole night, but it would have been even tougher and longer if not for Sergeant Walter Bowsher's all-civilian gun crew.

From the outset, Bowsher could tell that these men were willing to work as hard as any Marine in the garrison, and when moving the guns regularly became a necessary part of their routine, they showed even seasoned artillerymen some tricks. Otherwise, Bowsher figured, the whole bunch of them might have worked themselves to death. Relocating the battery by hand took from sunset on the eleventh to almost dawn on the twelfth and wore every man to a frazzle. But on the next move, the civilians brought in a crane that could pick up one whole gun at a time, and the job was finished in an hour and a half.

It was 4:45 A.M. when Captain Godbold reported to Major Devereux that the new position was manned and ready, and Goldbold's gunners staggered to their foxholes. Their fondest hope was to be able to catch a two- or three-hour nap before the enemy bombers made their usual late-morning run.

On this day, though, they were in for a rude awakening—in the most literal sense. Just fifteen minutes later, at about 5:00 A.M., two enormous, four-engine Kawanishi H6K4 flying boats paid an unexpected visit, each carrying 2,200 pounds of bombs, four machine guns, and a 20-millimeter cannon in its tail. It was the first time that this type of long-range warplanes had appeared over Wake, and the surprise dawn raid sent the gun crews scrambling back to their batteries.

It was a futile gesture. Low clouds and a violent rain squall prevented the antiaircraft batteries from getting a single clear shot at the raiders. But the weather also hampered the attacking planes, whose bombs and bullets hit nothing but the lagoon and unoccupied parts of Wake and Peale.

Captains Tharin and Elrod, already aloft in their Wildcats on morning patrol, didn't see the intruders, either, until the Japanese planes completed their bombing and strafing runs and headed back out to sea. Then Tharin caught sight of one and struck out in pursuit. Twenty miles south of Wake, he caught up with the slow-moving flying boat and pounced from above. Moments later, with flames spurting from two of its engines, the enemy craft plummeted into the sea.

There was brief excitement at the airfield when Tharin and Elrod returned with news of the fighter squadron's latest kill. But among the gun crews in the batteries and the rest of the First Defense Battalion, it was just another day—arduous, miserable, even dangerous at times, but generally routine.

That night, Battery A's Lieutenant Barninger took a few minutes to jot down some notes about the day in his journal. The first word that came to mind was "uneventful." His men had spent most of their time working on foxholes, freshening camouflage, and cleaning the guns. Right now they were trying to get a little sleep before the bombers came again—just another chapter in what was becoming an old story.

On the evening of the twelfth, Commander Cunningham reported the general status of the garrison to 14th Naval District headquarters at Pearl Harbor. A message from Pearl earlier in the day had asked for information about Wake's remaining facilities and equipment for aircraft maintenance and support. Cunningham replied that the airfield could handle two twelve-plane Marine fighter squadrons but the only spare parts available were those on wrecked planes. He added that facilities were also available for a squadron of Navy PBYs, long-range patrol bombers that could land in Wake's lagoon.

A half hour later, Pearl queried Cunningham again concerning the "ammunition situation" on Wake, and the commander reported a plentiful supply of several types of ammo: 5,000 cases of belted .50-caliber cartridges for aerial machine guns; 2,200 hand grenades; 250 hundred-pound bombs; a number of heavier bombs, which could be delivered only by PBYs or other larger aircraft; and ample supplies of ammo for rifles and ground-defense machine guns.

What the garrison lacked, Cunningham emphasized to Pearl, was other types of materiel, much of it essential in delivering American bombs and bullets to their targets. There was a shortage of everything necessary to keep Wake's batteries in operation—hydrolic fluid, range finders, firing pins, height finders, and ammunition for the three-inch and five-inch guns.

After sending back his responses to both inquiries, Cunningham found himself wondering why Admiral Kimmel's office was so interested in such details.

Could it mean that reinforcements might soon be on their way to Wake?

The next day was Saturday the thirteenth, but it brought Wake's defenders a lucky break—one of only two full days of respite from the bombing between the first Japanese raid on December 8 and the end of the siege on December 23. Nevertheless, the men still had to be on their toes and keep a wary eye on the skies to the south, and there was little time for rest or relaxation. For the gun crews, the routine included lengthy forays into the brush to collect fresh foliage to camouflage their batteries and getting rid of the old, dried-out material that would give away their locations to attacking planes. No dugout ever seemed deep enough, no gun pit sufficiently sandbagged, and the men worked constantly to improve their positions. They cleaned weapons ranging from five-inch guns to rifles, hauled tons of ammo, and grabbed what sleep they could in between. After nightfall, some of them slipped out to the lagoon in the darkness to indulge themselves in the luxury of a brief bath. The seawater left a salty residue on their skin and hair, but it was cool enough to clear some of the cobwebs out of their heads and ease some of the aches in their limbs, at least temporarily.

Late on that relatively peaceful afternoon, however, calamity again struck VMF-211. Just as Captain Freuler was starting to take off for the dusk patrol, something went wrong with his plane. Without warning, it veered sharply to the left, barreling toward a group of civilians working with a large crane at the edge of the runway. Freuler fought to straighten up, but the plane refused to respond. Then he tried to force it into the air, but it had no lift. At the last possible second, he gave up and jerked the

Wildcat hard to the left, narrowly missing the work crew and smashing into the dense underbrush. Freuler climbed out unhurt, but the plane was wrecked beyond repair. This time, even the extraordinary abilities of Lieutenant Kinney and Sergeant Hamilton weren't enough to resuscitate it.

As a fighting aircraft, the plane was a total wipeout, but the aviation Marines found it could still be useful. They towed the hulk back to the edge of the runway, where it became a very efficient decoy.

Still, Kinney and Hamilton—along with Navy Machinist's Mate First Class James F. Hesson, a staff member of the nonfunctioning naval air station who had been assigned to help out, and a small group of civilians—somehow managed to keep two of the F4F-3s in action. Wildcat No. 8, which had been written off as a permanent loss after Freuler nursed it home with a shot-up engine on December 11, was brought back to life by these miracle workers, using scavenged engine parts from one of the bomb-wrecked casualties of the first air raid. Fortunately, the engines on most of the planes lost in the first raid were still salvageable, so Kinney, Hamilton, and Hesson were able to pull two cylinders out of No. 5 and recycle them in No. 8.

Meanwhile, Wildcat No. 9 developed severe problems and had to be grounded for further around-the-clock repair work by Kinney, Hamilton, and company. The planes had now become such a patchwork of transplanted parts that it was hard to tell them apart. When Major Putnam's main fuel tank ran dry one day at 18,000 feet, he assumed he was in a plane with no auxiliary tank and barely made it back to the field. But after making a perfect dead-stick landing, he discovered he was in a different Wildcat—one that still had sixty gallons of auxiliary fuel supply left.

The bomb-free interlude ended abruptly in the predawn hours of Sunday, December 14. At 3:30 A.M., three of the big Japanese flying boats came rumbling out of the darkness and dumped some 6,000 pounds of bombs, all of which exploded harmlessly on the reef off the south beach of Wake proper or in the brushy wasteland around the airfield. The raiders rudely cut short the night for Wake's sleep-deprived garrison, but otherwise they caused no damage.

The Japanese seemed determined to compensate for their missed opportunity of the day before, however, and there was worse to come. Shortly
before noon, the now-familiar Nells of the Chitose Air Group streaked in
from the south at about 20,000 feet. Both Cunningham and Kinney
counted forty-one planes, and Devereux set the number at forty, but postwar Japanese records indicate that only thirty bombers took part in the
high-level enemy attack. Regardless of which figure is most accurate, it was
one of the largest Japanese aerial assaults of the entire Wake campaign.

Kinney and Hamilton, along with Hesson, Corporal John S. Painter, and
a few civilian volunteers, had been hard at work since sunrise trying to
cure the persistent engine problems of Wildcat No. 9. They'd taken parts
cannibalized from two of the wrecked fighters to produce one complete replacement engine, and they were so busy that the sound of the incoming
bombers didn't register at first.

"What's that?" one of the civilians yelled, raising his head. "I hear planes!"

"Aw, don't be so damned scared," Painter said. "That's our own patrol
coming back in."

Hamilton and Kinney caught their breath and turned to look. The
sound couldn't be from returning Wildcats; it was too high and deep-
pitched. Besides, there was only one Grumman aloft. To their horror, they
realized that Wildcat No. 10 was still sitting in its revetment, where it was
hidden from enemy view but still vulnerable to a direct hit by a bomb. An
eight-foot-deep, steel-reinforced bunker was being prepared as a secure,
twenty-four-hour repair hangar for the planes, but it wasn't ready yet.

Seconds later, the repair crew heard bombs exploding in Camp One and
started running for an open dugout about a hundred yards away. As they
ran, a string of bombs punched their way along the runway toward them.
One exploded close enough to cover them all with dirt, slamming a chunk
of shrapnel into Hesson's hip and knocking him down. At almost the same
instant, another bomb struck several yards away, killing two aviation
Marines, Sergeant Robert Garr and Corporal John F. Double. Yet another
exploded directly on top of Wildcat No. 10's revetment, and the plane
erupted in flames.

As the Nells flew away, Kinney jumped up and stared at the blazing
fighter. The tail section looked like a massive torch, and the oil tank and in-

tercoolers were blown away, but the engine—the best engine in the squadron, in Kinney's estimation—didn't appear to be damaged at all.

If only there were some way to get that engine out of the burning plane. Kinney ran toward the revetment as hard as he could go with Hamilton and the others who were still able to move close behind.

Two men started unbolting the engine while another ran to get a rubber-tired hoist to lift it out of the flaming plane. The engine was almost more than the hoist could handle, but they finally managed to remove it after six men climbed onto the rear of the hoist, using their weight to keep its back wheels on the ground.

At this point, Kinney had a tractor brought over to pull the engine clear of Wildcat No. 10 and haul it to where Hamilton and other crew members were already removing No. 9's defective power plant. All this time, of course, No. 10 was blazing furiously and throwing out intense waves of heat, but the crew finally managed to haul the engine to safety.

Other parts of Wake were catching the same kind of hell. Inside Devereux's command post, men listened to the ominous sounds of bombs coming closer and closer.

A massive blast shook the whole CP, sending streams of sand sifting thickly from the roof and raining down on the occupants' heads. The next one was going to be damned close, and everyone knew it. But all they could do was wait, squeeze their eyes tightly shut, and listen to the bone-chilling whistle of bombs coming straight at them. A few feet from Devereux, muffled, mumbling sounds were coming from Corporal Robert Brown, the major's phone man.

"What the hell are you doing, Brown?" a voice growled.

"I'm praying, you goddamn fool," Brown yelled.

An instant later, that "next one" hit with a deafening roar and a force that seemed to splinter the earth. It landed right outside—only a few feet away—sending a sheet of flame across the doorway and filling the CP with a whirling, choking maelstrom of dust and debris. The concussion bounced men into the air, knocked them off their feet, and sent them sprawling.

To Sergeant Donald Malleck, it felt as if the whole roof of the bunker were lifted off the ground, then hurled back down by a giant hand. The bunker was filled with choking smoke and dust. Malleck crawled into one corner near the door, desperately trying to dig deeper into the coral.

Just then, another blast shook the command post, and more dust and fumes filled the air. But now the blasts were moving away, receding gradually into the distance. Finally, it was quiet. Stunned Marines coughed and rubbed their eyes, staring uncomprehendingly at each other, amazed that they were still alive.

Devereux was shaken but intent on the business at hand, as usual. As soon as he was sure the bombers had moved on, he ran to the entrance of the dugout and looked outside to assess the damage.

He was almost afraid of what he'd find. The enemy's bombs had pulverized that whole section of beach so completely that it seemed impossible for anything to have lived through the pounding. But to his amazement, Devereux found that not a single man had been lost in that area. By some strange turn of luck, the only places the bombs had missed seemed to be those where they would have blown Americans to bits.

The most sobering sight confronting Devereux and the others was the gaping bomb crater right at one corner of the dugout. Just five or six feet nearer and it would have turned the whole command post into one mass grave.

It was by far the costliest enemy bombing raid on Wake since the first and second days of the war. In addition to the two aviation Marines who died at the airfield, the attack also killed Navy Coxswain George J. Wolney, assigned to the naval air station staff.

The most serious material losses were Wildcat No. 10 and its revetment, although several other revetments were also damaged, and a number of bomb holes were left in the runway. Because of the near miss at his command post, Devereux decided that Japanese aerial observers had pinpointed its location. After deciding to move into one of the empty reinforced-concrete powder magazines at the east end of the airfield, he and his staff spent most of the night of December 14–15 making the transfer.

Devereux had picked the old spot because it gave him an unrestricted view of Wake's south beach and the ocean beyond. But Major Potter,

Devereux's executive officer, had been openly critical all along of the old command post's relatively exposed site.

"The first location on the beach was terrible," said Potter, an officer whose military experience matched Devereux's and who didn't mince words when he disagreed with his commanding officer. "It violated practically every military rule and doctrine on how CP locations should be selected. They are *not* supposed to be the first place overrun by a potential enemy." The second command post, Potter noted, was closer to everything—the aviation unit, the airfield, the three-inch batteries, the hospital, and to Cunningham's own CP.

Sergeant Malleck also liked the new digs much better than the old, and he gave the bunker his wholehearted approval. He found it almost elegant compared to the crude, cramped dugout they'd occupied before. It was larger, roomier, and better ventilated—and even more important, it was safe. Malleck had never seen Devereux show the slightest fear in the old dugout, even while bombs were raining down around it. But the sergeant made no secret of the fact that he was damned glad to get out of there.

On that second weekend of the war, as Wake's defenders hunkered deeper into the coral and sweated out whatever fate might hold in store for them, two large task forces were taking shape half an ocean apart. One was charged with reinforcing and resupplying the beleaguered island garrison; the other's assignment was to wipe it out once and for all and claim the atoll for the Japanese.

At Pearl Harbor, on direct orders from Admiral Kimmel, every ship, plane, fighting man, and piece of military equipment that could be spared by the depleted Pacific Fleet was being assembled into a relief force for Wake. Simultaneously, at Kwajalein, what was left of Admiral Kajioka's ill-fated December 11 invasion fleet was being hastily repaired and incorporated into a much larger, more powerful Japanese strike force. Although disgraced and embarrassed, Kajioka was allowed to remain in command.

Amid the dismay and confusion that followed the surprise attack on Pearl Harbor, America's highest military leaders fully expected an all-out

Japanese invasion of Hawaii, and some were even ready to concede its temporary loss. The raid had killed 2,403 Americans and wounded 1,178 more; 5 battleships and 13 other vessels had been sunk or damaged; 188 planes had been destroyed and scores of others disabled. But in the stunned aftermath of the raid, the psychological devastation was even worse than the physical losses.

On December 9, Admiral Stark, chief of naval operations, warned Kimmel by radio from Washington to expect prompt additional enemy attacks. Stark expressed the belief that these attacks could "render Hawaii untenable as naval and air bases," then added ominously: "It is believed Japanese have suitable forces for initial occupation of islands...including Midway and Hawaii."

By the very next day, however, CinCPac had made a more accurate assessment of the situation, convincing Kimmel that it was far less perilous than Stark believed. All three of the Pacific Fleet's operational aircraft carriers had been absent from Pearl at the time of the attack. The *Enterprise* and *Lexington* had been well to the west of Oahu on their way back from delivering Marine aircraft to Wake and Midway, and the *Saratoga* had been at San Diego, picking up its own complement of planes, plus those of Marine fighter squadron VMF-221. With their dozens of fighters and dive bombers, Kimmel saw the carriers as the cornerstone of the Pacific Fleet's defense, as well as the potential spearhead for an aggressive U.S. counterstrike.

Although often dismissed by history as inept, negligent, and ill-prepared for war, Kimmel was a gutsy, perceptive strategist. The man who was about to become one of the war's chief "sacrificial lambs" had accurately read Japan's intentions well in advance, warned of them early on, and pushed hard to beef up defenses on Wake and other island outposts. Now, in spite of his fleet's massive losses, Kimmel still firmly believed that Wake was far from a lost cause. It could be saved, he told his staff, and he set out to do exactly that—but he realized that any rescue of Wake would have to be done in a hurry.

"Landings on outlying islands for purposes of [enemy] occupation are unlikely except for Wake and possibly Samoa," he predicted. "The possibility of a landing attempt against Midway is not to be discarded. It will be influenced by the results from Wake."

By December 10, Guam had already fallen. This left Wake as the westernmost U.S. bastion in the Pacific, and as long as its little garrison held out, Kimmel reasoned, other American bases to the east, such as Midway, Palmyra, and Johnston Island, would be safe from invasion. Just at this crucial juncture, the first news of Kajioka's defeat at Wake reached CinC-Pac headquarters, where it bolstered everyone's spirits and helped seal Kimmel's decision to reinforce the island "if practicable."

Before the end of that day, a preliminary plan had been drafted. A relief force formed around the carrier *Enterprise* would resupply and reinforce the Marines on Wake, take them a new squadron of fighter planes, evacuate their wounded, and remove as many of the civilian workers as possible.

Marines all over Oahu—including the whole detachment aboard the cruiser *San Francisco*—scrambled to volunteer for the relief expedition, and Kimmel wanted to get reinforcements on their way immediately. "Marines, hearing of attacks on Midway and Wake, have insisted on being sent there," he wrote in a letter to Admiral Stark on December 12. "Morale of all officers and men is high. They have but one thought, and that is to be able to get at the enemy."

That same day, the first elements of the relief force were being readied to embark from Pearl. They included two destroyers and the seaplane tender *Tangier*, which carried units from the Fourth Marine Defense Battalion as well as tons of crucial supplies for Wake, including the long-awaited and sorely missed radar unit. Kimmel's plan originally called for these ships to rendezvous at sea with a task force led by the carrier *Lexington*, but bad weather, rough seas, and midocean refueling problems forced a change that delayed the mission.

For Kimmel's plan to work properly, all three of the Pacific Fleet's carrier-led task forces had to be carefully positioned, and this coordinated deployment couldn't be carried out until the *Saratoga* arrived from San Diego. The big flattop, loaded with 117 planes, including the 14 fighters designated for Wake, had gotten under way on the morning of December 8, less than twenty-four hours after the attack on Pearl. If the *Saratoga* had been able to travel at its maximum speed of about thirty-four knots, it would have reached Hawaii in plenty of time for the relief expedition to leave for Wake on December 11 or 12. Unfortunately, though, wartime Navy regulations required a screen of escort vessels to protect the carrier against submarine attack, and the three decrepit destroyers assigned to the convoy weren't able to keep pace against the high winds and heavy seas.

By the time the *Saratoga* finally got to Pearl on the morning of December 15, Kimmel had altered his plan. Instead of sending the *Lexington*-led task force to Wake, he decided to build the relief expedition around the *Saratoga*, while the *Lexington* group attacked the Japanese base at Jaluit in the Marshalls as a cover for the Wake operation.

About noon on December 13, Marine Colonel Harold S. Fassett had boarded the *Tangier* with 7 other officers, 197 enlisted men, and a 5-member medical team including a Navy doctor. Fassett had been tapped to become the new island commander, replacing Cunningham—a fact that almost certainly added to later confusion about Cunningham's role. Fassett was also scheduled to supersede Devereux as the atoll's senior Marine officer, but his arrival would represent a far more serious reduction in authority for Cunningham.

Along with the rare early-warning radar unit—reportedly the only one in the Pacific that wasn't already in use somewhere—the *Tangier*'s cargo included two other radar devices for use as range-finding and fire-control equipment on Wake's antiaircraft batteries. These devices would give the islands' crews the ability to "see" and track incoming enemy planes long before they were visible to the human eye. In addition, the ship carried enough conventional fire-control equipment for every battery on Wake, a dozen .50-caliber machine guns, and a month's supply of every type of ammo, from five-inch shells down to .30-caliber machine gun rounds.

At twilight on the evening of the fifteenth, the heavily loaded *Tangier*, along with the oiler *Neches* and the destroyers *Flusser, Lamson, Mahan,* and *Porter,* sortied from Pearl Harbor while the *Saratoga* took on fuel for the voyage to Wake. Task Force 14, as it had now been designated, was under the command of Rear Admiral Frank Jack Fletcher. It also included the cruisers *San Francisco, Minneapolis,* and *Astoria,* and nine additional destroyers, the *Bagley, Blue, Helm, Henley, Jarvis, Mugford, Patterson, Ralph Talbot,* and *Selfridge.*

These were all the vessels that could be scraped together for Wake's relief, but the size of the force was far less a problem than its speed—or, more correctly, its lack of speed. Most of the ships waited until the next day to depart Pearl, mainly to give the *Neches* a head start. The ponderous old oiler could make only twelve knots under ideal conditions, and the zigzag course mandated by open-ocean security procedures added to the delay. Together, these factors set back the expedition's anticipated arrival at Wake until December 23—thirteen long days after the initial decision to reinforce the garrison there.

As Admiral Fletcher's Task Force 14 inched its ponderous way toward Wake, other frenetic preparations were under way nearly 3,000 miles to the southwest at the big Japanese naval base at Ruotta Anchorage in the Marshall Islands. The surviving ships of Admiral Kajioka's mauled invasion force dragged themselves into port about daybreak on December 13 and immediately began undergoing repairs and refitting.

Mainly because Kajioka's force had had no air cover on its first attempt, his superiors decided to give him another chance. But this time, the assault had to succeed; there were no excuses for failure. For the second invasion, Admiral Yamamoto, the Japanese navy's supreme commander, approved the addition of more ships, a much larger landing force, and—most important of all—the support of not one but two aircraft carriers.

On December 15, Yamamoto ordered Vice Admiral Chuichi Nagumo, commander of the four-carrier task force that had struck Pearl Harbor, to detach the carriers *Hiryu* and *Soryu,* the cruisers *Tone* and *Chikuma,* and the destroyers *Tanikaze* and *Urakaze* and send them to bolster the second Wake invasion force. Kajioka's old armada was also beefed up with the addition of three destroyers to replace the two that had been sunk, four older cruisers, another transport, and a seaplane tender. Just a few days earlier, Wake had been considered a low-priority target, but suddenly it was at the top of the list on Japan's overall plan of conquest.

But events that unfolded the very next day at Pearl Harbor cast an even darker shadow over Wake's future. On the afternoon of December 16, Admiral Kimmel was notified by President Roosevelt that he was being relieved as commander of the Pacific Fleet. After a fact-finding mission to Pearl, Navy Secretary Frank Knox had decided to make Kimmel a scapegoat for the tragedy of December 7. Kimmel's firing cost Wake a key friend in high places and couldn't have come at a worse time for its defenders.

At 3:00 P.M. on December 17, Kimmel's staff watched the formal transition of command with heavy hearts. "Although his dismissal was not unexpected, we all regarded it as premature," said Commander Edwin Layton, Kimmel's intelligence officer. "We wondered what would happen to the Wake operation."

Worse than Kimmel's demotion for those committed to Wake's rescue, however, was Knox's failure to designate a permanent replacement. Instead, Knox named Admiral William S. Pye to serve as interim Pacific Fleet commander. Pye was a well-qualified commander and a respected strategist, but the transient quality of his assignment, plus the fleet's depleted strength and ongoing fears of an enemy ground assault on Hawaii, made caution his top priority. From the start, Pye showed signs of being uncomfortable with the Wake rescue operation, and the man he appointed as his chief of staff, Rear Admiral Milo F. Draemel, vocally opposed the mission. It added up to one bad omen after another.

There was no hesitation, however, on the part of the Japanese as they converged on the atoll from north and south. By the morning of December 21, the carriers *Hiryu* and *Soryu* would be about 200 miles northwest of Wake and their planes within striking range of the defenders, but the *Saratoga* and the rest of the slow-moving U.S. relief force would still be more than 600 miles to the east.

Between them, the *Hiryu* and *Soryu* carried about a hundred dive bombers, torpedo bombers, and fighters. These numbers included some thirty-six Mitsubishi A6M2 Navy Type O Model 21 carrier fighters—Japan's infamous Zeroes, at the time the fastest, most maneuverable warplanes in the air. Scores of carrier-based enemy planes were about to make their first appearance over Wake, and the only aircraft the Marines had left to oppose them were two patched-up Grumman F4F-3s. It's hard to imagine worse odds.

No one on Wake knew the situation yet, of course—and it probably was just as well that they didn't. If an observer could have watched the scene unfold from high above the Pacific, it would have been obvious that the Japanese were going to win their race with the would-be rescuers by dozens of hours and hundreds of miles.

Things were about to get very ugly very fast—but in the meantime, the dazed, deadly tedium for Wake's defenders dragged on.

To many of the survivors who lived through it, the period between December 14 and December 22 is little more than a disjointed blur. "We were like a bunch of zombies," said Wiley Sloman. "We were so dead on our feet that whenever we got still for a few seconds, we just automatically went to sleep. I got to the point where I could sleep right through a bombing raid."

Devereux and other officers witnessed the same sort of thing every day, but there was little they could do about it. Men would stare at them with their eyes wide open yet fail to hear an order when it was given. If the order was repeated until it finally registered, the men frequently drifted back into a fog within a few seconds and forgot what they were supposed to be doing almost as soon as the officer walked away.

Every creature on the atoll seemed somehow affected by the wearing intensity of the siege. Upset by the bombing, the always hyperactive rat population became even crazier than usual, swarming by the thousands through dugouts and foxholes, running in mindless circles, and sometimes even attacking men in a wild frenzy. During one raid, a large rat went berserk and attacked a Marine crouching in a foxhole. The man was severely bitten and had to beat the rat to death while it hung by its teeth from his nose. "The Marine didn't think the incident was nearly as funny as his mates did," Devereux reported.

Hundreds of Wake's exotic birds were killed by the concussions from shellfire and exploding bombs, and their corpses had to be disposed of for sanitary reasons. The surviving birds were restless and disoriented, constantly squawking, flapping their wings, and running along the beaches.

On numerous occasions, someone would sound an air raid alarm, and bleary-eyed gun crews would stumble out to their batteries, only to find that some equally groggy lookout had panicked unnecessarily. The reason for such mistakes was obvious. Flocks of birds soaring high above the islands with their wings totally motionless bore an uncanny resemblance to enemy planes.

Many of the men came down with diarrhea or dysentery. Some became so sick and weak that they required hospitalization, but most tried to carry on between emergency trips to the head. The military personnel were well trained in field sanitation, and they and the civilians working with them did their best to dispose of waste and garbage properly. But some of the contractors who had gone into hiding in the brush weren't nearly so fastidious, and flies were everywhere.

There was simply no way to maintain adequate personal hygiene. The men worked and slept and lived in the same grimy, stinking clothes they'd worn since the war started. Usually the only way to wash anything—themselves included—was in salt water, although there were some rare exceptions.

"We found an elevated storage tank at the Pan Am compound that still had hundreds of gallons of water in it," said Walter Bowsher of Battery D on Peale. "A couple of the civilians rigged up a shower under the tank, and for a few days we were actually able to take a bath in fresh water. Then one of the Jap bombers spotted the thing and blew it full of holes. That was the end of our showers, and we really hated the Jap who did it. We called him 'Washing Machine Charlie,' and we'd have given anything to shoot him down."

Despite Dan Teters's efforts to keep the garrison fed, getting enough to eat was always an iffy situation. "If you were at the end of the chow line, like we were down on Peacock Point, you got the sour leftovers, and not very much of those," said Frank Gross.

Fortunately, caches of food were scattered around all three islands to supplement what Teters and his mess crews provided, and there were other "unofficial" sources of sustenance. "Some of our civilians went foraging over at the Pan Am compound, which wasn't far from our battery on Peale," said Bowsher. "They came back with canned shrimp, canned fish, and lots of other exotic foods. We ate pretty well there for several days."

"We'd have come close to starving if it hadn't been for a civilian named

Sonny Kaiser," Gross said. "He was one helluva scrounger, and he always came back with loads of good stuff—canned fish, coconut, candy, even cigars. He never said where he got it, and we never asked."

On Wilkes, Sloman and other Marines in Battery L subsisted largely on stores of pork and beans, hardtack, and an occasional can of salmon. "We were supposed to get at least one hot meal every day, but I don't remember one that was really hot when it got to us," Sloman said. "About the closest we ever came was some lukewarm stew."

The hungry men found out—sometimes too late—that what looked like a treat on the surface could harbor a toxic surprise inside. "I thought I'd made a real find when I came across a whole case of Oh Henry candy bars," said VMF-211's Sergeant Robert Bourquin. "Several of us chomped on those things all night long, and in the dark, we never noticed that they were full of worms. God, were we sick the next day!"

During this time, Wake's sick and well alike drifted in a twilight world somewhere between harsh reality and vague fantasy. When they weren't struggling to maintain their fortifications, men continued to write letters. They did so with little legitimate hope of getting them delivered, but the mere act of scribbling a few lines and addressing an envelope to someone special offered a slight psychological lift. It provided the writer with a sense of connection to those far away and a momentary respite from the unreality surrounding him.

Those who had managed to hold on to old letters from home also hauled out the smudged, dog-eared pages and reread them. Others started journals and diaries, trying to describe this godawful place and these godawful circumstances so that someday their children and grandchildren might comprehend what it was like.

Sergeant Bourquin had been keeping a diary since the first day of the war, and he managed to find a few minutes every twenty-four hours to jot down his thoughts. He was also fortunate enough to have a color photograph of Charlotte "Chotty" McLain, the girl back in Washington State that he planned to marry. Two or three times every day, he'd take the picture out of his pocket and stare at it. It didn't really keep him from being lonely, and his fingers often shook as he held it, but it gave him a sense of connection that motivated him to stay alive.

Sometimes he whispered to the face in the photo, promising Chotty that he'd make it home somehow, come hell or high water. As long as Bourquin had the picture to hold on to, he could make himself believe it.

As the days melted into each other, many other Wake Islanders lacked even the small comfort of a treasured photo or letter to cling to. For them, home and loved ones became half-forgotten memories. Parents, brothers, sisters, wives, fiancées, and girlfriends seemed as remote as beings from another planet. It was as if nothing existed anymore except coral and sand, sea and sky, onerous labor, falling bombs, and the perpetually pounding surf.

Each day, the faint hope for reinforcements dimmed a little further. Each day, fears grew about what the enemy was planning next—and when. Each day was indistinguishable from all the rest, except that every man was sleepier than he'd been the day before. Apprehension and despair were often held in check only by sheer weariness.

Eventually, it began to seem as if this stupefying, slow-motion phase of Wake's ordeal might last forever. But for many of the sleepwalking defenders, even that interminable fate would have been preferable to the one now heading toward them.

Captain Herbert C. Freuler of VMF-211 was awarded both a Navy Cross and a Bronze Star for his heroic feats in the skies over Wake. On December 22, 1941, after shooting down two Japanese "Kate" bombers, he was wounded and forced to crash-land his riddled plane on the beach in the fighter squadron's last mission. (Marine Corps Historical Center)

The Beginning
of the End

On December 20, the second Saturday of the war, the monotony was finally broken by the most eventful day on Wake in well over a week. Just after seven o'clock that rainy morning, Commander Cunningham was handed a brief but electrifying radio message from Midway:

DEPARTED MIDWAY FOR WAKE EIGHTEEN TWENTY GCT ONE PREP SAIL PREP.

Not since the arrival of what proved to be the final Pan Am Clipper flight on the afternoon of December 7 had the embattled atoll received any friendly visits from the outside world, either by sea or air. But the message to Cunningham meant that a Navy PBY was on its way to Wake at this very moment. No one knew the meaning of its mission, what cargo it might be carrying, or how long it would stay. But the very fact that *something* was finally coming—and bringing human beings who knew firsthand what was happening in Hawaii and back in the States—touched off a wave of excited speculation.

But along with the excitement came the strain of waiting and wondering what kind of news the PBY would bring. Some men speculated that the plane represented the first of Wake's reinforcements. Soon, these optimists insisted, the garrison would be getting enough new men and weapons to hold the islands against anything the Japanese could throw at them. Others, though, weren't so sure, and Devereux just tried not to think about it.

Along with their anticipation, Wake's battle-savvy veterans also worried about the danger to a lone patrol plane flying through the heart of a war zone. The worries intensified when radio operators heard the pilot sending out uncoded hourly weather reports in plain English. "Why doesn't this damn fool just send the Japs an invitation to come and get him?" joked one of a group of aviation Marines gathered around the radio. Ironically, though, the very quantity of the PBY's transmissions may have served to deter any enemy planes that picked them up.

A number of bets were made on whether the PBY would arrive in one piece, but the plane made it without incident. About 3:30 P.M., the big, blue, twin-engined flying boat glided to a smooth landing on the lagoon and taxied up to what was left of the dock.

A cluster of grubby, disheveled Marines kibitzed nearby. As the crew disembarked and approached them, the islanders realized just how ridiculously uninformed the average member of the U.S. military really was about conditions on Wake.

The first crewman down the ramp was the flight commander, a young Navy reserve ensign named J. J. Murphy. He carried a natty little overnight bag, and his freshly starched whites stood out in stark contrast to the Marines' ragged, battle-stained khakis.

"Hey, where's the Wake Island Hotel?" he inquired.

The Marines stared back at him in silence for a moment, long enough for Murphy to begin losing his patience. Then one of them pointed to the jumble of charred debris where the Pan Am Inn had once stood.

"That's it, sir," he said softly.

Murphy's jaw dropped. His eyes moved slowly around the remains of the Pan Am compound, from one pile of blackened rubble to another. He shook his head.

"My God," Murphy said. "Why didn't somebody tell us?"

The other two crew members were also spick-and-span youngsters, virtual carbon copies of their pilot. They acted more like tourists on holiday than naval officers on a perilous, top-secret mission, and they seemed equally shocked by what they saw. The Marines were quick to note that all were lowly reserve ensigns, green as gourds and clearly expendable as far as the brass hats at Pearl were concerned.

As the three of them moved away, one Wake Islander elbowed the guy beside him and rolled his eyes. "Jesus, we must be in a hotter spot than I thought," he said.

The newcomers were still wandering around from one bomb-wrecked building to another when Cunningham drove up. He loaded Murphy and Ensign Howard Ady, the PBY's copilot, into his pickup and took them back to the bunker that housed his command post, treating them to more stunning sights on the way.

As the truck bounced along past scores of bomb craters and the ruins of Camp Two, Murphy and Ady remained wide-eyed with awe. Their surprise clearly indicated how little the dispatch writers back at Pearl understood about Wake's situation or how much damage the Japanese had wreaked there.

The sealed papers the visitors brought from CinCPac, hand-carried because of persistent rumors that the enemy had broken the Navy's radio code, contained amazingly good news—better, in fact, than anything Cunningham could have anticipated. The dispatches promised everything the island commander had asked for and a great deal more. A carrier task force was now at sea and bound for Wake, loaded with fresh troops, more machine guns, millions of rounds of ammo, range-finding equipment, and spare parts for the three-inch and five-inch batteries.

Cunningham was told to prepare to receive another squadron of fighter planes and that ground-troop reinforcements and needed materiel were also on the way. About three-fourths of the civilians would be evacuated by the relief force. The other 350, selected by specified trades, would stay to work on construction projects. In spite of everything, CinCPac was still clinging to the notion that the ship channel across Wilkes had to be completed.

Conspicuously missing from the orders was the anticipated date of the task force's arrival. But from the information at hand, Cunningham estimated that the expedition would make an appearance by December 23 or 24, giving every man on Wake the best Christmas present he could possibly hope for. The news gave the the island commander's drooping spirits a tremendous boost. With a transfusion of manpower, supplies, equipment, and planes, Cunningham believed that Wake would be strong and secure enough to repel any future invasion attempt. Because of the beating the Japanese had taken ten days earlier, he also felt it would be "many days or even weeks" before the enemy dared to try another landing.

Cunningham was so pumped up that he grabbed more paper and scribbled a quick letter to his wife and daughter. He was filled with a new sense of well-being, and his words reflected it: "We're having a jolly time here, and everything is in good shape. The situation is good and getting better. Before long, you won't hear of a Japanese east of Tokyo."

As he sealed the letter, Cunningham was almost giddy with optimism. He couldn't suppress a smile when he thought of the relief force now steaming for Wake and the good news that his wife, Louise, would be receiving shortly. His faith had been justified, after all, and the civilians under his jurisdiction would soon be safe. He felt as if a great weight had been lifted from his shoulders.

It all seemed too good to be true.

To Wake's rank and file, many of whom had no advance knowledge of its coming, the PBY's arrival was sudden and unexpected, and it started the atoll's rumor mills working overtime.

Even to those who knew nothing about the orders Cunningham had received from Pearl, the plane was a strong indication that help was on its way. When Cunningham shared parts of the information with Major Devereux, Major Putnam, and Dan Teters, as well as key members of his own staff, it triggered a spreading chain reaction and generally sent hopes soaring.

The Wake Islanders got a particular kick out of learning from the PBY crew that Japanese radio reports had been claiming Wake's capture since December 8—and still were. It seemed to prove the truth of an old Marine adage: Apparently, there *was* always some dope that didn't get the word. Tired as they were, it made the men laugh.

After being alerted to expect additional aircraft, Putnam moved quickly to get construction moving on more protected revetments for planes and more personnel shelters at the airfield. Teters started compiling lists of the contractors who would stay on Wake and those who would be evacuated. Cunningham went to work writing the first detailed reports he'd been able to send back to Admiral Bloch at Pearl. In them, he gave generous credit to the Marine batteries and airmen.

"Our escape from more serious damage may be attributed to the effectiveness of AA fire and the heroic actions of fighter pilots, who have never failed to push home attacks against heavy fire," he wrote. "The performance of these pilots is deserving of all praise. They have attacked air and surface targets with equal abandon. That none has been shot down is a miracle. Their planes (two now remain) are full of bullet holes."

Lieutenant Commander Greey, who had been supervising construction of the naval air station on Wake when the war started, told his superiors it was time to get all nonessential civilian workers off the atoll. He also painted a grim picture of the station's current condition and its prospects for the future, since practically every building and structure on the island had been damaged, and 90 percent of the construction materials needed for repairs had been destroyed or rendered unusable.

"The morale of the contractors' personnel is very low," Greey reported, "and [it's doubtful that they] can again be used advantageously for construction work. Many men now refuse to expose themselves even after the danger of raids is past."

Putnam also offered a sobering assessment of conditions at the airfield. "Present facilities for handling land planes are practically nil," he wrote. "There is no gas storage at the field. Protective measures for aircraft consist of eight open bays...and two roofed hangars or workshop dugouts which can be made light-tight for night work. More protective bays are planned for the immediate future, but work is slow. There is one generator, capable of operating the radio, lights and small tools. Other tools and equipment consist of what had been salvaged from the wreckage of blasted and burned tents and airplanes, and consists of practically nothing."

Besides carrying official documents and letters from officers, Ensign Murphy also put out word that there was room on the PBY for personal mail from enlisted men. Some didn't hear about the offer soon enough to take advantage of it, but many dashed off hurried notes and postcards in time to get them aboard the plane.

After completing a report to Colonel Bert A. Bone, commander of the First Marine Defense Battalion and a longtime personal friend, Devereux himself tried to compose a letter to his wife and his eight-year-old son, Paddy. He had no trouble telling Bone of his pride in his officers and men or expressing his irritation with such "idiotic messages" from Pearl as one ordering all personnel to wear long trousers and rolled-down shirtsleeves to protect against bomb blasts. But when he tried to express his feelings to his family, Devereux simply couldn't find the right words.

There were many deeply personal thoughts that he wanted to convey to them, especially some things he wanted to tell his son in case he didn't make it back. In the end, though, he didn't seem able to put any of it down on paper. Finally, he tore the letter up and threw it away, not realizing that he was missing Wake's last outgoing mail call of the war.

No one was happier to see the PBY than Major Walter Bayler. The Harvard-educated Marine radio specialist's temporary assignment on Wake had stretched out far longer—and turned out to be much more perilous—than he'd expected. As the siege had dragged on, his thoughts had turned increasingly to his home in Coronado, California, his wife, and his daughter, Vam, and he'd wondered if he'd see them again. His orders were to proceed to Midway by the first available transport for a similar radio installation job after completing his work on Wake, so the PBY offered a golden opportunity to carry on with his mission and improve his chances of getting back to his family.

Major Putnam knew about Bayler's orders, and he lost no time checking with Ensign Murphy to see if there was space for a passenger on the flight back to Midway, along with the mail Murphy had agreed to take.

"Sure, there's plenty of room," the pilot said. "We'd be glad to have him." Even more important, he added, the PBY also carried a spare life jacket and parachute, both of which were required under Navy regulations for every person aboard.

The only stipulation, Murphy told Putnam, was that Bayler would have to be ready to leave bright and early the next morning. "I want to be airborne by 7:00 A.M.," he said. Now that he knew the gravity of the situation on Wake, the young ensign was even more anxious than Bayler to get the hell out of there. If he'd had any choice, he would have left that night, but taking off from the lagoon in the dark was too risky. Bayler was glad for the extra time, and he hustled to get ready.

It didn't help to learn that his written orders no longer existed. They'd been filed in Cunningham's office at Camp Two when it was hit by a bomb, but to Bayler's relief, Cunningham remembered the gist of the orders and gave him a verbal directive to that effect. Bayler also became the designated courier for the various reports and official papers being sent back to Midway by other officers. And, as a thoughtful gesture, Bayler arranged to take Lieutenant Conderman's sword back to the States to give to the dead pilot's family.

One of Bayler's last stops during his final evening on Wake was at the magazine near the east end of the airstrip that housed the hospital. "It was late at night before I could tie up the loose ends of my radio job and get to the hospital," he said, "but none of the boys minded being awakened when he learned it meant an opportunity to send a word or two home. I told them the messages had to be extremely brief, and I promised to get them off by telegraph at the earliest moment."

Some of the terse greetings that ended up in Bayler's notebook that night included these:

> To Mrs. J. R. Lanning, 320 D Street, National City, California: "OK, Chick."
> To Mrs. Neil Gooding of Gooding, Idaho: "OK from Boyce."
> To H. O. Pace, Casa Grande, Arizona: "OK from John."
> To V. F. Webb, 110 Military Street, Oxford, North Carolina: "OK, everything fine, from Gorham."
> To Mrs. Luther Williams of Stonewall, Mississippi: "Solon is OK. Tough fight—but OK."
> To Mrs. C. E. Compton, 2419 Fernleaf, Los Angeles, California: "Just say Clair is OK."

To F. W. Reeves, 334 Hawthorne Avenue, Palo Alto, California: "OK
from Wayne."

Bayler spent a few minutes visiting with wounded fighter pilot "Spider"
Webb, whose bomb-mangled foot and other injuries suffered in the first
air raid were slowly healing. Webb still couldn't get out of bed, but he was
moving around on his elbows regularly for exercise, and he seemed in
good spirits.

"I'm feeling a little better, Walt," he said, shaking Bayler's hand. "I can't
wait to get another crack at those bastards."

By the time Bayler left the hospital and stopped by Devereux's command post to pick up a packet of messages, there was only time for a short
catnap before the PBY's scheduled departure. It was barely first light the
next morning, December 21, when he reached the dock in the lagoon to
find an impatient Murphy fidgeting to get under way and glancing nervously "from the eastern sky to his wristwatch and back again."

Bayler had made numerous friends on Wake, especially among the officers and men of VMF-211, and a sizable group of well-wishers was on
hand to see him off. There was just time enough for some handshakes and
backslaps, a laugh or two, and a few hurried good-byes.

"Good luck."

"Take care of yourself."

"I'll be seeing you . . ."

It wasn't quite seven o'clock when Bayler climbed aboard the PBY and
paused to gaze out across the little atoll that had taken such hellacious
punishment over the past two weeks. He glanced up at the flag rippling in
the breeze at the top of its pole, where it had flown constantly since December 8. He looked at the grinning, confident young Marines on the
dock. As he waved a final good-bye and took his seat in the plane, he was
cheered by the sight. Because of them, he had the feeling that everything
was going to be okay on Wake.

Then Murphy revved the engines and the plane pulled slowly away from
the dock, leaving behind a foamy trail and a crowd of wistful Marines
whose faces quickly turned solemn as the PBY gathered speed and rose
into the misty, gray dawn.

One person who wasn't on hand for the fond farewells was Herman Hevenor, the official from the Bureau of the Budget who had missed the last outbound Pan Am Clipper flight. The evening before, Hevenor had urgently sought his own seat on the PBY, but his request was denied because Bayler had already claimed the only extra parachute and life jacket.

Thus, while Bayler escaped to safety and would soon be relaxing in Honolulu, Hevenor was left behind in the jaws of a closing trap. The hapless minor bureaucrat from Washington had planned to spend only a few days on Wake gathering information for a routine report on construction of the naval air station. When he heard the sound of the PBY's engines receding into the distance, he surely must have worried that his last hope of escape was fading along with them.

At nine o'clock that morning, barely two hours after the flying boat had disappeared into the overcast eastern sky, Wake was pounded by its fourteenth enemy air raid of the war. And along with the holocaust they rained down on the Marine batteries and other positions, the attackers delivered an ominous message.

There were forty-nine planes in the enemy formations this time—by far the largest number yet—but even more significant was the type of aircraft used in the raid. These weren't the high-level, hit-and-run Nells of the Chitose Air Group or the bulky, slow-moving seaplanes from the far-away Marshalls. These were speedy dive bombers that streaked in at less than 1,000 feet—too fast and too low for the antiaircraft batteries to have a chance of hitting them—then circled lower and lower. Worse yet, they hung around for a solid hour, making run after run over the same targets and pulverizing everything in their path with machine gun fire and high explosives. The raid seemed to go on forever.

Still worse, these bombers were accompanied for the first time by a fighter escort of no less than eighteen Zeroes. With their rugged agility and 330-mile-per-hour top speed, they not only provided cover for the larger planes but made their own damaging strafing runs. While VMF-211's Wildcats came close to matching the Zeroes in speed and maneuverability, they came up a little short in both categories.

The scariest part, though, was that the December 21 raiders were all carrier-based aircraft, the first the Wake Islanders had seen. Obviously, at least one enemy carrier now lurked within striking distance just beyond the horizon. This meant that a major enemy armada of destroyers, cruisers, and other vessels was also massed out there to shield and support the carrier. If a Japanese force of such size was that close, it could mean only one thing: another invasion attempt.

One particularly maddening aspect of this new type of air raid was the defenders' inability to respond with effective fire from their antiaircraft batteries. The raiders' low altitude made it impossible for the Marines' three-inch guns to track them, and the enemy's swift, circling style of attack made random fire ineffective.

As a result, Devereux ordered his three-inchers to remain silent and let his .50-caliber machine guns handle the whole task of aerial defense. To observers in a position to see the machine guns in action, they did an extraordinarily effective job. Lieutenant Barninger of Battery A gave special credit to the four .50s on Peacock Point commanded by Corporal Frank Gross for keeping the dive bombers from scoring any direct hits on the battery. Gross himself praised the .50-caliber machine gunners all over the island for filling the skies with a near-record volume of rounds.

Near the airfield, Lieutenant Kliewer was pinned down in a machine gun pit for close to an hour with two gunners who kept their .50s chattering constantly. He admired the fact that they stayed at their guns, "attacking the enemy wherever possible" despite their apparent lack of success. The machine guns didn't pose nearly as much danger to the raiders as the three-inchers normally did, but some witnesses reported seeing at least one raider go down.

PFC John R. Himelrick watched from a dugout on the south beach of Wake proper as one Japanese plane came spinning out of a cloud and exploded. "Boy, that sure looked good," he yelled to the men around him.

Cunningham, meanwhile, couldn't understand why the three-inch batteries were lying silent while the atoll was being pounded by the heaviest

Japanese air raid to date. When the island commander rang up Devereux's command post to demand an explanation, he sounded rattled.

"Why the hell aren't we firing at them?" Cunnigham yelled above the din outside.

"We are," Devereux said.

"I don't hear them," Cunningham shouted. "I don't hear your guns."

"The guns aren't shooting," Devereux shouted back in exasperation. "The machine guns are."

This information failed to placate Cunningham. From the depths of his bunker, the commander couldn't tell that these raiders weren't the same as all those that had come before. He simply didn't comprehend what was happening, and so he continued to fume and ask, "Why?"

Devereux had to explain to him that, because of the antiaircraft batteries' limited angular rate, it was impossible to shoot effectively at attacking planes of this type with a three-inch gun.

When the raid started, VMF-211 had been temporarily reduced to just one flyable plane—Wildcat No. 9. And for reasons that are hard to fathom, considering the squadron's catastrophic losses on December 8, it had been left in the most dangerous imaginable circumstances.

Major Putnam was horrified when he heard the first bomb blasts, and he had every right to be. He was in a dugout several miles away near Camp Two, talking with Dan Teters about airfield construction priorities, and he realized instantly that No. 9 was sitting out in plain sight at the edge of the main runway. Fully fueled with 160 gallons of gasoline, fully armed with bombs and machine gun rounds, and ready to take off on the midday patrol, the Grumman couldn't have presented a more tempting, vulnerable target.

Undoubtedly blaming himself for this latest sitting-duck situation, Putnam gave no thought to caution or his own personal safety. He jumped into his truck and tore out along the coral road that curved north, then back to the south around the lagoon. He didn't get far before he found himself squarely in the path of one wave of strafing Zeroes after another.

Crouching behind the steering wheel and dodging for his life, Putnam swerved and zigzagged from one side of the road to the other. Twice, with machine gun bullets pelting around him like hail, he had to abandon the truck and dive for cover off the road. Each time, he pulled himself back into the driver's seat after the planes veered away and tried again. And each time, to his amazement, the truck started and ran with no problem.

The same couldn't be said for the Grumman, however. When Putnam eventually got to it, the patchwork fighter steadfastly refused to start. By this time, the squadron had depleted its supply of the shotgun shells normally used to trigger ignition in the F4F-3's 1,200-horsepower engine, and the ground crew was having to improvise with a slingshot system that was slow and inefficient.

Again and again as this tense process continued, the Japanese planes swooped down with guns blazing, but through some improbable quirk of fate—or simply because the raiders' aim was incredibly bad that day— both Putnam and No. 9 remained unscathed.

As the raiders were breaking off their attack and retiring toward the open sea, the Wildcat coughed, sputtered, and finally started. Once airborne, Putnam opened the throttle, coaxed the plane up to near-maximum speed, and roared after the enemy bombers. But the raiders had too big a head start, and before he could begin to close the gap, they vanished into the clouds. Putnam continued out for forty miles or so, about as far as he dared to test the temperamental F4F-3's range, scanning the blue Pacific for any sign of enemy ships but finding nothing. Soon he gave up and headed home, too disappointed and disgusted to comprehend how fortunate he was to be alive after his potentially suicidal mission.

Overall, damage from the raid was unbelievably light, and the only casualties were a few minor injuries. One of the slightly wounded was Sergeant Bourquin, who had inherited the job of driving a new VMF-211 gasoline truck after the old one was hit by a bomb, killing the three Marines aboard it and hurling their bodies so far that they weren't found for ten days. "It wasn't a job I coveted, for obvious reasons," Bourquin said, "but when Captain Tharin told me I'd just 'volunteered' for it, I figured I didn't have much choice."

Like his commanding officer, Bourquin was also pursued relentlessly in

The Pan American Airways Inn on Peale Island as it appeared in 1940.
(National Archives)

A Pan American Clipper taxis up to the dock in the Wake Island lagoon
in the late 1930s. (National Archives)

Sergeant Robert Bourquin, who along with three other aviation Marines of VMF-211 held off scores of Japanese for several hours while trying to blow up the airstrip on Wake to keep it from falling into enemy hands. A faulty generator caused their harrowing mission to fail on December 23, 1941.
(Courtesy Robert Bourquin)

Sergeant Robert Bourquin carried this photo of his fiancée, Charlotte "Chotty" McLain, in his shoe during his forty-four months as a POW. The picture almost cost him his life when it was taken from him by a Japanese guard and Bourquin retaliated with his fists. As of mid-2002, Bourquin still had the picture in his billfold.
(Courtesy Robert Bourquin)

John Johnson, whose .30-caliber machine-gun section was instrumental in the Marines' counterattack and victory on Wilkes Island, is shown with his sister, Norma, on his graduation from military school in 1939.
(Courtesy John Johnson)

In this photo, originally published in a Japanese propaganda magazine, a grinning member of Japan's Chitose Air Group describes a direct hit by his bomber during a mission over Wake. (National Archives)

Gunnery Sergeant John Cemeris, credited by some observers with shooting down a Japanese plane with a .30-caliber machine gun on December 23 before he received word of the American surrender. This photo was made in 1940. (Courtesy Arlene Cemeris)

The light cruiser Yubari, flagship of the Japanese invasion fleet on January 11, 1941, was severely damaged by American artillery fire but was repaired in time to lead the enemy's amphibious assault when the invaders returned on December 23. (National Archives)

The "Grumman graveyard" of wrecked Marine F4F-3 Wildcat fighters litters the beach on Wake in this Japanese photo made after the surrender. The plane in the foreground was the one flown by Captain Henry T. Elrod when he sank the Japanese destroyer Kisaragi *on December 11, 1941. (National Archives)*

Major Paul A. Putnam, commander of VMF-211, saw two-thirds of his fighter planes demolished in the first Japanese raid on December 8, 1941, but directed the air defense of Wake that destroyed at least a dozen enemy planes and two major Japanese ships over the next two weeks. (Marine Corps Historical Center)

*In this 1956 photo, retired Marine General James P. S. Devereux enjoys a
reunion with three of the enlisted men who served under him in the
First Marine Defense Battalion during the Battle of Wake Island:
(from left) Ewing LaPorte, Mackie Wheeler, and Artie Stocks.*
(Courtesy Artie Stocks)

Robert Doyle.

Current photo of Chalas Loveland.

Current photo of Ed Doyle.

*All small photos on this page are
from the "blue book" published in 1945
by the Morrison-Knudsen Company as a
tribute to its employees who were taken
prisoner or killed on Wake.*

Current photo of Glenn Newell.

Bowsher, Johnson, and Gross at Bowsher's home in December 2001.

Wiley Sloman (left)
with Dr. Shigeyoshi Ozeki
during a reunion in Japan
in 1995. (Courtesy Ed Borne)

In a 2001 photo, John Johnson displays pages from
the handwritten daily diary he kept from the first
day of the war until his release from POW camp.
(Photo by Lana Sloan)

One of the two five-inch guns of Battery A on Peacock Point still points seaward a decade after firing its last rounds. (Courtesy Jack Skaggs)

The shell-riddled hulk of Patrol Boat No. 33, one of the Japanese destroyer-transports used to land troops on Wake on December 23, 1941, still sprawls on the barrier reef in a photo taken some ten years after the battle. (Courtesy Jack Skaggs)

The bunker that served as Devereux's command post on Wake during the last days of the battle for the atoll is shown shrouded by trees and brush in this 2000 photo. (Courtesy Artie Stocks)

his truck by strafing Japanese planes, but he didn't fare as well as Putnam. The truck was riddled by machine gun fire, and Bourquin was cut by fragments of the blown-out windshield and clawed by tree limbs as he crashed the vehicle into the brush.

Many of the gun crew at Lieutenant Barninger's Battery A on Peacock Point narrowly escaped a cluster of bombs that bracketed the large communal dugout where they were huddled and exploded in rapid succession just a few yards away. Barninger called the bomb craters the biggest ones he'd ever seen, but except for knocking over Sergeant Jack Cook, a gun captain on one of the five-inchers who was closest to the blast, and wrecking the dugout entrance, they did little actual harm.

By far the most damaging effects of the raid were psychological, not physical or material. To many of those on the receiving end of the attack, the sudden entrance of carrier aircraft into the battle for Wake changed everything and brought with it an aura of doom. Staff Sergeant Clifford Hotchkiss of the Army radio team interpreted the turn of events as "probably the beginning of the end." Even Devereux conceded that the Americans' luck may have run out.

The defenders had little time to fret about their future or try to analyze the meaning of that morning's unprecedented attack. The Zeroes and Kate dive bombers from the *Hiryu* and *Soryu* hadn't been gone much more than an hour and a half when the now-familiar land-based Nells from Roi made their ninth appearance over Wake. By 12:30 P.M., the second bombing raid of the day was in full flower.

On this visit, the raiders came in at 18,000 feet and concentrated most of their attention on Peale Island, where Captain Godbold's antiaircraft battery had exacted a heavy toll from the beginning on the Chitose Air Group. As was often the case, there were again conflicting reports as to how many Japanese planes were involved. Some observers claimed to see as many as twenty-seven, but Godbold himself placed the number at only eighteen, and on this day, no one was in a better position to know that number.

Not since their initial attack on December 8 had the Japanese pilots and bombardiers shown much tactical expertise or bombing skill—much less any stomach for braving the accuracy of Wake's sky gunners. With God-bold's Battery D leading the way, the Marines' three-inchers had downed at least eight or nine planes by now, and very possibly twice that many, considering those that limped back toward their distant base trailing smoke. Today, however, the attackers changed their strategy, and it paid off in spades against Battery D.

It was clear from the beginning—and came as absolutely no surprise—that the battery position on Peale was the enemy's main target on this trip. Unexpectedly, the bomber squadron split into two sections as it ap-proached, with about nine of the Mitsubishis flying straight up the north-ern leg of Wake proper toward Peale, while the rest of the planes veered away and looked to be heading out to sea.

After a moment's hesitation, Battery D opened fire, and Battery E, lo-cated down between the airfield and the south beach on the opposite end of Wake, immediately followed suit.

Godbold's gunners sent thirty-five rounds into the Japanese formation and were rewarded by seeing one of the Nells belch smoke as it passed over their position. But they had no time to congratulate each other before they realized—too late—that they'd been tricked. The first wave of bombers was acting as a decoy and baiting a clever trap, while the other half of the enemy squadron circled around and watched. Up to this point, frequent moves had kept the enemy confused about Battery D's exact location, but the flashes from their guns had given the secret away. The second wave of Japanese fliers had seen precisely where the three-inchers were concealed. Now they were streaking in from the opposite direction, and there was go-ing to be hell to pay.

"Look out," somebody yelled. "Here comes the other run."

There was no time left for the gun crew to adjust their aim or take cover. Before they could react, the second wave was right there on top of them, bombs screaming.

The enemy bombardiers dumped their payloads in a tight pattern that saturated the battery with earth-shattering explosions. "It was just one continuous rumble from dropping bombs," as civilian volunteer Oscar Lent described it.

Squatting in the battery's director pit and calmly supervising the anti-aircraft fire was Sergeant Johnalson E. Wright, a 320-pound giant, who may have been the biggest man in the entire Marine Corps. "Big" Wright was a legendary figure, both for his ability to down a keg of beer with unbelievable speed and for his professionalism and coolness under fire. While other members of the gun crew scrambled for cover when things got rough, Wright invariably stayed in his usual spot in front of the direction-finding device, with nothing above him but the sky, trusting in the lucky silver dollar clenched in his huge fist to protect him from harm.

Wright always followed the same routine in every enemy raid. He'd wave the dollar and shout reassuringly to his battery mates: "Don't worry, you guys. I'm squeezing my lucky dollar for you."

Once the raid was over and the danger past, Wright would stand up, brush himself off, and stick the charmed coin back in his pocket. Somebody would inevitably say, "Hey, that lucky dollar worked again," and Wright would grin.

The sudden appearance of the second wave of bombers caught several Battery D Marines in the director pit along with Wright and left them no time to take cover. As the bombs rained down at them, they heard Wright's familiar yell: "Hey, don't worry. I've got my lucky dollar right here."

Seconds later, one of the bombs struck the sandbag barrier at the very edge of the director pit. The earth-heaving concussion sent men flying like rag dolls and knocked Second Lieutenant Robert Greeley, the battery's range officer, out cold. Volleys of sand from disintegrating sandbags were hurled with such force that they dissolved the clothing—and skin—of those in their path. Sergeant Steve Fortuna was stripped of his uniform and temporarily blinded by the flying sand. PFC Leonard Mettscher fared even worse, losing every shred of hide from the back of his head to below his belt line.

The force of the explosion tore Wright apart, killing him instantly. Other Marines in the pit escaped death only because they were on the opposite side of the director from Wright, and the bulk of the device shielded them to some degree. But a half dozen were wounded, four of them severely enough to be hospitalized. After taking the direct force of the bomb blast, the director itself was nothing but a pile of useless junk.

Wright was mourned by everyone in the battery. Some of the men buried him a few yards from where he died, while others cursed and vowed revenge. "We were fighting mad," said Mettscher.

From the very first day, Battery D had been Wake's most effective anti-aircraft defense. Its gunners usually got the last shots at departing enemy planes and scored more kills and possible kills than any other gun crew. But now, with its director ruined, Devereux was left with no choice but to break up Battery D and move its guns and usable components to other locations. One three-inch gun, along with the battery's generator and range finder, went to Battery E at the base of Wake proper, which now became the atoll's only fully equipped, fully manned AA emplacement. It was a sound, sensible move. Battery E was in the best location to cover the airfield, and it hadn't yet been found by the Japanese and would be difficult for bombers to hit, if and when they discovered it.

Two of the remaining guns, now worthless against aerial attack, were moved to the north beach of Peale to defend against any Japanese landing attempt in that area. The fourth and final gun was left in Battery D's old position as a decoy, along with some hastily erected wooden dummies. Devereux reasoned that any enemy bombs wasted on an unattended position would be that many fewer that fell where they could actually do harm.

With the help of 125 civilians, Godbold's 60 Marines started moving the guns as soon as darkness fell. Around dusk, Devereux paid the work party a visit and took note of an odd change in the attitude of the toiling troops. Like any soldiers, they'd shown a tendency to bitch and grumble about hard, dirty assignments. But now, with their nerves rubbed raw, their bodies sapped by fatigue and sleeplessness, and the odds stacked solidly against them, they'd quit griping entirely. Maybe they just didn't have the strength to gripe and work at the same time, but Devereux sensed the birth of a "stubborn pride" that went beyond mere morale. From this point on, these men could be killed, but their fortitude and resolve could never be broken.

It was the third time in two weeks that the tons of weaponry in Battery D had been picked up bodily and moved. It had never been easy, but this final move was the hardest of all. When it was complete, the battery basically ceased to exist as a functioning unit.

"The Japs had just bombed us right out of business," said PFC Charlie Harrison, who had avoided serious injury or death by the thinnest of margins when the bomb hit the director pit. "Up to now, we'd been artillerymen, but from this point on, we were back to being riflemen."

It took until 1:00 A.M. the next morning to finish the moving job, and a number of the civilians continued to work on camouflage for the three-inchers on the beach until about daybreak. Meanwhile, at the airfield, other men also worked through the night on revetments for the new squadron of planes that was supposed to be on its way to Wake.

In the light-proof hangar, Lieutenant Kinney was so weak and sick with diarrhea that he could hardly stand up, but he and Sergeant Hamilton labored through the night to breathe life back into yet another battered Grumman. By midmorning of December 22, they'd somehow managed to get redoubtable old Wildcat No. 8 running for the first time in five days, again giving the squadron two planes capable of getting off the ground.

About 10:00 A.M., Captain Herb Freuler and Lieutenant Carl Davidson took off for the midday patrol and climbed quickly to 12,000 feet in near-ideal flying conditions. For once, the usual cloud cover over Wake had given way to clear skies and bright sun, and visibility was excellent. Even the Wildcats' temperamental voice radios were working perfectly that morning—another apparent good omen.

It was a few minutes before noon when Davidson reported masses of enemy planes approaching out of the north. A total of thirty-three carrier-based Kates—sixteen from the *Soryu* and seventeen from the *Hiryu*—were boring in at 12,000 feet. Streaking along above the bombers at 18,000 feet was a fighter escort of six Zeroes.

Since no U.S. planes had appeared to challenge yesterday's raiders, the Japanese felt sure that all of Wake's fighters had been knocked out. Led to believe that their Zeroes were strictly "along for the ride" today, the enemy fighter pilots weren't as alert as they should have been.

Freuler was south of the atoll in venerable Wildcat No. 8 when he got Davidson's message. He opened his throttle and streaked north across the center of Wake. Moments later, he spotted six of the Kates flying in a tight

V and tore into them. The enemy planes never saw him coming, and his ferocious surprise attack sent them scattering. One of them spun away, streaming smoke and plunging seaward as Freuler wheeled quickly for a second pass.

This time, he came at the Kates head-on as they tried to get back in formation. Taking maximum advantage of the fact that the enemy bombers had no forward machine guns, Freuler singled out another one and delivered a vicious burst of .50-caliber slugs from point-blank range.

Freuler was only about fifty feet away when the Kate exploded in a blinding ball of flame. With no time to veer away, he had to fly directly through the remains of the disintegrating bomber. For an instant, he was totally engulfed in a cloud of smoke and fire, but then he broke into the clear again.

Freuler had no idea that one of his two confirmed kills that noon had avenged the U.S.S. *Arizona* and the more than 1,100 American sailors entombed inside her at Pearl Harbor. Aboard one of the Kates was Petty Officer Noboru Kanai, the Japanese bombardier whose flawless aim had exploded the American battleship on December 7.

What Freuler *did* know was that the force of the blast from the second Kate had severely crippled his own plane. Old No. 8 was scorched, battered, losing manifold pressure and speed, and reacting sluggishly to his tugs on her controls. He could see the white beaches of Wake in the far distance, but he wasn't sure No. 8 could make it that far. And as if that weren't enough, the Zeroes, shaken out of their reverie, were descending on him in an angry swarm.

One of them was right on Freuler's tail now, and its machine guns were punching holes in his wings and fuselage. He felt a white-hot stab of pain as a bullet tore into his shoulder. Then a second slug plowed into the parachute pack on his back. Another Zero joined the chase, and Freuler searched desperately for a cloud to hide behind, but there was nothing in sight except blue sky and the pursuing enemy planes.

Out of the corner of his eye, he caught a glimpse of Davidson's Wildcat a mile or so away. Davidson was hot on the heels of one Zero, but another enemy fighter had come up behind the lieutenant's F4F-3 with its guns blazing.

The last Freuler saw of them, the three planes were receding into the far distance over the ocean with the Grumman still tightly sandwiched between the two Zeroes. Then Freuler had too much trouble of his own to watch any longer.

By now, his wounded Wildcat was a veritable flying sieve. Even on its best day, it had never possessed the speed or maneuverability to shake its present tormentors. For a second, Freuler felt trapped, doomed, but then an idea came to him. He had just one long-shot chance of living beyond the next few seconds: put his plane into a sheer dive, play dead, and pray.

He shoved the stick forward, and the Wildcat fell like a rock.

When the Japanese pilots saw Freuler plunging headlong toward the sea, they thought for sure he was going down—just as Freuler hoped—and they broke away. At the last possible second, Freuler pulled out of the dive, wondering if his riddled ship would fall apart around him from the strain. It held together, and a minute or two later, the gallant old Grumman rolled to a stop on the runway just as its engine gave up the ghost. No. 8 was an utter wreck, but its last landing had been almost picture perfect, and its pilot was able to climb out of the cockpit under his own power.

Lieutenant Davidson and his plane were never seen again.

For more than two weeks, the Wake Islanders had withstood everything the enemy could throw at them. Considering the tons of high explosives dumped on them during sixteen air raids, their losses in military personnel had been incredibly few. With the exception of the heavy casualties on December 8, only a handful of Marines and sailors had been killed or seriously wounded.

Nevertheless, the persistence of the Japanese attacks had taken a ruinous toll on Wake's ability to defend itself. Where earlier raids had barely nibbled at the atoll's defenses, the coordinated mass assaults of the past two days had started taking huge bites out of American armaments and fortifications.

Like Godbold's Battery D, Putnam's fighter squadron was now officially out of business. Nearly half of its pilots were either dead or in sick bay, and there were no planes left to fly, anyway. Even Lieutenant Kinney and

Sergeant Hamilton had run out of miracles. Kinney, in fact, had finally yielded to an order by Putnam to check into the hospital, where he was so spent from fatigue and diarrhea that he could barely sit up.

Late on the afternoon of December 22, Putnam reported to Devereux that the surviving able-bodied members of VMF-211 were volunteering as infantry. Devereux gratefully accepted the additional hands and assigned them to positions in his thin defensive perimeter between the airfield and the main island's south beach.

That evening, Devereux made a stoic assessment of the situation facing his Marines. He still hoped for reinforcements within the next twenty-four hours, but he knew it was foolish to pin the fate of his entire garrison on the slim chance of getting help. He also knew that it was impossible to cover all twenty miles of coastline with the men and weapons he had available. The only reasonable alternative was to try to determine the likeliest location for a landing and get his meager forces ready to meet the enemy there. This was what he'd done. If he was guessing wrong, there'd be no second chance.

Devereux's strategy was based largely on Wake's treacherous coral reefs. Except for the small break near the boat channel, the reefs completely encircled the atoll, but they were closer to shore on the south side of Wake and Wilkes than anywhere else. If the Japanese got across the reefs there, they'd be almost on the beach and, once ashore, within easy striking distance of the airfield. The logical conclusion was that the enemy's main attack would come somewhere along the south shore between Peacock Point and Kuku Point.

There was no longer any question that another enemy landing attempt was coming. What no one could predict with equal accuracy was *when* the strike would come. It might be preceded by a heavy artillery barrage by an enemy who now knew to stay out of range of the Marines' shore batteries. Or the Japanese might try to sneak their troops ashore under cover of darkness.

Late on December 22, Devereux pushed his papers away and yawned. Further thought about the problem seemed pointless. He'd done everything he knew to do. Now it was better to try to get a little sleep.

Meanwhile, the U.S.S. *Saratoga* and the rest of Admiral Fletcher's Task Force 14 had inched its way to a point approximately 475 miles east of Wake. Even with the pathetically slow pace being set by the antiquated oiler *Neches,* a few more hours would put the *Saratoga*'s planes within striking distance of Wake if the task force continued on its present course.

As he paced the bridge of the cruiser *Astoria,* Fletcher worried about his destroyers' fuel situation. Although the task force was maintaining strict radio silence, regular reports from CinCPac told Fletcher just how urgent Wake's situation was becoming. Still, caution had become a byword with Admiral Pye, Fletcher's interim boss back at Pearl, and although the destroyers had an adequate supply of fuel, the task force commander felt that if a fight developed near Wake, it might not be enough.

Early on the morning of December 22, rather than pressing on, Fletcher ordered the *Neches* to begin a refueling operation. While this was in progress, the admiral altered his course to a more northerly direction that brought his ships no nearer their destination. In effect, the ships were merely marking time while the refueling dragged on all day and into the night because of rough seas, snarled fuel and towlines, and other problems.

By the time the task force resumed its plodding westerly course toward Wake, the invasion fleet of Admiral Kajioka was already moving into position to launch its ground assault.

*Sublieutenant Shigeyoshi Ozeki, a Japanese
medical officer who landed with invading
Japanese troops on December 23, 1941, was
later credited with helping save the lives of
wounded Americans following the
surrender of Wake.*
(Courtesy Shigeyoshi Ozeki)

⋆ 11 ⋆

A Battle That
"Made the Gods Weep"

In years to come, most Wake Island survivors agreed that the night of December 22–23, 1941, was the darkest they could ever remember. Lookouts were literally unable to see their hands in front of their faces. The weather was foul, too, with a light rain falling out of a heavily overcast sky and a chill, penetrating wind blowing. The night hung above the atoll like a soggy blanket, so thick you could almost feel it. Even the snow-white beach that stretched away from right to left was as dark as a blot of India ink. The sound of the wind-driven surf pounding against the reef seemed strangely intensified by the blackness.

A few hundred yards from one of the lookout towers on Wilkes Island, at a .30-caliber machine gun emplacement near Kuku Point, Corporal John Johnson was feeling upbeat in spite of the wet gloom surrounding him. At the stroke of midnight, the quietly intense young Missourian would officially turn twenty years old, and he was looking forward to this milestone. Occasionally his thoughts turned to Dorothy David, a girl back in St. Louis, and the Hawaiian grass skirt he'd sent her as a high school graduation present. She'd asked for it, half jokingly, in one of her letters, and he would have loved to see her face when she opened the package.

Johnson also thought about First Sergeant Mike Hogan, his drill instructor back at boot camp. For a long time, it seemed as if Hogan had had it in for him, but then Johnson had figured out that Hogan was actually taking him under his wing as a mentor. Hogan was the main reason for Johnson becoming one of the younger corporals in the Marine Corps, and he wondered where Hogan was right now. Anyway, being a corporal and a teenager just didn't seem to go together. Before his promotion, Johnson had felt he looked and acted more mature than most guys his age, and as he waited out the last few minutes before his birthday, he utilized that maturity to ease the mind of a worried civilian volunteer from East St. Louis, Illinois, named Leo Nonn.

"They say these planes that hit us the last two days came from a Jap carrier," said Nonn, who was three years older than Johnson but seemed younger. "Does that mean they'll be trying another landing pretty soon?"

Johnson smiled and shook his head. Despite his fretfulness, Nonn was an affable guy whom the corporal considered the most dependable of the six civilians assigned to him. Before the shooting started, Nonn had never been any closer to a machine gun than the soda fountain in the contractors' canteen, where he worked. But since then, he'd taken an active interest in learning about the .30s and how to fire them. If the Japanese did try to land on Wake, Johnson knew he could trust Nonn to fight and fight well.

"Nah, that carrier was probably just passing by on its way to somewhere else," Johnson assured him. "Before they try to invade us again, I figure they'll send in ships to lay down an artillery barrage, like before. Until that happens, there's no reason to worry. So come on, lighten up. Tomorrow we'll have a big party to celebrate my birthday."

The mysterious flashes of light started around midnight. At first, they looked like glimmers of heat lightning dancing beyond the northwestern horizon. But as they went on, it became increasingly evident that the illuminations originated from ships somewhere far out at sea. The mysterious yellow and white flashes continued for close to an hour, and to this day, no one knows for certain what caused them. Several plausible theories emerged, but there's still no official explanation.

Wiley Sloman, who watched the strange spectacle from a point just below the Battery L command tower, and a number of other Marines heard later from Japanese sources that the flashes were caused by two groups of

Japanese ships mistakenly shooting at each other. But there were other reports as well.

Devereux went outside and climbed on top of his dugout to watch the lights. He described them as vivid flashes far beyond the horizon. Lookouts on Wake had seen occasional distant lights blinking for the past couple of nights, and they were interpreted as probable signals between scouting elements of a nearby Japanese task force. But on this night, the flashes were different—much brighter, more numerous, and much longer in duration. They gave every indication that a naval battle was raging far at sea, but there was no way to be sure.

Regardless of what caused the peculiar light show, however, it hardly seems likely that it was deliberately staged by the Japanese. The lights served to jar weary Wake Islanders into a heightened state of alert, seriously undermining enemy hopes of a surprise landing. They brought many Americans out of their foxholes and dugouts and tipped them off that something big might be about to happen. The men had been jumpy enough before, but the far-off pyrotechnics put them even more on edge.

Gradually, the lights lessened in intensity, then stopped altogether. After a while, men drifted back to their makeshift beds, but despite their exhaustion, many found it impossible to go back to sleep.

In his command post, Devereux had just closed his eyes when he heard a shout from Corporal Brown. It was a few minutes before 2:00 A.M. on December 23, and, as usual, Brown was on the phone, monitoring Wake's emergency warning network. The net linked every position on the atoll, and its lines were kept open constantly.

"I've got a report of an enemy landing on Toki Point," Brown said.

Devereux was off his bunk in an instant and headed for the phone. "Any confirmation?" he asked.

"No, sir, but it came over the warning net," Brown replied.

The major frowned. Toki Point was at the northwestern tip of Peale—a most unlikely spot for a landing, in Devereux's opinion. It could be either a feint by the enemy or some sentry simply "seeing things" as he stared into the curtain of darkness. But the mystery lights had also been to the northwest, so there could be some connection. Besides, Marines listening in all over the island heard the report on the telephone warning network. Men were already scrambling to their battle stations.

Devereux immediately rang Lieutenant Kessler on Peale. "What about this report of a landing at Toki Point?" he said.

"There's some lights out there," Kessler said. "No landing yet, but some lookouts report what looks like small boats pretty close to the north shore. We've got the beach defenses manned and ready."

Devereux checked quickly with other positions. He still thought the likeliest spot for a landing in force was the south beach between Peacock and Kuku points. When he heard that Lieutenant Poindexter was speeding from Camp One toward Peale with eight Marines and four machine guns mounted on a truck, Devereux sent a runner to intercept them. He ordered Poindexter to stand by until the situation was clarifed but warned him not to be "sucked out of the defense" in the main area of risk by enemy diversionary tactics.

A steady stream of reports was coming in now. All batteries and machine gun emplacements along the shore were manned. What personnel could be spared from the gun crews—about 200 men in all—were being deployed as infantry on the beaches, and small patrols of three or four men each were scouting the long open sections of shoreline for signs of the enemy.

Then Kessler called back. "There's plenty of lights out there, but that's all."

"Any boats beached?" Devereux asked.

"Negative," Kessler said. "I sent out a patrol, but they didn't find anything."

Devereux hurriedly put out the word over the warning net to all positions: "The Toki Point landing looks like a false alarm, but we definitely have enemy activity offshore, and it appears to be in strong force. I want everybody to be extremely alert."

Just then, an unsettling question crossed Devereux's mind. What if the boats seen off Peale had swung west around Toki Point and slipped into the lagoon? With the garrison's entire defensive focus directed seaward, any invaders who landed from the lagoon could attack the unexpecting defenders from behind. It was a chilling thought, one that sent Devereux back to the phone.

"Watch your back," the major warned Captain Platt, his strongpoint commander on Wilkes. "There's a chance the Japs could hit us from the lagoon side."

During the next few minutes, the frenetic rash of phone messages continued without letup, and Corporal Brown fielded what he called "a constant babble" of often-conflicting reports.

"I see lights off Peacock Point," one observer yelled over the line.

"Where are they?" Devereux demanded. "Do you see boats?"

"Yeah, I see boats," a voice rasped.

"No, I don't see nothin'," another voice said.

Then: "There's movement offshore. I'm sure of it."

"Some kind of craft very close in."

"Looks like two big barges off Peacock Point."

By now, it was obvious that things were happening all over the place and that they were all somehow connected. But in the inky blackness, it was anybody's guess what was real and what was a figment of blurred vision or imaginations rubbed raw by lack of rest.

"No matter how alert a man may be or how much he may strain his eyes, he can't see through a wall," Devereux observed later. "And the darkness around the island was a wall."

Yet in the midst of this melee of blind confusion, contradictory reports, and rising panic, some historians point to what may have been Devereux's only serious tactical mistake of the whole sixteen-day siege. With all reasonable doubt now removed that Japanese landing craft were no more than a few hundred yards off Wake's beaches, the major could have ordered his three five-inch batteries to fire salvoes of available star shells to illuminate the surrounding ocean. In the brilliant glare of these shells, the wall of darkness would have dissolved for several minutes, allowing Marine gunners to see the enemy landing vessels and have a chance to sink them before they reached shore.

But after all those days of relentless stress and sleeplessness, apparently this strategy never occurred to Devereux.

Admiral Kajioka's task force had, indeed, made a diversionary feint toward Peale Island, just as Devereux surmised, but as often happened with the Japanese commander's strategies, it went somewhat awry.

Kajioka had ordered the cruisers *Tenryu* and *Tatsuta* to circle north of Wake and direct a brief barrage from their 5.5-inch guns at Peale Island to distract the Americans' attention from the intended landing sites along the atoll's south beaches. But in the rough seas and rainy darkness, the two ships lost their bearings and ended up shelling only a patch of empty ocean dozens of miles from Wake.

Both the *Tenryu* and *Tatsuta* had been damaged in the costly invasion attempt of December 11, and their captains may have been as reluctant as Kajioka himself to venture anywhere near Wake's shore batteries. The Japanese commander and his officers were convinced that the devastation wreaked on their ships couldn't possibly have been inflicted by mere five-inch guns. They firmly believed the Americans had twelve-inch batteries—the same size ordnance mounted by older Dreadnought-class battleships—hidden in underground bunkers on Wake.

After finishing their pointless barrage, the two cruisers steamed northeast to join four other cruisers in a picket line intended to block any potential intrustion by U.S. naval forces. While undertaken in the name of caution—Kajioka's reticence today more than matched his arrogant carelessness on December 11—this deployment itself was laden with potential risk. The Japanese carriers *Hiryu* and *Soryu* were still 250 miles away, too far to protect the six picketing cruisers in the event of a U.S. aerial attack. If the cruisers had been discovered by Admiral Fletcher's Task Force 14, dive bombers from the *Saratoga* might easily have sunk all six before planes from the enemy carriers could intervene.

Kajioka had no intention of putting his hastily repaired flagship, the *Yubari*, back into range of the coastal guns that had come so close to sinking her twelve days earlier. As the troops of the Special Naval Landing Force headed for shore, the admiral ordered the *Yubari* and all his destroyers to hang back well out of range of Wake's batteries. In defiance of established procedures for amphibious assaults, the landing parties were left on their own—in choppy, pitch-black seas with sustained thirty-knot winds buffeting them from the northeast and sheets of rain swirling around them.

Kajioka's superiors had made it clear that no failure would be tolerated this time around. They'd given him all the tools they considered necessary to capture Wake, plus the authority to use those resources as ruthlessly as he deemed expedient.

Accordingly, the invasion force was split into two main groups with a third group available in an emergency. The first wave consisted of three companies with a combined total of about 1,000 officers and men. Uchida Company was aboard a former destroyer that had been converted into a transport and renamed *Patrol Boat No. 32.* Itaya Company was on a virtually identical destroyer-transport now designated as *Patrol Boat No. 33.* The crews of both these ships were under orders to get their troops ashore in a highly unorthodox fashion—by deliberately running aground on Wake's barrier reef at a point just south of the airfield. Crewmen of the two ships had been told before they ever left Kwajalein that they should consider themselves "disposable objects." A senior officer advised them: "Drink plenty of sake now, because you will not be coming back."

One of those expendable Japanese sailors was young Senior Petty Officer Hisao Tsuji from the central Japanese city of Nagoya. Like all the other members of the crew, he'd been told the mission would be very difficult. When Tsuji, a member of a deck gun crew on *Patrol Boat No. 33,* saw his ship burning, he was resigned to his own death but determined to try to obey his orders as long as he was able.

Meanwhile, about two-thirds of the other landing force unit, Takano Company, would come ashore in four conventional steel barges capable of carrying fifty or more men, two landing on Wilkes and two on Wake proper near Peacock Point. The remaining third of the company would land in scattered locations, via about twenty rubber rafts carrying five or six men each.

In reserve was a second wave, also of approximately 1,000 men, which would land after sunrise to secure the beachheads with the aid of close air support from the carriers. If this still wasn't enough manpower to subdue the defenders and secure the atoll, Kajioka was prepared to form a third wave from the crews of all six of his destroyers—about 1,000 more men—who would run their vessels aground and go ashore as infantry.

On Wilkes Island, Gunner Clarence McKinstry stared out over the three-inch guns set up near the water's edge for beach defense. He strained his ears against the roaring surf as he rang Captain Platt's dugout.

"Something's out there, sir," he said. "I hear a motor turning over, and it's getting louder."

"Can you see anything?" Platt asked.

"Not a damned thing, Captain, but I'm sure it's there. I can hear it."

"Then fire," Platt told him.

As he sprang for the guns, McKinstry repeated the order down the line: "Machine guns number nine and ten, open fire. Give us some tracers."

From the two .50-calibers just west of McKinstry's position, a sudden bright stream of tracer bullets cut through the wet darkness about ten feet off the ground—the first shots of the morning by Wake's defenders. In the dim light, McKinstry and his men could make out a large landing craft nearing the beach. The enemy barge was squarely in front of the defenders' two workable three-inchers and tantalizingly close.

"Fire!" McKinstry yelled. "Cut your fuses short."

It was 2:35 A.M. on December 23. For the first time in World War II, ground forces of the United States and Japan were about to meet face to face, hand to hand, and bayonet to bayonet.

In the words of Japan's naval minister, Admiral Shigetaro Shimada, it was a battle "which would have made the gods weep."

As the first enemy soldiers waded ashore and dashed through spotty machine gun fire on Wilkes, Admiral Fletcher's Task Force 14 was still more than 425 miles away.

The sluggish old oiler *Neches*, which sometimes had trouble maintaining a speed of even seven or eight knots in a rough sea, offered a convenient excuse for this slow progress, but there were also other, less obvious factors involved. Fletcher was clearly nervous about venturing so far into hostile waters with a scraped-together handful of ships and especially about putting the *Saratoga*—which now constituted fully a third of the U.S. Navy's offensive aerial muscle in the Pacific—in harm's way.

Worse yet, there was every indication from Pearl that CinCPac was ready to abort the Wake mission at the slightest pretext. Admiral Pye kept fiddling with the relief plan, ordering changes, then countermanding those orders, and generally making it apparent that his heart wasn't in the operation. And the closer the task force crept toward Wake, the deeper Pye's fears became. He ordered Fletcher to keep the *Saratoga* at least 200 miles from Wake to protect the carrier from enemy bombers from the Marshalls. But this would deprive Fletcher's ships of air cover as they unloaded men and materiel at Wake—and this, in turn, only added to Fletcher's uneasiness.

Late on the evening of December 22, Commander Cunningham had learned—much to his dismay—that CinCPac had ordered the submarines *Triton* and *Tambor,* which had been patrolling the waters off Wake since the war began, to withdraw from the area. Although *Tambor* had developed a leak, the withdrawal was mainly to avoid any possibility of the subs mistakenly attacking ships of Fletcher's task force, if and when they arrived. But to Cunningham, the order was just one more indication that Wake was being abandoned. All he knew for certain as the Japanese began to swarm ashore was that help wasn't coming and, in fact, that some of the previously existing help that Wake's defenders had counted on was being withdrawn.

"If Admiral Fletcher had been endowed with some of the energy exhibited by the Japanese invaders in the closing days of December 1941," Cunningham said later, "he could have arrived ahead of them and forestalled their landing."

From the perspective of any Wake defender, Cunningham's critique was justified. But in Pye's defense, no U.S. military decision maker in the early stages of World War II found himself in a worse no-win situation than the one Pye faced. On December 31, Admiral Chester A. Nimitz would arrive in Honolulu to take command of the U.S. Pacific Fleet, but until then, the full responsibility of CinCPac rested squarely on Pye and his thoroughly shaken command staff. The perceived threat of an enemy invasion of Hawaii hung over them, and the whereabouts of the Japanese fleet that had launched the attack on Pearl Harbor was still unknown. But the hottest potato of all to fall into Pye's lap was the Wake Island relief expedition, inherited from his fired predecessor.

The plan to reinforce Wake was Admiral Kimmel's last major brainchild, but Pye had never shared Kimmel's enthusiasm for the plan, and neither did his staff. In Washington, Admiral Stark, chief of naval operations, had dismissed Wake as a liability and left its fate entirely up to CinCPac. Stark's implied message was: *Go ahead with this thing if you want, but if it costs us more ships—especially a carrier—God help you.*

Undoubtedly, Pye would have canceled the whole operation at the earliest possible moment and with few serious qualms, except for one thing: By the time he took command, the ships of Task Force 14 were already bound for Wake, and a sequence of coordinated strategic moves was under way.

Even so, Pye came within an eyelash of scrubbing the mission on December 21, after receiving the first reports of enemy carrier-based planes raiding Wake and hearing Ensign Murphy, the PBY pilot who had just returned from the island, describe the situation there as "grim, grim, grim." Only an emotional outburst by members of Kimmel's old staff, particularly Marine Colonel Omar Pfeiffer, kept Pye from ordering a recall.

But finally, before sunup on December 23, Pye was handed the "out" he needed to abort the Wake mission—and it would be delivered by Cunningham himself.

For a few fleeting seconds, the glow of a red flare cut through the inky darkness above the south beach of Wilkes. It had been fired by a Japanese officer as a signal that his men had successfully reached shore, and its brief, flickering light revealed a budding disaster for the Americans trying to stop them.

Red-bearded Gunner McKinstry was doing all he could with his mostly civilian gun crew, and their two three-inch guns were keeping up a steady fire at the Japanese landing barges. But as the barges lowered their ramps and enemy troops leaped into the surf, their fire did little, if anything, to slow the invaders down.

"Damn," McKinstry yelled. "Cut your fuses at zero, and see if we can scorch 'em with a muzzle blast."

Although the landing craft were maddeningly close—only a hundred or so yards away, and almost in point-blank range—it was impossible to lower the converted antiaircraft guns' trajectory enough to aim them directly at the landing craft because the ground below the guns sloped away too sharply. The only option was to fire short-fused overhead bursts and try to rain enough shrapnel on the barges to inflict some casualties.

The machine guns just to the west, though, were doing a more effective job. McKinstry saw a burst of .50-caliber fire cut down at least six or seven Japanese in one of the barges, but he wasn't sure his three-inchers were accomplishing anything except making a lot of noise. With the invaders moving steadily closer, the gun crews' situation was deteriorating fast.

Meanwhile, Lieutenant McAlister had positioned most of his Battery L personnel in the undergrowth above the beach adjacent to the new channel and sent a few others over to the lagoon side of the island to watch for a possible enemy incursion there.

When McAlister found out that enemy landing parties were headed for shore, he ordered Wiley Sloman and his mates in Battery L to leave the five-inch guns unmanned, get their rifles, and take up defensive positions close to the beach near the new channel. They had no time to dig in, and much of the brush in the area had been burned or blown away, leaving them with a scant amount of cover.

McAlister had set up his own command post near one of the two searchlights on Wilkes, just east of McKinstry's two beach guns. Even in the gloom, McAlister could see one of the landing barges just a few yards offshore. He phoned Platoon Sergeant Henry Bedell.

"Send two men down there to grenade that damn boat," McAlister said.

"Yessir, they're on their way," Bedell replied.

The gravel-voiced sergeant didn't exactly obey McAlister's order to the letter, however. In his twenty years in the Corps, Bedell had never been known to duck a dangerous assignment. So, instead of sending two other Marines, he scrambled down toward the barge himself. On the way, he grabbed PFC William Buehler, a youngster from the prison town of Joliet,

Illinois, and the two of them loaded themselves with as many grenades as they could carry.

They used the sparse brush for cover as long as they could, but the last fifty yards or so was wide-open beach with no concealment except the darkness. Bedell spotted numerous dark shapes running across the sand in groups of twos and threes, and he knew the invaders were already pouring ashore and heading inland.

"Come on," he growled to Buehler. "Let's go for it."

Buehler was scared, but just having Bedell with him reassured him. The gritty old sergeant had been a Marine almost forever and lived through so many scrapes that he seemed indestructible.

They ran as fast as they could, hurling grenades as they went, but they never got close enough to the barge to hit it. They were still some distance away when a burst of machine gun fire came from somewhere, and Buehler saw Bedell sprawl facedown in the sand. In the same instant, Buehler felt a searing streak of pain as a bullet found him, too, but he managed to stay on his feet. As he staggered back toward the brush, he was sure Bedell was dead, and the shock of it was greater than the pain from his own wound.

A few minutes later, Buehler dragged himself back into his mates' position near the new channel, bleeding and gasping for breath.

"They got Bedell," he panted. "There was nothing I could do but come back. There's a landing barge beached around the bend, and there's more Japs on the island than there are of us."

From one end of Wilkes to the other, the ghostlike enemy was on the move. The landing force troops had been instructed to use their bayonets whenever possible instead of their rifles. Bayonet attacks conserved ammunition and offered the advantage of stealth, and the Japanese also believed they had a powerful demoralizing effect on their foes. Hence, there was only sporadic small arms fire as the invaders advanced, but shadowy forms were moving quickly up from the beach toward McAlister's position, yelling occasionally as they charged.

Squinting through the gloom from a hundred yards northeast of the landing site, McAlister felt a fierce urge to lead his men out to meet the enemy head-on, but he quickly stifled it and kept them where they at least had some cover. An impulsive movement in this dark morass could get his Marines killed by friendly fire as quickly as it could get them ambushed by the Japanese.

"Just keep up a steady fire toward the beach," he ordered, "and toss a grenade out now and then just to keep 'em from getting too cocky. If we can hang on until sunup so we can see the bastards, we'll have the advantage."

The desperate need for light was also on Platt's mind as he phoned Devereux. "Request permission to use searchlights."

"Go ahead," Devereux replied. "Just remember, it probably won't take the Japs long to shoot them out."

The nearer of the two searchlights on Wilkes was just to the east of McKinstry's three-inch battery and even more squarely in the invaders' path. When it flashed on, its eight-million-candlepower beam lit up the beach like broad daylight, and what it showed was hardly encouraging. One red and black landing barge was already aground and looked empty. A second barge was on the reef with its ramp down, in the process of discharging its human cargo.

The glare lasted for no more than sixty seconds, long enough for the nearest .50-calibers to rake the second barge with fire, leaving a half-dozen enemy dead on its deck. Then Japanese riflemen on the barge quickly shattered the searchlight and plunged the beach back into darkness. In that minute or less, however, the defenders were able to get their first real sense of the location and composition of the enemy invasion force.

Platt had somewhat more productive—although equally brief—results when he activated his second searchlight, this one on the tip of Kuku Point. It revealed three enemy-packed rubber rafts trying to sneak past the point toward the lagoon. PFC Erwin Pistole, captain of machine gun No. 12, the nearest .50-caliber, immediately opened fire. The onetime bridge builder from Texas had been eager for a hittable target ever since December 11, when he'd watched Battery L sink the destroyer *Hayate* from a point so close to one of the five-inch guns that the concussion had sent his helmet flying. Nothing had been within range of Pistole's machine gun yet that day, but now he had a chance to make up for lost time. He and Private Joe Reeves, an eighteen-year-old Oklahoman at Pistole's elbow, were wide awake and ready. They could see their tracers going right into the rafts, and they knew they were scoring hits.

This second light also failed after a few seconds, not from enemy gunfire but a faulty generator that had caused problems for weeks. Subsequent reports showed that all three of the rafts were sunk and no passengers made it ashore.

By now, however, McKinstry's position had become untenable. Further attempts to direct three-inch fire on the landing craft were pointless, and Japanese troops were now massing around the gun pits, making it clear that they were the main initial objective of the enemy's advance from the beach. The only effective defensive fire was from machine guns Nos. 9 and 10, and it wasn't enough to hold the Japanese in check. McKinstry's contractors had some grenades but no rifles or sidearms, and the invaders were now close enough to start lobbing grenades of their own. The gun pits were seconds away from becoming death traps.

"Fall back," McKinstry shouted. "Fall back toward the brush! On the double!" As the civilians clambered out of the gun pits and ran, McKinstry yanked the firing locks out of the guns, making them unusable by the enemy. A few contractors tried to help, but he waved them on.

"Move out! We're done here. Move!"

When the last of the crew was gone, McKinstry paused at the edge of the gun emplacement long enough to pull the pins of two or three grenades and toss them into the piles of three-inch ammo he was leaving behind. Then he ran like hell.

As soon as the sound of the grenade blasts died away, McKinstry heard the enemy pursuers behind him. Then, in the pitch blackness, he stumbled into a lifesaving miracle—a squad of Marines led by Tech Sergeant Edwin "Peepsight" Hassig, a longtime member of the Marine rifle team and widely renowned as the best marksman in the whole garrison.

Hassig and his riflemen laid down a blistering fire with their Springfields that drove back the pursuing Japanese. These nick-of-time reinforcements gave McKinstry fifteen riflemen, enough to set up a defensive skirmish line near the new channel and wait for sufficient light to find some targets.

At approximately this same moment, all telephone contact was abruptly cut off between Wake proper and the sixty-seven Marines of Platt's command. The Japanese had easily found the main phone lines on Wilkes—lying on top of the ground in plain sight—as they crossed the coral road that curved down south of the new channel near their beachhead. When these lines were cut, Platt not only lost all communication with Devereux's command post and the rest of Wake proper but with most of his own positions on Wilkes, as well.

One of the few posts still reachable from Platt's dugout was machine gun No. 9 a short distance to the west, where PFC Sanford K. Ray, the husky Arkansan who served as the gun's captain, reported a situation that was about as tenuous as it could get. No. 9 was the nearest .50 caliber to the enemy beachhead, and Ray knew he was virtually surrounded by SNLF troops. He couldn't see much of anything, but he could distinctly hear the Japanese shouting at each other no more than forty yards away.

"The Japs are all around us, sir," Ray gasped when Platt reached him.

"Can you keep the gun in action?" Platt asked.

"We can try, sir." Ray grabbed four grenades from a box beside him and threw them toward the shouts as quickly as he could pull the pins.

Before the sound of the grenade blasts died, Platt heard wild bursts of machine gun fire, punctuated by rifle shots and screams. In the echoing silence that followed, Platt feared the worst. Then he heard Ray's voice come back on the line.

"We're still here, sir," he said softly.

Above left: *Corporal Ralph J. Holewinski, who help man the three-inch gun that destroyed a Japanese destroyer-transport attempting to land troops on Wake before dawn on December 23, 1941. This photo was made the previous summer in Hawaii.*
(*Courtesy Ralph Holewinski*)

Above right: *Lieutenant Robert M. Hanna, commander of a makeshift crew and a sightless three-inch gun that destroyed a Japanese landing ship and inflicted a bloody toll on enemy forces attempting to land on Wake's south shore early on December 23, 1941.*
(*Marine Corps Historical Center*)

✶ 12 ✶

Hanna, Holewinski,
and Hellfire

Minutes after the first shots were fired on Wilkes, the enemy's amphibious assault punched ashore at two points along the main island's south beach, where there were precious few defenders in position to resist the landings.

Two of the same type landing craft used to put men on Wilkes reached shore undetected near the remains of Camp One. The only serious opposition facing them was Lieutenant Poindexter's small mobile reserve force—twenty Marines and fourteen civilians—and four stationary .50-caliber machine guns near the water tower manned by Navy bluejackets.

Poindexter's first inkling of trouble in the area came when he heard the sailors' .50s open fire. At first, he thought the inexperienced Navy gunners might be shooting at shadows, but when he jumped in his truck and sped to the nearest emplacement, he saw the two enemy landing craft bobbing in the surf. He also saw that the tracer rounds were bouncing harmlessly off the craft's steel sides and quickly decided on a grenade attack.

Kansas-born Art Poindexter exuded the kind of confidence that inspired others, and when he picked three men to go with him—Navy Boatswain's Mate First Class James Barnes, Marine Mess Sergeant Gerald Carr, and civilian Raymond R. "Cap" Rutledge—they followed eagerly. Rutledge, a graying Army veteran of World War I, had worked as a clerk in the contractors' office prior to December 8, but he'd seen more battlefield action than the rest of the group put together. He'd been in the thick of the fighting in France in 1918 and had earned a commission there, so when Poindexter decided to split his grenadiers into two two-man teams, Rutledge was his logical choice to lead the second one.

"Cap, you take Carr and go after the first barge," Poindexter said as each of them grabbed a half-dozen grenades out of a box. "Barnes and I'll get the other one."

The first time they charged the barges, they didn't get close enough, and all eight of the grenades they threw exploded harmlessly on the beach. As the .30-caliber rounds from four nearby machine guns rattled off the steel sides of the barges, the defenders fell back to regroup.

"Let's try it again and get closer this time," Poindexter panted.

All four Americans still had four grenades apiece—one in each hand and two in their pockets. On their second attempt, Poindexter led them out into thigh-deep water where they couldn't possibly miss.

Just then, the searchlight at the edge of Camp One flashed in their direction. It briefly illuminated the inside of the barges—both completely empty. The Japanese who had slipped ashore in them were no longer on the beach. Instead, approximately a hundred invaders were now lurking somewhere in the darkness behind Poindexter and his men.

Poindexter's problem was a relatively small one, however, compared to the one descending on Wake proper a thousand yards to the east at approximately the same moment. The epicenter of the Japanese invasion was aimed midway between Peacock Point and Camp One, where about 80 percent of the first wave of landing force troops was about to be slammed ashore with jarring suddenness aboard the two destroyers turned troopships, *Patrol Boats No. 32* and *33*.

The Japanese strategy here was brutally simple. The destroyer/transports would steam directly into the shore at a speed of about twelve knots, enough to drive the bows of the ships over the jagged coral reef and onto the beach by sheer force. Short of multiple direct hits by the Marines' five-inch batteries before the ships could be run aground—a virtual impossibility in the pitch darkness—there was no way the Wake Islanders could stop a forced landing of this kind.

The downside for the invaders was that the ships would be immobilized on the reef for at least the duration of the battle, and their hulls would be significantly damaged by the impact. Although there was a chance of salvaging the vessels later, their crews had already been warned to consider themselves expendable. The Japanese were fully prepared to sacrifice the ships' crews in order to throw some 800 of their best fighting men into the battle for Wake.

The chosen site for this mass landing was a mere stone's throw from the airfield, and while it was near the center of the area Major Devereux thought most likely to be invaded, it was very lightly defended. Five .50-caliber machine guns under the command of Second Lieutenant Robert M. Hanna were scattered at wide intervals along the southern perimeter of the airfield, and the surviving twenty-two members of VMF-211, along with a handful of civilian volunteers and a few sailors, had set up a thin skirmish line in the same area. But that was about it.

Devereux had also given Hanna, a gangly, soft-spoken, twenty-seven-year-old Texan, the added responsibility of defending a mile-long chunk of the main island's south beach. To cover this vast expanse, Hanna had only about ten Marines, a half-dozen civilians, and four .30-caliber machine guns. Devereux had ordered the .30s grouped just west of Peacock, rather than spread out over the whole distance. It was a logical defensive move, but one that put the guns out of range of the main enemy landing site.

The only other potential weapon at Hanna's disposal was a solitary three-inch gun similar to the one that Gunner McKinstry had unsuccessfully tried to use against the enemy landing craft on Wilkes. One major difference was that the sight on Hanna's gun was totally wrecked; the only way to aim it was to look down the bore, line up a target visually, and blaze away. Another, more fortuitous difference was that Hanna's gun was much better situated to the lay of the land, allowing it to bear directly on the beach, the reef, and the surrounding sea.

The three-incher originally had been part of Lieutenant Lewis's Battery E, but without a range finder, it was worthless for aerial defense, so Lewis left it behind when the battery was moved. Now it was positioned between the main road and the airstrip and just to the east of the two troopships' intended landing points, a nearly ideal spot for an antiboat gun. But in addition to its broken sight, there was an even bigger problem: It didn't have a crew to man it.

If the Japanese established a secure beachhead in the targeted area, they'd be able to seize the runway at the airfield, control the midsection of the south leg of Wake proper, and push east and west from there. All the defenders to the west would be bottled up between the main Japanese force and those that had landed near Camp One, and except for Hanna's and VMF-211's meager forces, the nearest fortified positions down the coast to the east were around Battery A at the very tip of Peacock Point.

As the enemy ships plowed toward shore, the only thing standing between the invaders and their objective was a hastily assembled hodgepodge of military and civilian defenders. All told, within the four-mile stretch of beach from the Wilkes Channel to Peacock, there were no more than about eighty Americans—some of them without rifles or sidearms—close enough to offer any resistance to the main Japanese landing force.

Lieutenant Hanna was with his .30-caliber machine gun section when he caught sight of *Patrol Boat No. 32* gliding west through the darkness and still several hundred yards offshore. Hanna was probably the first American to spot the destroyer/transport, and when he sensed what was about to happen, he immediately called Devereux on his field phone.

"There's a good-sized ship headed for the beach just below the airfield, and it looks like the Japs may plan to run it aground," he told Devereux. "I'd like to take a few men and see if we can get that three-inch gun in action."

"Have you got anybody to spare?" Devereux asked.

"I think I can find one machine gunner to take," Hanna replied. "The rest will have to be civilians."

"Go ahead and do what you can," Devereux said.

As Hanna hung up and took off at a run down the beach, two civilians tagged along behind him. Contractors Bob Bryan and Paul Gay had overheard the lieutenant's conversation with Devereux, and both were eager to volunteer as cannoneers.

After a couple of minutes, the trio came to a .50-caliber machine gun pit where Corporal Ralph Holewinski, a muscular, dark-haired twenty-year-old from rural Michigan, was trying to fire at the enemy ship.

"This gun's not working right, Lieutenant," Holewinski told Hanna. "It won't put out but one round at a time, and there's no tools to fix it."

"Just leave it and come on," Hanna said. "We're heading to the three-inch gun to see what we can do there, and I'm looking for another volunteer."

Holewinski hadn't met Hanna face to face until December 10, but he'd taken a quick liking to the young officer. Hanna was friendly and easygoing—never one to "pull rank" like some shavetails—and the corporal had had no trouble making small talk with the lieutenant about everything from family to favorite desserts. When Hanna boasted that his wife made "the best banana cream pie anywhere," Holewinski countered with glowing descriptions of his mother's "melt-in-your-mouth cream puffs."

Hanna also seemed to know what he was doing, so Holewinski had no qualms about following him now. The corporal jumped to his feet and ran with Hanna and the two civilians toward the three-incher. After growing up with eleven brothers and sisters for company, Holewinski didn't like long periods of enforced solitude. He was just glad to be *with* somebody for a change, instead of sitting there alone with total responsibility for about two miles of beach.

Hanna had accumulated more than nine years in the military since joining the Army as a private in 1932, and his first duty station had been with the 77th Field Artillery. But he knew next to nothing about the M3 three-inch antiaircraft gun he was about to fire. He'd never been on the platform of a three-inch gun before, much less fired one, but he'd been around artillery enough that he had a vague idea of how to do it.

Hanna and his three accomplices reached the gun just as *Patrol Boat No. 32* veered north and began its run straight toward them. At that moment, almost as if he were purposely doing the little group of Americans a favor, a Japanese sailor hung a lantern over the bow of the ship. Intended to help light the way for the disembarking enemy troops, it also gave Hanna and his men a distinct advantage. Now they had something visible to aim at.

Panting from the run down the beach, Holewinski grabbed a round from a pile of three-inch shells stored beside the gun and handed it to Hanna. The lieutenant cut the fuse to two seconds and jammed it into the breech, then sighted directly down the bore to line up the target. Meanwhile, Bryan and Gay tussled over the privilege of pulling the lanyard for the first shot.

"I want to do it! I want to pull the trigger!" Both of them were yelling at once and shoving at each other.

"Come on, you guys, knock it off," Holewinski snapped. "Just take turns."

To settle the issue, Hanna handed the lanyard to Gay. "Go ahead," he said calmly. "Fire away."

Gay's shot went slightly wide, but Hanna quickly rammed home another shell. This time, he yanked the lanyard himself and scored a direct hit.

Holewinski clearly saw the second shot hit the ship and set it ablaze. After that, in the light of the leaping flames, the gunners had no problem seeing where to aim. Hanna judged the ship to be no more than 400 yards away when they first opened fire. When it was beached, only about 150 yards separated the vessel from the gun, and Hanna found it easier to hit than he'd expected.

With Holewinski serving as first loader and the civilians as ammo handlers, Hanna poured three more shells into the oncoming ship before it ground to a halt on the reef. Then he resighted the gun, reduced the fuse setting to one second, and opened up again.

As Hanna and his fledgling crew grew more familiar with the gun, their rate of fire gradually increased. It also helped when a third civilian, Eric Lehtola, happened along and joined the group. They were still well short of the seven to nine men ordinarily assigned to a three-inch crew, but it's hard to imagine how one gun could do more damage under any circumstances.

For the next half hour or more, Hanna, Holewinski, and company rained unmitigated hellfire on *Patrol Boat No. 32*. By Hanna's count, they hit it a total of twenty-one times, but the thirteenth or fourteenth round achieved the most spectacular results, hitting the magazine and setting the ship afire.

The ship looked like one huge Roman candle, spewing exploding munitions skyward in brilliant flashes of red, orange, yellow, and white. To Hanna, the scene resembled a fireworks show on the Fourth of July. As the explosions died down, a raging fire engulfed what was left of the ship, and a searchlight from Camp One flashed on, bathing a wide area of the beach and surf with vivid light.

In this brilliant illumination, Hanna and his gun crew spotted the second ship, *Patrol Boat No. 33,* for the first time. It had hit the beach some distance to the west of *No. 32* and was also coming under machine gun fire as it attempted to discharge its landing party. For the moment, Hanna elected to keep pounding away at the blazing remains of the nearest boat, but he eventually turned the gun on *No. 33,* firing six rounds at the second ship and watching it catch fire, too. But one of the five-inch guns also started firing at it about the same time, and Hanna couldn't be sure which gun did the major damage.

All four of Hanna's .50-caliber machine guns joined in the barrage on both ships from their positions to the east and west. Dozens of men from Uchida Company were cut to pieces as they tried to escape *No. 32* on rope ladders or leaped blindly into the sea, and the surrounding surf was clogged with the bodies of dead and wounded invaders.

The nearer ship itself became a veritable slaughterhouse. One of Hanna's high-velocity rounds struck the bridge, hurling shrapnel and the mutilated bodies of sailors in all directions. Both the ship's captain and navigation officer were fatally wounded by machine gun fire.

"The enemy put down a barrage in our direction by performing a terrific net of fire," wrote Kiyoshi Ibushi, a Japanese news correspondent aboard the ill-fated vessel. Ibushi was obviously unaware that the bulk of this devastation was coming from a single broken gun, but for every Japanese on the receiving end of it, Hanna's "net of fire" looked like the end of the world.

"Shore ahead!"

This sudden shouted warning from the ship's captain broke an ominous silence aboard *Patrol Boat No. 32* as it bored in on the beach. These were among the captain's last few words. Moments later, he was mortally wounded by a blast from Hanna's gun. With his dying breath, the captain ordered his crew to abandon ship, an order that none of them wanted to obey.

An unidentified member of Uchida Company described the quick sequence of events that followed the ship's impact against the reef: "As we started to rise to our feet, the enemy opened fire all at once. Out of the darkness in front of us, shells came shrieking like a thousand demons let loose. One shell exploded on the ship's bridge. Simultaneously, several men fell where they stood.... Artillery shells, machine gun bullets, rifle bullets—the resisting fire of the enemy grew to a mad intensity."

Sub-Lieutenant Shigeyoshi Ozeki, the only son of a prominent Japanese family, had received his M.D. degree just a few months before the war began. Faced with induction into the Japanese army, he had joined the Imperial Navy because he believed its doctors to be better trained and more "honorable" than their army counterparts. Now, as the only medical officer among the 600 troops of Uchida Company, he was caught in the middle of this bloodbath—and just another enemy invader to the Americans shooting at him.

Although Dr. Ozeki displayed the symbol of the International Red Cross on his clothing, there was little else to distinguish him from other landing force personnel, especially in the uncertain light and panicked confusion of the landing. Like other Japanese officers, he was armed with a pistol and a sword, and he wore the same type of steel helmet and naval uniform as the rest of the invasion force.

"Fortunately or unfortunately, I had the honor of taking part in carrying out the forced landing operations on Wake Island as the only surgeon of Uchida Corps," Ozeki recalled. "We landed at around 3 A.M. on December 23 and found ourselves face to face with an American pillbox built hurriedly on the sand dune at the seaside."

It wasn't a "pillbox," of course, although it certainly must have looked like one to Ozeki. In fact, it wasn't even an actual fortified position. There'd been no time to fill sandbags or other barriers around the three-inch gun, and other than the scant protection offered by its firing platform and out-rigger legs, no cover was available in the gun position. Except for the pro-tection of the gun itself, Hanna and the others stood completely out in the open. But the invaders were so confused and in such disarray that none even tried to fire back at the gun crew with small arms until much later.

By the time Ozeki scrambled over the side of the ship close behind Cap-tain Kinichi Uchida, his popular young commanding officer, the vessel was already in flames, and the combined machine gun fire and explosions from Hanna's gun were taking an awesome toll.

"As I dropped off the rope into the water, I could see men being hit all around me," Ozeki said. "There were so many fallen and wounded soldiers that we had a hard time collecting them all after the battle."

Many of the Japanese troops plunged into water that was neck deep, desperately holding their rifles above their heads to keep them dry as they struggled toward the beach with machine gun fire hammering at them. Even those who managed to reach solid ground found only a few coral rocks and outcroppings for protection, and the slaughter went on.

Ozeki was only a few feet away from Captain Uchida when the com-mander was killed by a bullet between the eyes as he rallied his troops toward Hanna's gun.

"Only twenty meters left to go," Uchida shouted a second before he was hit. His death stunned the troops around him and ended their attempts to advance for several minutes.

"He was shot right on the glabella beneath his steel helmet," Ozeki said. "There was only a little ooze of blood from the shot-open wound, but I guess he was killed on the spot. I was at his side, but I did not see him get hit. He was a great officer, admired both for his personality and his combat operations. I respected him so much that I would have been willing to be killed in action under his orders."

By authoritative estimates, up to half the men of Uchida Corps lost their lives that morning along with their commander. Several hundred yards farther west, Itaya Corps also suffered heavy casualties aboard *Patrol Boat No. 33*, which was hit repeatedly by both Hanna's gun and the three- and five-inch batteries on Peacock Point.

"Our boat sank because of the U.S. attack," said Senior Petty Officer Hisao Tsuji, one of the men desperately trying to escape *No. 33.* "I had to jump into the sea. I crawled about fifty meters and reached the shore, but I was so soaked that I could not proceed. I had to lie down on the ground."

In the aftermath of the battle, Japanese officers told Hanna that more than 350 landing force dead were counted the next day along the stretch of beach where the two troopships had gone aground. In Hanna's words, "Their bodies were stacked up like cordwood."

At the time the enemy troopships were grinding onto the reef, Major Putnam and the other remaining members of VMF-211 were lined up along the southern edge of the runway in defense of the airfield. But around 3:00 A.M., just after the aviation Marines heard the three-inch gun on the beach open fire, Putnam got a call from Devereux directing him to move his men south to form a screen around Hanna's position.

Putnam moved quickly in response, but he refused to leave the airstrip totally undefended, so he handed one of the toughest assignments of the day to shy, soft-spoken Lieutenant Kliewer. With Staff Sergeant John Blandy, Sergeant Robert Bourquin, and Corporal Carroll Trego, Kliewer was to occupy a pair of dugouts at the west end of the runway. In one of the dugouts, a generator was set up and wired to a network of powerful dynamite charges positioned to destroy the airfield if the enemy should overrun it.

"If the Japs break through and get to the field, your orders are to blow it up and then try to get out of there and rejoin us," Putnam told Kliewer.

After the foursome settled down for their grim vigil, Robert Bourquin took time to jot a quick notation in the day-by-day journal he'd started on December 8: "Lieutenant Kliewer and I are in position on top of the dugout with grenades and the two tommy guns. Staff Sergeant Blandy and Corporal Trego are below us at the generator and are to keep the lieutenant and me supplied with ammo."

As Putnam and the rest of his men started south toward the sound of Hanna's gun, the major was approached by fourteen civilians, all of whom had been filling in for VMF-211's dead and wounded mechanics since the first day of the war. The group was led by John "Pete" Sorenson, a tall, muscular steel worker in his early fifties who had helped build dams across the West for Morrison-Knudsen before going to Wake. Sorenson had been one of Dan Teters's construction superintendents when the war broke out, and he'd led a group of civilian volunteers to the airfield to offer their help to VMF-211 immediately after the first raid. Since then, they'd worked day and night with the aviation unit, repairing aircraft engines, guarding the airfield, hauling ammo, and doing anything else that was needed. Sorenson was one of the most cheerful, bighearted men Putnam had ever met, but he was also tough as nails.

"We're going with you, Major," he said flatly.

"I can't let you do it, Pete," Putnam said. "If you're captured in combat, you won't stand a chance. Now take off and join the other civilians."

Sorenson had asked repeatedly for weapons for himself and the others, but Putnam had had none to give. Now he grinned and shook his head. "Sorry, Major," he said, towering a good six inches above Putnam, "but you're just not big enough to make us go away."

When the Marines marched off, Sorenson and the other civilians grabbed up all the ammunition they could carry and followed silently in the darkness, picking their way through the undergrowth. Most of the aviation Marines were equipped with Thompson submachine guns, Browning automatic rifles, or Springfields in addition to their sidearms, although Putnam's only weapon was a .45 automatic.

The civilians, on the other hand, were totally unarmed—but if Sorenson was bothered by the fact that he had nothing to fight with but his bare hands, he never showed it.

Despite the heavy toll exacted by the three-incher and the four nearby machine guns, the invaders kept coming. There were just too many of them, and to Hanna and his little crew, it was becoming more apparent by the second that it was utterly impossible to stop them all.

Slowly, inch by inch, the survivors kept creeping forward, taking advantage of every slight bit of cover, then jumping to their feet and running a few steps before throwing themselves back to the ground. The very intensity of the defenders' fire forced the invaders to risk advancing as their only means of reaching safer ground. They knew there was no going back. They also realized that their risk of sudden death could never be any greater than it already was there on that beach.

Hanna, Holewinski, and the three civilians helping them were in a very unenviable position for repelling hordes of enemy troops charging with fixed bayonets. Holewinski had the only rifle in the group, and Hanna had a .45 automatic but only two seven-shot clips of ammunition. Paul Gay also had a pistol, and someone had thought to leave two boxes of hand grenades beside the gun, but that was the extent of their "arsenal." Bryan and Lehtola were weaponless, although each was quite capable of throwing grenades.

Realizing the precariousness of Hanna's position, Devereux was doing whatever he could from his command post to slow the Japanese advancing from the beach to menace the antiboat gun. While dispatching Putnam's men from the airfield, Devereux ordered Captain Godbold to send a gun crew from his Battery D on Peale, where no action was taking place, to relieve Hanna's makeshift crew. Devereux also told Lieutenant Lewis at Battery E on Peacock Point to fire airbursts over the area around the two burning troopships.

Unfortunately, neither of these latter measures proved very effective. The replacement crew from Peale found itself pinned down under heavy fire before it could get anywhere near the landing site, and by then the three-incher was out of operation, anyway. After some adjustments, Lewis's battery exploded a few shells no more than fifty feet above the beach, momentarily stalling the enemy advance. But for reasons that remain unclear, Devereux ordered the battery to cease fire after only a few minutes, and the Japanese moved rapidly to take advantage of the lull.

On the fortunate side, Putnam and about thirty Marines and civilians from VMF-211 arrived just in time to save Hanna's crew from being overrun. But in doing so, they almost walked into an enemy ambush themselves.

From the elevated vantage point of the firing platform where Hanna stood, he heard Japanese voices in the undergrowth just to the west. He also spotted three enemy riflemen moving to the north, then crouching behind a boulder and aiming their weapons toward the path on which Putnam's unit was approaching.

Hanna calmly drew his .45 and fired, killing the nearest Japanese with one shot. He fired twice more at the other two and saw them also disappear, but he wasn't sure whether he'd hit them or they'd simply ducked.

No more than a minute later, the men of VMF-211 trotted into view with Putnam in the lead. Hanna didn't bother to tell them what had just happened. There was no time for talking, anyway, as Putnam's men hurriedly formed a fragile semicircular defensive line facing west, anchored on the left by the three-inch gun and extending on the right to a point just short of the airfield.

By this time, the invaders were closing in all around Hanna's position, and he and his crew were finally forced to break off their one-gun barrage and take cover.

With rifle bullets ricocheting off the barrel of the gun, Hanna dropped the three-incher's lanyard for the final time. "We'll make a stand here," he said. "This is as good a spot as any. Come on."

He motioned Holewinski and the three civilians, Bryan, Gay, and Lehtola, into the empty space under the firing platform, where they were protected to some degree from above by the heavy metal platform itself and from the sides by the gun's steel outriggers.

"We'll dig in right here around the gun," Hanna said, jumping in after the others.

They didn't get under cover an instant too soon. As their own gun stopped firing and the shell bursts from Lewis's battery abruptly halted, Hanna saw knots of Japanese infiltrators moving toward them from all directions. They got around the gun on both sides and also slipped over onto the airstrip, encircling the small band of defenders.

Almost immediately, a firefight broke out between Putnam's men and increasing numbers of enemy in the brush. The Japanese pressed forward now, regaining some of the confidence they'd lost on the beach and challenging the aviation Marines up and down the line. Now that the three-inch gun was no longer firing, they showed no interest in charging it—or the men hiding under it—at least for the moment.

While the Special Naval Landing Force troops were well armed with bolt-action Arisaka rifles, light machine guns, and even some 50-millimeter grenade launchers, they much preferred to use their bayonets in close-order combat. Many of the Japanese marines who landed on Wake were veterans of the China campaign, and all had extensive training in bayonet tactics. Theoretically, this may have made them better prepared for hand-to-hand fighting than their U.S. counterparts. American training emphasized the power of the gun over the intimidation of the bayonet.

In this first pitched battle between Japanese and American fighting men, the enemy's stubborn faith in the bayonet, plus a belief that he was naturally stronger than any western foe because of greater "purity of spirit," cost him dearly in casualties. Only an overwhelming superiority in numbers kept the Japanese from suffering a total rout in the final show-down on Wake, but that numerical edge was never more obvious than along the tenuous line held by VMF-211 and Hanna's handful of men.

Again and again in the predawn darkness, the enemy employed the same instilled tactic: A small squad, or even a lone soldier, would crawl stealthily toward the American line, then leap up with bloodcurdling cries and charge blindly into the concentrated fire of the Marines' automatic weapons.

Sometimes the Japanese shot off flares to locate Marines hiding in the brush, but the tactic inevitably backfired. The flares illuminated the charging invaders long before they got close enough to do any damage with their bayonets, and the defenders simply mowed them down.

When all else failed, some of the SNLF soldiers turned to sheer savagery. After flushing several unarmed civilians out of the undergrowth and capturing them, the Japanese stripped the men's trousers off and jabbed their testicles with bayonets. They hoped the victims' screams would bring other Americans rushing rashly to their aid, but the Marines cursed under their breath and stayed where they were.

Around 4:30 A.M., still using the darkness to their advantage, more invaders began coming ashore in rubber boats and landing craft west of Peacock Point. Along with the survivors of the two troopships who were steadily infiltrating to the east, they posed a growing threat to the network of bunkers housing Devereux's and Cunningham's command posts and the hospitals.

By now, the Japanese had found all the phone lines running across the airport and severed them, leaving Devereux cut off from most of his units on Wake proper as well as Wilkes. His only available response to the threat was to send a small, thrown-together force under Major Potter to form a last-ditch defensive line between the approaching Japanese and the bunkers. This line was only about a hundred yards from Devereux's command post. If it were pierced, the whole command structure of the garrison would be open to direct attack.

Meanwhile, near the east end of the airfield, Corporal Winford McAnally commanded a .50-caliber machine gun section manned by a half-dozen Marines and three or four civilians. "Mack" McAnally was a wiry Oklahoman with a reputation among his mates for being "good with his dukes" and having a temper to match. But he was also known as a bright guy with a knack for analyzing tough situations and coming up with quick solutions. Right now, he knew his men were in a key location to thwart the Japanese advance because their position overlooked the main road running north from Peacock toward the bunkers housing the hospitals and command posts. Devereux still had phone contact with McAnally, and McAnally, in turn, had contact with other machine guns several hundred yards to the south.

If the fire from these machine guns could be coordinated, McAnally figured, they could set up a crisscross pattern that the invaders couldn't penetrate. So, in addition to keeping his own gun busy, the corporal took on the job of coordinating the fire of all the machine guns north of Peacock. He told them when to fire and when to duck down so that he could fire in their direction. Being closer to the enemy, he was in a better position to spot Japanese movements in the dark, and Devereux credited him with keeping the area under such closely interlacing fire that the invaders couldn't push through.

It didn't take the enemy long to figure out that McAnally was a major fly in their ointment. In a desperate bid to overrun his position, they first tried a sneak attack, but McAnally heard them coming.

"Hold your fire till they get closer," he whispered as the Japanese rustled through the brush only a few feet away.

"Now fire!" McAnally yelled, and every gun in the position exploded at once. The invaders retreated, leaving several dead and wounded behind, but they soon came back. This time, the Americans waited until the last possible second, then blazed away with everything they had when the closely packed Japanese were in point-blank range. When the firing stopped, the ground was covered with enemy bodies.

But again the Japanese regrouped. Moments later, they attacked en masse for the third time with the same identical result. The position was surrounded by riddled corpses and screaming wounded. Not a single one of McAnally's men was hurt, but he didn't know how they could hold out much longer. The supply of Japanese out there seemed inexhaustible.

"Sir, we gotta have some help if we're gonna hold this," McAnally panted into the phone.

"Sorry, but I've got nobody to send," he heard Devereux saying. "You and your men have permission to withdraw."

McAnally sighed. He thought of his wife, Trudy, with whom he'd spent exactly twenty-two days after their marriage in California the previous June before he'd shipped out for the Pacific.

"Well, sir," he said, "I reckon we can make out a little longer."

The stalemate between Putnam's and Hanna's men and the enemy continued until dawn finally broke about 5:30 A.M. But from what Hanna could see in the first dim light of December 23, the situation was steadily sliding from desperate toward untenable. On all sides of his position, he caught glimpses of Japanese troops on the move. The noose was tightening.

A burst of small arms fire to the north attracted Hanna's attention. He turned in time to see a Japanese rifleman stalking someone beyond Hanna's field of vision. The lieutenant waited while the invader dropped to the ground and raised his rifle. Then Hanna took careful aim and killed him with a single shot from his .45.

The young Texan drew a deep breath. He'd fired his pistol four times so far. That meant he had ten rounds left.

Farther away through the brush, the invaders took advantage of the growing light to swarm all over Putnam's men. Wave after wave charged the thin line held by VMF-211, pushing the defenders back toward Hanna's silent three-inch gun.

The aviation Marines made the enemy pay for every yard, every inch, but they were coming under heavy fire now from both north and west. The right flank of Putnam's line was exposed, and it began to give way. Then it broke completely.

"Fall back!" Putnam yelled. "Fall back on the gun position."

The retreat became a melee—a churning quagmire of struggling bodies, chattering automatic weapons, flashing bayonets, angry shouts, and cries of pain.

As Putnam hurried to obey his own order, he paused under a bush and turned in time to see two green-clad Japanese soldiers suddenly loom over him. He fired twice with his .45 and both invaders fell dead practically on top of him—one so close that his helmet and Putnam's banged together.

A few yards away, burly Pete Sorenson, leader of the civilian mechanics, leaped out of the brush and darted headlong into the path of a group of charging Japanese. Having no other weapon, Sorenson threw rocks and screamed curses at the enemy while their bullets ripped through him and slammed him to the ground.

Enraged by the fate of Sorenson and others around him, Captain Henry Elrod also jumped in front of the advancing invaders, swinging a stuttering tommy gun and blazing away wildly from the hip. When one of his bursts cut a Japanese machine gunner in half, he coolly handed his weapon to one of his fellow Marines, jerked up the enemy gun, and continued to fight.

Incredibly, Elrod's unbridled one-man fury momentarily stopped the Japanese onslaught and sent the enemy reeling backward. They recovered quickly, but Elrod's rampage bought enough time for Putnam and seven of his men to reach the gun position and take cover there.

Elrod, Captain Tharin, and several others from VMF-211 stayed behind in the brush, still fighting, while scores of Japanese formed a solid ring around the three-inch gun. The invaders finally seemed to have lost their taste for bayonet charges and settled for keeping up a steady rate of rifle fire on the position.

On the east side of the gun, Holewinski and the two civilian volunteers, Gay and Bryan, continued to hold the Japanese at bay. Holewinski killed three enemy riflemen who crawled within twenty feet of his position. Gay sniped away with his pistol, and Bryan kept tossing grenades toward enemy voices in the brush.

"Just be sure you save a couple of rounds on that pistol," Bryan told Gay between shots. "We're not gonna be tortured by those bastards."

At least half of Putnam's original group had been lost, and no one knew for sure how many were dead or wounded, but the Japanese losses had been many times greater. There were so many green helmets and green-clad lumps lying on the surrounding two or three acres that, in the words of one Marine, "It looked like one big watermelon patch out there."

Yet, somehow, the little band around Hanna's gun still managed to hang on.

*Commander Winfield Scott Cunningham,
who took overall command of Wake's
garrison a few days before the outbreak of
war, remained in the background during
battle but issued the controversial surrender
order on December 23, 1941.*
(National Archives)

✲ 13 ✲

"It's Not My Order,
Goddamn It!"

As the darkness slowly dissolved in the gray dawn of December 23, the first thing PFC Artie Stocks noticed from his position in the brush on Wilkes Island was the rising sun. Not the blazing sphere that had climbed above the horizon beyond the clouds and misty rain, but the vivid, red-orange emblem on scores of Japanese battle flags now fluttering over the sand and coral.

The flags—"flaming assholes" in Marine Corps parlance—had been stuck up in all directions during the night. Stocks could see them fluttering all over Wilkes and across the channel on the main island, too. They were prominently displayed even in places where there wasn't a single Japanese in sight.

The rough-hewn, demonstrative Stocks had grown up as one of a handful of white kids on the Utah Indian reservation where his father worked. His mother had died while he was still young, and he'd never been particularly close to his dad, but he'd found a "second family" in the Marines. He made friends easily—and usually for keeps—with all kinds of people. But as his mates in Battery L knew, Stocks also had a hot temper and two hard fists to go with it. As one of his buddies put it: "Artie could be throwing a punch at some guy one minute and buying him a beer the next."

Stocks had never thought of himself as biased toward any ethnic group, but over the past fifteen days, he'd come to despise the Japanese in a fierce, uncompromising way. He couldn't wait to get a shot at one of them, but so far they'd stayed too well hidden. Now that the sun was almost up, it'd be a different story. He cradled his Springfield in his arms and waited.

The profusion of enemy flags drew varied reactions from the Americans as morning broke. Some of Stocks's comrades tore down those within reach, only to regret it later. As the Marines on Wilkes belatedly realized, the flags weren't there merely for bragging rights; they'd been carefully spotted around the main combat areas as guides for the pilots from the Japanese carriers. The flags conveyed a simple but critically important message: Any point that *wasn't* marked by an enemy flag was fair game for aerial attack.

To Lieutenant Kliewer, as he peered out from his dugout at dozens of the flags now visible along the south beach and to the east and west, they sent an urgent warning. Their numbers indicated that the Japanese were in control of much of the main island. Kliewer decided it was time to activate the generator and blow up the runway.

Even before seeing the flags, Kliewer and his little group could tell that the defenders' situation had deteriorated drastically since the enemy landing. They'd heard nothing from the rest of VMF-211 for several hours—or from any other Americans, for that matter—because their phone line had been cut. But the proof of their predicament was all around them. The four men huddled in the dugout at the edge of the airstrip were totally surrounded by Japanese. It was almost light enough to see, and within the next couple of minutes, they expected the enemy to start attacking.

Sergeant Robert Bourquin cradled his tommy gun against one arm and pulled the well-worn picture of Charlotte McLain, his fiancée, out of his shirt pocket with the other hand. In the past hour or so, he'd touched the photograph in the darkness a dozen times at least, but now he could actually see Chotty's features, and that made him feel better. Then he reluctantly stuck the picture back in his pocket and picked up his weapon.

Among them, Kliewer, Bourquin, Sergeant Blandy, and Corporal Trego had considerable firepower at their disposal—two tommy guns, three .45s, a Browning automatic rifle (BAR), and a couple of boxes of hand grenades. From their strong defensive position, they managed over the next little while to fight off wave after wave of attackers, helped along by two important advantages. For one thing, the Japanese couldn't seem to get past the persistent idea that they could overrun the dugout by charging it with bayonets. For another, some sharpshooting American machine gunners nearby came to the rescue more than once.

Bourquin was scared as hell, and he knew that the other three men were scared, too. But all they could do was try to keep their heads and hold the Japanese at bay with the tommy guns. So far, they hadn't even used the BAR, but it was there if needed, and they were getting some welcome help from the guys manning two .50-caliber machine guns at the west end of the runway. In fact, Bourquin figured, they already owed their lives to those guys.

Now, with the situation turning desperate, it was time to make a decision.

"I'm not sure we can last here much longer, so we'd better go ahead and blow the field," Kliewer said. "After we set the stuff off, we'll make a run for it to the nearest of those machine guns. It's only 150 yards or so."

Blandy and Trego immediately went to work on the generator while Kliewer and Bourquin stayed alert with the tommy guns. Once the generator got going, it wouldn't take more than a few seconds to touch off the seventy-five cases of dynamite buried along the length of the runway. It would be one hellacious blast, assuming everything went according to plan.

Only it didn't.

"Something's wrong," Blandy yelled. "The generator won't start. I think the rain must've fouled it up."

"Well, keep trying," Kliewer said.

When the lieutenant looked back outside, he saw a half-dozen enemy soldiers rushing toward them again. He and Bourquin raised their tommy guns and fired.

The bleeding remnants of Putnam's unit and Hanna's gun crew were already in desperate straits. "Hammering Hank" Elrod was dead, cut down by enemy fire as he hurled a grenade after his tommy gun ran dry. Many of those who were still alive were wounded. They were trapped under a three-way crossfire that made every slight movement an invitation to sudden death, and their ammunition was almost gone.

Corporal Holewinski had started the morning with fifty rounds for his Springfield, the only rifle protecting the east side of the gun. Now dead invaders were strewn everywhere, some no more than fifteen or twenty feet away. Holewinski had long since lost count of how many he'd killed, but a Marine later pressed into service to bury enemy dead reported finding thirty-four Japanese bodies in close proximity to the gun and within Holewinski's field of fire.

He'd done all this with a damaged rifle that wouldn't accept a full five-round clip but had to be hand-fed with a single bullet at a time. One of the civilians had broken down the clips and handed the individual cartridges to Holewinski. The nerve-grinding process seemed to take forever when enemy soldiers were only a few running steps away, but it had, at least, forced them to make every bullet count. Now Holewinski had exactly three rounds left. It wasn't much to fight a war with.

It reminded Holewinski of those cowboy-and-Indian movies he'd always liked, the ones where the cavalry always arrived just in the nick of time to save the wagon train. And he kept wondering: *Where's the cavalry? Isn't it about time for the cavalry to show up and get us out of this mess?*

As any hope of rescue faded, the men hugging the coral around the base of the gun prepared themselves for what seemed inevitable. No matter how many attackers they felled, more always seemed to spring up to take their place.

"I'd given myself up for dead," said Hanna, "and I'd decided I'd die fighting."

Holewinski closed his eyes for a moment and his mind dredged up mental images of home. He could see the rolling green pastures of his family's two-hundred-acre dairy farm, dotted with grazing milk cows. Every day of his boyhood he'd milked twenty cows by hand morning and night. He guessed that was what had given him the hand strength that made him a good machine gunner and rifleman. But with only three rounds left, that wasn't going to be enough.

At 7:00 A.M., massive waves of carrier-based Japanese planes zoomed in on Wake at little more than treetop level. There were fifty-nine of them in all, and one Val dive bomber in particular singled out the three-inch gun position for repeated punishment.

Fire from the Val's forward machine guns beat a deafening tattoo on the gun and its legs and platform as the plane made its first strafing run. But it was the rear gunner's deadly accurate fire as the Val streaked away that did the worst damage. The plane swooped so low that Holewinski could clearly see the goggles on the gunner's face.

A few feet away, he also saw Bryan and Gay killed instantly. Gay was riddled by at least a dozen slugs, while a single bullet slammed through Bryan's skull. At the same instant, Holewinski felt a fiery streak of pain ram through his left leg, and he knew he was hit, too. But almost before the first wound had a chance to register in his mind, the Val whirled around for a second pass, hitting Holewinski in both legs this time.

On the plane's third pass, Holewinski had the presence of mind to play dead, and the gunner ignored him. But he could tell he was bad enough off as it was. Not only had the machine gun fire hit him in the back, the buttocks, and both legs, but he'd also taken some fragments from a grenade that exploded on the gun platform right above him.

By this time, every American around the gun was either dead or wounded, with the exception of VMF-211's Captain Tharin. Hanna had a bullet in his right knee, a fragment in his back, and was missing a piece of his right ear. Putnam was bleeding so profusely from wounds to his cheek and neck that he was about to pass out from loss of blood. Thirteen men— three Marines and ten civilians—were dead.

Holewinski lay in a puddle of his own blood, drifting into a state of shock. He was pretty sure he was dying, and he wished he'd had the foresight to take out a big insurance policy for his mom and dad. That way they'd at least have had something to show for his life. Then, gradually, this worry gave way to a strange feeling of serenity.

While one group from Itaya Company, the invaders who reached shore aboard *Patrol Boat No. 33,* moved east before dawn to challenge the defenders led by Putnam and Hanna, another body of enemy troops split off to the west toward Camp One—where they soon bit off more than they could chew.

Waiting in the darkness for the unsuspecting Japanese was Lieutenant Poindexter's mobile reserve force, consisting of twenty Marines, fourteen civilians, two trucks, and four .30-caliber machine guns. Poindexter's men had been ordered by Major Devereux to take up defensive positions in the area between Camp One and the west end of the airstrip, and they got there in time to spring a lethal surprise on the enemy.

Poindexter smiled tightly as he and his men waited, holding their breath and listening to the invaders moving toward them along the beach road. The Japanese were shouting so openly back and forth to each other that the Marines could easily follow their approach as they blundered closer and closer. Now they were only a few yards from the Americans' hiding place.

"Fire!" Poindexter barked, and every machine gun and rifle in the unit seemed to explode at once. Their muzzle flashes reflected on enemy soldiers falling in droves and others staggering back in confusion.

To Poindexter, a quick-witted veteran officer, the enemy seemed disorganized and out of control. Their sporadic return fire was generally inaccurate, nicking only one Marine. But by the light from the two blazing troopships, the lieutenant could clearly see scores of invaders crossing the road and ducking into the brush just to the north, and he directed his machine gunners to concentrate on that area to keep the enemy from infiltrating his line.

For the next hour or so, the Japanese showed little stomach for tangling directly with the deadly marksmen of the mobile reserve. Shortly before first light, however, the Americans started taking enemy fire along their left flank and from the left rear, and, as dawn broke, the defenders came under heavy attack from grenade launchers directly in front of them.

"They're all around us," Sergeant Q. T. Wade, leader of a machine gun squad, reported to Poindexter.

Now it was the defenders' turn to be surprised by the intensity of the landing force's counterstroke. After several Marines and civilians were wounded and one .30-caliber machine gun was put out of action by grenade fragments, Poindexter ordered his men to withdraw toward Camp One, with the disabled gun section going first.

They reached Camp One without further losses, and Poindexter immediately ordered ten extra .30-caliber machine guns brought up from the rear. With a perceptiveness that more than matched his thirst for action, he ordered the new guns aimed to the east to set up interlocking fields of fire that stretched across the entire width of the island. Meanwhile, he sent a runner to round up every Marine, sailor, and civilian with a weapon in the vicinity of Camp One. Enough recruits were located to swell his force to about fifty-five men.

When the runner arrived at a bunker where some twenty rear-echelon personnel had taken cover and called for volunteers, at first the response was less than enthusiastic. Then twenty-year-old Corporal Cyrus Fish, a small-town boy from northern Minnesota whose usual job was supply clerk, picked up his rifle and glared at the others. "What are we sitting here on our asses for?" Fish yelled, and ran outside. After a few seconds, everyone else in the dugout followed.

Poindexter waited for two hours for a new Japanese attack, but none came. Except for a few probes and desultory rifle fire from the brush, the invaders avoided contact with the formidable defensive line now facing them.

So, at 9:00 A.M., eager for a fight and convinced he could win it with Marines like Corporal Fish and civilians like World War I veteran "Cap" Rutledge, Poindexter ordered an all-out counterattack. He assumed that American resistance near the airfield had been crushed, but he still sensed victory within reach. With Lieutenant Barninger and the men of Battery A pushing west from Peacock Point and the mobile reserve force pushing east, he reasoned, the enemy beachhead could be squeezed to death and the invaders chased into the sea.

"To hell with gallant last stands like the Little Big Horn," Poindexter said later. "The Marine Corps had taught me that the only way to accomplish anything is to take the offensive. If we were going to fight to 'the very last man,' we might as well die on the attack."

Within minutes, the Japanese—who hadn't bothered to dig in because they thought *they* were on the offensive—were retreating in disarray. The SNLF line fell apart, leaving behind little pockets of frightened soldiers who hid in bomb craters and died as Marines threw hand grenades in on top of them.

"We had a long, hard night, but things are looking up a bit," Poindexter told his men quietly. "Let's keep moving ahead."

An hour and a half later, Poindexter's force had driven forward some 900 yards, all the way to the western edge of the airfield. Only a thin, ill-defined line of Japanese skirmishers stood between them and a major breakthrough. Quickly assessing the situation, the lieutenant dispatched a message to Sergeant Wade: "Bring up your .50-caliber sections to the center of our line, and let's finish this."

Poindexter smelled a surrender in the offing.

By 4:00 A.M., Devereux and Commander Cunningham had lost contact with virtually every position where defenders were actively engaging the enemy. Devereux could still reach Captain Godbold's strongpoint on Peale Island and a few of the machine gun sections on Peacock Point and near the airfield, but the phone lines between the major's command post and Wilkes had been dead for close to an hour. Communications had also been cut with Hanna, VMF-211, Camp One, Poindexter's mobile reserve, and Barninger's Battery A.

The consequences of this massive communications failure could hardly have been more profound. It robbed Devereux of any ability to direct his forces and coordinate their movements—or even to know where they were and what was happening to them—in the very early stages of the final fight for Wake.

The only decisive move Devereux was able to make after the phones went out was to order Godbold to send as many men as he could spare from Peale, where all was quiet, to reinforce Major Potter's defensive line between the airfield and the command posts. Leaving Lieutenant Kessler and a skeleton crew to man the five-inch guns of Battery B, Godbold put together a contingent of just over sixty men, including Sergeant Walter Bowsher's all-civilian three-inch gun crew from Battery D. A few of the civilians had no weapons to bring with them, but they lugged bags of grenades and as much extra ammo as they could carry. Others sported a weird assortment of hunting rifles, shotguns, target pistols, and .38 revolvers retrieved from the ruins of the Pan Am hotel.

None of these men had been trained as infantry, Bowsher knew, but they were all experienced hunters, and he thought they'd do all right if a firefight broke out with the Japanese.

Beyond this move to bolster Potter's "last-ditch" line, Devereux ceased to be a real factor in the battle. In effect, Wake's garrison no longer had an overall command structure or strategy. Every tactical decision had to be made in the heat of battle by officers in the field, based on their own limited perspective.

Cunningham, meanwhile, was totally out of the loop and even less aware than Devereux of what was happening beyond the reinforced-concrete roof and walls of his bunker. He wisely left Devereux in complete charge of Wake's ground defenses. Before their disruption, the phone lines from all Marine positions had fed directly into Devereux's command post, while Cunningham had phone contact only with the dugout shared by Dan Teters and Commander Keene, plus two or three other positions on Peale and Wake proper. The island commander had to depend on Devereux for all information on positions that were actually engaged with the enemy—but now Devereux had no hard information to pass along.

Wake's unique geography and the multiple Japanese landings made it almost certain from the start that the defenders would be separated into small pockets of resistance. The early breakdown of communications only added to the isolation and made each unit's situation more perilous—and more unknown to the officers in command.

Yet by 5:00 A.M., Cunningham felt that he had sufficient information to respond to a request from Admiral Pye that CinCPac be kept informed of any significant developments. He knew beyond doubt that the enemy had landed at three places and perhaps more, and although no enemy planes had yet arrived, they were expected by dawn.

Although Cunningham spent considerable time working on its wording, the message he finally sent to Pye and Admiral Fletcher giving them an acceptable excuse for abandoning the Wake Islanders ran to just six words:

ENEMY ON ISLAND. ISSUE IN DOUBT.

About 7:00 A.M. Wake time, with the issue still very much in doubt, CinCPac ordered Fletcher's Task Force 14 to reverse its course and return to Pearl. On the flight deck of the *Saratoga*, Marine aviators beat their fists against the wings of their planes, and some wept openly. On the bridge of the cruiser *Astoria*, Fletcher's flagship, some of the admiral's staff pleaded with him to disregard the order and push on. Rear Admiral A. W. Fitch found the talk so mutinous and himself in such total agreement with its tone that he had to excuse himself and leave the bridge. Aboard the seaplane tender *Tangier*, replacement Marine ground troops cursed the "chickenshit" Navy for "selling out" their comrades.

In the absence of factual reports by reliable officers and enlisted men on the scene, Devereux was forced to weigh the validity of any information that came his way, including scare stories from panicked witnesses and anonymous voices over the phone. One wild-eyed civilian, cut off from Poindexter's unit during its retreat, staggered into the major's command post babbling about the Japanese knocking out machine guns near the airfield and bayoneting the crews.

"They're killing 'em all!" the man cried. "They're killing 'em all!"

Devereux tried to question the man, but he was too shaken and exhausted to give coherent answers. He appeared on the verge of collapse, but he stuck to his story. It was Devereux's first news of the fighting west of the airport since the lines had gone dead, and the major had no reason to doubt it.

Yet the civilian's hysterical account was highly exaggerated and left a completely erroneous impression. Even as the man spoke, Poindexter's counterattack was in full sway, and he was steadily driving the Japanese back. But Devereux had no way of knowing this, and he could only wonder: What had happened to Poindexter? There was still fighting in that area, but was it only the Japanese mopping up the last pockets of resistance?

And what about Kliewer? Were he and his men going to be able to blow up the airstrip, or were they lying dead out there at this very moment? Beyond the airfield, the sound of gunfire, intense at times, indicated that Putnam was still holding out, but there was no way to be sure. Then there was the riddle of Wilkes. Were any defenders alive there, or had they been annihilated to the last man?

The questions went on and on, and from where Devereux sat, there were no answers to be had. As he wrestled with his own negative feelings, he heard a shout from Corporal Brown, who was monitoring the open line on the warning network.

"I've got something, sir," Brown said.

Devereux took the phone and listened to a faint voice that kept repeating the same message again and again.

"There are Japanese in the bushes," the voice said. "There are definitely Japanese in the bushes."

"Who is this?" Brown asked. "Where are you?"

But the only reply was "There are Japanese in the bushes... There are Japanese in the bushes..."

In Devereux's words, "It was like hearing a dead man talk. He was speaking so carefully, so monotonously, over and over, every now and then repeating that word 'definitely.' "

The whispered warning went on for a couple of minutes. Then there was a sharp burst of sound and the whispering abruptly stopped.

"I guess they got him," Brown said.

Devereux nodded. He was becoming more convinced by the second that the Japanese were in full control of Wilkes and the entire southern leg of Wake proper. That would mean that most of the defenders on Wilkes and the main island had been either killed or captured. It would also mean that those on Peacock Point were hopelessly cut off and that the enemy would soon be close enough to menace the bunker where Devereux sat.

★

With the attention of Wake's defenders focused solidly on concerns much closer at hand, it was well after daylight when they began to notice the unbroken ring of Japanese ships now surrounding the atoll. At Battery B, Lieutenant Kessler and his gunners continued to pump five-inch rounds into the burning remains of *Patrol Boat No. 33* until about 6:30 A.M., when Kessler looked over his shoulder toward the north shore and made an unpleasant discovery.

While Kessler and his battery had been concentrating on the south shore of Wake, a large Japanese naval force had slipped in behind their backs. When Kessler spotted the ships, they were an ominous sight, and he found it incredible that they weren't yet firing at the American position. A range-finder reading placed them at over 16,000 yards, well beyond Battery B's effective range.

As they stared seaward, many Wake Islanders tried to count the ships, but they came up with widely varying numbers, and some estimates were surely exaggerated by a mixture of distance and apprehension. Kessler's well-trained eyes saw "at least a dozen ships" off to the north, including four heavy cruisers, but other observers misidentified the cruisers as battleships. Major Potter reported sixteen men-of-war, both light and heavy cruisers, and Lieutenant Barninger counted twenty-seven ships of all types. Navy Yeoman Glenn Tripp, Cunningham's former office aide who had joined the Battery L gun crew on Wilkes, claimed to see sixty-nine vessels in all.

Regardless of the exact number, the sight of the huge invasion fleet drove home the terrible one-sidedness of the situation. Wake was surrounded by a solid ring of Japanese steel and firepower. As Devereux put it: "Whatever force the enemy had in that far, slow-moving circle, it was more than enough, and every man of us knew it." And, of course, the Japanese aircraft carriers and the ships screening them were much too far away to be seen.

Out of the whole armada, only three enemy destroyers refused to profit from the lesson of December 11 and ventured into the range of Marine gunners. Kessler spotted the interlopers as they came around Kuku Point on Wilkes, where they drew no fire from Battery L, the nearest five-incher, because Captain Platt had assigned all his artillerymen as infantry. The trio steamed unconcernedly north, led by the destroyer *Mutsuki,* heading almost directly toward Peale and Kessler's Battery B near Toki Point.

The enemy skippers assumed, just as Admiral Kajioka had assumed twelve days earlier, that none of Wake's coastal batteries was capable of firing. That assumption was rudely shattered by the first of four salvoes from Kessler's guns.

The first three tries were near misses, but both rounds of the fourth salvo scored direct hits on the *Mutsuki,* killing and wounding an undetermined number of Japanese sailors and damaging the ship so severely that it looked to be sinking. Confident that his first target was crippled and could be disposed of at will, Kessler then shifted his fire to the second destroyer but was unable to hit it before it fled out of range.

Moments later, when Kessler's crew turned their guns back toward where they'd last seen the *Mutsuki,* it was nowhere to be found. Its disappearance was so abrupt that several Marines felt certain it had gone down. Actually, though, as postwar records revealed, the stricken destroyer had managed to escape.

In books published after the war, Devereux and Cunningham gave sharply conflicting accounts of just how the decision to surrender was made—and who made it. About the only things both men fully agreed on was that they were in constant touch with each other during the critical period when Wake's fate was decided and that they discussed what they knew of the garrison's situation at some length before acting. As much as their stories clashed, however, each man shared a bitter determination not to accept final responsibility for throwing in the towel.

According to Cunningham, he and Devereux had been in regular contact throughout the battle, and each time they talked, Devereux described the situation in more dismal terms. When Cunningham relayed the information received a short time earlier from CinCPac that no relief could be expected, it made the major's mood even gloomier. At 6:30 A.M. that morning, Devereux reported that his position appeared to be the only one not yet overwhelmed and that enemy pressure there was growing heavier. In Devereux's opinion, Cunningham said, the command post area wouldn't be able to hold out much longer.

"I knew the time had come to consider the question that only a few hours ago had been unthinkable," the island commander added, and posed this question to himself: "Would I be justified in surrendering, in order to prevent further and useless loss of life?" When he repeated the question to Devereux, Cunningham said, the major "evaded" answering it directly and said he felt the decision was solely up to the commanding officer. Cunningham replied that he was well aware of this but wasn't willing to act without reviewing the situation "as fully as possible," and the two talked a while longer.

"He asked if I knew Wilkes had fallen," Cunningham recalled. "I said that I did. At last I took a deep breath and told him if he felt he could hold out no longer, I authorized him to surrender."

For the next hour, however, neither man pressed the issue, and the question of whether to fight on apparently remained unresolved. By his own admission, Cunningham's actions during this interval were those of a man who had, in effect, already written off his cause. He told of sending a final dispatch to CinCPac, reporting the two grounded destroyers and the presence of the enemy fleet "closing in."

Then, he added, "I had all codes, ciphers and secret orders destroyed and ordered the communicators to haul down our transmitter antenna. It would be too easy for the Japanese dive bombers to spot. Besides, I had no more messages to send."

Around 7:30 A.M., Cunningham would later charge, Devereux more or less took matters into his own hands.

"He called me again... and asked whether I had reached the Japanese commander by radio," Cunningham said. "I told him I had not. He said he was not sure of his ability to contact the enemy and asked me to try. I promised to see what I could do. But before I could do anything, it was all over. Devereux rigged a white flag, left his command post, and moved south down the road toward the enemy, giving our troops the cease-fire order as he reached them."

Cunningham claimed that he became aware of the actual surrender only after receiving reports that bedsheets had been hoisted above the civilian hospital bunker.

At that point, he said, he tossed his .45 into a latrine, got in his truck, and drove to the badly damaged cottage where he had lived during the early stage of the siege. There amid the debris, he dug out his dress blues and cleaned himself up. He took off the soiled khakis he'd been wearing night and day for close to two weeks, then found enough fresh water to shave for the first time in days and wash his face. He put on the clean dress blues, carefully knotted his tie, glanced briefly in a mirror to make sure that he looked presentable. Finally, he walked back outside to where his pickup was waiting, climbed back into the truck, and drove down the road until he encountered several Japanese.

The first enemy soldiers Cunningham met had no knowledge that a surrender was in progress, and they were shocked to see a high-ranking American officer driving alone in the midst of a battle. To Dr. Shigeyoshi Ozeki, the Japanese navy surgeon accompanying the invading troops, the sight came as a total surprise.

"At the time we didn't know which side the tide of battle was running in favor of, or what our prospects were," Ozeki said. "Then I saw a vehicle with a white flag driving up right under my nose, and I heard Commander Cunningham shouting, 'Stop the fire!' "

Ozeki's comrade, Senior Petty Officer Hisao Tsuji, said he initially assumed that Cunningham was conducting a patrol mission. Several Japanese pointed their rifles at the pickup's occupant but held their fire when they saw he was offering no resistance. "We believed at the time that our capture of the American commander was the cause of our victory," Tsuji said.

At the very moment Cunningham was handing over his sword, Lieutenant Poindexter's force was on the attack a mile or so away and driving the Japanese steadily backward toward the airfield. Lieutenant Kliewer's small band at the airfield was still holding the invaders at bay, and on Wilkes, Captain Platt's Marines were mopping up the last Japanese resistance on the island.

★

Devereux gives a far different account of this dark and crucial moment in U.S. military history.

"Now, about 7 A.M.," he said, "I reported to Commander Cunningham the way the situation looked from my CP. We had no communication with Wilkes Island or any other forward position, so my estimate of the situation had to be based largely on guesswork and possibilities.

"This was how it seemed to me: Jap flags were reported flying 'all over Wilkes.' In the absence of any indication to the contrary, I had to assume that Wilkes Island had fallen. On Wake proper, all along the front of the Japanese advance, the enemy had pushed through to the airstrip and even beyond. Our firing line set up by Major Potter—our secondary line—lay across the road only one hundred yards from my CP, and now it was our first line."

Devereux went on to talk about Potter's line coming under heavy fire from enemy troops as near as 300 yards away and getting strong pressure from the brush along its right flank. Devereux believed that Potter's men were opposed by 250 or more enemy troops. But later evidence indicates that, at most, only a few dozen Japanese skirmishers were in the area immediately in front of the line, and none of these was in any shape to threaten the command post. Some historians have faulted Devereux for failing to send out patrols to get a better fix on actual combat conditions before jumping to unrealistically negative conclusions, and the criticism seems justified.

Simply stated, the Marines on Wake were smarter, tougher, and more capable than their commander realized. Contrary to what Devereux believed, Potter's defenders were actually on the attack and moving forward—as was every other major American unit on Wake proper and Wilkes at this moment.

Captain Godbold, who had just rushed some sixty of his artillerymen from Peale by truck to serve as infantry in Potter's line, was directly involved in the action:

"About 7 or 7:30 A.M., I brought my men over to Wake, and we took up a position about 150 yards from Major Devereux's command post. There were no Japs near us, so we began to move forward, toward the airport, to set up our defense line as far as possible from the command post. We advanced a couple of hundred yards and encountered only a few Japs and no organized resistance. We sustained no casualties at all, but we did inflict a few on the enemy."

To Godbold and other observers, the invaders seemed disorganized and lacking any leadership from their officers. What little return fire they put up against Potter's reinforced line was sporadic and inaccurate. They moved foolishly, haphazardly, and often individually, never seriously threatening to penetrate the American defenses.

At one point, Marines watched incredulously as a lone Japanese came walking right down the middle of the road, making no effort to take cover. Sergeant Bowsher saw at least one SNLF soldier apparently trying to surrender. "He came along carrying a white flag, but somebody thought it must be a trick and shot him," Bowsher said.

Devereux witnessed none of this action, however, and because of the thick layer of gloom overlaying his perceptions, it might not have made any difference if he had. "I had to assume that our forward positions had been overrun, or, at best, broken up and isolated in a few helpless 'last stand' pockets that could do us no good," he said. "I had to report to Commander Cunningham that it looked to me as though the Japs had secured Wilkes Island, Camp One, the channel, the airstrip, and probably Barninger's position [on Peacock Point] as well, and that now the enemy was eating his way into the island with Potter's line as the next bite."

According to Devereux's account, Cunningham hesitated for a long moment when he was presented with this overall assessment, then replied: "Well, I guess we'd better give it to them."

Devereux claimed to be thoroughly stunned by Cunningham's response. In the major's own words: "I couldn't believe he had said it. I hadn't contemplated even the possibility of surrender...I don't think any of us had thought further than trying to hold the enemy as long as possible at each position, buying time...But now he was saying we had to surrender."

Devereux later recalled asking for a little time to mull things over. He tried to think of "something—anything—we might do to keep going," but he was forced to admit that he could see no viable options for fighting on.

"I'll pass the word," he said finally.

Regardless of who ultimately took the final, fatal step that ended the Battle of Wake Island, there's no question which commander bore the heavier physical and psychological burden in making the order effective. While Cunningham went to spruce up in anticipation of the formal surrender, the complex—and dangerous—ordeal of conveying the bad news to the widely scattered units on the three islands fell squarely on Devereux's shoulders.

The major had just stood up and started toward the door of his bunker when Gunner John Hamas came in to tell him that the last of Godbold's men had joined Potter's defensive line.

"What are your orders now, sir?" Hamas asked.

"It's too late, John," Devereux said heavily. "Commander Cunningham has ordered us to surrender. Fix up a white flag and pass the word to cease firing."

Hamas looked as if someone had just clubbed him between the eyes. The twenty-year Marine veteran had spent his whole life in the military, serving in the Austro-Hungarian army in World War I and later as an officer in the Czech infantry. As Devereux remembered it, Hamas's jaw dropped, and he stared disbelievingly at his commanding officer as if he were crazy.

But all Hamas did was bite his lip and mutter, "Yes sir." Then he turned quickly away and went outside.

Devereux followed and stood at the entrance of the command post, listening to Hamas's voice breaking as he shouted the order to cease fire:

"Major's orders! We're surrendering! Major's orders!"

For a moment, the usually unflappable Devereux completely lost his composure. The major later claimed that he couldn't remember doing it, but a number of men in the vicinity of the command post saw the tears streaking Devereux's face and heard him howl out his rage and anguish.

"It's not my order, goddamn it!" he yelled at Hamas.

At that moment, Walter Bowsher was standing only a few yards from the CP, and even sixty-plus years later, he vividly remembered the fury in Devereux's voice. "I heard every word," Bowsher recalled. "He was absolutely livid."

For the major, considering surrender in the abstract was one thing, but facing the excruciating reality of it was something else entirely. It defied everything that the Marines who served under him had ever been taught and everything he himself had ever believed in. Given a choice, Marines preferred physical death to the "death of pride" signified by surrender. But now they had no choice, and the task confronting Devereux was as painful as having the flesh torn from his body.

One of the first officers in the field to receive the stunning order was Lieutenant Barninger of Battery A on Peacock Point. One of Barninger's men had found and repaired the severed phone line between their position and the command post, and Barninger eagerly called in to report his battery was secure, ready for attack, and awaiting orders.

The order Devereux delivered was a crusher: "Cease firing and destroy all weapons. The island is being surrendered."

A few minutes later, as the word of the cease-fire spread from man to man among Potter's unit, Devereux tried to phone the Marine hospital but found the line was dead. Afraid that his undefended wounded might be massacred unless he moved to protect them, he asked for a volunteer to rig a white flag that could be carried by hand and accompany him on foot to the hospital.

Sergeant Donald Malleck stepped forward, tied a white rag around a mop handle, and followed Devereux outside. Major Potter also volunteered to go with them, but Devereux told him to stay where he was.

"Under the circumstances, I considered that an act of great courage," Potter said later, "and under any circumstances, who the hell would've wanted that humiliating and onerous job?"

Before Devereux and Malleck reached the hospital, they were intercepted by a Japanese soldier who ordered them to drop their helmets and sidearms and empty their pockets. Then he motioned with his bayonet for them to march ahead of him toward the Japanese lines. They'd gone only a few steps when a second Japanese appeared. As they approached the second man, a rifle cracked from the brush, and the man fell.

"The order has been given to cease firing," Devereux yelled, "and, damn it, you'll obey that order!"

When they reached the hospital, the Japanese had already occupied it. Random, ricocheting bullets fired by landing force troops who burst into the bunker had killed at least one civilian patient and rewounded several other previously injured men. All the other patients, except for those unable to move, had been forced outside, along with the hospital staff. About thirty Americans in all now sat on the ground in four rows with machine guns aimed at their backs.

Several Japanese were standing at the hospital door. One of them was a lieutenant who spoke English, and Devereux told him he was surrendering. About that time, another group of Japanese arrived with Cunningham in tow, and the Japanese lieutenant looked indecisively from Devereux to Cunningham.

"Who number one?" he asked.

Devereux pointed to Cunningham. "I said that while he arranged the formal surrender, I'd go around the island with Malleck to be sure everybody got the word," the major said.

That job would take six white-knuckle hours to complete, a fact that Devereux and Malleck couldn't possibly foresee when it began. As they started out, they could still hear heavy firing to the west, a clear indication that many defenders were in no mood to give up. Scores of Marines would receive the dispiriting news at a time when they thought they were on the verge of victory. More than once, the prolonged surrender mission came close to costing Devereux his life—and not always at the hands of the Japanese.

Even small pockets of Marines who were pinned down and cut off from the other defenders reacted in angry disbelief. One of them was Sergeant Bourquin, a member of Lieutenant Kliewer's foiled demolition team, still holed up with a dead generator in a dugout near the airfield.

"I came within an inch of shooting Devereux when he came up with this escort of Japs and told us to lay down our weapons and come out," Bourquin admitted. "I was convinced it was some kind of trick, and I told Dave Kliewer, 'Don't listen to him, Lieutenant. It's a hoax. Marines never surrender.'"

*Captain Wesley McCoy Platt, strongpoint
commander on Wilkes Island, led the
counterattack that swept the island of Japanese
forces on the morning of December 23, 1941.
(Marine Corps Historical Center)*

✦ 14 ✦

Wilkes—The Victory
Nobody Noticed

Unfortunately for the Japanese, Captain Platt and his sixty-plus Marines on Wilkes Island knew nothing of the surrender. They were totally cut off from communication with the rest of the garrison, and they could only guess what was happening on Wake proper. In fact, in the eerie predawn hours of December 23, they weren't any too sure of the situation on their own island, either.

As nearly as Platt could tell, close to a hundred enemy troops had come ashore on two large barges, and they'd suffered relatively few casualties in the landing. After chasing Gunner McKinstry and his crew away from the ineffective three-inch gun above the beach, some of the invaders had occupied the useless gun and the other abandoned three-inch emplacements of Battery F, as if these were their major objective. They'd seemed satisfied to plant their flags around the area and then sit there without making any significant effort to push the fight or try to gain more ground.

More worrisome, though, was the fact that an undetermined number of the landing force troops had slipped into the undergrowth and disappeared. Their voices could be heard clearly as they shouted back and forth, and some of them crept to within thirty or forty yards of American positions, but the Marines' Nos. 9 and 10 machine guns manned by PFC Sanford Ray and Sergeant Raymond Coulson held them at bay.

Early on, Platt had decided to vacate Battery L and convert his five-inch gun crews into two platoons of infantry to meet the invaders in strength when they landed. The five-inchers had been so badly bunged up in the last couple of enemy air raids that they were no longer usable anyway.

Because of the battery's condition, the garrison on Wilkes was as well prepared for ground combat as any of Wake's defenders. But the inky blackness, coupled with the failure of the three-inch beach gun and the need to send men to the lagoon side of the island in response to Major Devereux's mistaken fear of an enemy landing there, prevented any show-down at the time of the invasion.

Now, with enemy troops scattered through the brush in the middle of the island, others embedded around the abandoned beach gun, and phone communication lost to his own positions as well as to the main island, Platt faced a desperate situation. A less nervy commander might well have stood pat and allowed his separated, outnumbered units to be destroyed piecemeal. Platt, however, planned to attack the enemy at the earliest pos-sible moment.

With his boyish face, athletic build, and mildly wisecracking manner, Wesley McCoy Platt looked—and sometimes acted—younger than his twenty-seven years. Few officers have been more popular and admired by those who served under them than Platt, and virtually every Marine who knew him sang his praises. He did more than lead them; he inspired them, encouraged them, and taught them to believe in themselves.

PFC Henry Chapman, an ammo handler on Battery L, found Platt to be the kind of officer men could follow into hell "and have fun doing it." To machine gunner John Johnson, Platt was most admired because he never asked any of his men to do anything he wouldn't do himself.

Tech Sergeant Edwin F. Hassig had joined the Marines in 1929 to escape the frigid winters and bleak prospects on a North Dakota farm, and he was widely known as a tough judge of commissioned officers as well as one of the Corps' top marksmen. To Hassig, who was in charge of one of the searchlights on Wilkes, Platt was a rarity in that he could be both a trusted friend and an effective commander without letting either role interfere with the other.

★

It wasn't Platt's style to lie back and let the enemy dictate the terms or tenor of the battle. But before dawn on December 23, he was handicapped by the fact that his force was divided into three small groups, none of which had phone contact with the others, and no one knew how many Japanese lurked in the scrub separating them.

Platt had only a handful of riflemen assembled near the center of Wilkes, along with four .50-caliber machine guns (Nos. 9, 10, 11, and 12) spread along the south beach all the way to the west end of the island. At the moment, he didn't know the exact location of the group sent to the lagoon side of Wilkes. The rest of the Marines from Platt's strongpoint, including the crew from McKinstry's abandoned three-incher, were concentrated to the east—on the other side of the enemy beachhead from Platt—with Lieutenant McAlister in command.

PFC Artie Stocks was among a small group sent to check out the lagoon side of the island. There were only four or five men in the patrol, and as long as it stayed dark, they "might as well have been blindfolded," as Stocks put it. But as the sky lightened, they could tell there were no Japanese around the lagoon. Now they could see all the way to the far side of the island, and they could also hear a lot of small arms fire coming from that direction, a clear indication of where the enemy was concentrated.

For more than an hour, meanwhile, Platt bided his time in the darkness. He kept his own little band of artillerymen-turned-infantry in protected defensive positions while his machine guns peppered the brush with continuous fire to discourage enemy movement. Until there was something visible to shoot at, Platt's immediate goal was to hold the Japanese in check and keep them from pushing west toward the battery's vacated five-inch gun emplacement.

Like any number of other Marines, Wiley Sloman didn't fire a single round from his Springfield before daylight that morning because there were no visible targets. The Japanese riflemen weren't doing much shooting, either, but Sloman and his mates had to stay low because of frequent bursts of tracer bullets, including some that may have come from their own machine guns. The situation on Wilkes was as confused as it was tenuous.

By 4:30 A.M., however, Platt was fed up with lying low and playing a waiting game. He was determined to end the uncertainty—and the stalemate—and the first logical step was to get a better idea of exactly where the Japanese were and what they were up to. So, in true Platt fashion, instead of sending some of his men out on a high-risk reconnaissance mission, the agile South Carolinian undertook his own one-man patrol to see what was going on.

First, he picked his way through the brush to check on machine gun No. 11, which he couldn't reach by phone. Then he spent a half hour crawling over the jagged coral to scout the enemy beachhead itself. By 5:00 A.M., it was light enough—and Platt was close enough—to see the disposition of the Japanese force. What he saw made his pulse quicken.

To a man, the invaders massed around the three-inch gun position were all facing eastward, away from Platt, and directing sporadic rifle fire in the direction of the new channel while ignoring the area behind them. From the east, Platt heard the throaty roar of Marine Springfields—readily distinguishable from the staccato *pop-pop* of the Japanese Arisakas. Not only were McAlister's and McKinstry's men still fighting, but they were also commanding every iota of the enemy's attention. Believing the Marines east of them to be the only Americans left on Wilkes who posed a significant challenge, the Japanese had overlooked the need for security in the other direction.

Platt couldn't help but grin as he scrambled back toward his unit. Not a single rifle or light machine gun was positioned to cover the invaders' backside. In Platt's book, that was an open invitation to kick it as hard as he could.

On Kuku Point at the western end of Wilkes, meanwhile, Corporal Johnson noted a near-total lack of enemy activity in his sector and ordered his two .30-caliber machine guns to cease fire. The .30s had had few targets over the hour and a half since the landing, but they'd been keeping up a steady sequence of tracer bursts to illuminate the lagoon on the chance that more Japanese were sneaking ashore on that side of the island. Now, with no invaders apparently nearby, Johnson concluded that continued firing was not only a waste of ammunition but also risked giving away his location for no good purpose.

At approximately the same time when Platt was eavesdropping on the Japanese beachhead, Johnson was trying to decide what course of action he and his seven-man squad should follow. Except for PFC Marvin Mc-Calla, the other six men under Johnson were all civilians with extremely limited experience on machine guns. The corporal was well aware of Mc-Calla's passive nature and his extreme religious beliefs, but he also considered McCalla a good soldier and trusted him to do what had to be done. Finally, Johnson decided they should leave the position where they'd spent the night and head southeast in search of the enemy.

He attempted to phone Platt for permission to make the move but got Sergeant Coulson at machine gun No. 10 instead. Although separated by rank, Johnson and Canadian-born Ray Coulson had been friends since machine gun school in San Diego, and they'd pulled a lot of liberties together. They knew each other well enough not to mince words.

"What's it look like over there?" Coulson asked.

"There's no sign of any Japs, and I think we ought to move the guns," Johnson replied. "Should we quit this position now or wait for Captain Platt to reassign us?"

"Hell, no, don't wait," snapped Coulson, who hadn't heard from Platt since he'd gone to scout the beachhead. "Platt may be dead for all I know, and they're killing us over here. The Japs have gotten in the woods behind us, so move as quick as you can, and give us some help."

"Okay," Johnson said, "but make sure the guys on the other .50s know we're coming. We don't want to get wiped out by our own people."

Johnson elected to move the guns on their tripods without breaking them down, leaving their ammo belts and water-cooling systems in place. Handling them this way was slow, cumbersome work, but it also allowed the guns to open fire immediately if they encountered enemy troops. It took two men—one Marine and one civilian—to carry each of the .30s. Two civilians hauled two boxes each of belted ammo, and the other two carried Johnson's and McCalla's rifles, plus one box of ammo each.

Along the way, Johnson and McCalla played a dangerous game of leapfrog with their machine guns. They alternated their moves, going about twenty feet at a time and keeping one gun in position to fire while the other one was being moved, then reversing the process.

As they made their way along the empty beach in the faint early light, there was no hint of movement among the brush and scrubby ironwood trees on their left and no evidence of any other invaders approaching shore on their right. But if anyone happened to notice the little entourage as it struggled past, Johnson thought they must have resembled a line of "pack animals and Mexican bandits."

They passed the first three .50-caliber positions—Nos. 12, 11, and 10—without incident. But as they approached PFC Ray's No. 9 gun, Johnson spotted a Marine waving for their attention and gesturing toward the brush behind the gun pit.

Ray was a big, lighthearted kid from Arkansas whose dream was to buy enough dollar-an-acre land in the Ozarks to start a hog farm. He didn't look like he could hurt a fly, but he and his crew had already more than proved themselves that morning. Johnson took the man's gestures to mean that Ray wanted Johnson's .30s to fire into this brushy area, and he hurried to comply.

Using the same leapfrog method of advancing the guns, Johnson and McCalla moved forward alternately about thirty feet apart, with Johnson on the left and McCalla on the right. Johnson made it nearly to the edge of the woods without disturbing the surrounding quiet, then motioned Mc-Calla to come ahead. But McCalla was only a few feet into the trees when he drew rifle fire.

In the gloom, Johnson couldn't make out anything to shoot at, not even any muzzle flashes, but he fired a burst toward the sound of the rifles. When he heard somebody scream, he knew he was firing in the right spot. Hugging the dirt, Johnson swung his gun in a sixty-foot arc and sprayed the area fifteen feet in front of him. There were more screams and shouts. Then, as Johnson expended his belt of ammo and McCalla's gun opened fire, Johnson's position allowed him to get his first actual glimpse of the enemy soldiers—or, more correctly, of their lower extremities.

Through a clear area directly in front of him and just below the lower limbs of the ironwood trees, Johnson saw the wildly pumping legs and feet of Japanese trying to escape the line of fire and flank the American positions. He couldn't see anything much above the enemy soldiers' knees, but their feet were going up and down like pistons as they ran.

Both .30s poured simultaneous streams of fire into the brush. Johnson heard more screams, and after three long bursts, all the feet and legs stopped moving. In the echoing silence that followed, Johnson heard soft mumbling sounds coming from McCalla. It took him a second to realize that the other Marine was praying for the souls of the men he had just killed.

Forty or fifty feet deeper into the woods, Johnson and company attracted more rifle fire and repeated the process. The next time they moved forward, they found the bodies of four dead Japanese. Their greenish landing party uniforms and helmets with leafy tree branches stuck through the netting for camouflage had made them almost invisible in the undergrowth.

The oddest thing that struck Johnson about the dead men was their shoes. They had split toes, similar to mittens, with a separate section where the big toe went. He'd never seen anything like them before.

Johnson glanced around uneasily while his civilians went on gaping at the enemy dead. The corporal had the feeling that other invaders weren't far away, and it was anybody's guess where the next volley of hostile rifle fire would come from.

"Come on. Let's get moving," he said, "before we end up like that ourselves."

They moved on a few yards, but Johnson wasn't sure which way they should go from there. He thought about pushing on east and firing directly on the enemy beachhead, but there was no telling what he and his little group might encounter on the way. If some of the Japanese had slipped past them on the left, they could be behind them right now.

It was about 5:30 A.M., while Johnson was still trying to decide how to proceed, when he looked around and saw Captain Platt leading eight Marine riflemen through the brush toward him. Johnson breathed a quick inward sigh of relief. Now the decision was out of his hands, and he was glad. From this point on, he was more than willing to let his captain call the shots.

On the opposite side of the Japanese beachhead from Johnson and Platt, McKinstry's detachment of fifteen Marines and five civilians was moving cautiously west in the early light, hoping to recover some of the ground they'd lost after abandoning the three-inch gun.

A short distance away, McAlister's range section from Battery L was also on the move in the same area when they spotted five invaders crawling toward them along the beach. A half-dozen rifles cracked in ragged unison, and one of the enemy soldiers slumped dead. The other four scurried behind a large coral boulder, where they were immediately pinned down by rifle fire.

McAlister glanced over the skirmish line of Marines drawn up in the sparse brush beside him, and his eyes lit on his "master builder," Wiley Sloman.

"Hey, Sloman," the lieutenant said over his shoulder, "see if you can get over to the other side of that rock." He nodded toward PFCs Robert Stevens and Ernest Gilley. "Take Stevens and Gilley with you, and try to flush those Japs out of there."

Taking advantage of their mates' covering fire, the trio inched their way around the boulder. There was a rapid exchange of fire between the three Marines and the four invaders, then silence. Sloman and the others waited, but there was no sound or movement from behind the rock.

"What does it look like?" McAlister yelled.

"Can't tell for sure," Sloman called back.

McKinstry and his men came up about this time, and "Big Mack" sized up the situation at a glance. "Somebody's got to climb up on that rock and see what the hell's behind it," McKinstry said.

The burly gunner started forward to do it himself, but McAlister grabbed his arm and stopped him. "Let somebody else go," the lieutenant said.

"I got it, gunner," said Corporal William C. Halstead, one of the shortest—and normally one of the quietest—Marines on Wake. Halstead sprinted across the beach and reached the rock ahead of Sloman and the others. He leaped on top of it and fired a single shot, killing the only living invader cowering there.

Halstead, Stevens, and Gilley made it back to their line with no further trouble. Sloman, however, found himself briefly trapped by machine gun fire that may have originated from Platt's unit, which was now closing on the enemy beachhead from the west, rather than from the Japanese. Sloman's unit didn't know that Platt's men were coming up on the other side of the Japanese and raking the area in front of them with Johnson's and McCalla's machine guns.

With two dozen riflemen between them now, McAlister and McKinstry started a slow, determined advance on the three-inch gun position where the main force of Japanese huddled. The enemy had had almost three hours to dig in, but the landing party troops had contented themselves with planting flags all around the disabled guns and done practically nothing to secure the position.

They showed precisely the same lack of organization and preparation as those who were being overrun at about the same time by Lieutenant Poindexter's unit on the main island. The last thing the Japanese expected on Wilkes this early morning was a forceful American counterattack—especially one that smashed into them from all four sides at once.

In the growing light to the west of the Japanese-held gun emplacement, Platt gathered his men around him in a tight semicircle for a final briefing before they attacked. There were only seventeen of them in all, and little more than a squad of riflemen, so he knew they'd have to wait to open fire until they were as close to the enemy as possible.

"We're going after that three-inch gun position," Platt told them. "We crack it, and the Jap beachhead falls apart. We want to get our two .30s set up on each flank, just like it says in the manual, to give us a base of covering fire for the riflemen. Machine gunners, keep your aim low and pick your targets carefully. Johnny Mac and McKinstry and their guys are somewhere over there on the other side of the Japs, and I sure as hell don't want to hit them. Now hug the dirt, keep moving forward, and be as quiet as you can. Hold your fire till I give the word."

With that, Platt slithered forward on his belly, and the others followed close behind.

East of the enemy position, meanwhile, McAlister and McKinstry were also urging their men forward. Their riflemen were keeping up a steady fire against the Japanese, but they were receiving heavy return fire, as well. The closer the Marines inched toward the three-inch guns, the more American casualties began to mount.

As the firefight intensified, Battery L's PFC Jack Skaggs could see small arms ammunition hitting everywhere around him and taking a bloody toll among his battery mates. PFC Ernest Gilley was just to his right when Gilley took a fatal bullet, and Skaggs was within thirty feet of Corporal Alvey Reed when Reed was killed in a bayonet-to-bayonet fight with an enemy soldier. Moments later, Skaggs saw another Marine he knew, PFC Clovis R. "Skinny" Marlowe, sitting dead on a rock with a bullet through his temple.

Beyond Skaggs's field of vision, Corporal Halstead, the diminutive Marine who had finished off the last invader behind the boulder, was also mortally wounded.

But the Marines advanced tenaciously, spurred on by fierce rebel yells from Skaggs's feisty fellow Oklahoman, PFC Gordon "Gunny" Marshall, whose regular job was a "spotter" on Battery L's range finder. Other riflemen in the skirmish line joined in, and their yells swelled momentarily into a thunderous roar that covered up the invaders' own defiant shouts.

This vocal outburst, coupled with the Marines' relentless concentration of fire, was starting to panic the invaders. They were huddling together in scant or no cover, making themselves much easier to kill.

Now Wiley Sloman found himself with plenty of good targets. The Japanese were bunched so closely together that Sloman found if he missed the one he was aiming at, he had a better than even chance of hitting one of the others.

Armed only with a .45 automatic and a shirtful of grenades, and seemingly oblivious to the men falling around him, Gunner McKinstry charged up and down the line like a raging, red-bearded bull. He was everywhere at once, throwing grenades, exposing himself to enemy fire, and yelling curses at anybody he thought was dallying:

"Come on, you guys, move! Keep moving forward or, by God, I'll shoot you in the ass!"

A few seconds earlier, Sloman had crawled into a slight depression about fifty yards from the water's edge. From there, he had a good angle on the Japanese position, and he was firing continuously, as fast as he could empty one five-round clip and jam a new one into his rifle. Out of the corner of his eye, he noticed PFC Bill Raymond, who'd reached the three-inch gun emplacement just to Sloman's right and was banging away steadily from a kneeling position.

By now, the invaders were caught in a murderous crossfire. Dead Japanese already lay in tangled piles around the disabled antiaircraft gun, and others were falling quickly. Incredible as it seemed after the reversals and uncertainty of the night, the enemy beachhead was rapidly collapsing, leaving only a few scattered invaders out in the brush to be mopped up. The Marines were clearly winning the battle for Wilkes, but it was much too early to celebrate.

Some of the Japanese were still shooting back. Sloman could hear their bullets whizzing past his ears, and he figured he'd make a much smaller target lying there in his little dip than he would out in the open. But when he heard McKinstry yelling at everybody to keep moving, he got up and started running again.

Sloman didn't hear the shot that hit him. He was moving ahead and to his right in a crouching position when "a great big flash of fiery light" exploded behind his eyes. The initial impact didn't knock him out, but it stunned him. The force of it straightened him up, and then he fell forward.

Within that searing flash was a 6.5-millimeter slug fired from an Arisaka rifle. It punched a dime-size hole in Sloman's skull just above his right temple, then tore a jagged exit wound about three inches farther back, driving bullet and bone fragments deep into Sloman's brain.

He had a live round in his rifle, and somehow he was able to squeeze off one last shot and pull back the bolt to eject the shell, but by then his left arm was dead, and he couldn't hold the rifle to shove the bolt forward and put another round in the chamber.

As the rifle slipped out of his fingers, he could feel his senses shutting down. The white-hot pain had ebbed into numbness, but now everything was getting dark, fuzzy, and vague. The last thing Sloman heard before he slipped into unconsciousness was rebel-yelling "Gunny" Marshall. This time, Marshall's shouts seemed to be directed at McKinstry.

"Hey, Mac, looks like Sloman got his! You want his rifle?"

Sloman dimly remembered hearing McKinstry wishing several times that morning for a rifle to augment his grenades and his .45 automatic. But Sloman's rifle was as dear to him as his own flesh, and he wasn't ready to give it up quite yet.

Now wait a damn minute! I may need that old Springfield.

Sloman thought he uttered the words aloud, but they were only a silent, fleeting thought that dissolved almost instantly in his stricken brain. Then the beach, the coral, the shooting, the shouts, the rifle, and all the rest of it quietly faded to black.

Moments later, when Marshall himself fell mortally wounded by a shot to the gut from a "dead" Japanese, Wiley Sloman was floating in a netherworld from which no one present—Sloman included—ever expected him to return.

"Even though each and every one of you fall," a wounded Japanese officer beseeched his men as American fire ripped through them, "defend this position to the last man." Seconds later, the officer was cut down by a volley of shots.

For a few moments, the firing reached a deafening crescendo, then finally tapered off. When the last enemy machine gun was silenced, the slaughter pen around the three-inch gun position became the scene of a lethal game of hide-and-seek.

Platt spotted about a dozen landing force troops holed up behind a large Caterpillar tractor used earlier by the contractors to dig fortifications. The tractor was little more than ten yards in front of Platt and his men, who lobbed a barrage of well-placed grenades and blew the invaders apart. Not far away, more than a score of other Japanese frantically clambered over the bodies of their dead and wounded comrades, trying to find shelter under a bombed-out searchlight truck.

While Platt's unit converged on the devastated enemy beachhead from the east, McAlister's remaining men struck the Japanese right flank from the west, and McKinstry's unit attacked from the front. Meanwhile, Artie Stocks and the other Marines from the lagoon side of the island arrived in time to hit the enemy from the north.

The carnage they encountered when they came together was like nothing any of them had ever seen before. In the words of one Japanese correspondent who visited the site later, the clearing around the old three-inch gun was covered with "mountains of dead and rivers of blood."

But among the heaped corpses, a number of invaders were still alive—and still intent on carrying out their dead commander's final order.

Lugging the same .30-caliber machine gun he'd dragged halfway across Wilkes Island, John Johnson paused at the edge of the clearing and sank to his knees in exhaustion. Immediately in front of him was a scene that defied description. Dozens of dead and wounded Japanese were piled around the ruined searchlight truck. A dead officer, his head and helmet partially torn off by an American grenade, still clutched his pistol and sword. Nearby was an enemy soldier with the lower half of his face blown away.

But it was also obvious that not everyone in this gory jumble of humanity was dead or helpless. Johnson could clearly see some of the bodies in the pile moving. It made him uneasy, and he kept his machine gun trained toward them.

As Johnson watched warily from behind the .30, he saw Private Severe R. Houde, one of the crewmen from Battery F, come into the clearing.

"You'd better get down," Johnson said.

Houde grinned. "Those Japs can't hit me," he said.

As if on cue, a rifle cracked from somewhere in the direction of the truck, and Houde's head exploded.

"They got him right between the horns," Johnson said. "He never knew what hit him."

At almost the same instant, an enemy grenade went off just to Johnson's right, bloodying the side of his face with coral fragments. Realizing that he'd waited too long to do what he should have done in the beginning, the corporal lined up the searchlight truck in his gunsights and opened fire.

Johnson later recalled with calm deliberation the scene that unfolded before him as he emptied his machine gun:

"I kept the trigger depressed and watched the bullets going where I wanted them to go, making minor movements with my hand to correct the flow of bullets if they weren't going where I intended. I realized how severe the machine gun fire was as shrieks and screams came from the Japanese as their bodies winced and contorted, and their arms and legs flailed in the air. Methodically from right to left, I attempted to spray bullets into every Japanese body visible, and when the tracer bullets showed me that the bodies on the right had been struck, I backtracked from right to left."

When Johnson's belt of ammo ran out and he quit firing, the Marine riflemen surged forward with fixed bayonets.

"Make sure the dead ones are really dead," Gunner McKinstry hollered. His men did all they could to obey his order, but there were still some harrowing near misses.

With enemy resistance apparently crushed, PFC Henry Chapman had his rifle on safety as he checked out a patch of brush near the south beach. One of the crewmen on Battery L who had left their five-inchers to become infantry, Maryland-born Chapman was also one of the few Marines without a bayonet on his rifle. But he wasn't thinking about that when he spotted what looked to be a dead enemy soldier on the beach and moved closer to investigate.

Chapman's buddy, Artie Stocks, was just a step or two ahead of Chapman, when Stocks heard a terrible scream and whirled around to see a Japanese sergeant jump from the tangle of bodies and charge Chapman with a bayonet. Stocks shot the man a split second before he ran Chapman through with the blade.

Stocks claimed to remember nothing of what immediately followed. Chapman and a few other witnesses, however, said they watched Stocks walk deliberately over to the fallen invader, put his foot on the man's midsection, shoot the Japanese a second time at point-blank range, then pound his chest with his fist and yell like Tarzan.

"Damn, Artie, you're crazy as a loon," Chapman said in a shaking voice. "But if I ever get a million bucks, you'll get half of it. You just saved my life."

Asked later if the incident actually happened that way, Stocks smiled and shrugged. "I honestly don't know," he said. "All I know is what people told me later, plus the fact that there was a lot of emotion running through everybody right then. I did shoot the son of a bitch, though, and I think he was the last Jap killed on Wilkes that day."

Except for two wounded prisoners whom Platt ordered taken alive for questioning, every Japanese who had set foot on Wilkes since the invasion began over four hours earlier now lay dead.

"Well, we've secured the island," Platt said quietly as he glanced around, first at the piled-up enemy corpses, then at his own dazed, disheveled troops. "Good job, men."

Over the next couple of hours, as the Marines scoured the island for any possible stragglers, ninety-four enemy bodies would be counted, with a few others likely lost in the surf. Eight members of Platt's command had been killed defending Wilkes, and a half-dozen more had been wounded. In addition to his skinned face, John Johnson had a flesh wound in his right arm from a rapid-fire weapon, and Artie Stocks had a helmet filled with blood from a large chunk of shrapnel that ripped his scalp before slamming into the bank behind him.

"I don't know what that piece of shrapnel was, but I know exactly where it came from," Stocks said. "Printed right there on the metal were the words 'made in Ohio U.S.A.'"

By far the most seriously hurt of all, however, was Wiley Sloman. He was barely clinging to life, but nobody realized it until the enemy was beaten.

With his right hand, Sloman gingerly touched the coral on which he was lying. It was hard and scratchy, same as always, but it was reassuring just to know he could still feel something. His left eye was plastered shut with drying blood, but with his right eye he could make out the bloody mess on the shoulder of his sweatshirt. Then he heard the faint voice of his friend, Bill Raymond. It seemed to be coming from somewhere far away, but in reality, Raymond was leaning right over him, his face only inches from Sloman's own.

"Hey!" Raymond yelled. "Sloman's still alive. Get a corpsman over here!"

Another face materialized out of the misty gloom, and Sloman recognized Pharmacist's Mate Third Class Ernest C. Vaale, a tall, blond Norseman from Minnesota and one of only eight Navy corpsmen on Wake. Sloman had noticed Vaale several times that morning as the unarmed medic exposed himself repeatedly to enemy fire to tend to wounded men. Now he was doing the same for Sloman, gently lifting his head and turning it ever so slightly, just enough to shake some white powder on the wound and slip a field bandage over the gaping cavity in Sloman's skull.

"Pretty bad, huh?" Sloman mumbled.

The medic bit his lip. "Just lie still and try not to move. You're gonna be all right."

"Hell, I couldn't move if I had to," Sloman whispered. Everything was starting to fade out again. "What happened to the Japs?"

"They're all dead but two, and those two are prisoners," Vaale said. "We've secured the island."

Sloman smiled and closed his eyes. "That's nice," he said—at least he thought he said it. "Does that mean we can go home now?"

*Captain Henry T. "Hammering Hank"
Elrod, who sank the Japanese destroyer
Kisaragi with two 100-pound bombs from
his Grumman Wildcat on December 11,
1941, and later fought valiantly on the
ground during the invasion of Wake, was
posthumously awarded the Congressional
Medal of Honor.*
(Marine Corps Historical Center)

☆ 15 ☆

"We'd Rather Have Died Fighting"

Outside of those in the immediate command post area and Potter's line, the Marines of Lieutenant Barninger's Battery A and Lieutenant Lewis's Battery E, both on Peacock Point, were the first major units to receive Major Devereux's order to cease firing and destroy their weapons.

Strips of bedding were stuffed into the muzzles of the five- and three-inch guns, and the guns were fired to destroy the barrels. Then, for good measure, grenades were dropped down the muzzles and set off. All cables were cut, all gun dials broken, all firing locks destroyed.

Lewis's men used twenty pistol shots to ensure that their director and height finder were wrecked beyond repair. One of the bullets ricocheted and struck Sergeant Robert Box, who wasn't injured seriously enough to keep him from cursing the quirk of fate. He'd gone unscratched through sixteen days of attacks only to be wounded in a freak accident when the fighting was over.

Nearby, Corporal Frank Gross, commanding four .50-caliber machine guns on Peacock, also got a call from Devereux's command post conveying the same grim instructions: Cease firing. Destroy all weapons. The island is being surrendered.

"We were one of the few posts still in contact with Devereux," Gross said. "I didn't believe it when a guy ran up to me and said we'd surrendered, and

I had somebody call back twice to make sure, but we got the same order every time."

Like scores of other Marines on Wake, PFC Clifton Sanders, one of the gunners serving under Gross, was in no mood to throw in the towel. "I was prepared for the worst, but I just wasn't ready to give up," Sanders said. "I used my .50-caliber till I ran out of ammo. Then I moved to a .30-caliber on the beach and kept firing."

When the surrender order was repeated, Sanders's first concern was keeping the Japanese from using the machine guns they were leaving behind. He pulled the firing pins out of as many of the .30s and .50s as he could reach and threw them as far as he was able.

After the guns were disabled, Gross got all four of his gun crews together—a dozen men in all—and they walked down toward the five-inch battery but found no one there when they arrived. Some of them climbed up on the command tower and looked around, but they didn't see a soul. Barninger's and Lewis's men had apparently already reached the area of the command post and given themselves up.

Gross and the others tied an undershirt around a stick and walked on a little farther. Then six or eight Japanese approached and started yelling and jabbing at them with bayonets. They put the Marines in a group, tied their hands with wire, and trained a machine gun on them. Gross felt certain that he and his men would be gunned down within the next few seconds. "Damn," he told himself, "if this is how it's gonna end, I'd rather have died fighting."

For the next hour, Gross and the other Americans waited helplessly, staring at the barrel of the machine gun and expecting it to spit fire at any second. "I was determined I was going to see it when it happened," Gross recalled. "I guess that's the only thing that kept me going."

The fatal shots never came.

As Devereux's group warily approached Lieutenant Hanna's gun position south of the airfield, they found the ground covered with scores of enemy dead. Several dozen live Japanese had taken cover in the airplane revetments at the edge of the airstrip, where they seemed content to keep the defenders pinned down by a steady stream of rifle fire and try to wait them out. From the number of bodies littering the landscape, it was easy to see why the Japanese weren't eager to charge the gun emplacement.

Two Japanese lieutenants had now taken charge of the surrender mission. One spoke reasonably good English and was talkative and friendly. The other also understood English well enough but maintained a silent, hostile demeanor and made menacing gestures with a huge samurai sword. They watched Devereux climb atop one of the revetments and shout toward the gun position:

"This is Major Devereux! The island has been surrendered! Cease firing and put down your weapons!"

There was no reply from the gun position, only an eerie silence. Devereux yelled the same order again, but there was still no answer. Then, as the major walked slowly toward the three-incher, a few tattered, bloody Marines dragged themselves out into the sunlight. Devereux recognized Major Putnam, but barely. He'd been shot in the jaw, and most of his face was a red smear of blood.

"Jimmy, I'm sorry," Putnam mumbled in a daze. "Poor Hank is dead."

Captain Henry Elrod lay faceup in the gun pit, his eyes wide open, defiance still frozen on his face, a grenade still gripped in his hand. The bodies of civilians Paul Gay and Bob Bryan sprawled nearby. Of the twenty-six men who had defended the gun position for more than six hours against overwhelming odds, sixteen were dead. Of the ten still alive under the gun, nine were wounded. Hanna and Corporal Holewinski were too badly shot up to move on their own and had to be pulled out by the Japanese. Only VMF-211's Captain Tharin was unhurt.

The enemy soldiers separated Putnam, Tharin, and Hanna from the enlisted men and left both groups under guard while Devereux and the rest walked on toward Camp One.

Like a slow-spreading stain, word of the surrender seeped across the rest of Wake proper that morning. And at almost every new stop along the way, Devereux, Sergeant Malleck, and the group of Japanese soldiers and American prisoners accompanying them encountered the same dismay, disbelief, and defiance from the Marines.

As they approached Lieutenant Poindexter's advancing mobile reserve force, Poindexter took one look at their white flag and assumed that the enemy his unit had been whipping soundly for the last couple of hours was giving up. Poindexter stepped out of the bushes with his pockets stuffed with grenades, a .45 automatic strapped to his hip, and a Springfield in his hand. His face was smeared with black ointment for flashburns he'd suffered during the fighting, but it was also split with a wide grin as he walked down the road toward the approaching surrender party.

When the unthinkable reality sank in, Poindexter's grin dissolved. His jaw dropped as his gaze shifted from Devereux to the white flag and back again. As the men who fought with him knew, the lieutenant's usually quiet, thoughtful demeanor gave way under battle conditions to a surprising, no-quarter toughness firmly backed by sound thinking. They used such terms as "brilliant," "inspiring," and "interested in people" to describe Poindexter. "He was too optimistic," Corporal Cyrus Fish recalled later, "to ever think he was going to lose."

Known by his fellow officers as a "very cerebral guy," Poindexter would enjoy a long second career as a college political science professor after retiring from the Marines, but on this morning, he was pure warrior. Shock, denial, and fury mingled in his eyes as he faced his commander.

"Drop your rifle, Lieutenant," Devereux said. "We've been ordered to surrender. Tell your men to stand up and leave their weapons on the deck."

For a long moment, Poindexter stood motionless, and every American present could sense his inner struggle as he searched his mind for a response. Finally, he let the rifle slip from his grasp and fall to the ground, then unbuckled his pistol belt and dropped it, too. When he pulled the grenades out of his pockets, some of the Japanese jumped back, but Poindexter carefully laid the grenades on the ground beside his other weapons and stepped away.

Then he shook his head, snapped his fingers, and muttered a couple of words under his breath. Devereux later said he thought the lieutenant's final comment was "Aw, shucks." Others within earshot heard it somewhat differently.

★

At Camp One, the American flag still billowed in the breeze from the water tower, where it had been moved after the flagpole was knocked down by enemy planes. In one spot or the other, the Stars and Stripes had flown continuously above Wake, day and night, since the morning of December 8.

When the Japanese troops in the burgeoning surrender party saw the flag, several of them broke into a run, yelling, cheering, and racing each other for the privilege of pulling it down.

With a guard's bayonet poking him in the back and his hands raised above his head, Devereux anxiously surveyed the sullen faces of the Marines around him as one of the landing force soldiers scaled the water tower. The major sensed a potential calamity in the making. The Marines' eyes were burning, their fists clenching, their hearts clearly weighing so heavily in their chests that they didn't give a damn what happened to them anymore. Devereux could tell that some of them were dangerously close to "the crazy point where a man will go against a gun with his bare hands."

"Hold it!" Devereux shouted. "Keep your heads, all of you!"

Somehow, they forced themselves to obey the order. They watched silently as the exultant invader cut their colors down, stuffed them into a camouflage bag, and climbed down from the tower with his prize.

But the men in Devereux's group weren't the only Americans to witness this wrenching spectacle. The water tower was by far the tallest structure on Wake, and defenders all over the main island—both the surrendered and the unsurrendered—could see what was happening with perfect clarity. Few of them ever forgot it.

To Sergeant Walter Bowsher, who watched as a bound and helpless prisoner, that crushing moment would never have an equal—not in all the next sixty years. When he saw the Japanese tear down the flag that day, he called it "the lowest point of my whole life."

Platoon Sergeant Dave Rush, captain of one of the five-inch gun crews on Peale, who had come to Wake proper to man a machine gun in Major Potter's defensive line, didn't know about the surrender when he saw the Japanese on the water tower. Known as a likable, mild-mannered guy—particularly for a gun captain—Rush quickly lined up the climber in his sights and drew a perfect bead on the enemy soldier. Fortunately he held his fire just long enough to spot the approaching surrender party.

From another machine gun pit west of Camp One near the Wilkes boat channel, Gunnery Sergeant John Cemeris was also staring at the figure on the water tower. The brawny product of a rough-and-tumble Russian-Polish neighborhood on Chicago's South Side, Cemeris was almost certainly the only man on Wake who had served in three different branches of the U.S. military—first the Army, then the Navy, and finally the Marines.

As one of the noncoms who often drove Devereux around the atoll on inspection trips, Cemeris would never have ignored one of the major's orders. But like Rush, he hadn't heard about the surrender, and he also had a personal score to settle with the Japanese. His wife and ten-month-old daughter had been quartered at Hickam Field in Hawaii when the Pearl Harbor raiders struck. Hickam had suffered heavy damage, and the sergeant had no way of knowing if his family was dead or alive. He'd been thinking of them moments earlier as he sprayed .30-caliber tracers at a low-flying Japanese dive bomber.

By some accounts, Cemeris had sent a stream of bullets into the attacking plane, then grinned as it pulled away coughing smoke. Devereux claimed to have seen the plane jettison its bombs over the ocean and said he later heard reports that it eventually crashed. The major called it "beautiful shooting."

J. J. Coker, Cemeris's young civilian ammo handler, who was at the sergeant's side behind the machine gun almost constantly that morning, told a different story, however. Coker said he never saw the .30-caliber Browning, a weapon designed for ground defense, score a direct hit on the enemy plane. "The Jap buzzed us several times, and Cemeris fired at it each time, but I didn't see any of the bullets actually hit the plane," Coker said.

Nevertheless, with the Japanese prodding their captives toward the Wilkes Channel with bayonets, Devereux and Poindexter led a desperate rush toward Cemeris's position to tell him to cease firing. In the meantime, Cemeris was giving serious thought to testing his marksmanship on the invader scaling the water tower.

"I bet I can get that son of a bitch," the sergeant told Coker, squinting at the climber through his sights.

The idea put Coker's nerves on edge. The twenty-two-year-old native of the Texas Panhandle had come to Wake as a clerk in the contractors' canteen, and a few days earlier, he'd voluntarily made the transition to machine gun duty. He'd hauled can after can of heavy ammo belts out to the gun pits along the beach and even fired a few rounds himself, but now he had an ominous feeling about what lay ahead. Even though he didn't know at the time that his best friend, Paul Gay, had been killed earlier that morning defending Lieutenant Hanna's three-inch gun, Coker felt time rapidly running out for the Americans on Wake. The last thing he wanted to do was tempt fate.

Coker had seen a group of Japanese moving toward the machine gun position, and he had the feeling they were pretty close by now. He figured he had about five minutes to live at best—and less than that if Cemeris started shooting at the tower.

"Sergeant," Coker said, "before you shoot that guy, why don't you let me crawl back through those bushes behind us and see if there's any Japs closer than that?"

Cemeris glanced at Coker and frowned. "Okay," he growled. "Go have a look, but make it fast."

Coker made as much racket as possible—"like a bull in a china shop going through that brush"—and about that time, he heard somebody yell: "Hey, you! Stand up and come out of there with your hands over your head."

Coker did as he was told, then saw Devereux's party approaching. "I never felt so relieved in my life," he said later.

As a truck driver, PFC Ed Borne enjoyed operating "at large" wherever he happened to be needed and not being permanently attached to any particular unit. The downside of his job was that he could find himself alone and separated from the rest of the garrison at critical times. The morning of December 23 was one of those times.

Borne had been at a searchlight position near Camp One when the invasion started, but as the fighting intensified, he took cover in a bomb crater at the edge of the brush. Shortly after daylight, he heard heavy firing to the north and west, and it grew steadily closer. Soon Borne detected scattered Japanese troops retreating in disarray through the bushes. He realized that Poindexter's mobile reserve was driving the invaders directly toward him and that he was in an ideal position to intercept them. He was on their left flank, and he could hear them distinctly in the brush.

Borne had a dozen hand grenades carefully hooked in his various buttonholes so as not to impede his mobility. His rifle was fully loaded, and he had two bandoliers and a cartridge belt of ammo. He was in good shape to do some damage.

"My finger was on the trigger, but I held off firing and giving away my position until the Japs were so close I couldn't miss," he said later. "I was pretty sure I wouldn't live through the next few minutes, but I was calm. It was almost like I could feel God's presence, and I didn't care what happened to me."

Then, Borne said, he heard a sudden shout behind him, and when he turned, he saw Devereux coming toward him. "He was hollering, 'Lay down your arms! We've surrendered the island!' I couldn't believe it. I didn't want to surrender. We never should've done it."

Hiding in a foxhole near the south beach of Wake proper with three other civilians, young Idahoan John Rogge had also ceased making any long-range plans for the future. When the war started, Rogge had traded his job as an office clerk for duty on a searchlight crew, and when the searchlight was knocked out, he'd gone to work filling sandbags. Now there was nothing left to do but hunker down and wait for the end—whatever it might be.

Shells from a Japanese warship were bursting on all sides of the dugout, and Rogge was waiting as stoically as possible for the direct hit that he was sure was coming. To make matters worse, the foxhole was knee deep in water.

"After all the bombs they'd dropped on us, we thought the deeper we could dig into the coral, the better," Rogge said. "But we dug down so far that seawater started seeping in. We were wet and miserable, but it was better than being outside. Those shells were shaking the whole damned island."

As he contemplated his fate, a fly buzzed past his ear and plunged into the puddle of water in which Rogge squatted. The fly struggled mightily to escape the puddle but couldn't pull free. After a few moments, it appeared to be drowning, and Rogge found himself intently observing the fly's predicament. At first, he thought of it as just a momentary diversion from the exploding shells, but it gradually grew into something more meaning-ful, as if the fly's fate and Rogge's own were somehow linked together.

"Any other time, if I'd paid any attention to that fly at all, I probably would've just smashed it with my hand," Rogge said. "But instead I reached down and scooped it out of the water and threw it outside into the air. And I remember thinking: Okay, you little bastard, I guess you want to live as bad as I do, so just get the hell out of here."

Not long afterward, the shelling stopped. A few minutes later, when Rogge and the others heard about the surrender, he knew how the fly had felt when he set it free.

By early afternoon, Devereux and his party had slowly carried their sur-render message along the south leg of Wake proper all the way to the west-ern end of the main island. Another group of Japanese had taken Cunningham up the north leg of Wake to Peale, spreading the word and collecting prisoners as they went.

When he reached the narrow channel separating Wake proper from Wilkes Island, where he supposed the enemy had been in full control for hours, Devereux assumed his dispiriting mission to be at an end. He learned differently when his captors motioned him toward the boat dock and a launch tied up there.

"We must cross the channel and arrange the surrender of the other is-land," the more congenial of the two Japanese lieutenants told him.

Only then did Devereux comprehend how mistaken he'd been about the situation on Wilkes. Now, as he stared across the water, he realized that at least small pockets of defenders probably were still holding out on Wilkes. Another major concern was the dynamite-laden barge still anchored in the channel, and he felt the only intelligent thing to do was tell his captors about it. This delayed the actual crossing to Wilkes a little longer.

Meanwhile, Captain Platt and his Marines were still trying to work their way toward the boat channel—and still hoping to get back into the fight, utterly unaware that it had been called off hours before.

After searching every inch of their island and finding no live Japanese, other than the two they held prisoner, Platt's men did as much as possible to prepare for another wave of invaders. Platt had his captives' wounds bandaged, gave them some pineapple juice and hardtack, then tried to interrogate them, using mostly gestures and sign language. Their responses indicated no knowledge of any further landing attempts scheduled for Wilkes, but Platt wasn't convinced. All the enemy officers on Wilkes had been killed, and the captives were only enlisted men, who weren't likely to know what their commanders might be planning next. Platt believed a second landing was a distinct possibility.

At the same time, some of his men also urged Platt to cross the narrow boat channel between them and the main island to try to help their fellow Marines on Wake. "There were no boats on our side of the channel," recalled Artie Stocks, "but it was pretty narrow—only about sixty or seventy feet wide—and some of us could've swum over to Wake and gotten a boat in a pinch."

With his heavy guns battered and useless anyway, Platt ordered his men to move southeast and set up a defensive line among the craggy boulders that overlooked the beach on the west bank of the channel. From there, he figured they'd be positioned to meet a new wave of invaders head-on as they came ashore and to try to drive them back into the sea. And, if circumstances warranted, they'd also have a chance of crossing over to Wake and joining the action there.

While they attempted to make this move, however, the Wilkes garrison was harassed more or less constantly from before 8:00 A.M. until early afternoon by assault planes from the Japanese carriers. In an effort to keep the Zeroes and dive bombers away, the Marines replaced some of the Japanese flags they'd torn down. But by then, the low-level enemy planes had spotted the Americans concentrated near the old Japanese beachhead, and they kept coming back anyway. Even if all the flags had been left standing in the first place, enemy commanders likely would have realized that something had gone terribly amiss on Wilkes and that more manpower was needed to overcome the defenders there.

PFC Robert Stevens was killed by an enemy bomb during the persistent aerial attacks, becoming the ninth Marine to die on Wilkes that day and the last American casualty in the battle for Wake. Otherwise, the dozens of bombing and strafing runs by Japanese planes inflicted no casualties, but they laid waste to the already-damaged batteries on Wilkes and forced the defenders to stay under cover, drastically curtailing their attempts to redeploy.

No sooner had the planes broken off their attacks than Platt noticed several Japanese destroyers moving in dangerously close. One was no more than 2,000 yards offshore, and a couple of others were within 4,000 yards—virtually point-blank range for their heavy guns.

Platt got Lieutenant McAlister on the phone and told him to send a gun crew back to Battery L to try to open fire on the destroyers. But McAlister called back a few minutes later to report the battery's five-inchers were damaged beyond repair.

Fueled by adrenaline, a reserve of stamina, and pure athleticism that most individuals lack, the captain then raced on foot down to the three-inch batteries to check on their condition. Unfortunately, he found them wrecked and useless from the air attacks.

"Bring the men on back," he told McAlister when he returned. "We'll just have to fight 'em on the beach."

Because of the aerial drubbing they'd sustained, none of Platt's Marines had reached the channel by the time Devereux, Malleck, and about thirty Japanese climbed into the launch on the other side and started toward Wilkes. Devereux was sweating heavily from the afternoon heat, the accumulated pressures of the last sixteen days, and the six-hour ordeal he was now trying to complete. The newfound knowledge that the Marines on Wilkes were still holding out did nothing to ease the pain of what had to be done.

"This is Major Devereux," he shouted. "The island has been surrendered! Put down your arms!"

There was no sound or movement of any kind among the boulders and brush of Wilkes. It was a few minutes before 2:00 P.M. when the launch touched the opposite bank of the channel. The Japanese made sure that Devereux and Malleck stepped ashore well ahead of them.

Devereux yelled again: "The island has been surrendered! Don't try any monkey business!"

The major glanced around. The only visible signs of life were the Japanese ships lying close offshore and several enemy landing craft plowing toward the beach. Platt's suspicions had been well founded. The Japanese were, indeed, about to make a second landing—but this time the Marines on Wilkes would be in no condition to do anything about it. With Devereux and Malleck in the lead with the white flag, the group moved slowly along the beach. Obviously nervous, the Japanese lagged behind, fingering their rifles.

The nearest enemy destroyer opened fire abruptly. Devereux saw a flash of light, and a shell burst at the water's edge. Seconds later, a second shell struck the beach, nearer this time. The surrender party was obviously the target. The gunners on the destroyer had seen the launch crossing the channel, but they were too far away to notice the white flag.

Malleck and Devereux resisted the urge to hit the deck and continued walking straight ahead. Devereux glanced at the sword-swinging Japanese lieutenant, but neither he nor Malleck said a word. When the Japanese lieutenant ducked, so would they, but not until then, Devereux vowed.

"We kept walking," he said. "The third shell burst within fifty yards of us. I wanted to crawl into a hole. I'm sure Sergeant Malleck must've wished the same thing, but we kept walking. We were scared, but we couldn't show it before the Japs."

Finally, the Japanese lieutenant told everybody to take shelter and ordered a signalman to tell the destroyer to cease fire. When the destroyer got the message and complied, the surrender party moved on. At intervals, Devereux called out his cease-fire order again and strained his ears for a response above the ever-present roar of the surf.

Still nothing. From all outward signs, Wilkes was a ghost island, as uninhabited as it had been the day Lieutenant Charles Wilkes gave it his name and sailed away. Devereux could only wonder if the Americans and Japanese who struggled there had somehow killed each other off to the last man.

★

Captain Wesley Platt was mad as hell. He knew that more enemy troops would soon be splashing ashore, but because of the damned Japanese planes, his dog-tired troops still weren't in position to intercept them. His men were exhausted, hungry, hollow-eyed zombies, but he knew they were still capable of fighting and fighting well. After what they'd been through over the past eleven hours and the victory they'd won, Platt believed these guys could do anything.

He was checking the two .45 Colts at his belt when he heard a rifleman calling to him.

"Hey, Captain! Somebody's coming up the road!"

Platt frowned. It couldn't be the second wave of invaders, he thought. Not this soon. They hadn't had time to reach land yet.

"Okay," he yelled back. "Hold your positions and hold your fire until I can check this out."

Platt's men stood their ground, their rifles at the ready, as the captain slowly stepped out into the open and got his first look at the white flag and a large group of uniformed Japanese. He apparently didn't recognize Devereux at first, even after he heard the major shouting: "Lay down your arms! Lay down your arms! The island has been surrendered!"

"What's going on here?" Platt demanded.

"We've surrendered," Devereux said.

"Who the hell gave that order?" Platt howled.

"It's me, Major Devereux. Now lay down your arms! The island's been surrendered!"

No one knows for sure just how near Wesley Platt came to mutiny during the next few moments. In his later writings, Devereux sought to minimize the tensions that flared when he and his fire-eating young strongpoint commander confronted each other that afternoon. Among the several Marines who witnessed the face-off at close range, accounts of exactly what was said and done vary somewhat, but all agree that it came perilously close to the flash point.

Corporal John Johnson and his machine gun crew were moving forward when they came face to face with Devereux and the surrender party. Until that moment, Johnson had been sure he'd never live through his twentieth birthday, and he only hoped his death would be quick. The sight of Devereux threw him into something of a state of shock. Then, when he heard the major say the Americans had surrendered, the first thought that raced through his mind was: *Hey, maybe I'm not going to die today after all.*

Johnson, who kept a handwritten daily record of the battle that survived the war and still remains in his possession, was probably the closest man to Devereux during his face-off with Platt. Platt had one of his pistols raised in the air, and the Japanese behind Devereux froze in their tracks at the sight of it.

"Major, do you know what you're asking us to do?" Platt demanded.

"Yes, Trudy," Devereux said. "Tell your men to lay down their weapons. It's an honorable surrender."

For many of the same reasons that Platt's men would have followed him into hell, Devereux was extremely fond of the young captain, Johnson explained, and "Trudy" was a nickname he often used in talking with Platt. Devereux invariably addressed all other officers in the garrison by their ranks—lieutenant, captain, and so forth—but Platt was an exception to this rule.

As Platt stared tight-lipped at his commanding officer, others present, including PFC Artie Stocks, recall Platt fuming: "Marines don't surrender, Major. Let us die right here."

"I'm not asking you, I'm telling you," Stocks quoted Devereux as retorting. "This is an order. You *will* surrender."

An electric silence followed. Then, with tears streaming down his face, Platt slammed his .45 to the ground, and the impasse was over.

Reports have circulated that Platt demanded, and received, a half hour to allow his men to destroy their weapons, but Johnson denied any recollection of such a demand.

"As soon as Platt threw his pistol down, the Japanese surged forward with their bayonets and swarmed all over us," Johnson said. "I was trying to take the back plate off my machine gun to disable it when a Jap rushed up and started hacking at my hands with his bayonet. I pulled a grenade out of my pocket, and the Jap left in a hurry, but he came right back with an officer. After the officer nodded okay, I threw the grenade out toward the ocean."

Within a short time, several hundred fresh enemy troops landed on

Wilkes from the barges that Platt had been planning to attack. Their commander stared at the dead Japanese littering the coral and scowled at the Marines. Platt released the two wounded Japanese prisoners and watched his own men herded down to the boat channel for transportation to Wake proper.

"They made us take off our shirts and helmets," Johnson said, "but we were luckier than most of the men on the main island. The Japs made them strip down to their underwear."

Platt pointed to the desperately wounded PFC Wiley Sloman, who had been placed on a stretcher, and asked one of the enemy officers to let him be taken over to Wake for medical attention. Either the officer didn't understand or he pretended not to, but he gestured excitedly at the hand grenades still hanging from Sloman's belt and bulging in his shirt pockets.

Two Japanese soldiers ran toward Sloman and raised their rifles, but Lieutenant McAlister stepped in front of them.

"For Christ's sake, leave the man alone," McAlister said. "He can't hurt you. Can't you see he's practically dead?"

The officer said something to the two soldiers and pointed to the grenades. The soldiers approached Sloman nervously, and McAlister helped them remove the grenades from his clothes. Then the soldiers dumped Sloman off the stretcher and used it for one of the two wounded Japanese that Platt had taken prisoner.

As the group moved toward the boats, a pair of civilians lifted Sloman and carried him a short distance. But several Japanese shouted angrily and jabbed at the would-be good Samaritans with bayonets until they put Sloman down again and left him next to a mound of enemy corpses.

While the Japanese lined the rest of the Americans up just a few yards away from where Sloman was lying, Artie Stocks tried to stop and help his fallen friend, but enemy soldiers blocked his way with bayonets. As they hustled him into line, Stocks took a last look back at Sloman and felt a choking sensation in his throat. "Leaving Wiley lying there helpless was the hardest thing I ever had to do," he said.

In a daze, Sloman saw his mates being marched away. He opened his mouth to yell at them, but the paralysis had gotten worse, and he couldn't make a sound. He tried to pucker his lips and whistle, but that didn't work, either. As the other Marines moved beyond his field of vision, he drifted off again.

It was about 2:30 P.M. when the boats pulled up to the dock on the other side of the channel to discharge their captive cargo. The siege of Wake Island was over. The last shot had been fired in the first battle of the Pacific war. But for those Americans who lived through it, the longest, harshest fight for survival was yet to come.

"If I'd had any inkling of what kind of torture was ahead, I swear I'd have gone out fighting right there on Wilkes," Stocks said. "There's no question I'd rather have died than go through what we went through later."

Christmas Dinner
on Wake Island

DECEMBER 25, 1941

RELISHES	Burr Gherkins	Celery en Branche	
	Pearl Onions, Vinaigrette		
	Queen Olives	Sweet Cucumber Pickles	
APPETIZERS	Norwegian Pepper Fish	Chilled Tomato Juice	
	Hawaiian Fruit Cup		
SOUP	Cream of Chicken — Queen Margot		
FISH	Grilled Fillet of Sole — Sauce Tartare		
ENTREES	Roast Young Tom Turkey — Old-Fashioned Savory Dressing		
	Spiced Giblet Sauce		
	Baked Virginia Ham — Sauce Demi Glace		
VEGETABLES	Cranberry Sauce	Hot Pickled Peaches	
	Southern Yams — Franconia		
	English Garden Peas — au Beurre		
	Whipped Snowflake Potatoes		
SALAD	Iceberg Head Lettuce — Quartered Tomatoes		
DRESSINGS	Wake	Wilkes	Peais
DESSERTS	English Plum Pudding	Fresh Fruit Sherbet	
	Brandy Sauce	Wafers	
CHEESE	American	Swiss	Brick
	Pimento	Roquefort	

. . . . .

Fresh Fruit Basket   Nut and Raisin Cup

Holiday Candies   After-Dinner Mints

Demi-Tasse

*This souvenir menu of a sumptuous holiday
feast planned for Wake Islanders on December
25, 1941, describes a Christmas dinner that
was never eaten. By Christmas Day, 1941, all
Americans on Wake were held prisoner at
machine-gun point by the Japanese, and the
only nourishment most received
was a bowl of thin rice gruel.*
(Courtesy John Rogge)

☆ 16 ☆

The "Alamo of
the Pacific"

After the war, when Major Devereux had become Colonel Devereux, he recalled a young Marine from Texas who earned the nickname "Sam Houston" because of his outspoken comparisons of the Wake Islanders to the defenders of the Alamo, the legendary "cradle of Texas independence."

"This is another Alamo," the Texan would say proudly—and repeatedly—during the siege. "That's exactly what it is."

Devereux couldn't remember the man's real name, and his identity has been obscured by time. As this book was being written, only a handful of the two dozen Marines from Texas who served on Wake were still living, and none could identify this latter-day "Sam Houston." But the aptness of his comparison wasn't lost on his comrades—or on newspaper writers of the time. Even today, there are good reasons why its ninety-plus living American military survivors still sometimes refer to the Battle of Wake Island as the "Alamo of the Pacific."

Not since the original Battle of the Alamo in 1836 has such a small, ill-equipped band of defenders held off such overwhelmingly superior enemy forces for so long or made them pay so dearly for their eventual triumph. The only appreciable difference, according to an editorialist for the *Tulsa Tribune,* was that Wake's defenders held out two days longer than "Davey Crockett and his comrades of the Alamo."

Fittingly, World War II's first presidential unit citation—and the only one ever signed personally by President Franklin Roosevelt—was directed at the men of the Wake detachment of the First Marine Defense Battalion and VMF-211 of Marine Aircraft Group 21. The citation read in part:

> *The courageous conduct of the officers and men who defended Wake Island against an overwhelming superiority of enemy air, sea, and land attacks from December 8 to 22, 1941, has been noted with admiration by their fellow countrymen and the civilized world, and will not be forgotten so long as gallantry and heroism are respected and honored.*

At the time, few Americans would have argued with the truth of that statement. Like the Alamo, Bunker Hill, Little Big Horn, and a handful of other storied moments in the nation's military annals, Wake seemed destined to live forever in the public memory. Unfortunately, though, it didn't. If they should run across FDR's citation today, most Americans of the twenty-first century—particularly those under the age of fifty—probably wouldn't have the slightest notion what he was talking about.

On Christmas morning, December 25, 1941, newspaper readers in towns and cities all over America learned to their sorrow that Wake had finally fallen. It was a grim and dispiriting Christmas present, yet in a strangely bittersweet way, it was uplifting, too. A front-page headline in the *Dallas Morning News* managed to capture the conflicting emotions that welled in the hearts of Americans everywhere:

DOFF YOUR HATS, U.S.,
TO MARINES ON WAKE!
Fighting Huge Odds, 385 of Them
Give Japs Hell for Fourteen Days

Other newspapers served up similarly stirring tributes to the atoll's defenders as families observed a somber holiday. In the *Honolulu Advertiser,* the headline read:

**WAKE FALLS
AFTER GALLANT FIGHT
Two Enemy Warships
Sunk in Last Attack**

In Boise, hometown of many of the civilians trapped on Wake, the *Idaho Statesman* tried to convey a note of hopeful uncertainty to loved ones seeking the tiniest shred of information on their sons, brothers, husbands, and fathers, as evidenced by this page-one headline:

**Fate of Idaho Boys on Wake
Still Surrounded by Mystery**

Aboard the U.S.S. *Saratoga,* now heading back toward Pearl Harbor, the issue of the ship's mimeographed newspaper dated December 27 carried the following exhortation to the carrier's Marine detachment:

> It is quite fitting and proper that this detachment make a resolution, since New Year's Day isn't far away, to...take up as our warrior call, "Remember Wake!" That garrison served the motto of the Corps to the end. Nothing more can be expected, and, being Marines, nothing less can be expected of us. Texas had its Alamo, and now the Marines have their Wake. There is little we can do for those gallant men except bow our heads in remembrance and resolve to be "Semper Fidelis" ourselves...As the Great Emancipator said, "They shall not have died in vain."

Along with the disaster at Pearl Harbor, the example of Wake, and the outpouring of patriotic sentiment it inspired, generated a tremendous recruiting boom for the Marine Corps. From July through November 1941, an average of about 2,000 men per month joined up. But between December 7, 1941, and January 7, 1942, the Corps added more than 18,000 new recruits, including over 1,300 in just one day, bringing its strength to 85,000—twice its size as of mid-1940.

The Navy also benefited. In one mass swearing-in ceremony in Los Angeles, 385 young men formed a huge block W as ex–heavyweight boxing champ Gene Tunney administered their oath as Navy recruits. Photos of the ceremony appeared on newspaper front pages from coast to coast, and not one out of every thousand readers had to ask what the "W" stood for.

Today, the horror and disaster of Pearl Harbor continue to dominate our collective memory of those times, but, ironically, the tenacity and raw courage of Wake Island have all but disappeared from America's consciousness. Six decades after one of the most soul-stirring dramas in U.S. history, the "Alamo of the Pacific" is largely forgotten.

Militarily as well as psychologically, however, what happened at Wake was of major significance. While giving the home front something to cheer about and serving notice to the enemy that "pampered" Americans were no pushovers, it tied up a huge Japanese task force, diverting it from other targets and buying sorely needed time for crippled U.S. forces in the Pacific to regroup.

All America mourned Wake's loss, especially since many citizens mistakenly assumed from the tone of the news stories that, like the defenders of the Alamo, the entire U.S. garrison had been annihilated. "Whether any Marines are left there or whether they died to the last man is not known," said a Christmas Eve dispatch from the Associated Press.

The illusion that no Americans survived the battle was perpetuated by the hit film *Wake Island,* the first major wartime movie depicting Americans at war. With a cast headed by Brian Donlevy, William Bendix, Robert Preston, and MacDonald Carey, the picture was rushed into production within days after the atoll fell, with the avid cooperation of the Marine Corps. By the time this "virtual documentary" hit the nation's theaters in August 1942, the Navy Department was well aware that most of the Americans on Wake were prisoners of war. But Paramount Pictures was allowed to end the film by showing all the defenders dying at their guns.

In that respect, of course, Wake differed sharply from the Alamo or

Custer's last stand. The vast majority of the Wake Islanders did, indeed, survive—only to face forty-four months of brutality, slave labor, and starvation.

When Devereux and Sergeant Malleck completed their surrender rounds, they were kept separated from the rest of the garrison, along with Commander Cunningham, Commander Keene, Captain Platt, Lieutenant McAlister, and several other officers. Later that afternoon, the group was confined to one of two damaged but usable cottages that still stood on the north leg of Wake proper near Camp Two, where they generally received much less abusive treatment than the rest of the American prisoners.

First, though, the group was driven by truck to a makeshift Japanese headquarters that had been set up amid the carnage surrounding Lieutenant Hanna's three-inch gun emplacement. There they were given some canned raw fish—the first food any of them had had in more than twenty hours—and questioned for the first of many times by their captors.

As Devereux ate, the full realization of what had happened descended on him, leaving him feeling "dead inside," as he put it. He watched listlessly as Keene drew diagrams to show the Japanese where Wake's supplies of food and water were stored and tried to communicate various nonmilitary information to the landing force commander by writing on a notepad.

At one point, the Japanese commander abruptly interrupted Keene to write a question on the pad:

"Where are the women's quarters?"

"No women on island," Keene wrote in reply.

The interrogator frowned in disbelief.

Most members of the Japanese military considered Americans spiritually corrupt and addicted to an immoral, self-indulgent lifestyle, so they naturally assumed that prostitutes would be available for the defenders' amusement. And although they were surprised at the total absence of women on Wake, they found confirmation for their scorn toward comfort-loving American materialism when they sorted through what was left of Camp Two. Japanese news correspondent Toshio Miyake, who observed the battle from Admiral Kajioka's flagship, came ashore for a tour after the atoll was secured. When he was shown the former civilian barracks, he mistakenly assumed they were where Wake's Marines had been quartered. Miyake offered these disparaging observations:

> *I was amazed to see that they had brought in all the machinery for living purposes, even on a tiny island like Wake. . . . Electrical appliances to kill flies instantaneously on contact, electric razors, electrical machinery to repair shoes, and living was completely mechanized. . . . They seem ridiculous to the Japanese, who can endure hardships and privations. . . .*
>
> *Extravagance and hedonism are, as you know, a part of the American soldier, but I was astonished to see that every soldier had a crude woman's picture pinned on the walls when I went around the barracks. How can they fight the war with this kind of spirit? The annihilation of this type of people before long is most certain.*

Given their disdain for "decadent" Yanks, the conquerors of Wake may have been severely disappointed not to find a full-fledged red-light district, teeming with voluptuous women of ill repute. But they were likely even more confounded by the resilient, unyielding defiance of their captives.

"As a Marine, I bowed to no man," said PFC Artie Stocks. "Because of that, I got the hell beat out of me a lot while I was a prisoner, but the Japs never broke my spirit. I made up this little tune, and I'd sing it under my breath to express my feelings. It had very simple lyrics, just 'Hirohito is an asshole, Hirohito is an asshole, Hirohito is an asshole,' repeated over and over."

As Devereux sat dejectedly over his meager meal that afternoon, he saw a column of disheveled Marines approaching. Guarded by bayonet-wielding Japanese soldiers, they were a picture of defeat and despair as they marched head down toward the airfield. Most of the men were stripped down to their underwear, and some were limping barefoot on the coral. They were exhausted, hungry, and covered with dirt, and there was an air of total hopelessness about them.

But at the head of the column marched Sergeant Edwin "Peepsight"

Hassig, whose squared shoulders, barrel chest, and bristling mustache made him look like something straight off a recruiting poster, even in these circumstances. To Hassig, moping was almost as big a sin as cowardice under fire, and when he spotted Devereux watching from up ahead, he turned and shouted back at the shambling column.

"Snap outta this stuff!" he yelled. "Goddamn it, you're Marines!"

Moments later, when they passed where Devereux was sitting, every man in the column was marching in perfect cadence—"heads up and eyes front, stepping out like a regiment on parade," as the major described it.

"I felt pride at the sight of them marching by," he said, "and at the bewilderment on the faces of the Japanese officers standing with me. The Japanese never did understand. As they used to say, 'But you don't act like prisoners!'"

Corporal Frank Gross was among those marchers, and he felt pride, too. "It was a feeling I'll never forget," he said. "It made me realize that the Japs could kill us, but they couldn't break us unless we let them."

By late afternoon on December 23, all American military personnel who could move under their own power and most of the civilians on Wake—about 1,600 men in all—had been rounded up and herded to the airfield. The Japanese had bound many of their captives with the most convenient material they could find—the miles of exposed telephone wires lying in plain sight all over the atoll, which they cut in short lengths and used as rope. Many of the men were barefoot and had been forced to strip to their underwear. A few were left without a stitch of clothing.

"When the Japs took me prisoner, they tore all my clothes off," said PFC Ed Borne. "I was bare-ass naked, and I knew I was dead. It was the most humiliating time of my life."

The Japanese used an ingeniously cruel method of restraining their prisoners and rendering them physically helpless. First they tied the Americans' hands tightly behind them with telephone wire, then pulled their hands up high on their backs, attached another length of wire to their hands, and looped it around their necks. If a prisoner tried to free himself or loosen his bonds—or even allowed his arms to relax—he found himself choked by the wire around his neck.

Even the sick and ambulatory wounded in the hospital were dragged outside, trussed up with the others, and forced to kneel or squat on the rough coral of the airstrip in the blazing afternoon sun. They were formed into long rows with lines of loaded, manned machine guns facing them on two sides.

VMF-211's Lieutenant Kinney, hospitalized with severe dysentery and exhaustion, was among them. "In spite of the coral sand digging into my bare knees and the pain beginning to throb through my arms and shoulders, I had time to ponder the possible outcome of the Japanese victory on Wake," Kinney said. "One scenario that kept running through my mind was that they were going to line us up in nice straight lines, so they could kill at least three or four of us with a single bullet."

Army Sergeant Ernest Rogers had similar thoughts as he eyed the machine gun trained on him from a few yards away. "This is it," he told himself. "They're going to wait until they get us all down here in these big rows, and then they're going to take that thing and go up and down the row and wipe us all out."

These fears were based on much more than mere despair or pessimism. Despite the "honorable surrender" that Devereux had worked so hard to secure, there is ample evidence that the Japanese seriously contemplated the mass execution of all their prisoners. Doubtless many landing force soldiers and junior officers fully expected this to happen, just as the Americans did. From all indications, the rank-and-file Japanese troops were ready, even eager, to carry it out when the order came.

"You have one hour to live," a grinning enemy guard informed Sergeant Malleck, bearer of Devereux's white flag, at one point that afternoon.

And after Captain Platt's Marines from Wilkes were told by several English-speaking Japanese that the whole lot of them would soon be put to death, Platt directed a blunt question to one of their officers: "What are you going to do with us, General—shoot us?"

At the time, not even the highest-ranking Japanese officer at Wake knew the answer to Platt's question.

Because of the ferocity and determination of the American defense, and the staggering losses they'd inflicted on Admiral Kajioka's Wake Invasion Force, the enemy commander was uncertain what to do with his prisoners when word of the surrender first reached him. Kajioka was as shocked and surprised as most of the men now at his mercy by the capitulation of a U.S. garrison that remained highly combative and basically intact. Chances are, Kajioka had never heard of the Alamo, but he expected the Marines' dogged resistance to end only when the vast majority of them were dead.

According to evidence obtained after the war, Kajioka considered the chances of taking large numbers of prisoners so remote that he hadn't thought to ask his superiors in advance what to do in such a situation. Disposing of a few survivors would have been no problem, especially if no white flag had been raised. But killing 1,600 Americans in cold blood—three-fourths of them civilians—after they'd voluntarily laid down their arms and given themselves up was an entirely different matter. Kajioka refused to make the decision on his own and radioed his headquarters at Truk for instructions. After a lengthy delay, the reply came back: "You are authorized to take prisoners."

It was around 5:00 P.M. when Kajioka arrived at the Wake airstrip, riding in an American staff car and wearing a starched white uniform resplendent with medals and a sword. The admiral strode up to the khaki-clad landing force officer in charge, and the two of them were soon embroiled in a loud, angry shouting match that lasted for close to a quarter hour. When the argument ended, Kajioka stalked back to his car and roared away. The commander, his face plainly showing his displeasure, climbed atop an aircraft revetment and shouted a string of orders to his troops—orders he obviously disagreed with.

Only then were the Japanese machine guns uncocked and their cartridge belts removed. The Americans had been spared—at least for now.

A short time later, a Japanese interpreter arrived and unrolled a sheet of paper. With much posturing, he read the following proclamation:

Here it is proclaimed that the entire islands of Wake are now the property of the Great Empire of Japan.

PUBLIC NOTICE

The Great Empire of Japan who loves peace and respects justice has been obliged to take arms against the challenge of President Roosevelt. Therefore, in accordance with the peace loving spirit of the Great Empire of Japan, Japanese Imperial Navy will not inflict harms to those people though they have been our enemy—who do not hold hostility against us in any respect. So they be in peace!

But whoever violates our spirit or whoever are not obedient shall be severely punished by our martial law.

issued by The Headquarters of
the Japanese Imperial Navy

When he was through reading, the interpreter added: "The emperor has gracefully presented you with your lives."

For a long moment, there was only a stony silence from the captives lined up on the airstrip. Then, from somewhere out in that miserable throng, a hoarse but clearly audible voice replied: "Well, thank the son of a bitch for us."

While being stripped and bound, surrendering Americans were roughly and routinely relieved of their personal possessions by the Japanese troops, who helped themselves to watches, rings, and other valuables, then often threw the rest away. Even Commander Cunningham had his Naval Academy ring taken from him, and few Americans, officers or otherwise, were in a position to protest when the Japanese seized their valuables as "spoils of war."

One who did protest—with his fists—was VMF-211's Sergeant Robert Bourquin, whose rather cherubic features masked an impulsive combativeness that could flash like lightning. Bourquin had left home and joined the Marines after a row with his domineering father, and he'd made up his mind that nobody was ever going to bully him again.

When Bourquin and the rest of Lieutenant Kliewer's small demolition team dumped their weapons, raised their hands, and came out of their dugout near the airport in response to Devereux's surrender message, they were promptly shaken down like all the other American captives.

Among the first things that fell out of the sergeant's clothes was his treasured billfold-size photograph of his fiancée, Charlotte McLain, that he'd carried constantly since the last time he'd seen her. The moment he heard the Japanese ordering the prisoners to strip down to their under-wear and shoes, Bourquin shoved the picture under the waistband of his shorts, but when the officer yanked his shirttail out, the photo fell to the ground. Bourquin lunged forward, trying to pick it up, but he was re-strained by soldiers, and the officer beat him to it.

The Japanese glanced at the photo, then at Bourquin. "Your wife?" he asked in English.

She was only his fiancée at the time, but Bourquin lied and told him "yes."

The Japanese nodded and thrust the photo back under the waistband of Bourquin's shorts. "Okay, you keep," he said.

Seconds later, Bourquin's hands were tied behind him with telephone wire, and soon he was marched to the airfield and placed under guard with a group of about twenty other prisoners.

Japanese marines kept mounted machine guns trained on the Ameri-cans, and Bourquin counted four guards with bayonets watching each group of prisoners. But Bourquin, Sergeant Blandy, and Corporal Trego surreptitiously began working on each other's bonds, trying to free them-selves. Bourquin had just gotten his hands loose when the picture fell to the ground again.

This time, one of the Japanese guards grabbed the photo. He looked Bourquin tauntingly in the eye, then spat on the picture, threw it down, and stepped on it.

Something inside Bourquin snapped like a rubber band, and he totally lost control for a second. Without thinking of the consequences, he lashed out at the guard with both fists. The blows—plus the fact that Bourquin's hands were untied—caught the guard by surprise, but he recovered quickly, and he and the other guards rushed forward with their bayonets.

At that crucial moment, however, the Japanese officer who had returned the picture to Bourquin earlier materialized again and stepped in front of the guards. The officer slapped the man who had stepped on the picture and yelled at him and the others until they backed off. Then he handed the photo back to the impulsive young Marine and apologized. "I'm sure I owe him my life," Bourquin said.

For the next forty-four months, Bourquin kept the prized photo safely tucked inside his shoe. But that wasn't quite the end of the story.

"I'm still carrying that same picture today," he confided in 2002. "It's right here in my wallet, where it's been ever since 1945."

The first forty-eight hours of captivity were sheer hell for the Americans held at the airstrip. They endured two days of blistering sun and two nights of chill winds without shelter and with little or no protective clothing. They also got practically no food or water.

"When the Japs finally brought us some water, it was in fifty-gallon fuel drums that hadn't been washed out very well, and it still tasted like gasoline," said Corporal Frank Gross. "It made some of the guys sick, but we drank it anyway. God, we were dying of thirst."

Under heavy guard, some of the men were sent out on work or burial details. A party of about thirty Americans, including Captain Tharin, Gunner Hamas, and Devereux's former phone man, Corporal Robert Brown, were handed the gruesome task of burying a number of bodies that had been stored for days in a refrigerated reefer. During the fighting, it had been impossible to carry out the order to bury the dead where they fell. The refrigeration system had been knocked out by bombs, and now the bodies were badly decomposed.

Some of the men were so hungry that they paused amid the overpowering stench in the reefer to eat the only food they found there—several large jars of maraschino cherries. Years later, when the men were safely back in the States, the very thought of a maraschino cherry was still enough to make them gag.

The bodies from the reefer, along with others, were buried in a common grave not far from Lieutenant Hanna's three-inch gun position. A large, four-foot-deep trench was gouged out of the coral by hand, and the bodies were laid in it side by side, then covered with rubber ponchos before the trench was filled. After a brief prayer, the burial detail was marched back to the airstrip.

The Japanese made no allowances for Christmas. Devereux and the other officers confined in the cottage near Camp Two had a holiday meal of crackers and evaporated milk. The men languishing at the airstrip got only a few gallons of thin gruel made from boiled rice and water with, as one Marine put it, "most of the rice removed."

As the Americans consumed their scant portions, it was fortunate that none of them had ever seen the fancy souvenir menus detailing the lavish feast originally planned for the Wake Islanders on Christmas Day 1941. The ten-course menu was replete with such delicacies as grilled fillet of sole with sauce tartare, roast young turkey with savory dressing and cranberry sauce, baked Virginia ham with sauce demi glace, English plum pudding, fresh fruit sherbet, five varieties of cheeses, assorted fancy relishes, candies, and so on.

On December 7, the cargo vessel bound for Wake with this holiday bounty, along with a large box of the full-color menus, was alerted by radio of the attack on Pearl Harbor and diverted to Johnston Island, where the food was eventually eaten—and doubtlessly enjoyed—by other Americans. Those Wake Islanders who heard later about the "dinner that was never served," as the *Idaho Statesman* newspaper called it, agreed it was just as well that they didn't know about it on that grim Christmas Day.

That afternoon, however, the suffering Americans did receive a gift of sorts from their captors. Several vehicles appeared at the airstrip, piled with articles of discarded clothing, collected around the main island at points where civilians and Marines had been forced to strip two days before.

The Japanese haphazardly tossed out shirts and pairs of pants to the prisoners, but virtually no one got his own clothes back. Civilian Glenn Newell, whose prewar job on a plumbing crew had given way during the siege to filling sandbags and digging revetments, was luckier than most. The man who ended up with Newell's trousers later returned his billfold, still containing fourteen dollars that had been in it when Newell was forced to strip.

That evening, probably in response to a letter from Devereux to the Japanese commander, protesting the treatment of American noncoms and civilians, the prisoners were finally moved from the airfield to the barracks at Camp Two. Virtually all the buildings there had been damaged by enemy air attacks, but they at least provided a measure of shelter from the elements and a respite from the jagged coral.

Once this transfer was made, the Japanese began allowing civilian cooks to prepare at least two meals a day for the rest of the prisoners. It was simple fare—hot cereal in the morning, beans or meat stew at noon, supplemented by a little bread and jam in the evening.

As they bedded down that night, some Marines still clung to a desperate hope. The most treasured Yuletide gift of all would have been the arrival of the U.S. rescue fleet promised for December 25. It hadn't come, of course, but they tried to tell themselves, even now, that an American task force could still be steaming toward them, that salvation was still possible.

When a few diehard optimists heard gunfire at sea the day after Christmas, they thought their prayers had been answered.

"This is it!" someone yelled. "Those are our ships out there!"

But it was only the Japanese trying out some new artillery. After that, even the diehards gave up. No help was coming. Wake's defenders had been abandoned to their fate—whatever it might be.

This obviously staged photo of smiling American POWs from Wake on their arrival at Yokohama after their harrowing voyage aboard the Nitta Maru *originally appeared in a Japanese propaganda magazine called* Freedom. *Seated in the center of the group are civilian construction chief Dan Teters and Navy Commander W. Scott Cunningham, commandant of the Wake Garrison. Note the Japanese guard holding a billy club.*
(Courtesy Artie Stocks)

✵ 17 ✵

The Terrible Voyage of
the Nitta Maru

No sooner was one fearsome struggle for survival over than another one began. The battle for Wake had seemed endless while it overshadowed their lives, but the defenders would look back on the sixteen days of warfare as a mere blink of the eye compared to what came next. As fearsome as the bursting bombs, whining tracer bullets, and banzai bayonet charges had been, the ordeal that started when they became prisoners of war would be even more debilitating, dehumanizing, and unbearable.

Worst of all, it would last almost a hundred times longer than the siege. When it finally ended, those who were strong enough, stubborn enough, or lucky enough to live through it would be nearly four years older and forever changed by the experience.

Although it was only the beginning of their ordeal, the misery suffered by the American prisoners between the surrender on December 23 and the evening of Christmas Day, their first two days of captivity, is hard to exaggerate. Except for a couple of dozen officers, the rest of the almost 1,600 military and civilian survivors of the battle were kept squatting on the runway at the airfield, blistered by the sun in the daytime and soaked by rain at night. They had minimal protective clothing—most of it worn by someone other than the original owner—no sanitary facilities, and almost no food or water. But even these conditions were a relief for the more than one hundred prisoners who had spent their first hours of captivity trussed up with telephone wire and packed so tightly into one of the hospital bunkers that sick men vomited on each other and others came close to suffocating.

Scores who had received minor to moderate wounds during the fighting and a few with more serious injuries received no medical attention during this interval, and the Japanese generally ignored their plight. At considerable risk to himself, Gunner John Hamas approached a Japanese officer and managed to convince him to let Lieutenant Kahn, the Navy doctor, attend to those in the worst condition, although Kahn had next to nothing to work with.

During the two and a half weeks after the prisoners were moved from the airfield into the damaged barracks at Camp Two, their living conditions improved markedly. They weren't allowed to talk or move around, and they remained under the constant watch of guards with fixed bayonets, but they were protected from the elements, provided with adequate food and water, and basically left alone. It was only a temporary respite, however, before the ordeal that lay ahead.

On January 11, 1942, a former Japanese passenger liner, the *Nitta Maru*, arrived at Wake. The ship had once carried carefree tourists on Pacific pleasure cruises, but it had been stripped of its luxurious appointments and converted into a floating prison as forbidding and inhumane as the black hole of Calcutta.

About noon the next day, January 12, Japanese guards informed the prisoners that they were being transferred to a "safer place" and that they had exactly one hour to prepare for departure. Each man would be allowed to take along only one small bundle of personal possessions—a restriction that didn't bother most of the men since they had nothing left but what they were wearing. But a few tried to hide items under their clothes.

Corporal Cyrus Fish, one of the stalwarts of Lieutenant Poindexter's counterattack on Wake proper, had found approximately 10,000 U.S. first-class postage stamps—with a cash value of $300—in a building at Camp Two, and he was determined to try to keep them. Fish showed them to Corporal Frank Gross, who urged him to bury them under one of the barracks, but Fish insisted on trying to smuggle them aboard the *Nitta Maru*. Gross couldn't understand what good Fish thought this contraband was going to do him in a Japanese prison camp, but it didn't matter. The stamps started falling out of his shirt before Fish even got on the ship, and all he got for his trouble was some extra kicks from the guards.

About 1,150 Wake Islanders—both civilians and military enlisted men— would be crammed into the ship's barren cargo hold. The only furnishings were a little straw ticking for bedding and a few five-gallon buckets for sanitary facilities. There was no heat whatsoever as they headed into a colder climate, and barely enough room for each man to huddle in one spot. Here the prisoners would endure the most excruciating experience of their lives as the ship transported them to a prison camp near Shanghai, China.

The journey aboard the *Nitta Maru* would take twelve days, but for the men who experienced it, it seemed like a lifetime. Almost without exception those who survived the trip would remember it as the most terrible period of their lives.

The organized brutality began for the prisoners as they boarded the ship. They were shoved into cargo nets, hoisted up to the main deck, then forced to run a gauntlet of kicking, club-swinging Japanese sailors en route to the steel ladders leading to the hold.

Commander Cunningham, Major Devereux, and twenty-eight other American officers were herded into less crowded, more comfortable quarters in what had been the ship's mail room. Although no heat was supplied there, either, the space was directly above the engine room and remained much warmer than the hold. But they, too, had to make their way past the punitive Japanese "welcoming committee."

Cunningham, who thought that as Wake's "number-one" officer he might be able to take more than the allotted one bundle of clothing aboard, was picking up one of his bundles when a Japanese sailor struck him and tore it out of his hands. The hostile move was like a signal to the rest of the double line of sailors, who lashed out against Cunningham and the other American officers with a barrage of kicks, blows, and slaps as they ran the gauntlet.

The enlisted men got even rougher treatment. "They made us jump onto the ship, and if we didn't move fast enough to suit them, they beat the living hell out of us," PFC Artie Stocks remembered. "Then they beat us again on our way to the hold. When we got down there, most of us had to stand up because there was no room to sit."

"We were piled on a steel floor like sticks of cordwood," said PFC John Dale of Battery L. "Making the slightest sound or movement was enough to get you kicked or beaten."

Posted in the prisoners' quarters immediately before their scheduled embarkation and later on the *Nitta Maru* itself were crudely typed notices that read:

Commander of the Prison Escort
Navy of the Great Japanese Empire

REGULATIONS FOR PRISONERS

1. *The prisoners disobeying the following orders will be punished by immediate death.*
   a. *Those disobeying order and instructions.*
   b. *Those showing a motion of antagonism and raising a sign of opposition.*
   c. *Those disordering the regulations by individualism, egoism, thinking only about yourself, rushing for your own goods.*
   d. *Those talking without permission and raising loud voices.*
   e. *Those walking and moving without order.*
   f. *Those carrying unnecessary baggage in embarking.*
   g. *Those resisting mutually.*
   h. *Those touching the boat's materials, wires, electric lights, tools, switches, etc.*
   i. *Those climbing ladder without order.*
   j. *Those showing action of running away from the room or boat.*
   k. *Those trying to take more meal than given to them.*
   l. *Those using more than two blankets.*

Following these twelve "capital crimes" was a lengthy set of instructions, which ended on this reassuring note:

Navy of the Great Japanese Empire will not try to punish you all with death. Those obeying all the rules and regulations, and believing the action and purpose of the Japanese Navy, cooperating with Japan in constructing the "New order of the Great Asia" which lead to the world's peace will be well treated.

The wording of the notice put the Americans in a dark, apprehensive mood even before they had to run the gauntlet.

"These Jap bastards have us by the short hair on a downhill pull," Sergeant Robert Bourquin noted in his journal entry for January 11. "I pray to God that I will live thru all this to go home someday. We are getting enough to eat now, but I know that the worst is yet to come. I found two jars of cheese that I will eat before going on the ship. Our spirits hit rock bottom after reading this Jap proclamation, especially the part about 'punish you all with death'..."

The first leg of the POWs' trip to "destination unknown," as Bourquin put it, ended in Yokohama on January 18. By the time the *Nitta Maru* docked there, all the Americans aboard had been introduced to the Japanese practice known as *bushido*. Although it seemed little more than orchestrated savagery to the Americans, it was a time-honored system in the Japanese military designed to initiate those who suffered through it to the "way of the warrior." At the heart of *bushido* was a pecking order in which Japanese officers and higher-ranking noncoms used physical punishment to discipline and indoctrinate their own subordinates. It was employed in a particularly merciless fashion against the helpless POWs from Wake Island in order to teach them humility and cooperation.

The Japanese soldiers and seamen who now controlled every aspect of the Americans' lives had been trained to hold their prisoners in utter contempt. And, paradoxically, their disdain toward foes who surrendered, rather than fighting to the death, was more than matched by their fury over the heavy toll inflicted on their comrades at Wake.

"You will be treated worse than a Japanese soldier," the prisoners were told by a Japanese army colonel, "because you have no honor."

The colonel's warning was prophetic. Virtually every prisoner aboard the *Nitta Maru* was either a personal victim of *bushido* or an eyewitness to its inhumanity. In addition to the regular crew, about fifty prisoner guards were assigned to the ship. They were specially trained in judo, and their commander, Lieutenant Toshio Saito, was fond of polishing his martial arts skills on the defenseless captives.

"Saito liked to come down in the hold and practice judo on the prisoners," said Artie Stocks. "If you cried out in pain, he'd just keep hitting you again and again. I still have nightmares about him."

Keeping prisoners half starved was a standard *bushido* procedure. Twice a day, POWs were served a bowl of thin gruel called *kanji*, which contained a little rice but was about 95 percent water. With the afternoon bowl, prisoners might also get a morsel of canned fish, an olive, or a slice of radish. Cunningham described the rations as "so scanty that we would hardly have been worse off with none at all." It was no exaggeration. Many prisoners reported going two weeks or more during and after the voyage without a bowel movement.

Neglect was also an integral part of the regimen. Captain Freuler, who took two bullets in his shoulder during his final flight for VMF-211, had received only cursory treatment for the wounds, which grew steadily more inflamed as the voyage progressed. Despite repeated pleas for medical attention from other officers, the Japanese ignored Freuler's condition until, as Cunningham expressed it, "an evil odor from the infections became noticeable even to the guards." Finally, the *bushido* policy was relaxed enough to allow Freuler to get his wounds cleaned and dressed.

Higher rank offered no protection from injury or indignity. Devereux himself was slapped soundly across the face when he leaned toward a Japanese officer to point out something on papers he was carrying, and Captain Platt, leader of the heroic victory on Wilkes, was severely beaten with a heavy club for whispering without permission.

Platt took his pounding from a bull-like guard without uttering a sound. When he was shoved back into the compartment with the other American officers, he managed to grin through bloodied lips.

"Twarn't nuthin," he muttered defiantly. But to those who witnessed the incident, even the irrepressible Platt seemed shaken by its viciousness.

★

After about a week at sea, the *Nitta Maru* docked in Yokohama harbor and remained there for two days, during which time the captured Americans were put on display for propaganda purposes. Japanese reporters and photographers swarmed around the prisoners, conducting carefully monitored interviews and taking staged pictures.

One particular photo, published in a Japanese English-language propaganda organ called *Freedom,* showed Cunningham and civilian boss Dan Teters seated in front of Lieutenant Kahn, the Navy doctor, and other POWs, all of them smiling broadly. A dead giveaway to the forced nature of the smiles was a grinning Japanese guard, standing just to Cunningham's left with a billy club tucked under his arm.

"Our captors seemed anxious to have the outside world believe they treated their prisoners well," Cunningham said. "On the other hand, they were equally anxious to convince their own people that they didn't treat us well."

After the war, Cunningham came across a transcript of a radio announcement of the Wake Islanders' arrival in Japan that was beamed to Japanese armed forces around the South Pacific. It included these sly, tongue-in-cheek comments, which undoubtedly drew a lot of laughs from the listeners:

"American prisoners of war arrived from Wake Island in Yokohama yesterday. They had a very sad expression on their faces, but they were admiring the *bushido* treatment they received on the boat from the Japanese. . . . During their voyage, they displayed their typical American individualism, but the Japanese trained them to be more cooperative. On the boat, the Japanese exerted every effort to thresh out American individualism. Now they are very cooperative with the Japanese."

During the stopover, Cunningham and several other Americans were invited to make recordings to be sent back home. They accepted the opportunity, since it at least offered some chance of letting their loved ones know they were alive. But they avoided any mention of their brutal treatment for fear the recordings would be thrown away.

In his recorded message, civilian Hudson Sutherland of Portland, Oregon, tried to walk a verbal tightrope between fact and fiction. "So far we have been treated fine," he said, "I think."

About thirty of the POWs were detained in Yokohama for questioning. They included Commander Keene, Major Putnam, and a number of officers and men who were either connected with military communications or had seen recent service with the U.S. Pacific Fleet.

When the ship put out to sea, the news that these detainees were no longer aboard triggered both apprehension and relief among the other POWs. Many preferred the idea of being confined in China to being held in Japan, if only because China was closer to Japan's enemies.

The men left behind in Yokohama were later taken to a prison camp at Zentsuji on the Japanese island of Shikoku. Once there, they generally fared no worse—and perhaps even somewhat better—than the rest of their shipmates, who went on to a grim compound near Woosung, a few miles down the Whangpoo River from Shanghai.

On January 20, 1942, the *Nitta Maru* set sail on the final leg of her voyage.

The first hint that something ominous was afoot came even before the ship left Yokohama, when several prisoners were taken out of the hold under heavy guard and hustled topside for questioning. Two of the men— Seaman First Class John W. Lambert and Seaman Second Class Roy J. Gonzales—were close friends of Navy Yeoman Glenn Tripp, Cunningham's former office aide, who occupied the space next to them when they were dragged away.

When the pair were returned to the hold a couple of hours later, they were excited and frightened. They told Tripp their interrogators had accused them of lying when questioned about their naval experience.

"They said they were going to punish us," the two sailors whispered, "but they didn't say how."

"These were young lads not long out of boot camp," Tripp recalled, "and when the Japs gave out questionnaires to all of us about what we'd been doing on Wake Island, I advised them to say they were cooks. But they both put down the truth—that they'd been to machinist's school and were assigned to the staff of the naval air station on Wake. That may have been what got them in trouble."

Some time later, the guards reappeared. They again ordered Lambert and Gonzales topside, but this time they instructed them to bring all their belongings with them.

"The guards told them, 'You won't be needing those things anymore,'" Tripp said. "I never saw either of them again."

Two days out of Yokohama, Lambert and Gonzales were marched out onto B Deck of the *Nitta Maru*, along with three other POWs—Seaman Second Class Theodore D. Franklin, Marine Master Sergeant Earl Raymond Hannum, and Technical Sergeant William Bailey.

Standing before them with a drawn sword was Lieutenant Saito, commander of the guards, who was in full charge of the proceedings and clearly enjoying them. Facing the prisoners in a semicircle were approximately 150 Japanese servicemen. Later, in testimony before the Allied War Crimes Commission, a member of the ship's crew described what happened next:

"Saito took a piece of paper from his pocket.... In his right hand, he also held his sword. I recall the following message was read by Saito to the five prisoners in front of him in Japanese and was substantially as follows:

"'You have killed many Japanese soldiers in battle. For what you have done, you are now going to be killed—for revenge. You are here as representatives of your American soldiers and will be killed. You can now pray to be happy in the next world—in heaven.'"

Although the Americans were undoubtedly fearing the worst by this time, they were apparently unaware of what was about to happen. "It is my personal belief that the five Americans did not know they were to be executed," the Japanese eyewitness said. "They were not advised of the contents of the death warrant as read to them in Japanese."

The victims were blindfolded, and their hands were tied behind them. They were forced to kneel on the deck, then methodically beheaded, one by one.

"[O]f the five victims, two of them had their heads completely cut from their bodies," the Japanese observer said. "Their heads rolled to one side. Three of the victims were not totally decapitated.... As the blade hit and pierced the flesh, it gave a resounding noise like a wet towel being flipped or shaken out."

After the men were dead, their bodies were used for bayonet practice, according to the crewman's testimony. Finally, the mutilated remains were thrown overboard.

The barbarism of this spectacle sickened many of the Japanese who witnessed it. "After it was all over, a Japanese warrant officer came down and told us about it," Tripp remembered. "He said he'd been made to watch and almost forced to participate in the executions, and he was nearly as shook up about the whole thing as we were."

For the bloodbath he directed, the War Crimes Commission tried after the war to find Saito and put him on trial for his life. But when he learned that U.S. authorities were on his trail, the self-appointed executioner vanished and never surfaced again. Four other participants in the beheadings received life sentences but were paroled after serving only about nine years. A fifth was acquitted.

Even today, it's never been explained how or why these particular five victims—all enlisted men or noncoms with nothing unusual in their backgrounds—happened to be singled out as objects for Saito's grisly revenge. Cunningham later wondered why he, as Wake's acknowledged "number one," wasn't at the top of the death list, or why other high-ranking officers weren't included. Possibly only Saito himself knew the answer.

The hand-picked victims shared few common characteristics, but one clue may lie in the fact that all five were involved in some aspect of military aviation, as members of VMF-211 or the naval air station staff.

Back on Wake, meanwhile, a strikingly different kind of story was unfolding—a story of compassion and human kindness that stands in sharp contrast to the horror on the *Nitta Maru*.

Left behind when the prison ship sailed were approximately 380 Americans. The vast majority of these were civilian contractors, who were kept on the atoll to repair damaged U.S. facilities and build new ones for Japanese use.

Twenty of the remaining Americans, however, were sick or wounded military personnel whose condition was too serious to allow them to be moved for the time being. Among them were Lieutenant Henry G. "Spider" Webb, severely wounded as he tried to reach his plane on December 8, then wounded again when enemy bombs struck the hospital; Corporal Ralph Holewinski, one of the heroes from Lieutenant Hanna's gun, suffering multiple bullet and shrapnel wounds; Seaman First Class James B. "Dick" Darden, whose leg was mangled by a fragmentation bomb at the airfield on December 8; and Sergeant Walter T. "Tom" Kennedy of VMF-211, suffering arm and leg wounds from the same bombing.

The list also included Sergeants Edwin Ackley, Andy Paskiewicz, Glen Gardner, Ellis Johnson, and Jesse Stewart of VMF-211, all hurt in the December 8 raid; Army Captain Henry Wilson, ailing with severe dysentery; Navy men Jim Hesson, Bill McCoy, and I. S. Wood; and six members of the Marine Defense Battalion—PFCs Berdyne Boyd, Warren Conner, Dick Reed, and Charles Tramposh; Corporal L. L. Johnston; and Sergeant Alvin Bumgarner.

As the heat of battle cooled, the invaders showed far greater concern and consideration for the wounded American servicemen than they had early on. They allowed them to be placed in the Japanese hospital, which was much better equipped than the Marines' makeshift facility, and actual friendships developed between some of the foes who had fought so bitterly against each other.

"When they found out there was a wounded American flier in our group, several of the Japanese pilots stationed on Wake came over to the hospital to visit Spider Webb," recalled Tom Kennedy. "Sometimes they'd bring a bottle of sake with them, and they'd lift up Spider's head and give him a snort. It was all very congenial."

The last American patient to be brought to the hospital—and the one closest to death when he arrived—was Wiley Sloman. At the time he was found on Wilkes, Sloman had had no food or water for four days or more. His horrendous head wound was flyblown, and blood and drainage oozed constantly from it. His brain was swollen and embedded with splinters of bone from his shattered skull. Nobody who saw him when they carried him in would have given a plugged nickel for his chances.

Once Sloman reached the hospital, Dr. Lawton Shank, the civilian physician, cleaned the wound as well as he could. Sloman was told later that Shank also picked maggots out of his head, but the wounded Marine was too sick to notice at the time.

Shank realized that the bone fragments in Sloman's brain could cause major problems, but he was reluctant to try to remove them for fear of aggravating the damage. All he could do was give Sloman some aspirin. That was the only painkiller available, except for strong narcotics that would have turned the patient into a hopeless addict within days. The pain was excruciating and endless, but Sloman felt hungry, and he was determined to try to eat something.

"The Japs brought me some seaweed and stuff, but I couldn't get it down," Sloman said. "The next morning, I woke up and saw a Japanese doctor standing over me. 'I understand you don't like our food,' he said. 'I'll see what I can do to get you something that will taste better.'"

A short time later, an American civilian cook showed up and asked what Sloman wanted to eat. "Soft-boiled eggs, toast, and milk," the wounded man muttered. A few minutes later, that's exactly what he got.

Sloman's brief meeting that day with Sub-Lieutenant Shigeyoshi Ozeki, the Japanese navy surgeon who intervened on his behalf, may well have saved the young Marine's life. Ozeki had landed on Wake with the landing force's hard-hit Uchida Company and narrowly escaped the carnage in and around *Patrol Boat No. 33*. Now he became an instrument of survival for a man who doubtless would have killed him on sight a few days earlier.

"Dr. Ozeki let this cook make special food for me every day, and I gradually got stronger," Sloman said. "There were no antibiotics then—and not much medicine of any kind, for that matter. So I have to credit Dr. Ozeki, and the good nutrition he made possible, with saving my life."

Ozeki himself saw nothing unusual in his willingness to try to help Sloman. Showing kindness toward wounded Americans was a "common practice" among many Japanese on Wake, he maintained many years later. "The fact is that our corpsmen treated wounded American soldiers as kindly as they treated Japanese wounded soldiers, following my instructions," Ozeki said. "I was more than strict about such fair treatment. Whenever I found Japanese soldiers behaving outrageously, I gave them a sharp verbal rebuke on the spot. I never used violence on any soldiers, Japanese or American."

While Sloman probably derived the greatest benefit of anyone from Ozeki's presence, other hospitalized Americans also remember his kindness. "Dr. Ozeki visited us in the hospital two or three times a week and brought us whatever he could in the way of medicine and medical supplies," said Sergeant Tom Kennedy.

Most of the day-to-day care for the Americans, however, was left up to Dr. Shank. "Dr. Ozeki probably changed my dressings once or twice," Sloman said, "but the rest of the time, it was Dr. Shank who took care of me. The drainage from the wound caused my hair to get all matted and made it hard to keep the wound clean. It was a terrible mess, and it also stunk like hell, so when somebody found some hand clippers, Dr. Shank used them to cut off all my hair."

Noticing Sloman's newly shorn head, a male nurse located a bottle of pomade and applied some to the patient's scalp. A little while later, Shank walked past Sloman's bed.

"Well, you're looking mighty dapper, Slick," he remarked lightly without breaking stride.

"From that moment on, I had a new nickname," Sloman said. "Pretty soon, everybody was calling me that."

By early January, it was increasingly apparent that "Slick" Sloman was going to live, but how fully he might recover from his wound remained a huge question mark. Even as his overall physical condition improved, the pain in his head grew more and more intense. A noticeable crease developed along the entire right side of his skull, and there was no way to gauge the extent of damage to his brain or how permanent it might be. His left side was still totally paralyzed.

"The headaches were terrible, and aspirin didn't faze them," Sloman said. "They went on for so long that I can't clearly remember when they stopped, but I'd say it took a good two years before they went away completely."

To focus his mind on something besides his pain, Sloman started giving himself a crude form of physical therapy. "Initially, I had no use at all of my left arm and left leg," he said. "I'd stand in a doorway and start swinging my left arm with my right one. At first, it was just like a dead weight hanging there, but after a while I found that once I got it moving, I could keep it going. Then I'd do the same thing with my left leg."

After six weeks, Sloman had taught himself how to walk again, although he still dragged his left foot. His arm was slower to respond, but he kept exercising it as long and as often as possible. Dr. Shank put him on the chow detail, getting food for the other patients, so that Sloman had to walk all the way to the galley and back a couple of times a day. "I'm sure he did it on purpose to give me more exercise," Sloman said.

Meanwhile, other patients also struggled to overcome their festering wounds and regain their strength. Although both his injured legs were stiffly splinted and it was extremely hard for him to move, Corporal Ralph Holewinski managed to scrounge his own hard-to-find bandages. He changed the dressings regularly and boiled the used ones so that they could be reused. While they boiled, he read a rumpled copy of *The Grapes of Wrath* that someone had dug out of the remains of Camp One and tried to concentrate on the plight of the characters fleeing the Oklahoma "Dust Bowl" to keep from thinking about his own agony.

"I made up my mind I wasn't going to die of gangrene if I could help it," he said.

Above left: *PFC Artie Stocks on his way back to the States from POW camp.*
(Courtesy Artie Stocks)

Above right: *This letter written by PFC Artie Stocks from a Japanese prison camp in China was one of the few to reach their intended recipient in the States. None of the letters written to Stocks by his father were ever delivered.*
(Courtesy Artie Stocks)

✷ 18 ✷

POWs—The Longest,
Toughest Fight

The *Nitta Maru* docked at Japanese-held Shanghai on January 23, 1942, exactly one month after the fall of Wake. By that time, word of the executions and rumors of other horrors that might lie ahead had filtered down into the hold and circulated among the POWs. Consequently, reports that the Japanese were planning a "nice little outing" for the prisoners on their arrival in China were greeted with nervousness and apprehension.

Word had circulated that the Japanese planned to parade the Americans through the streets of Shanghai for the "edification" of the city's diverse population of Chinese and numerous other nationalities. Cold, rainy weather apparently caused the Japanese to change their minds, and the POWs were at least spared that indignity.

Instead, the ship sailed on downriver to the port of Woosung, where the POWs arrived the following day—and were subjected to a final dose of *bushido* as they disembarked. A long, frenzied line of Japanese sailors was eager for a final crack at the Americans before they turned them over to the army. "I remember one of our tormentors especially," said Commander Cunningham, "a buck-toothed man who ran up and down the lines of prisoners, dealing out blows with a club and literally frothing at the mouth."

What clothes the Wake Islanders had were lightweight garments designed for tropical climates and hardly suited for the bitter midwinter temperatures in China. Although the hold of the *Nitta Maru* had been damp and frigid, the body heat from hundreds of men crowded into a small space had at least helped break the chill. But there was no buffer against the outside cold as the shivering, teeth-chattering Americans trudged toward their prison compound with the mercury hovering around freezing. The march was only about five miles, but it was an ordeal for the prisoners, who were exhausted and weak from hunger after twelve days of starvation rations and close confinement. A number of the men were wearing shoes that were either too large or too small for them, and their feet were raw and blistered by the time they reached their destination.

"The only clothes I had were a T-shirt, a pair of pants, and my shoes," said PFC Jack Hearn. "I wasn't much more than an icicle by the time we got to the camp."

On the positive side, the prisoners received their first substantial food in almost two weeks. "When we got to the camp, they gave each of us some stew and a small loaf of bread," said civilian Ed Doyle. "That was one of the best meals we had the whole time we were there."

The POWs' new home was a grim collection of seven unheated, unpainted wooden barracks surrounded by electrified barbed wire in the midst of a barren wasteland that had once been a military outpost. A small number of Americans and Britishers captured in China were already quartered there. Two hundred men were packed into each of the long, narrow structures, where they slept on thin straw ticks on crude wooden platforms eighteen inches from the floor.

The camp had been built hurriedly several years earlier to house an infantry battalion of the Japanese army, but as soon as more comfortable quarters could be arranged, it was abandoned. It had been standing vacant for some time, and the barracks, drafty and poorly constructed in the first place, were dingy and dilapidated. They were also totally without heat and furnished only with the sleeping platforms and a few shelves. However, the accommodations at Woosung, formally known as the Shanghai War Prisoners Camp, were considerably better than those in most other Japanese military prisons. The Japanese were actually proud enough of the camp to make it a sort of "showcase" for observers from the International Red

Cross. But to most American POWs, it wasn't a fit place to keep animals, much less human beings.

"Each barracks was divided into sections so that we only had about two feet per man of sleeping space," said civilian Glenn Newell, whose brother, Emmett, was also a prisoner. "A lot of us were about to freeze to death when they issued us some Jap clothes. I remember one of our biggest guys, Bill Okle from L.A., stood about six foot seven, and they gave him this little tiny coat that he couldn't begin to button. One little Japanese guard, who was barely four feet tall, enjoyed picking on Bill. He'd climb up on a stool and slap Bill across the face and yell, 'Button coat! Button coat!' But, of course, there was no way Bill could do it."

During that first interminable winter, overcrowding was the least of the prisoners' problems. They pooled their meager supply of blankets and slept four to a bunk to keep from freezing. The cold was among their bitterest hardships, and its ill effects were increased because they never had enough to eat. The winters in that part of China were comparable to those in the U.S. Midwest, and the cold was severe for about four months out of the year, but temperatures were much more comfortable during the spring, summer, and fall. By contrast, American and British POWs held in camps in the tropics suffered from the hot, steamy weather the year round—as well as the diseases associated with it.

Civilian Ed Doyle, a happy-go-lucky youngster from Boise, whose grandfather had helped build dams for Morrison-Knudsen Company, had been among one of the earlier contingents of CPNAB employees to arrive on Wake in April 1941. Ed's glowing letters about how much fun he was having there driving a dump truck and "wrestling sharks" had enticed his brother, Bob, to follow three months later. Now, as POWs at Woosung, they both found themselves shivering in the same frigid barracks, and Bob seldom missed a chance to remind Ed that he was to blame for their predicament. Meanwhile, though, the brothers clung resolutely to their sense of humor, as well as their Yankee ingenuity.

"Our second winter at Woosung, the Red Cross gave us a couple of stoves for our barracks, but we had nothing to burn in them, except what we could scrounge," recalled Ed. "We picked up scraps of wood and hid them under our clothes, and we mixed coal dust and mud into balls that would burn. We even tore pieces off the barracks themselves to use as fuel. Then the Japs found a cache of wood we were hiding under the floor in Bob's section, so they confiscated the wood and the stoves, too."

As punishment, several men from the offending barracks had sections of stove pipe hung around their necks and were made to parade around outside carrying signs scrawled in pidgin English that said: "We bloke the floor, we hid the wood—the stove made us guilty." All other residents of the barracks were ordered to stand outside and watch this little spectacle.

"The guys who were marching started beating on the stove pipes and laughing, and the first thing you knew, most of the rest of us were laughing, too," Doyle remembered. "It wasn't really funny at the time, but we laughed like hell anyway."

One of the Japanese guards gave the participants a tongue-lashing over the incident. "You damned Americans," he fumed. "We try to punish you, and all you do is laugh!"

Fortunately, the cold was only a seasonal problem, while physical abuse and hunger became the two great constants of the POW experience.

"The Japs had some real good torture schemes," said PFC Richard Gilbert. "They had what they called the 'water cure,' where they'd put you on your back and pour water down your nose and mouth till you were about to bust. But the worst thing for me was the way they messed up my legs. I got so weak from hunger that I was passing out and falling while I was trying to work. As punishment for that, they'd put a bamboo pole under the bend of your knees, then push you backward over it."

The permanent cartilage and ligament damage caused by repeated torture of this type eventually earned Gilbert a Purple Heart, although it wasn't awarded until some fifty-five years later—at a special ceremony on Veterans Day 2001.

Adding to the demoralization of some prisoners was the psychological warfare directed at them by their captors, who saw to it that every piece of negative "war news"—much of it false or exaggerated—reached the POWs. American officers, in particular, were subjected to repeated reports of such Allied military disasters as the fall of Singapore, and later of Bataan and Corregidor. They even made sure that the Yanks heard about the death of movie actress Carole Lombard in an airplane crash.

But as the tenor of the war began to change and the number of Japanese defeats mounted, the number of reports conveyed to the POWs gradually dwindled away.

Oddly enough, the most unremittingly vicious individual encountered by the Woosung prisoners wasn't a Japanese officer or guard but a civilian interpreter named Isamu Ishihara. In the words of civilian Glenn Newell, "He was one mean dude. He hated all Americans with a passion, and none of us ever knew why."

To Newell and others who felt Ishihara's wrath—and there were many—his lust for inflicting pain remains legendary, even today. Dozens of Wake survivors recall him lashing out with an ever-present riding crop at a victim's face or throat and devising intricate forms of torture for the smallest misdeed. He had lived in Hawaii for a number of years before the war and attended school in Honolulu, where he learned to speak English flawlessly. Later he worked as a truck driver, but he also apparently had enough bad experiences and suffered enough real or imagined mistreatment by Americans to leave him deeply embittered against them.

Ishihara was about thirty-five years old, slightly built, and wore horn-rimmed glasses that gave him a rather scholarly look during his calmer moments, but he could burst into a maniacal rage at the slightest provocation. His victims referred to him as the "Beast of the East" or the "Screaming Skull," and Devereux called him the "most insatiably brutal" of all the Japanese he encountered as a prisoner.

On one occasion, Ishihara came close to beating Second Lieutenant Richard Huizenga, one of the Marines captured earlier in North China while serving as embassy guards, to death with a club for the "crime" of borrowing some tools from another prisoner to make repairs in his quarters. Huizenga, a former football star at the U.S. Naval Academy, was knocked senseless in Ishihara's attack.

Ishihara was irate when he heard that some POWs were trading what few items of value they had to the Chinese laborers who sometimes worked with them for an occasional egg or other food. His tool for identifying the "culprits" and ending the practice was wholesale water torture.

Systematically, he singled out a lone prisoner or small group of prisoners for questioning. Then, if they refused to answer, as did the vast majority of them, Ishihara subjected them to repeated doses of the water treatment. The victim was strapped to a plank that was inclined at a sharp angle with the man's head at the lower end. Then a guard covered the prisoner's face with a wet towel and poured water on it until it was so saturated that any attempt by the victim to breathe would force water into his lungs.

It took only a few seconds of this to bring the prisoner to the verge of suffocation or drowning, and the process was continued until Ishihara either got the answers he wanted or the prisoner lapsed into unconsciousness. After a while, trade with the Chinese fell off noticeably.

Sir Mark Young, the British governor of Hong Kong, who was also confined at Woosung, incurred Ishihara's wrath himself. Young had been transferred to the prison camp after more than a month of solitary confinement in a hotel at Kowloon, across the bay from Hong Kong, and he had welcomed the chance to be with other POWs. The Wake Islanders found him to be a pleasant man and admired his sound judgment and keen intelligence. Even most of the Japanese treated Young with deference, allowing him several creature comforts that other prisoners were denied, including a small stove, a radio, and a few pieces of furniture.

To Ishihara, however, Young was just another westerner to be knocked around. In an incident that the belligerent interpreter would live to regret, he struck Young with a sheathed sword over some alleged misdeed but was disarmed by a Marine before he could do any further harm.

According to Artie Stocks, who witnessed the confrontation, the normally mild-mannered Young jumped to his feet and knocked Ishihara down, and, for once, the Japanese guards failed to retaliate. In fact, the camp commandant, Colonel Yuse, subsequently forbade Ishihara to carry a sword. After that, his weapons were limited to a club or riding crop, but he still managed to cause plenty of pain.

As Stocks recalled the face-off between Ishihara and Young many years later: "Sir Mark told Ishi, 'You son of a bitch, this war won't last forever, and when it's over, I'm going to see you get what's coming to you.' Sure enough, after the war, Young was a judge at the war crimes trials, where Ishi was sentenced to life in prison. He died there."

In looking back on their captivity some fifty-seven years after it ended, most Wake survivors classify Ishihara's viciousness as a cruel exception to the treatment they received from the Japanese. Although the *bushido* system to which the Americans were introduced on the *Nitta Maru* continued in the prison camp, most guards didn't make a habit of delivering punishment without some justification. When a POW broke the rules or failed to obey an order, swift kicks or blows were usually the result—one experienced now and then by virtually every Wake Islander.

Civilian Ed Doyle made a brief—but largely unsuccessful—attempt to learn to speak Japanese well enough to help other POWs converse with their captors, but all Doyle got for his efforts was pain. "The other guys in my barracks started laughing and calling me 'Tojo,'" Doyle said, "and the one time I tried to do some interpreting, it was for a mean little guard named Araki. I screwed up the translation really bad, and he beat the hell out of me."

Yet the consensus among Wake survivors seems to be that, except for a relative handful of bullies, the Japanese didn't go out of their way to inflict intentional serious harm on their prisoners.

"I got an occasional slap when I didn't move quickly enough to satisfy one of the guards," said Captain Bryghte Godbold, the erstwhile strongpoint commander on Peale Island. "That happened to almost everybody, but it was nothing serious."

Others, however, report more lasting physical and psychological scars from their imprisonment.

"I've been under a doctor's care ever since 1945 because of the abuse I suffered as a POW," said former PFC Leroy Schneider, an Illinois Marine who served on Godbold's Battery D on Peale Island. "Every day was traumatic in prison. The Japanese were very brutal, and they just loved to beat on people. They literally beat a kidney out of me—damaged it so severely that I had to have it removed when I got home. They tore my legs up, too, and I've had trouble with them ever since."

For twenty-two-year Marine veteran Artie Stocks, the most irreparable damage was psychological. Long after his physical injuries healed, he remained embittered and raging inside.

"After I retired from the Corps, I got fired from a job or two for hatin' Nips so bad," Stocks said. "I was hostile toward Orientals in general, but I was worse about Japanese. I started having such terrible dreams about them that I finally went to the VA [Veterans Administration] for counseling, and it helped me some. It was like getting rid of a hundred-pound bag of rocks I'd been carrying on my back."

At the other end of the scale was Sergeant Edwin "Peepsight" Hassig, the crusty twelve-year veteran who had inspired a dispirited group of captive Marines to march with pride on the day of their surrender. Hassig took justifiable pride in his toughness and said he had "no gripes" about his treatment as a POW. "As far as I could see, they treated us just about as good as they treated their own soldiers," Hassig said. "The Japs didn't have any food to throw away back then, and most of the time, they were just about as hungry as we were."

And some Japanese actually went out of their way to try to make the prisoners' ordeal less onerous. The POWs at Woosung especially remember a compassionate young officer, Captain Morita Matsuda, for his thoughtfulness. A graduate of the University of Missouri School of Journalism and a member of the Japanese propaganda corps, Matsuda was shocked when he came to the camp and learned that the Americans hadn't been allowed to communicate with their families in the States. "He did his best to intercede for us with the camp commander," said Corporal John Johnson, "and I think it helped."

Of all the Wake Islanders held captive by the Japanese, the small group of wounded men left behind on the atoll when the *Nitta Maru* sailed probably were the least-mistreated group of POWs. But as the Americans' injuries healed, the troops assigned to guard them toughened their discipline and exposed even these wounded men to the unforgiving harshness of Japanese discipline.

The gory fate of Julius M. "Babe" Hofmeister, a civilian giant who stood nearly seven feet tall, offers a particularly unsettling example of the kind of "justice" meted out to those who broke the rules.

Hofmeister was a roofer by trade, but he could handle just about any kind of general construction. The Japanese found ample work for him fixing damaged buildings, and whenever a building contained usable goods, Babe always left himself a way to get back inside. Those who knew him said he had the strength of a bull, the nerve of a hungry bear, and the cunning of a fox. But he also had an unquenchable thirst for alcohol and a rare talent for thievery, a combination that led to his downfall.

Babe's towering height was intimidating to the Japanese guards, most of whom were a good two feet shorter than he was, and he displayed a notable lack of fear of their weapons and angry gestures. The story was told of how Babe was once challenged by a guard, who prodded his belly with the point of a bayonet until Hofmeister simply reached down, shoved the bayonet away, then turned and walked casually away. He seemed to have some sort of sixth sense about what he could get away with.

Meanwhile, Babe proved a tremendous friend to the wounded prisoners. "He was a very likable guy, who was always bringing us stuff he'd stolen—cigarettes, medicine, food, just about anything you can think of," Sloman said.

Hofmeister was also quick to use his imposing strength to help a disabled man. Sloman remembered one such incident in particular in February 1942, when American ships were shelling the island and the prisoners had to take cover along with their captors. "After the shelling stopped, I wasn't strong enough to make it back from the dugout to the hospital under my own power," Sloman said. "But Babe picked me up and carried me as easily as he would've carried a pet puppy."

On the night of Sunday, March 8, 1942, as Hofmeister came down a ladder with a carton of cigarettes he'd just pilfered through a hole in the roof of a storage building, he found a reception committee of armed guards waiting for him. After a brief military trial, during which Babe was never allowed to speak in his own defense, his captors sentenced him to death.

About fifteen of the healthiest wounded Americans in the hospital were ordered outside to witness the execution in an adjacent lumberyard. Sloman, Holewinski, Webb, and a few others were allowed to stay inside but forced to watch through the windows from a hundred feet away as guards made the condemned man dig his own grave in the coral.

When the hole was judged to be deep enough, Hofmeister's hands were tied behind him, and he was ordered to kneel facing one end of the hole. An officer with a samurai sword positioned himself beside Hofmeister and took several practice swings similar to those a golfer might take before approaching the tee. Then he raised the sword high in the air and slashed it down with all his strength, cleanly severing Hofmeister's head from his body.

"Many of us had anticipated trouble for Babe because of the way he constantly stole and defied the guards, but never anything like this," Sloman said. "It was a horrible sight—almost too horrible to believe—and it left all of us feeling sick and shaken and scared of what might happen next."

In Sloman's opinion, the Japanese commanders were looking for an excuse to inflict the harshest form of punishment on a prisoner as a warning to the others, and Babe gave it to them.

"It was a pretty severe penalty for stealing a carton of smokes," Sloman said, "but it damned sure got our attention."

About two months later, in early May 1942, Wake's recovering wounded boarded the *Soma Maru,* another former Japanese luxury liner converted to military use, and sailed for Japan. Their journey was notably easier than it had been for the men on the *Nitta Maru.*

"The weather was warm and pleasant, and we were quartered in what had been the swimming pool area," Sloman recalled. "Since there were only twenty of us, it wasn't crowded, and we had adequate sanitary facilities."

Their eventual destination would be the same prison camp at Zentsuji in which a number of other Wake Islanders were already held, but first they were taken to another camp at Ofuna for several weeks of intensive questioning.

"This was just before the Battle of Midway, and the Japs knew I'd been stationed there before coming to Wake, so they asked me lots of questions about what kind of fortifications we had on Midway," Sloman said. "They asked me to point out the five-inch gun positions, but I knew the guns had been moved since I left. I denied knowing where any of the machine guns and three-inchers were, and I told them I'd never been on Eastern Island, where the airstrip was. I was lying, but I made them believe me."

Once the prisoners reached Zentsuji, they were put to work loading and unloading freight cars at five railroad stations in the area. It was backbreaking work for the weakened men, since most of the goods they handled were 300-pound bags of food. On the plus side, they were able to steal enough edibles to keep themselves relatively well nourished—a "fringe benefit" that was denied to the rest of Wake's POWs.

"We literally had to steal to live, but we never came close to starving at Zentsuji, the way the guys at the other camps did," Sloman said. "We also had good medical attention because all the doctors from Guam were there."

Sloman's supply of miracles wasn't exhausted yet. Somehow it had kept him alive and kicking when most men would be dead, or at least crippled for life, and his run of good fortune was still intact.

For the last Americans still held captive back on Wake, however, both luck and time were rapidly expiring.

One of the most tragic and macabre episodes of the Pacific war took place on the north beach of the northern leg of Wake proper on the dark night of October 7, 1943.

By that time, the enemy troops on Wake had been left in an isolated backwater as the major fighting bypassed them and moved steadily closer to Japan's home islands. They were under constant pounding by U.S. ships and planes, but an even greater peril was a critical shortage of food and medicine. Much of the garrison was too sick or weak from hunger to work more than an hour or two a day. Between early 1942 and the war's end, an estimated 600 Japanese soldiers were killed on Wake by American bombs and shells, but more than twice that many died there from disease or malnutrition—almost matching the number killed in action trying to capture the atoll.

Two-thirds of the 300-plus U.S. civilians left behind to work for the Japanese after the *Nitta Maru* sailed were themselves later transferred to POW camps in Japan. But in early October 1943, ninety-six contractors still remained on Wake, trapped there by a virtually impenetrable ring of American naval forces, which made it impossible for the Japanese to evacuate them. Among them was Dr. Shank, the courageous civilian physician, who could have left earlier but volunteered to stay.

To the Japanese commandant, Rear Admiral Shigematsu Sakaibara, whose men were dying almost daily, the Americans posed a perplexing dilemma. There was nothing left for them to build—indeed, there was nothing left to build *with*—and they were consuming indispensable rations necessary to keep Japanese soldiers alive.

Sakaibara had shown himself to be a cruelly efficient officer when necessary. The previous summer, he'd ordered a prisoner allegedly caught stealing food from a warehouse to meet the same fate as Babe Hofmeister. And now, with his command dying before his eyes, the admiral made a desperate decision.

On October 6 and 7, 1943, Wake came under unusually heavy assault by a U.S. carrier task force. During this two-day period, American planes flew 510 sorties against the atoll, dropping 340 tons of bombs, and accompanying cruisers and destroyers rained nearly 3,200 rounds of five- and eight-inch shells on Japanese positions. The civilian POWs were all in shelters at the time, and no Americans were hurt.

According to a report submitted to the War Crimes Commission by U.S. Navy Captain Earl A. Junghans, who assumed command of Wake after the war, these attacks gave Sakaibara the pretext he needed to solve the problem of the captive Americans once and for all.

On the evening of October 7, Sakaibara ordered the commander of his Headquarters Company, Lieutenant Torashi Ito, to take all the prisoners to a spot on the north beach near the northwestern extremity of Wake proper and execute them.

When Ito reached the site, which was within easy view of Sakaibara's command post, the prisoners were already there. They were seated on the ground in a single long line facing seaward. They were blindfolded, and their hands were tied behind their backs.

Three platoons of Japanese soldiers were positioned behind the Americans with rifles and machine guns. When the platoon leaders reported that everything was ready, Ito stepped forward.

"Go ahead as ordered," he said, and the executioners opened fire. They continued firing until they were satisfied that all the victims were dead.

Incredibly, one prisoner temporarily escaped the slaughter. No one knows the man's identity, but he was found eight days later, hiding in a warehouse. Sakaibara eventually admitted hacking this survivor to death with his sword at a spot just below the high-water line on Peale Island, where the rising tide would wash away the blood.

Major Walter Baylor, nationally known during the war
as "the last man off Wake Island," also becomes the first
American to return to Wake as he steps ashore from a
motor launch on September 4, 1945,
following Japan's surrender.
(National Archives)

✴ 19 ✴

The Peace and
the Price

During the POWs' first year at Woosung, the Japanese frequently had to search for jobs to keep the prisoners busy. Without making their intentions too obvious, the Americans did their best to botch or delay any productive assignment they were given. Partially as a result, they ended up with some totally pointless, even frivolous, chores.

"I remember sitting in fifteen-degree weather polishing brass artillery shells with straw ropes until they shone like new money," said civilian Ed Doyle. "Part of the problem was, the Japs took so many prisoners so fast early in the war that they didn't know what to do with them. But by 1945, they'd figured it out, and I was working as a riveter in Osaka, building and repairing cargo ships."

As Doyle noted, Japan's string of early territorial conquests in China, Southeast Asia, and the Pacific had left them with tens of thousands of American, British, and Dutch POWs. It took considerable time and effort merely to transport and house these captives, and it was months before the Japanese began fully utilizing the labor potential they represented. But as the war wore on and Japan's manpower shortage steadily worsened, all the men from Woosung were forced to labor up to eighteen hours a day in mines, factories, shops, shipyards, and other vital production facilities.

In December 1942, part of the Wake prisoners were transferred from Woosung to another camp at nearby Kiangwan, which Devereux labeled "the worst hellhole in our captivity." Supposedly, they were there to construct a "children's playground," but the project was actually a military rifle range, whose main feature was a gigantic earthen mound measuring 200 feet wide by 600 feet long by up to 60 feet high. The Wake Islanders who built it with spades and other small tools, augmented by a hand-operated, narrow-gauge railroad to haul dirt and stone to the top of the mound, still refer to it derisively as "the infamous Mount Fuji project."

The murderous work schedule on "Mount Fuji"—twelve to eighteen hours a day six days a week—dragged on for many of the POWs until early 1945 and took a heavy toll on their health. Tuberculosis, dysentery, and other illnesses spread among the Americans. Virtually all lost significant amounts of weight—in some cases a hundred pounds or more. But even those who were down to skin and bones were forced to keep working long, arduous hours.

"Most of us spent eighteen months or more building 'Mount Fuji,'" said PFC John Dale, formerly of Battery L on Wilkes. "The mountain part was the backdrop for the rifle range, and we had to push those rail cars filled with dirt to the top of it with our bare hands. Every carload had to go a little higher than the one before it. It was a killer."

Many of the POWs working on Mount Fuji were appalled by their captors' apparent disregard for human suffering and human life.

"I remember seeing a severely injured Chinese coolie lying beside the road as we went to work," Dale said. "He laid there for about a week before he finally died, but the Japs wouldn't let us do anything to help him."

"When you see dead and dismembered people often enough, you condition yourself to it," said civilian John Rogge. "You have to. If you don't shut it out of your mind, you go crazy."

In a gesture as farcical as it was cruel, the Japanese agreed to pay the POWs a small monthly wage for their Mount Fuji labors to allow them to buy a little extra food from the Chinese. "They paid us thirty dollars a month in Chinese money at a time when peanut butter cost forty-five dollars a pound," said civilian Chalas Loveland. "That was bad enough, but by 1945, peanut butter was up to $840 a pound."

Many of the food packages shipped to the POWs by the International

Red Cross were confiscated by the Japanese, but after persistent complaints from American officers and the intercession of Red Cross officials, more of the packages got through. "I guess we'd all have starved to death if it hadn't been for the Red Cross," said PFC Clifton Sanders. "Whenever we got our hands on one of their boxes, it was a cause for celebration."

Letters and packages from the States were routinely pilfered, destroyed, or held in limbo for months by the Japanese. Of about 1,500 pieces of mail that reached the prison camps in China by September 1943, only about half had been delivered, and Christmas mail that arrived in December 1943 wasn't distributed to the POWs until the following April.

Some prisoners went years without hearing from their families. "I only got one letter from home the whole time I was a POW," said PFC Artie Stocks. "My mother was dead, but I felt a lot of anger toward my dad because I wrote him but never heard back from him. It wasn't until I got home that I found out he'd been writing me all along. The Japs just never let the letters get through."

Wiley Sloman and the other Wake Islanders at Zentsuji, meanwhile, remained "lost" for many months, both to their families and the Red Cross. "It was about the middle of 1943 before I got my first letter from my parents and realized they knew where I was," Sloman said.

Numerous prisoners owed their lives to the efforts of Edouard Egle, a compassionate and resourceful Swiss representative of the Red Cross, who worked tirelessly to ease their suffering. In March 1944, with the prisoners in particularly desperate need, Egle personally delivered a half-dozen food packages, plus clothing and boots, to each prisoner at Kiangwan.

When Egle learned that the four American medical officers in the camp were performing surgery with razor blades and sewing up incisions with fishing line, he brought them the first up-to-date medical supplies and equipment they'd seen during their captivity. Before he was through, Egle used his logistical skills to outfit a complete operating room and a well-equipped dental facility at Woosung.

As a neutral country, Switzerland maintained a consulate in Shanghai, and Swiss citizens like Egle were able to stay in close touch with the prisoners and help provide them with a small window to the outside world. In addition to help from the Swiss Red Cross, the consular staff also took a sympathetic interest in the POWs' welfare, applying gentle diplomatic pressure on Japan to improve living conditions in the Woosung camp.

Many POWs also never forgot the kindness and generosity of "Shanghai Jimmy" James, an American civilian from Minnesota who operated four restaurants in Shanghai and provided the prisoners with food, medicine, cigarettes, and other supplies. At Christmas 1942, Shanghai Jimmy gave the prisoners' spirits a tremendous lift by bringing a decorated Christmas tree to the camp and treating each man to a hot turkey dinner with all the trimmings.

"It was the only really decent meal I ever had as a POW," said Corporal John Johnson. "Even today, I never sit down to Christmas dinner without thinking about good old Shanghai Jimmy."

Many Wake Islanders remember James's treat as the best Christmas dinner they ever had—before or since. It seemed miraculous that he'd been able to persuade the Japanese to let him bring it into the camp, and the prisoners never understood how he'd managed it.

Eventually, though, Shanghai Jimmy ran out of miracles. In early 1943, the Japanese shut down his restaurants and put him in prison with the rest of the Americans.

For some of the prisoners, thoughts of escape hovered constantly in the backs of their minds, especially as friendly Chinese forces moved closer to Shanghai. A number of Wake Islanders tried it, but only a small handful were successful.

Commander Cunningham had been at Woosung less than two months when he made the first of two escape attempts, both of which fell into the brave-but-foolish category. Along with CPNAB superintendent Dan Teters and three other prisoners, Cunningham slipped out of his barracks on the night of March 11, 1942. The five trenched their way under the electrified barbed wire, made it a few miles up the Yangtze River, and remained on the loose for two days before they were recaptured.

After being paraded through the camp by their captors, the escapees were confined to the notorious Bridge House in Shanghai, headquarters of the Kempeitai, an elite investigative unit of the Japanese army sometimes compared to the Nazi Gestapo. They were put on trial as deserters, rather than escaped prisoners, and faced a possible death sentence. Afterward, they spent seven weeks in solitary confinement, and Cunningham and two of his cohorts were each sentenced to ten years in prison. Teters got off with a two-year sentence.

After the war, Cunningham told civilian John Rogge, with whom he became close friends, that this initial bid for freedom was "the dumbest damned thing I ever did." The experience didn't keep Cunningham from trying it again two and a half years later, however.

In October 1944, Cunningham and several other prisoners, including Sergeant Raymond Coulson of the Wake Marines, smuggled hacksaw blades into their cells at the Shanghai Municipal Jail and sawed through the bars on their windows. This time, they never even made it out of the city before they were caught. Then it was right back to solitary confinement in the Bridge House again for Cunningham.

The commander later justified these abortive attempts by saying he felt it was "the clear duty" of a prisoner of war to try to escape and that he felt he had information that could aid the Allied war effort. "I longed for another chance...to avenge the humiliation of Wake," he added significantly.

But his preoccupation with flight—plus the consequences it brought down on him—kept Cunningham effectively removed for the duration of the war from the men he'd commanded. Devereux, on the other hand, was with most of the other Wake prisoners throughout the endless days at Woosung and the agony of the Mount Fuji project. He maintained a sense of both camaraderie and discipline with the military prisoners that Cunningham never shared. In the process, Cunningham became even more isolated and alienated from most of his former garrison than he was during the fighting.

But not all escape attempts by the Wake Islanders ended in disaster. On May 9, 1945, VMF-211's Lieutenant Kinney and Battery L's Lieutenant McAlister escaped with Lieutenants Huizenga and James McBrayer of the

North China Marines from a prison train en route from Kiangwan to a camp at Fengtai, near Peking.

The foursome planned their escape carefully, deciding to split up into pairs instead of jumping from the train together, and keeping their plans secret from most of the other POWs in their crowded boxcar. After dark, while the train was slowly climbing a hill, they slipped through the barbed-wire strands on the only unbarred window in the car and jumped into the night, leaving straw dummies in their beds to fool the guards. McAlister and Huizenga went first, with Kinney and McBrayer following moments later. Their plan called for the first two men to walk in the same direction the train was traveling and the second pair to walk in the opposite direction until they located each other.

When Kinney made his leap for freedom, he assumed McBrayer was right behind him, but he found himself alone as he fled from the railroad tracks. He ran along briskly for about ten minutes, then paused to try to get his breath and his bearings. As he lay there panting, he heard dogs barking and the sound of men slapping the ground with bamboo sticks. In a panic, Kinney jumped to his feet and started running again, not realizing he'd left his knapsack with all his worldly possessions behind until a half hour later.

He headed in the direction he thought was west, then turned north, and somehow managed to elude the search party behind him. In the first light of the next morning, he cautiously approached several Chinese peasants and tried to elicit their help.

"*Mei guo fi ji,*" he said, which he hoped meant "I am an American aviator" in Chinese.

The peasants understood, all right, but they were afraid for their lives. They made chopping motions at their necks with their hands and moved away hurriedly. After several similar encounters, Kinney was starting to lose hope when a younger Chinese man finally showed interest and guided him to a cluster of mud-and-straw huts. There a woman gave him food, and he traded his telltale prison clothes for the kimono, straw hat, and straw sandals of a Chinese coolie.

With the help of other friendly peasants, Kinney managed to hook up with a detachment of blue-uniformed Chinese Communist cavalry, and on May 15, he was reunited with his three comrades, all of whom were safe and well. Just over a month later, after a harrowing trip through country infested with Japanese patrols, all four were turned over to Chiang Kai-shek's Nationalist forces and taken to Chungking. On July 9, 1945, after an around-the-world flight that took them to Burma, India, Iran, Egypt, Casablanca, the Azores, and Newfoundland, they finally landed in Washington.

Kinney and McAlister thus became the first members of the surrendered Wake garrison to return to U.S. soil. But within a couple of months, others began to follow.

By spring 1945, with the noose of Allied power tightening, many of the surviving Wake POWs were moved from China to other parts of the shrinking Japanese empire to work as industrial slaves in coal and iron mines, steel mills, repair depots, shipyards, and freight terminals. And as Japan's situation grew more desperate and more of these facilities came under attack by U.S. planes, the prisoners were apt to be shifted abruptly from place to place.

"We were moved from Shanghai in May 1945, first to Peking, then to Manchuria, then to Pusan, Korea," recalled Chalas Loveland. "In early July, we were shipped on to Japan, then sent by train to the northern tip of Honshu to work in an iron mine."

After leaving Woosung, Corporal Frank Gross found himself at the Tsumori prison camp near Osaka, Japan, and laboring in a shipyard, where he developed a hernia from carrying massive steel plates used to repair damaged ships. "When the port at Osaka got bombed out, it was the best break of the war for me," Gross said. "They were working us to death in that place." Along with Major Potter, Lieutenant Kliewer, and a few other prisoners from Wake, Gross was soon sent to a new camp high in the mountains. The routine there was somewhat less strenuous, but the quarters were alive with biting fleas, and the rations grew increasingly meager.

Food in all the POW camps had always been skimpy and substandard, but now it was close to nonexistent, and men would go to any extreme for a mouthful of anything remotely edible.

"I very happily ate cat once during that period," remembered John Rogge, "and I have to tell you I'd have eaten it a lot more often if I'd had the chance. It was the best piece of meat I'd had in a long, long time. Hell, on second thought, it was the *only* one I'd had."

"I worked on a hog farm for a while, and I ate as much of the swill they fed the pigs as I could force down," said PFC Jack Hearn. "The stuff tasted terrible, and God knows what was in it, but it was either that or die."

Some POWs, especially those working in close proximity to livestock, were reduced to eating discarded, half-rotted animal parts. More than a few came down with near-fatal bouts of dysentery from their diet. Hearn had dysentery three times, and the third time was the worst. He developed terrible stomach pains, and Dr. Kahn told him, "If it's appendicitis, the only thing I've got to operate on you with is a pocket knife." Fortunately, Hearn recovered without surgery.

With the country's economy collapsing, vast numbers of Japanese civilians and servicemen were suffering from chronic hunger, too. But by early 1945, the men from Wake were little more than walking skeletons, who felt themselves being worked, starved, and brutalized to the edge of extinction.

"My weight dropped from around 200 pounds at the time of the surrender to about 110 in the summer of '45," said Loveland. "I was very sick with dysentery, and I didn't know how much longer I could hang on."

PFC Leroy Schneider was working up to nineteen hours a day in a steel mill and thinking every day was going to be his last. "We were all down to skin and bones," he recalled, "and we knew we were going to die."

"You had to make yourself believe that you were going to survive and come home," said John Rogge. "If you didn't, you were a dead man."

Then, in the space of a few weeks, everything started to change.

Radios were strictly forbidden to prisoners, but there was almost always at least one hidden jury-rigged receiver in every barracks, and at night men would huddle around the set to pick up whatever war news they could. They knew that B-29s were now conducting regular raids on Tokyo and other major cities and that U.S. ground forces were within a couple of hundred miles of the Japanese homeland.

Soon the B-29s were also hitting targets around Shanghai, and it was obvious that defeat was closing in on the Japanese. The clandestine radios brought news of the fall of Iwo Jima and the steady retreat of Hitler's armies in Europe. On May 8, 1945, Germany surrendered unconditionally. The end of the war was almost at hand, but the big question was how many of the Wake Islanders would live to see it.

The Kiangwan camp was located near two military airfields, and those POWs who were still there in early 1945 often got a too-close-for-comfort look at U.S. bombing raids and dogfights between American and Japanese planes. One of the Americans' biggest thrills came in the spring of 1945. A flight of P-51s passed over the camp so low that they were able to wave to the pilots. The fact that they were Army fighter planes meant there was now a U.S. base nearby. For the first time in three years, Marines could be heard whistling at their work.

The Japanese guards, for the most part, became less abusive toward their captives when they sensed their empire's impending doom. But sometimes their fear and frustration boiled up into near hysteria. In January 1945, when three P-51s pounced on a Japanese Nell bomber and shot it down in flames only a few hundred yards from the prison compound, angry guards jabbed three cheering POWs with bayonets.

In early May, all the prisoners at Kiangwan were loaded into freight cars for the 700-mile trip north to Fengtai—the same trip on which Kinney and McAlister escaped. A few days later, they traveled on by train to Pusan, Korea, then by ferry steamer to the main Japanese island of Honshu, then aboard another train to a camp about twenty miles from Takagawa on the island of Hokkaido.

The trains were always the same: dozens of men crammed into boxcars with only a thin layer of dirty straw to sleep on and two five-gallon buckets per car as the only sanitary facilities. The boxcars were similar to those in the States, only smaller, with sliding steel doors in the middle of each side and small windows at each end. Armed guards rode in the center of each car, beside the sliding doors, with the prisoners crowded into the two end sections. Often a car's last passengers had been horses, and there was a smelly residue of manure under the straw.

As they traveled, the prisoners craned their necks to look out the small windows at mile after mile of destruction and desolation spread across the Japanese landscape. Whole cities had been reduced by repeated bombings to piles of smoldering rubble. By the time the POWs reached the new camp, it was early July.

Initially, they were put to work clearing ground for a garden, but within a few weeks, most of the officers were transferred to a lumberyard and more strenuous duties carrying timbers and gravel to a nearby coal mine. Enlisted men from the surrounding camps, meanwhile, were sent underground to work up to fourteen hours a day in the mines.

Little by little, though, the guards were relaxing their iron grip on the prisoners. The food got somewhat better and more plentiful. A daily ration of cigarettes was restored after a long absence. The Americans were allowed to go swimming in the river below the camp. "Very soon we will all be friends again," a Japanese soldier told them.

On August 14, all the Japanese personnel in the camp gathered around blaring radios to hear an announcement that none of the POWs could understand. Some of the listeners screamed or sobbed. Others stood in stunned silence.

It was obvious that something big had happened, but the POWs had no idea that Emperor Hirohito had just announced Japan's unconditional surrender. They didn't know that, on August 6, an American B-29 had dropped an atomic bomb on Hiroshima or that a second A-bomb had devastated Nagasaki three days later. World War II had just ended.

It would be almost another week before a Red Cross representative arrived to give the prisoners the official word. In the interim, Japanese officers implied that it was a negotiated peace and that the emperor would remain in power. The Americans generally continued with a scaled-down version of their daily routine, but telltale signs were everywhere that the rising sun had finally set.

Jack Hearn was still working in the coal mine on Hokkaido when he realized the war was really over. "The B-29s flew over again," he said, "but this time they were dropping food—big canisters of it—and it was landing all around us."

For Hearn and many others, the air drop didn't come a moment too soon.

"I was down to about seventy-five pounds," he said, "and I started eating Hershey bars as fast as I could. I got such a sugar buzz I couldn't sleep that night, but the guy next to me was worse off. He ate a whole gallon of pork and beans—God, you talk about gas!"

On September 2, 1945, Hirohito's representatives signed the documents of surrender on the deck of the U.S.S. *Missouri* in Tokyo Bay. Less than two weeks later, the Wake Islanders were headed home.

Devereux, who learned in prison camp that his wife, Mary, had died of diabetes during his absence, was among the first to reach the States. Along with several other officers from Wake, he landed in Washington on a Navy plane on September 26. The last time he'd seen his son, in January 1941, the boy had been just seven years old; now he was twelve.

"I don't think any man who was a prisoner of the Japanese will ever be able to put down in words what he felt on coming home," Devereux said. "But for me, the high point was a single moment when I reached Washington. There was a crowd—kinsmen, old friends and a lot of others—but in that moment, the only person I saw was my son Paddy coming toward me."

Great and prolonged as their suffering was, the men from Wake had a much higher survival rate than Japanese-held POWs in general. Of 1,593 Americans and Guamanians taken prisoner on Wake, a total of 244—or just over 15 percent—died in captivity. This compares to an overall death rate of 28 percent among all Allied personnel taken prisoner by the Japanese.

Observers have cited various reasons for this unusually high survival rate. For one thing, unlike the scarecrows from Bataan and Corregidor, the Wake Islanders were well nourished throughout their siege and up until the time they embarked on the *Nitta Maru*. For another, the grim prison camps around Shanghai were actually model facilities by Japanese standards; prisoners held elsewhere were treated far more harshly and given much less to eat; and the winter chill around Shanghai was far less deadly than the stifling heat of the POW camps farther south. And finally, the POWs near Shanghai received various forms of assistance from the city's large, prosperous international community.

But the biggest lifesaving benefit to the Wake POWs may have been the moral support, psychological reinforcement, and physical help they received simply from being with each other. They'd been together long enough to develop friendships and a sense of cohesiveness, and unlike members of many other captured units, most of them remained together for the duration of their captivity. Their officers were there, too, and they continued to promote discipline, structure, and purposefulness among the enlisted men. Survivors agree that this was a major factor in keeping the Wake Islanders' morale high.

"The person most responsible for fostering this spirit of order, pride and self-respect was Major Devereux," said historian Gregory Urwin. "The same Marines who had cordially hated Devereux before the war had come to respect him for his conduct of Wake's defense.... That respect deepened over the next three and a half years as a result of the example Devereux set in prison camp."

"When your buddy's down, you picked him up, and when you were down, he picked you up," said Corporal Robert Brown, Devereux's "phone man" during the siege. "It happened all the time." Brown described the Wake Islanders' affection for each other as "one of the greatest cases of friendship the world has ever known."

These feelings spilled over into the civilian POW population, as well. "The thing that irked the Japs most," said Ed Doyle, "was that they couldn't break our spirit. We developed an inner strength that they didn't understand."

At 7:00 A.M. on the morning of September 4, 1945, three small U.S. Navy vessels appeared off the south coast of Wake Island to reclaim the atoll for the United States. The signing of the official documents of Japan's surrender was less than two days old, and although instructions regarding the transfer of authority on Wake had been dropped earlier by plane, the

destroyer-escorts U.S.S. *Levy, Lehardy,* and *Charles R. Greer* approached the shore with some degree of caution.

General quarters was sounded as the ships closed to within 1,000 yards of the Wilkes Channel leading into the lagoon, and the small force of Marines and sailors aboard took their stations. But the only evidence of enemy activity was two small boats cruising slowly toward them and bearing a white flag.

Aboard the lead boat, a battered American-built motor launch, were Admiral Sakaibara, the Japanese commander of Wake, and his staff. At about 8:00 A.M., with a notable absence of ceremony or honors, the unarmed group was taken aboard the *Levy* to meet with American officers. Introductions were made, and the Japanese were motioned to seats at a table set up on the boat deck. There were no handshakes.

A few moments later, Brigadier General Lawson H. M. Sanderson, the Marine officer chosen to accept the surrender, appeared on deck, accompanied by a Japanese-American interpreter. He nodded curtly to the Japanese officers, then took his seat. He didn't smile as two copies of the surrender documents, one in English and one in Japanese, were read and signed.

At about 1:30 P.M. that same day, a small group of photographers and film cameramen recorded a poignant moment for posterity. Now-Colonel Walter Bayler, the last American to leave Wake before it fell, also became the first American to return.

Bayler found only a few recognizable landmarks still standing. The rusty water tower above what had been Camp One leaned drunkenly on three legs, but except for a few sticks and bits of debris, the camp itself had vanished. The overgrown remains of three of VMF-211's Wildcats huddled in the brush near the airstrip. Heavy equipment and machinery were scattered in all directions, some of it still operable.

Moments after Bayler symbolically set foot on the atoll, a bugler sounded "To the Colors," and the Stars and Stripes were hoisted up a new flagpole and caught the breeze above Wake for the first time in 1,351 days. As the *Levy* fired a twenty-one-gun salute offshore and about forty U.S. sailors and Marines stood at rigid attention facing a similar number of defeated Japanese, General Sanderson formally turned the atoll over to the Navy.

Except for Bayler, most other survivors of the first battle of the Pacific war were still in Japan, awaiting transport for the long journey home. But the wave-swept little atoll they defended, which Hirohito had renamed Otori Shima, or Bird Island, was back in American hands for keeps.

"I accept this island proudly," said Navy Commander William Masek, "because this is Wake Island—not just any island. It was here the Marines showed us how."

During a detailed inspection tour, it quickly became obvious that no living Americans remained on Wake when Sanderson and his party arrived. The U.S. officers were shown two large mounds topped by freshly painted white crosses—so fresh, in fact, that the paint was still tacky—and told that these were the graves of Americans killed during the battle. But evidence was also found of a third grave—a long trench in which dozens of bodies had apparently been buried—and this led to questions about the ninety-eight civilians who were left on Wake after all other POWs were removed, and whose fate was unknown.

Under interrogation, Admiral Sakaibara; his adjutant, Lieutenant Commander Soichi Tachibana; and other officers admitted that the civilians had died on the island and told a far-fetched story about how their deaths supposedly occurred. About half had been killed when their shelter took a direct hit during an American air raid, the Japanese said. Others in another shelter had mutinied, overpowering and killing their guards, seizing two rifles, and fleeing to the north beach of Wake, according to the Japanese account. After refusing to surrender and firing at the soldiers pursuing them, the account continued, all the mutineers had been killed.

The identical story was repeated by a half-dozen Japanese officers, leading the questioners to conclude that it had been well rehearsed in advance. To Captain Junghans, the new officer in charge on Wake, it seemed highly unlikely that an almost-unarmed group of civilians would take such drastic action, especially after remaining docile captives for the better part of two years. Junghans was determined to get to the bottom of the matter, and after General Sanderson and his entourage departed, the investigation intensified.

By November 1, 1945, most of the 1,240 surrendered Japanese soldiers on Wake had boarded two transports and were either already home or on their way. Remaining behind were sixteen Japanese whom Junghans and his staff continued to question about the fate of the ninety-eight civilians.

Finally, the sordid facts emerged, both about the bloodbath on Wake's north beach two years earlier and the two prisoners who were previously beheaded. Sakaibara and two of his officers, Lieutenant Commander Tachibana and Lieutenant Ito, were charged with murder and taken to Kwajalein for trial by a U.S. military commission. While the proceedings were under way, Ito committed suicide in his cell, leaving behind a signed statement implicating Sakaibara. When the admiral was shown the statement, he made a full confession.

"All the incidents which took place on Wake Island took place because I ordered them," Sakaibara acknowledged at the trial, "and if there should be any guilt arising from the incidents that took place, I, as the person who issued the order, would like to take full responsibility for what happened."

Both Sakaibara and Tachibana were found guilty and sentenced to death by hanging, but Tachibana's sentence was later changed to life in prison. Following the trial, Sakaibara was imprisoned on Guam to await execution of the sentence. There, on the early evening of June 18, 1947, he was taken from his cell, handcuffed and accompanied by a Buddhist priest, then driven to a scaffold about twenty minutes away.

Sakaibara smiled as he made a final statement. "I think my trial was entirely unfair and the proceeding unfair, and the sentence too harsh," he said, "but I obey with pleasure."

Many of his countrymen agreed with the admiral's last sentiments. "I still feel misgivings that Commander Sakaibara was not saved from the death penalty," said Hisao Tsuji, who remained on Wake for nearly four years after his ship, *Patrol Boat No. 33,* was destroyed.

Tsuji, who lost more than a third of his total body weight during the last months of the war, was probably saved from death by the arrival of American occupation forces. "They gave us our first decent meal in a long time," he recalled in March 2002. "We were lean as rakes, and some men had lost down to thirty kilograms. I was at about forty kilograms, but I gained back what I had lost during the two months before the Americans sent us back to Japan."

Tsuji survived to become president of the Japanese Wake Island Veterans Association and play an active role in keeping the group together. Between 1969 and 1995, he led his former comrades in four return visits to Wake, where a memorial to the Japanese war dead was dedicated in 1980. "Our members are still tied to all our fallen comrades by very strong bonds," he said. "I still regret that Commander Sakaibara could not be saved from the death penalty."

On one visit to Wake in 1978, Tsuji and thirty-two former comrades searched the atoll for the scattered remains of dead countrymen who had never been properly buried. Today Tsuji and other Japanese survivors realize how lucky they were to get home alive. Counting those under Sakaibara's command who died of disease and starvation, the conquest and occupation of Wake probably cost at least 4,500 Japanese lives between December 1941 and September 1945.

Of the 1,700-plus American civilians and military personnel on Wake when the war broke out, a total of 366 died either of combat injuries or the ill effects of captivity.

★

Top: *Civilian survivor John Rogge wears his*
original POW number pinned to
his shirt in this 2002 photo.
(Photo by Lana Sloan)

Bottom: *Wiley Sloman in 2002*
with his pet poodle Gigi.
(Photo by Lana Sloan)

✲ 20 ✲

Fading Images and
Forgotten Heroes

As the survivors of Wake made their way back to their homes and loved ones in America, they found a nation too busy celebrating victory and looking ahead to peace and prosperity to take much notice. In the fall of 1945, millions of veterans were streaming homeward from scattered points around the globe. Thousands were arriving daily, and it was easy for a few hundred Wake Islanders to get lost in the shuffle.

On September 13, 1945, an estimated six million cheering onlookers packed the streets of New York to welcome home General Jonathan M. Wainwright, the hero of Corregidor, and make front-page news from coast to coast. But the welcome for Wake's heroes was generally more subdued, and there was little hue and cry from the public.

When Seaman Dick Darden landed in California that same day as one of the first enlisted men from Wake to reach the U.S. mainland, not even his own mother knew about it. As Darden's hometown newspaper, the *Clinton* (North Carolina) *News,* explained in its edition of September 20, 1945:

> Mrs. Eva Bell Darden is the happiest woman in Clinton, and rightfully so.
>
> Her son, J. B. (Dick) Darden, who had been a prisoner of the Japs for 45 months, called Saturday afternoon from Oakland,

Calif., advising that he had arrived there by plane from Tokyo on September 13. He was two days getting the phone call through. A telegram filed before he reached the States was delayed....

Similar homecoming stories about the men from Wake appeared in local newspapers around the country, but for reasons that still aren't totally clear, returning Wake Marines were routinely asked to sign a form agreeing not to give media interviews concerning their wartime experiences. In many cases, they signed without thinking and later regretted it.

"The editor of the Texas City paper asked me for an interview several times after I got home, and I probably made him mad because I kept saying no," said Wiley Sloman. "But I'd signed that paper, so I didn't feel like I could do it."

One newspaper that did give the returning Wake Islanders extensive coverage, however, was the *Idaho Daily Statesman,* which trumpeted the first homecomings in an eight-column headline atop page one of its September 14 issue:

SEVEN IDAHO WAKE SURVIVORS REACH STATES

The seven were identified as Forrest Don Read, Raymond George Quinn, Robert Eugene Brown, William R. Carr, Joseph Hugh Arterburn, Wilbur Merel Masoner, and Roland Edwin Young. No less than 210 of the survivors were from Idaho, almost all of them civilians employed by the Morrison-Knudsen Company, headquartered in Boise.

M-K itself paid special tribute to the workers trapped on Wake at the outset of the war in the form of a hardbound commemorative "Blue Book" containing the names and photos of all 1,146 men, plus a complete list of those killed, wounded, and still designated as missing. The consortium of companies known as Contractors Pacific Naval Air Bases, of which M-K was a part, also set up a charitable foundation, which paid each worker and his dependents a portion of the wages lost during their captivity. It wasn't until 1980, thirty-five years after their release from prison camp, that full veterans' benefits were extended to Wake's civilian survivors.

Elsewhere, though, the news coverage and recognition were considerably more muted. Even a brief Associated Press dispatch out of Tokyo, quoting a just-promoted Lieutenant Colonel Devereux on the fact that relatively few men had been killed during the battle for Wake, received less than prominent play.

By October 1945, most of the Marines and sailors from Wake were once more on American soil. Some were in hospitals for treatment of long-neglected hurts and ills. All were eager to be reunited with their families, but there was also an undeniable feeling of loss as their units were disbanded and they parted company for the first time in four years or more. They exchanged fleeting farewell toasts and handshakes, then drifted their separate ways—pulled apart by peace as surely as they had been united by conflict, imprisonment, and privation.

Their heroic stand in the war's earliest true battle was overshadowed now by the magnitude of Hiroshima, Nagasaki, and all the other historic events that had occurred since. Memories of Wake Island and the men who fought there had already begun to fade from the public consciousness, and as time passed, they would fade still further.

For most Americans, the postwar period was a time for catching up on all they'd missed and sacrificed during the war. They rushed to get their names on waiting lists for new cars, new washers and refrigerators, new houses, and a miraculous new gadget called television. They found new jobs in burgeoning new industries, moved to new places, and pursued new dreams. Millions of veterans got married and started having kids in record numbers.

As thousands of returning POWs prepared to spend their first Christmas season at home in five years or more, President Harry S. Truman took time to sign a personal note to many of them. Some still have their copy of the letter, dated December 4, 1945. In it, Truman wrote:

> *It gives me special pleasure to welcome you back to your native shores, and to express, on behalf of the people of the United States, the joy we feel at your deliverance from the hands of the enemy...*
>
> *You have fought valiantly and have suffered greatly. As your Commander in Chief, I take pride in your past achievements and express the*

thanks of a grateful Nation for your services in combat and your stead-
fastness while a prisoner of war.

The sound and fury of World War II had scarcely subsided, however, when a new global conflict began dominating the headlines and consuming the full attention of Truman and his administration. The Cold War was on, and our former Soviet allies were suddenly our enemies. In Asia, the same Chinese Communist troops who had helped Lieutenants Kinney and McAlister escape to freedom were chasing Chiang Kai-shek's forces off the mainland. Meanwhile, an "Iron Curtain" fell across Europe, imprisoning tens of millions of Czechs, Hungarians, Poles, Germans, and Romanians behind it. West Berlin was under a siege that dwarfed Wake's in magnitude, and only a massive airlift kept it from being strangled and swallowed by the Soviets.

In this atmosphere, Wake Island became a distant, hazy image from another time. Even those who fought and bled for it were swept up in America's new priorities and its irrepressible march toward the future. Most soon disappeared from the public eye and blended quietly into the ever-changing tapestry of their country—but there were exceptions.

Major James P. S. Devereux, the diminutive officer whose steel nerves and artillery skills on December 11, 1941, won him a permanent place of honor in Marine lore, spent the last four decades of his life piling one success on top of another.

In 1947, Devereux, by now a full colonel and Wake's most celebrated hero, published a best-selling book entitled *The Story of Wake Island*, in which he gave previously unknown details of the battle and his role in it. His account contained more than a few misstatements and exaggerations, but few readers seemed to mind, and the book enjoyed several reprintings.

Devereux retired from the Marines in 1948 as a brigadier general and later served four terms in Congress. He spent his last years raising thoroughbred horses on a picturesque Maryland farm, and he remained in close touch with many of the men who served under him until his death in 1988.

As testimony to the high caliber of the men who led Wake's defense, at least six other officers from the Marine garrison reached the rank of general before the end of their military careers. They included **Major George H. Potter,** Devereux's exec; **Major Walter L. J. Bayler,** the atoll's noted "last man off"; **First Lieutenant Woodrow M. Kessler,** who commanded Battery B on Peale; **Major Paul A. Putnam,** commander of VMF-211; and two other members of the fighter squadron, **Captain Frank C. Tharin** and **Second Lieutenant John F. Kinney.**

Captain Wesley McCoy Platt would almost surely have become the seventh Wake Island Marine officer to make general if his life hadn't been tragically cut short. The leader of the counterattack that routed Japanese forces on Wilkes Island was mortally wounded by shrapnel from an enemy artillery shell in Korea on September 27, 1951.

Then-Colonel Platt was serving on the headquarters staff of the First Marine Division at the time. Never the rear-echelon type, he'd left the safety of a command post to inspect front-line troops engaged in heavy fighting. Only thirty-seven years old when he died, Platt was the highest-ranking Marine officer killed in action in the Korean War. He was posthumously awarded the Legion of Merit to go with the Silver Star he received for his gallantry on Wilkes. He was buried in Arlington National Cemetery on January 11, 1952, and was survived by his wife, Jane; an eight-year-old son, Thomas; and a four-year-old daughter, Valerie.

By and large, though, the defenders of Wake were deplorably "under-decorated" in comparison to Americans who fought in later Pacific battles. In many cases, their decorations were delayed for decades, and as this book was written, some still hadn't been received.

For his courage both in the air and on the ground, **Captain Henry T. "Hammering Hank" Elrod** was posthumously awarded the only Congressional Medal of Honor won by a Wake Islander, and a Navy guided missile frigate is also named in his honor. But **Second Lieutenant Robert M. Hanna,** whom many Wake survivors feel also qualified for the nation's highest award for valor, had to settle for a Navy Cross. VMF-211's **Captain Herbert C. Freuler** received both a Navy Cross and a Bronze Star for his courageous feats in the skies above the embattled atoll.

To date, the only valor-based medal received by **Corporal Ralph J. Holewinski** is the Bronze Star—and it wasn't presented until fifty-nine years after the battle. Yet Holewinski probably killed at least as many enemy soldiers on Wake as Sergeant Alvin York, World War I's most storied Medal of Honor winner, felled in France. (York is credited with killing 20 Germans but also single-handedly captured 132 others.) Holewinski, who served for thirty-four years as sheriff of Otsego County in his native Michigan after the war, has also been recommended for a Navy Cross, but no official action had been taken by early 2003. The delay continues to upset his former comrades.

In many cases, even Purple Hearts have been hard to come by. **Corporal John S. Johnson,** who suffered an arm wound in the final firefight on Wilkes—a fight he was instrumental in helping to win—had to wait until 2000 for his medal. And **PFC Richard C. Gilbert** didn't receive his Purple Heart for permanent knee injuries suffered in prison camp until Veterans Day 2001, when its presentation came as a "complete surprise." Other eligible military veterans are still waiting, as are the vast majority of civilians who suffered wounds while defending Wake.

Commander Winfield Scott Cunningham retired as a rear admiral in 1950. He also coauthored a book, published in 1961, called *Wake Island Command.* Much of it was devoted to lashing out at those who failed to recognize his authority or extend the respect he felt he deserved as Wake's commandant. He was awarded a Navy Cross for his service on Wake but never got over the omission of his name and role from FDR's presidential unit citation, and when he belatedly received a unit citation ribbon, he confessed to wearing it "with some bitterness."

He was bitingly critical of Lieutenant Colonel Heinl's official report, *The Defense of Wake,* which was prepared for—and highly favorable to— the Marine Corps but which contained a generally accurate overview of Cunningham's part in the battle. In a fiery article in *Cavalier* magazine, Cunningham also railed against the "Marine myth" surrounding Wake.

He staunchly defended the role of the civilians during the sixteen-day siege—and rightly so. He refuted reports that only a few contractors participated in Wake's defense, while the rest were a "sorry lot" that hid in the brush and thought only of themselves. He cited a list of "at least 312" civilians who had actively aided and fought beside their military comrades. Because of this, and because of his friendship with construction boss Dan

Teters, some civilians remain sympathetic toward Cunningham and feel his rancor was justified.

"He was a fine gentleman, who was very badly mishandled by history," said the commander's onetime civilian orderly, John Rogge. "It's tragic that he never got proper credit."

The closing sentence of Cunningham's book sums up the thirst for vindication that dominated his final years. "The Wake Island legend remains alive," he wrote. "Someday, I am confident, it will be replaced by the facts."

But historians and military experts have never rallied to Cunningham's cause. While considering it unfortunate that his name wasn't on the unit citation, they generally agree that he got about as much credit as he deserved. "On the basis of the evidence now available," wrote author Gregory Urwin, "the honor for directing the defense of Wake Island must go to Devereux and Putnam."

At any rate, the real and imagined slights from his superiors and fellow countrymen clearly continued to rankle Cunningham until his death in 1986.

Although he never personally received medical care from Dr. Shigeyoshi Ozeki, retired career Marine **Joseph E. "Ed" Borne** became the Japanese physician's biggest postwar booster in the United States. After Wake's surrender, truck driver Borne was chosen to chauffeur Ozeki on his rounds among the wounded and was deeply impressed by the doctor's humanity and compassion. Along with Wiley Sloman and other Wake veterans, Borne visited Ozeki in Japan in 1995, then played host to Ozeki on three visits to the United States. In 1999, Borne persuaded General James L. Jones, commandant of the U.S. Marine Corps, to write a letter to Ozeki, thanking the doctor for his "generous, kind and decent actions" toward wounded American prisoners and praising his "moral courage and superb character." When Ozeki died in October 2002 after several years of failing health, no one mourned his loss more deeply than Borne, who called the Japanese physician "my best friend." Borne lives in Haynes City, Florida.

David D. Kliewer was never officially credited with his kill of an enemy sub, but he was awarded the Bronze Star and two air medals for his stalwart service with VMF-211. He entered Harvard Medical School soon after his discharge, earned an M.D. degree there, and served for a half century as a practicing physician. Always a deeply religious man, he credits his experiences between December 1941 and August 1945 with transforming him into an ardent pacifist, and he tries to avoid doing or saying anything that might "glorify war." He lives in Corvallis, Oregon.

Civilian construction boss **Nathan Dan Teters,** whose heroic actions on Wake and during his captivity in China earned him a Bronze Star, continued his work with Morrison-Knudsen following the war. In 1957, the French government designated him a knight in the National Order of the Legion of Honor for his role in building French air bases in Morocco. He died in 1960.

After seeing extensive service in Korea and retiring from the Marines in 1958 as a colonel, **Bryghte D. Godbold,** whose gun crews on Peale exacted a heavy toll on enemy aircraft, moved to Dallas, where he still lives. He later served as vice president of the Southwest Center for Advanced Studies, now the University of Texas at Dallas. He travels extensively and remains active in a number of business ventures.

Since retiring from the Marine Corps in 1958, erstwhile machine gunner **Franklin D. Gross** has become a veritable encyclopedia of information about Wake survivors. For the past thirty years, he has written, published, and distributed the *Wake Island Wig-Wag,* a quarterly newsletter, which he mails free to all his living former comrades and the families of many who have died. His latest project is a Wake Island Defenders Scholarship Fund, established at Southwest Missouri State University and aimed at helping deserving youngsters attend college. He lives in Independence, Missouri.

With the fortune-seeking curiosity that had taken him to Wake in the first place still unsatisfied, civilian **Ed Doyle** bought a sleek '41 Packard after the war and went to Hollywood to try his hand at show biz. He sang for a while with a troupe of young nightclub performers, but the only steady work he could find was as a soda jerk in Beverly Hills. After a year or so, he went home to Boise for good and became a restaurateur, operating five different dining establishments before retiring in the late 1980s. His brother, **Bob,** who was separated from Ed for the last two years of their captivity, also returned to Idaho. He died of bone cancer in 2001.

Another set of civilian brothers from Idaho, **Glenn and Emmett**

Newell, also returned permanently to their home state following their release from prison camp. Glenn got home in late October 1945 and soon got a job at Idaho Power Company. He worked there for nearly forty years, part of that time as a lineman—a job he called "as hard as anything I did on Wake." He's now retired and living in Boise. Emmett, who spent some time on Guam after the war, was killed in an auto accident in 1987.

Artilleryman **Charles Harrison,** a PFC on Wake, lived through the long ordeal in a Japanese POW camp only to be captured again a decade later by Red Chinese troops in Korea, where he was held for five months before managing to escape. He also served two tours in Vietnam. Harrison's thirty-year career in the Marines began with his enlistment as a private in 1939 and ended with his retirement as a lieutenant colonel in 1969. "These are the good times; I've had the bad," he said in 2001 from his home in Grass Valley, California. "I've learned to blank out the worst of the three wars I was in. Otherwise, I'm sure I'd have cracked up long ago."

In late 1945, **Robert E. Bourquin** of VMF-211 married Charlotte "Chotty" McLain, the girl whose picture he almost died for, then carried all the way through prison camp. Surviving along with the treasured photo was the handwritten day-to-day journal kept by Bourquin from December 8, 1941, to August 26, 1945. After leaving the service, he returned to college and received a degree in education, subsequently teaching high school science for more than thirty years. He and Chotty live in Sequim, Washington.

After losing about forty close friends and relatives in World War II, **Artie J. Stocks** decided he'd had enough of military life and became a civilian. But after the Korean War broke out in 1950 and the Marines got involved, he reenlisted. "I was the oldest corporal in the Corps when I went back in in 1952," he recalled, "and probably the only one who'd never even had an M-1 in his hands, much less fired one." He retired as a gunnery sergeant in October 1967 after nine disturbing months in Vietnam, during which he "lost a bunch of kids because we were ordered not to fire until we were fired on" and developed posttraumatic stress syndrome as a result. He lives in Layton, Utah.

Walter A. Bowsher, who molded a group of civilian novices into a fully functional three-inch gun crew on Peale and later saw action in Korea, traded one kind of uniform for another when he retired from the Marines in 1954. He served for twenty years as a police officer for the San Francisco Port Authority before retiring again and returning to a picturesque corner of the Ozark Mountains that he remembered from his youth. He lives quietly in the deep woods beside a large lake and gets his mail at Bull Shoals, Arkansas.

Chalas Loveland, whose prewar job of making milk shakes in the contractors' canteen gave way to carrying ammo for machine guns and moving three-inch batteries during the siege, helped form and lead a civilian survivors' group after the war. He currently serves as president of the Survivors of Wake, Guam and Cavite, Inc., which circulates a bimonthly newsletter to civilian Wake Islanders and their relatives and sponsors an annual convention. Like a number of other civilians who worked on Wake, Loveland still lives in Boise.

Proud of the fact that thirty-two of his fellow Oklahomans fought with him at Wake, **Jack R. Skaggs** has been a major force in helping Marine and Navy veterans of the battle maintain contact with each other over the past six decades. For many years, Skaggs, who served three terms in the Oklahoma legislature, hosted an annual reunion for Wake veterans in Oklahoma City. He was also instrumental in getting the only stateside monument to the Wake Islanders—a red granite marker bearing the names of all servicemen stationed there in December 1941—erected in a city park in Bristow, Oklahoma, in the late 1980s. Skaggs made his first trip back to Wake in August 2002 to participate in the filming of a TV documentary on the battle. He lives in Edmond, Oklahoma.

Arthur A. Poindexter, who was awarded a Bronze Star for his "exemplary conduct" in the counterattack he led on Wake proper on December 23, 1941, retired from the Marine Corps as a full colonel in 1963. He later served on the political science faculty at California State University, Long Beach, and, at the age of seventy-three, earned a Ph.D. degree from the University of Hawaii. "He was a military man to the end, though," said his wife, Patricia Poindexter, in a recent interview. "He was big and gruff, but underneath it all, he was a real pussycat—an extremely intelligent man who loved people and was interested in just about everything." Poindexter died on January 5, 2000, at Huntington Beach, California, and is buried, as he requested, in Arlington National Cemetery.

Discharged as a platoon sergeant after a series of operations to remove bone and bullet fragments from his brain, **Wiley W. "Slick" Sloman** finally made it home to stay in May 1946 and soon found employment as a building inspector for the city of Texas City. Less than a year later, on April 16, 1947, one of the worst domestic catastrophes of the twentieth century almost wiped the Gulf Coast town off the map, and, true to form, Sloman was right in the midst of it.

He was only a few blocks away when a chemical-laden French ship, the S.S. *Grandcamp,* blew up in the Texas intracoastal waterway, killing 512 people and injuring more than 3,000. He not only escaped without a scratch but helped set up an emergency aid station in a local high school gym where scores of injured were treated.

"I was sitting in the mayor's car when the ship went up," he said. "I jumped out and ran behind a building on the leeward side and got flat on the ground just before the concussion hit. The blast was a lot more powerful than anything we saw on Wake. The ship's anchor came down a mile and a half away."

In 1995, Sloman traveled to Japan with several other ex–Wake Island defenders for an emotional reunion with Dr. Ozeki, the man he credited with saving his life. "It was an unforgettable experience," said Sloman, "and Dr. Ozeki was an unforgettable man."

Like other members of the gun crew of Battery L, who sank the first major enemy ship of the war, Sloman received no special official recognition for this historic feat. But he was proud of a letter of commendation he received in 1992 from retired Brigadier General Woodrow Kessler. Published that same year in *Fortitudine,* the bulletin of the Marine Corps historical program, it reads:

> To Wiley W. Sloman, whose great work at Wake Island helped
> to bring the great victory against Kajioka on 11 December 1941,
> and who served as a true Marine throughout the battle for Wake
> Island.

Sloman's wound left him with a pronounced limp and a tendency to drag his left foot slightly that lasted the rest of his days. Otherwise, he showed no permanent aftereffects from the bullet that almost killed him in December 1941. Out of his ordeal grew a quiet, unassuming philosophy on his miraculous journey through life, which he expressed in one of his last interviews during the summer of 2002. "It's either fate or just dumb Irish luck," he said. "That's the only way to explain the past sixty-one years."

On October 23, 2002, several months after moving from Harlingen, Texas, to Houston and a few weeks before his eighty-first birthday, Sloman checked into a VA hospital in San Antonio for what was expected to be routine oral surgery. He was given an anesthetic to have three bad teeth removed, and the operation was completed successfully with no apparent problems. Shortly afterward, however, Sloman died in the recovery room without regaining consciousness.

"After all he'd been through, for Wiley to leave this world peacefully in his sleep at the age of eighty-one is totally amazing," said his longtime friend and fellow Wake Islander Frank Gross. "If he could've chosen the way he wanted to go, that probably would've been it."

Sloman's only survivors were his second wife, Misty; a pet poodle named Gigi; and a steadily dwindling "family" of aging Marines.

Above left: *Major James P. S. Devereux.*

Above right: *Commander Winfield Scott Cunningham.*

AFTERWORD

Could Wake Have Been Saved?

Wake Island's value to the U.S. Navy in late 1941—and to America's entire early war effort in the Pacific—went well beyond whatever strategic advantage might have been gained by hanging on to three isolated chunks of coral on the enemy's doorstep.

As Admiral Kimmel correctly deduced when he ordered Wake's relief and reinforcement, the Navy needed a clear-cut victory as desperately at that juncture as at any time in its history. Inflicting major harm on the Japanese was the only way to help offset the disaster at Pearl Harbor and the string of defeats that followed—and, at the time, Wake was the only spot in the Pacific that offered a chance for this kind of victory. It presented a prime opportunity to lure Japan into exposing its navy in a location where U.S. forces could "get at them," as Kimmel phrased it.

That's exactly what the Japanese did when they sent a huge, carrier-supported naval armada to Wake on December 23. Considering the hesitancy and ineptitude already demonstrated by the enemy at Wake, plus their smug belief that the U.S. Pacific Fleet was too shattered to launch an effective offensive strike, some historians believe Admiral Kajioka's force was extremely vulnerable. But when Kimmel was removed from command, Admirals Pye and Fletcher squandered the opportunity.

The real key to an out-and-out U.S. victory was for the *Saratoga*-led Task Force 14 to reach Wake ahead of the Japanese, disembark its 200 fresh

Marines, and challenge Kajioka's fleet by sea and air before it could carry out a landing. If the task force had arrived by December 22, as Kimmel originally planned, the *Saratoga*'s dive bombers could have wreaked havoc on the Japanese ships, particularly their picket line of four unprotected cruisers, before enemy planes from the *Hiryu* and *Soryu* could intervene from 200 miles away. Clearly, this would have put the *Saratoga* herself at risk, but the carriers *Lexington* and *Enterprise* were also within a few hundred miles, close enough to offer aerial support and more than even the odds.

Even after Pye's indecisiveness and Fletcher's dawdling allowed the Japanese to reach Wake first and put an invasion force ashore, Fletcher's task force still could have struck a telling blow on the Japanese armada by staying on course and engaging Kajioka's unsuspecting flotilla. It seems doubtful that the estimated 250 to 300 landing force troops left alive on Wake as of 8:00 A.M. on December 23, when the surrender decision was made, were strong enough to subdue the defenders—or perhaps even hold the ground they'd taken—without substantial reinforcements. And if a battle had been raging off Wake between U.S. and Japanese naval forces, the enemy might have found it impossible to land additional troops.

"I'm sure we could've pushed all the Japs who were already there off the island," Frank Gross said sixty years later, "but as long as they could just keep sending more and more men in, it wouldn't have done much good. If we'd kept fighting without outside help, we'd all be buried under the coral right now."

Noted World War II historian Samuel Eliot Morison was particularly critical of Pye and Fletcher for their refusal to risk going in hot pursuit of the Japanese ships and, at the very least, forcing a naval battle at Wake. As Morison noted: "Kimmel was inclined to make up his mind what the enemy would do, and act accordingly; Pye, on the contrary, could apprehend everything the enemy might do, but was inclined to wait and see what developed before doing anything himself.... The general impression was one of irresolution at Pacific Fleet headquarters, which was correct. But that was the more reason why Fletcher should have pressed forward to meet the enemy."

Morison's criticism was strongly supported by Commander Cunningham's own observations following the surrender on December 23: "I saw a division of cruisers, which I took to be heavy cruisers, steaming not far off shore from the island," Cunningham said. "Several submarines were also sighted from time to time. Two transports came in and moored to the buoys south of the island on the same day, I believe. All in all, the Japanese, by these actions, presented a picture of perfect relaxation, and also exposed themselves to the likelihood of heavy losses had our task force attacked even after surrender, which is naturally what I fervently hoped for."

"I call this the blackest day in the history of the U.S. Navy," added fleet Marine officer Colonel Omar Pfeiffer. "All of us believed . . . that a glorious victory was at hand and had been let slip away."

When an aide to Navy Secretary Frank Knox asked Admiral Stark, chief of naval operations, to give President Roosevelt the word that Wake had been abandoned, Stark refused. "I wouldn't have the heart," the admiral said. "Please ask Secretary Knox to do it."

Knox accepted the distasteful assignment but later told his aide that FDR "considered this recall a worse blow than Pearl Harbor."

There's definitely another side to this story, however, and Pye's defenders have been every bit as vocal as his detractors. "Had Fletcher endeavored to push on to Wake, it would have resulted in our forces going into action piecemeal," said Admiral Milo F. Draemel, Pye's chief of staff, in backing the decision to scrap the relief mission.

Like Pye, who cited "conservation of our forces" as his primary concern in calling off any offensive action at Wake, Draemel called for "caution— extreme caution." Wake and the Americans trapped there, he argued, simply weren't worth the risk of further losses to the already weakened Pacific Fleet.

In ordering the retirement of both Task Force 14 and the *Lexington*-led Task Force 11, Pye said he merely followed a set of criteria for writing off Wake issued by Admiral Stark himself. These criteria included (1) the belief that Wake had become a strategic liability, (2) concern for holding Midway, (3) fears that Hawaii was in imminent danger of another air raid or an actual invasion, and (4) concern about keeping shipping lanes open to Australia.

Another factor, although unrecognized at the time, also supports the decision not to commit a sizable naval force to Wake's relief. Backers of the rescue mission relied on the fourteen planes of VMF-221, the Marine fighter squadron carried by the *Saratoga* to replace Wake's decimated VMF-211, to give U.S. forces a vital edge in the air. But these planes were slow, unwieldy F2A-3 Brewster Buffalos—probably the worst aircraft ever flown into combat by the U.S. military. Their impotence was tragically demonstrated five and a half months later in the Battle of Midway, where Japanese Zeroes made mincemeat of virtually the whole squadron and killed thirteen of its pilots.

"We called those damned things 'flying coffins,' and that's exactly what they were," said VMF-211's Sergeant Bourquin. "The Brewster Buffalo was one piss-poor airplane—a deadly joke to the poor guys who had to fly them."

Surprisingly perhaps, even Major Devereux expressed approval of the decision by Pye and his subordinates that cost Devereux three and a half years in a Japanese POW camp. "The Navy had too little left after Pearl Harbor to gamble the ships on an attempt to retake Wake," he said. "I believe they did the right thing. They had a more important job—defeat the enemy in another place."

For years before the war, both the United States and Japan had envisioned Wake as being of extreme strategic importance to the other side, but to a large extent, this idea turned out to be more illusion than reality.

Given Japan's temporary aerial superiority and the weakened state of the Pacific Fleet, Wake would almost surely have been subjected to continual enemy air and sea attacks—although perhaps not a third invasion try—if it had remained in American hands. Realistically, because of its remoteness and attendant supply problems, it would have had little chance of playing a viable offensive role for U.S. forces. Merely keeping it supplied with basic necessities could have become a nightmare for the Navy, and any idea of using it as a base for air strikes against the heart of Japan's Pacific empire was probably an impossible dream.

Meanwhile, except for depriving U.S. forces of its use for the duration of the war and denying them the victory they might have achieved there, Wake's capture brought surprisingly little practical value to the Japanese, who found it far less useful than originally perceived. While their bases lay just half as far away as the nearest other American outpost, supplying Wake and defending it against U.S. attack posed constant headaches for its conquerors. Indeed, one of the great ironies of the war, considering how much they sacrificed to take it, is that Wake quickly became for the Japanese exactly what Stark, Pye, and Draemel had believed it to be for the United States: a liability.

From the spring of 1942 on, Wake was pounded regularly by American planes and shelled frequently by passing U.S. warships en route to or from higher-priority targets. The Japanese hoped to make the island a staging point for an invasion of Midway, but because Wake's defenders disrupted their timetable, they were never able to utilize it effectively. Japan's crushing defeat at the Battle of Midway in early June 1942—in which the *Hiryu* and the *Soryu* were both sunk, along with two other Japanese carriers— stripped Wake of most of its strategic value to the enemy. For the last eighteen months of the war, what few supplies reached its Japanese garrison had to be slipped in at night by submarine. By war's end, enemy troops on Wake were literally dying of starvation.

In outspokenly blaming Pye and Fletcher for the loss of Wake, Cunningham conveniently ignored his own pivotal role in that loss. It was, after all, the island commander himself who contributed the proverbial "last straw" to Wake's demise. On the morning of December 23, Cunningham made two costly mistakes, both of which were instrumental in the American defeat. Two and a half hours before he issued a surrender order based mostly on bad guesses and misinformation, his ill-conceived radio message to Pearl triggered the decision to scrub the relief mission.

Cunningham's principal failing as island commander was allowing himself to remain totally out of touch with the garrison under his command and hence to be completely unaware of what was happening on his watch. Devereux also failed in this regard after the invasion, but as officer in overall charge and the one person with the power to relay informa-tion—and impressions—to CinCPac, Cunningham had a larger, more crucial obligation.

He had the authority, for example, to order Devereux to send out pa-trols to determine the true state of affairs on Wake and even on Wilkes. At the very least, a few men could have gone to Wilkes Channel to listen for gunfire on the smaller island. If they had, they certainly would have heard enough to know that the Marines on Wilkes were still fighting. Yet Cun-ningham apparently never considered any such step. Instead, he blindly accepted Devereux's flawed perspective and took no initiative of his own. To the end, Cunningham remained a commander *in absentia,* as he'd been all along.

"I was damned glad we had someone like Devereux out there," said Ma-jor Walter Bayler, the "last man off Wake Island," after the war. "The only time we saw Cunningham was each day when the fight was over, and then all he wanted to know was how much ammunition was expended, how many shells were fired—nothing else."

Cunningham's second major misstep on that last morning—and the one that effectively slammed the door on any rescue attempt by Task Force 14—was his painstakingly worded final radio message to Pearl Harbor:

"Enemy on island. Issue in doubt."

Cunningham thought the message had a forceful, hopeful, even poetic ring to it, and he was pleased to learn after the war that many Americans viewed it as a final gesture of defiance by Wake's defenders. He steadfastly maintained, however, that no bravado was intended.

"At the moment I began to write the dispatch," Cunningham recalled, "a phrase I had read sixteen years ago came into my mind. It was from Ana-tole France's *Revolt of the Angels.* He was describing the assault made on the heavenly ramparts by the legions of Satan. 'For three days,' he wrote, 'the issue was in doubt.'"

In later years, Cunningham vigorously denied any intention of imply-ing by these words that all was lost on Wake. In France's story, he insisted, the victory had gone to the side of the angels, and while he knew the atoll's defenders were outnumbered and outgunned, he was still unable "even to consider the prospect of defeat."

If this is true, Cunningham apparently was capable of changing his mind in a hurry. Just two and a half hours later, he would issue the order to surrender. As for Pye and his staff, they wrote Wake off almost as soon as the commander's message reached them.

"The use of offensive action to relieve Wake had been my intention and desire," Pye said in a dispatch to Admiral Stark, chief of naval operations. "But when the enemy had once landed on the island, the general strategic situation took precedence, and the conservation of our naval forces became the first consideration. I ordered the retirement with extreme regret."

In essence, the message achieved the exact opposite of what Cunningham should have wanted. If he'd been less concerned with dramatic prose and literary style, he might have realized how ominous—how devoid of hope or spirit—his six words sounded when they were decoded and read 2,000 miles away.

It's impossible, of course, to argue with the basic truth of the message. Enemy forces *were* on the island, and the issue *was* in doubt. But one of the main reasons for the doubt was that it was still too dark to get any kind of fix on where the enemy forces were concentrated and what they were doing. Understandably, Cunningham felt a need to report the situation to his superiors. The problem, however, was that he didn't *know* the situation. Besides, the invaders had already been ashore for two and a half hours, so there was justifiable cause to wait a while longer, until daylight cleared up some of the confusion.

There was also a certain negative urgency about the wording that subtly invited recipients of the message to stretch and distort the truth it contained. The transmission's brevity was remindful of an SOS from a ship breaking apart in stormy seas. Its very lack of detail and specifics seemed to imply the worst. Its tone somehow suggested that hostile troops were battering at the door even as the radio operator tapped out the message on his key. (The movie *Wake Island* included just such a scene, in which the Japanese burst into the radio room and riddled the operator with bullets as he called for help.)

In fact, though, none of this was true. Cunningham himself later recalled that, when the dispatch was sent at 5:30 A.M. on December 23, surrender was still the farthest thing from his mind. But the "between-the-lines" implications of Cunningham's message gave Pye the impetus he needed to order Task Force 14 to turn back.

Some people may argue that it serves no legitimate purpose to play the what-if game more than sixty years after the fact. Yet a key part of Cunningham's responsibility to the men under his command was to do everything possible to get them the help they needed—and his message to CinCPac had a totally opposite effect.

It's tempting to wonder what Pye would have done if Cunningham had rephrased the message to make it less poetic but more positive, informative, and to the point. For instance:

"Heavy fighting on island. Enemy landing ships destroyed. Urgently need reinforcements."

Would Pye have reacted differently to that kind of exhortation? No one knows, of course. But it surely wouldn't have made it any easier for him to desert the man who sent it.

Based on prevailing combat conditions across Wake proper, Wilkes, and Peale as of 8:00 A.M. on December 23, there was no valid military reason for American forces to lay down their arms when the surrender order was issued. Former servicemen who survived the battle agree, almost unanimously, that Wake's defenders probably could have held out for at least another day or two—even without reinforcements—if given the chance. Many more American lives would have been lost if the fight had continued, and deprived of outside help, the garrison had no real chance of holding off the Japanese indefinitely. At some point, surrender likely would have become the only alternative to death for the defenders, but as it happened, the order was clearly premature.

Captain Bryghte Godbold, Devereux's strongpoint commander on Peale and the highest-ranking officer on Wake still living as this book was written, offered a unique overview of the situation during a 2002 interview.

"From my local perspective, there was no immediate need to surrender," Godbold said. "I think we could have hung on for another two or three days, but, of course, Devereux was working with incomplete information, and he thought Wilkes was gone. The Japanese held the airfield at the time, no question about it, but none of the batteries themselves had been overrun, and our casualties had been amazingly light. My unit had sustained only one man killed and about five wounded in fifteen days of bombing and shelling, although we were constantly a target."

Even the massive attacks by Japanese carrier-based planes were generally ineffective. Hours of sorties by Zeroes and Val dive bombers on December 23 produced only one fatality among the Marines, and enemy naval bombardment never caused any serious casualties. Several of the three-inch batteries were wrecked during the last two days of bombing, but except for Battery L on Wilkes, all of the Marines' five-inchers were still functional when the white flag was raised.

"I don't think we should've surrendered under any circumstances," said PFC Ed Borne. "I was one of very few Americans to see two Japanese landing barges stuck on the barrier reefs just like those two transports. If our guns had still been in action when they came in, we could've done the same thing to them that we did to those big ships. If the Japs had tried to put more men ashore in daylight before the surrender, it would've been one helluva slaughter."

The toll exacted by Wake's coastal batteries on December 11 had left the Japanese in awe of the Marines' five-inch guns and their sharpshooting crews—so much so that they thought they were dealing with much larger weaponry. Time and again, as they questioned captive American officers, Japanese interrogators demanded, "Where are your sixteen-inch batteries? Where do you have them buried?"

They couldn't believe that so much havoc had been rained on them by mere five-inchers, and fear of the guns was their chief reason for scheduling the December 23 landing during the darkest part of the night. Trying to land a second wave of troops several hours later against Marine gunners with the advantage of broad daylight would have been courting disaster. But the heavy casualties suffered by the first wave of invaders left them too weak to secure their objective unaided. If the Americans hadn't surrendered when they did, a second contested landing would have been essential to a Japanese victory—and the enemy might well have been forced to make that landing without close air support.

Strong evidence exists that the *Hiryu* and *Soryu* were critically short of fuel for the combined total of sixty-four planes they had available at Wake (more than a third of their aircraft were "Kate" torpedo bombers, which were of no use in attacking ground troops). If this is true, the enemy squadrons would have been forced to withdraw from the action after flying their final sorties around noon on December 23. Even if no surrender was in progress, they would have had no choice.

Several historians have alluded to this fuel shortage and to warnings issued by Vice Admiral Chuichi Nagumo, commander of the Pearl Harbor strike force, that the Japanese carrier planes had only enough gasoline for limited duty at Wake.

"Nagumo warned the Fourth Fleet that [there was] only enough fuel to deliver one air raid against Wake," wrote historian Gregory J. W. Urwin in his book *Facing Fearful Odds: The Siege of Wake Island.* "After that, the carriers had instructions to retire."

As Urwin pointed out, this order was later countermanded by Nagumo's superiors, who insisted on repeated attacks to knock out Wake's aircraft, artillery, and machine guns. But, although Nagumo may have exaggerated the situation somewhat, the shortage of fuel was real. If not already at the critical stage, it soon could have been—thereby impairing not only the Japanese ability to continue the aerial assault on an unsurrendered Wake but also to defend their own ships against a U.S naval attack.

Could Wake have been saved? And could it have been saved without more crippling losses to American naval forces? Any definitive answers to these questions lie obscured beneath an interwoven tangle of "ifs":

If a radar unit had been delivered as promised before hostilities broke out... *If* two-thirds of VMF-211's planes and over half its personnel hadn't been lost in the first air raid... *If* the defenders' telephone lines had been buried, or a reliable field radio system had been available... *If* the powers in Washington had waited a few more days to relieve Admiral Kimmel as commander of the Pacific Fleet... *If* Admiral Fletcher's task force had moved as fast and decisively as it was capable of moving...

Once enemy forces landed on the atoll in strength and enemy ships surrounded it on all sides, it was probably too late for a clear-cut American victory. Yet changing one or more of the interacting factors listed above from might-have-been status to reality could very well have altered the overall outcome at Wake.

From both a moral and military standpoint, the inordinate delay of the relief expedition seems harder to justify than the ultimate decision to call off the rescue effort after the Japanese landing.

As Lieutenant Colonel R. D. Heinl put it in his Marine Corps–commissioned report, *The Defense of Wake*: "Had it been possible at any time for United States surface forces to intervene, or for substantial reinforcements to reach Wake, the results might have been entirely different."

The decision to surrender was "reasonable," Heinl wrote, "in light of the civilian situation and the fact that relief was no longer in prospect," as well as because the defenders had exacted a "more than honorable toll" on the Japanese and Wake's defensive resources had been "sapped to a great extent.

"Without more airplanes, fire-control instruments, radar, spare parts, and personnel to bring the defense to full strength (all of which and more had been embarked with Task Force 14)...Wake could not have carried on," he concluded.

Warranted or not, this defeat served at least one positive military purpose—as a valuable learning experience for U.S. combat forces. In months to come, American fighting men at Midway and Guadalcanal would draw from the bitter lessons of Wake to hand the Japanese their first major reversals and turn the tide of the Pacific war. If their commanders had been as tentative and unwilling to accept losses or take risks in the spring of 1942 as Pye and Fletcher were at Wake the previous December, those two pivotal battles might well have ended in defeat as well.

Largely because the surrender came when it did, American losses during the sixteen days of fighting were incredibly light.

Between December 8 and December 23, 1941, the 522 U.S. Marine, Navy, and Army personnel on Wake came under attack by combined forces totaling tens of thousands of Japanese. During this period, forty-nine

Marines and Navy bluejackets were killed in action defending Wake, and PFC Wiley Sloman was among thirty-six American servicemen seriously wounded.

Sixty-five civilian construction workers also were killed during the battle—a number of them while fighting shoulder to shoulder with Marines and sailors—and a dozen more suffered severe wounds. In addition, ten Chamorros employed by Pan Am were killed in the first bombing raid.

Despite Japanese attempts to conceal the full extent of their losses on Wake, the atoll proved to be an extremely costly prize for its conquerors. Lieutenant Colonel Heinl's "conservative" estimate of 700 or more enemy deaths on December 11, coupled with the near certainty that a minimum of 500 to 600 invaders were killed on December 23, would put Japanese dead in the area of 1,300. In addition, the submarine sent to the bottom with all hands by Lieutenant Kliewer carried a crew of about 60, and losses aboard Japanese aircraft—most of them twin-engine bombers with five-man crews—could add another 100 to 150 enemy fatalities. A number of crewmen also were killed aboard an enemy destroyer that came under American fire on December 23. Taking all these losses into consideration, the Wake campaign may well have cost the Japanese 1,500 or more dead— or about 13 enemy fatalities for every American serviceman and civilian killed.

The Japanese also suffered their first serious material losses of the war at Wake. When the five-inch battery on Wilkes Island blew the destroyer *Hayate* in half, she was the first major Japanese warship to go down in the Pacific. Captain Henry Elrod's kill of the destroyer *Kisaragi* a couple of hours later was the second. The two Japanese destroyer-transports used to land troops on December 23 were shelled into oblivion, although not technically sunk, by Lieutenant Hanna's makeshift gun crew. At least five other Japanese ships, including two light cruisers, were disabled or damaged.

According to reliable estimates, between twenty-one and twenty-nine Japanese planes were shot down over Wake. Reports obtained from Japanese sources after the war indicated that as many as fifty-five enemy aircraft were lost or damaged in the Wake campaign.

When no relief arrived for the American garrison by the evening of

December 21, 1941, the fall of Wake was virtually inevitable. The atoll surely would have fallen much sooner if not for the bravery and endurance of its defenders.

Their victory on December 11 marked the first and only time during the war that an amphibious landing force was repelled by coastal guns. Wake was the scene of the first sinking of enemy surface ships, the first enemy ship sunk by aircraft, and the first full-size enemy sub destroyed. Hank Elrod was posthumously awarded the war's first Congressional Medal of Honor won by a Marine aviator.

Wake Atoll, 2003

E xcept for the sound of the surf, still endlessly pounding against the barrier reef, Wake is quiet today. Most of the few twenty-first-century Americans who make their way to the atoll these days are struck by the same sense of remoteness and solitude that travelers on the Pan Am Clippers found there in the mid-1930s.

"It's a great place to be a beach bum," said Paul Golden, a geologist at Southern Methodist University who visits Wake periodically to conduct federally funded infrasound and hydro-acoustic studies. "And it really kind of grows on you."

The same airstrip from which the intrepid pilots of VMF-211 flew their Wildcats in 1941 is still in use, with many improvements, including wide concrete runways and a well-equipped terminal. But there are no regularly scheduled flights to Wake anymore—neither commercial nor military— and the strip is maintained only for emergency landing purposes.

Today the resident population of Wake consists of about 120 civilians. Two or three dozen of these are Americans, who live in neat, apartment-style housing near the former site of Camp Two and enjoy such recreational amenities as a nine-hole golf course, a bowling alley, a protected swimming area in the lagoon, and a cozy cocktail bar. Some are employed by the Air Force, which assumed administration of the islands in October 2002, and a few Federal Aviation Administration personnel are also stationed there. Others work for the Space and Missile Defense Command, which monitors undersea and atmospheric disturbances for possible nuclear test ban violations, or for various contractors supplying goods or services to the federal government.

No military personnel have been stationed on the atoll for several years, but some classified tests of the U.S. missile defense system have been carried out recently, although these operations were reportedly being transferred to Kwajalein and Johnston Island as of late 2002.

Thanks to a vigorous eradication program, the notorious Wake Island rats that besieged its defenders along with the Japanese in 1941 are nowhere to be found. They have been succeeded by profusions of bright yellow canaries, originally brought to Wake as pets but now flourishing in the wild. Meanwhile, once-unheard-of palm trees, planted during a postwar landscaping campaign by the Navy, sway gracefully above the beaches, although the atoll's most predominant foliage continues to be underbrush and scrubby ironwood trees.

The rusty steel framework of the long-gone Pan Am hotel still stands on Peale Island, along with a series of broad concrete slabs where the airline's shops and storage facilities once stood. Beyond them are a number of hand-built huts and cabins occupied by several score Thai maintenance and service workers and their families, who have been warned against digging or excavating on Peale because the island has never been thoroughly cleared of unexploded World War II ordnance.

A designated bird sanctuary, Wilkes Island remains mostly wilderness. Except for a few storage tanks and a protective seawall, it's nearly as undeveloped today as it was in 1941. A bridge across the Wilkes Channel now connects it to the main island, however, so it's no longer accessible only by boat.

Among the trickle of visitors to Wake, all of whom require advance U.S. government authorization, are geologists, meteorologists, oceanographers, bureaucrats, occasional filmmakers, and more than a few survivors of the battle. Marine and Navy retirees may travel there free of charge aboard military planes, which drop them off en route from Hawaii to the Far East, then pick them up a few days later on their return trip. Over the past fifteen years, dozens of Wake's former defenders have taken advantage of the opportunity to return, some several times.

"The mess hall has an incredible variety of great food—as good as you could find anyplace, and all of it elegantly served by waiters in white coats," said Jack Skaggs following his first return visit in 2002. "It's a far cry from what we had there back in '41."

Returning veterans find that many of the outward signs of their epic struggle have been smoothed away by time and the typhoon-driven tidal waves that sweep periodically across the atoll. The ravaged hulks of *Patrol Boats No. 32* and *33*, which were still sprawled on the reef off the main island's south beach more than fifteen years after Lieutenant Hanna's gun gutted them there, are gone now. Yet many other signs of the battle remain.

"There's a sense of history that you can feel in the air," said Paul Golden after a recent trip to Wake. "A couple of the old Japanese shore batteries are still there, and you can see shell and bomb craters everywhere."

If visitors venture into the undergrowth just east of the airfield, they may stumble across the remains of Major Devereux's command post, its earthen roof thickly matted with scrub brush and vines. If they dig in the sand and coral almost anywhere along the south beach of Wake proper, they may unearth corroded bits of shrapnel and other wartime debris—like the two corroded .50-caliber machine gun shell casings found by Skaggs more than sixty-one years after they were fired. If they search out the site of Camp One, where the Marines pitched their tents, they'll find it obscured by junglelike growth.

And, if they bother to look, they'll discover three separate monuments to the memory of those who suffered, bled, and died here. One pays tribute to U.S. servicemen, and another honors the American civilians who fought beside them. The third commemorates the thousands of Japanese who lost their lives at Wake.

Over the years, veterans from Japan have joined their former foes in revisiting the atoll where they battled. Here in this place of fierce, no-quarter combat, some on both sides have found a surprising feeling of peace and closure. To them, Wake is hallowed ground.

In a letter to President George W. Bush, written in the spring of 2002 in response to reports that Wake was being considered as a hazardous waste disposal site, Dr. Shigeyoshi Ozeki described the atoll as "a holy place for both American and Japanese soldiers" who fought there. He asked President Bush to use his influence to prevent any future industrial dumping on Wake.

A number of aging American survivors—virtually all are now past eighty—also voiced their concern. No one on either side who was here in December 1941 comes back without a surge of conflicting emotions. Returning can be both a disturbing and soul-satisfying experience.

"I didn't see much I remembered, except the steel net that kept the sharks out of our swimming hole in the lagoon," said Artie Stocks, who went back for several days in 2000. "But it's beautiful there now, nothing like it was before, and it made me stop and think. It made me sad and even angry in a way, but it also helped me understand what it was all about. I'm glad I went."

Ex-artilleryman Walter Bowsher, who also made his first pilgrimage back to Wake in 2000, came away even more deeply touched. He found that the bloodstained, bomb-blasted bits of coral he remembered from fifty-nine years earlier had been miraculously transformed. They'd become a place of idyllic tranquillity—one that seemed to reach out and embrace him.

"Everything had changed, and it looked entirely different," Bowsher said. "But I felt like, well, like I'd come home after all this time, and I just wished I could stay there and never leave. If I had my choice of any place in the world to live out the rest of my life, I can honestly say it would be Wake Island."

NOTES

Chapter 1

p. 20 *Major Walter Bayler, a Marine...* Bayler's observations in the following paragraphs about the unusual birds on Wake are from his book, *Last Man Off Wake Island.*

Chapter 2

p. 34 *"The strategic importance of Wake..."* Admiral Kimmel's letter to Admiral Stark is quoted in historian Gregory Urwin's book *Facing Fearful Odds: The Siege of Wake Island.*

Chapter 3

p. 48 *On one occasion that hectic fall...* Devereux describes this encounter in some detail in his postwar book *The Story of Wake Island,* but he doesn't identify the British diplomat or his wife by name.

p. 52 *"It was not good," he said...* Cunningham's quote and his description of his first day's activities after his arrival on Wake are from his postwar book, *Wake Island Command.*

Chapter 4

p. 67 *In the midst of all this...* Cunningham reveals his inner confusion at this moment in *Wake Island Command.*

p. 72 *Cunningham himself was in his...* Cunningham's book details his reaction to the attack on his headquarters.

Chapter 5

p. 86 *...Gunner John Hamas...* The rank of Marine gunner was the equivalent of warrant officer and was a designation used primarily in Marine artillery units.

Chapter 7

p. 130 *As Devereux described the scene...* The major's quote is from his book, *The Story of Wake Island*.

p. 133 *After the men of Battery L...* The admission by the Japanese of nineteen casualties aboard the *Oite* is cited in *Facing Fearful Odds: The Siege of Wake Island* by Gregory Urwin.

p. 135 *In spite of everything...* The casualty count aboard the *Yayoi* is also cited in Gregory Urwin's book.

p. 141 *The pilots of VMF-211...* Japanese confirmation of the loss of the *Kisaragi* and the other ships in the attack by the four Marine fighters is mentioned in Urwin's *Facing Fearful Odds: The Siege of Wake Island*. The fact that the Japanese frequently failed to reveal the full extent of their casualties is cited by Devereux, Urwin, and various other authors.

Chapter 8

p. 145 *Evidence suggests that two other ships...* "Japanese personnel casualties can be fixed only approximately," said Lieutenant Colonel R. D. Heinl Jr. in *The Defense of Wake*, a postwar summation of the engagement prepared for the Marine Corps. "Assuming that the two sunken destroyers were manned by crews comparable to those required by similar United States types (about 250 officers and men per ship), it would be logical to claim approximately 500 for these two losses with the fair assumption that no survivors escaped in either case. Seven more ships were damaged, but with what personnel losses we do not know. Two hundred does not seem an excessive figure, all things considered; if this is anywhere near correct, we may well believe that their ill-fated attack of 11 December cost the Japanese at least 700 casualties, mostly dead, and possibly more." Not counted among Heinl's figures were fifteen Japanese airmen later confirmed dead aboard the three bombers that were lost and the eleven others that were damaged over Wake that day by AA fire and the attacking Wildcats.

Based on hearsay reports from Japanese sources, Major Devereux later concluded that 5,350 Japanese lost their lives on December 11, but that figure has been shown to be totally unrealistic and unsupportable. In all candor, there probably weren't that many Japanese personnel in the entire invasion fleet, yet official Japanese attempts to conceal the extent of their losses have only added to the guessing game. Japanese naval records indicate that each of the lost destroyers carried about 167 men, but the validity of this number remains open to question.

p. 148 *Japan's top military leaders could dismiss...* After the war, Commander Masatake Okumiya, a flight training officer at the Imperial Japanese Navy's Kasumigaura Air Station, offered a brutally frank assessment of the events of

December 11. "Considering the power accumulated for the invasion of Wake Island and the meager forces of the defenders," he said, "it was one of the most humiliating defeats we had ever suffered." It was unfortunate, Okumiya added in *Zero*, a book that he coauthored after the war, that Japan's otherwise unbroken string of early triumphs allowed the "valuable lessons obtained at such a high price" at Wake to be forgotten all too quickly by the Japanese high command. "Japan was much too jubilant at the news of victory which rolled in from all corners of the Pacific to heed the bitter lesson of Wake Island," he said.

p. 148 *Hamas: "Lieutenant McAlister reports..."* This exchange between Cunningham and Hamas is recounted in Cunningham's *Wake Island Command*.

p. 153 *Cunningham was still brooding as he...* Cunningham describes his mood and the encounter with the radio operator in his book, but he is apparently mistaken in saying that the report of the sub sinking occurred on December 11. Other published accounts, as well as sources interviewed by the author, place the sinking on December 12.

p. 156 *...one of these subs, identified as RO-66...* More circumstantial evidence emerged after the fall of Wake, when Lieutenant Kinney and several of Kliewer's other squadron mates were questioned by a Japanese naval intelligence officer. While inquiring about a number of well-documented enemy naval losses, the officer specifically asked about the fate of a sub that disappeared near Wake at this time. The fact that the other losses had been established beyond doubt led Kinney to conclude that Kliewer had, indeed, destroyed the sub.

One more piece of evidence goes a long way toward proving Kliewer's claim beyond any reasonable doubt, despite some disagreement among knowledgeable sources about the date of his encounter with the sub. Both Devereux and Cunningham, as well as one respected historian, place the action on the afternoon of December 11. Cunningham went so far as to describe how he learned of Kliewer's feat as he was returning from the burial service on the evening of December 11. But Lieutenant Kinney, Lieutenant Colonel Heinl, and other knowledgeable observers—including Kliewer himself—set the time of the sinking a full day later, on the afternoon of December 12. "I always thought it was the twelfth, and I still do," Kliewer said years later. "I'm sure I'd remember if it had happened on the same day as the landing attempt on the eleventh."

Even on the off chance that the earlier date is correct, it does nothing to disprove Kliewer's claimed sub sinking. The only raid on December 12 came early in the morning rather than at the usual midday hour, and it wasn't by the familiar Nells of the Chitose Air Group based at Roi but by flying boats from the Yokohama Air Group. These latter planes came from a base on Majuro in the Marshalls, a considerable distance from Roi, and their vast range of more than

2,500 miles made it less risky for them to fly long missions over water without radio guidance.

Finally, Japanese records examined after the war confirmed that two subs were, indeed, lost during this period in the very same locale where Kliewer had dropped his bombs. One sinking was attributed to a "noncombat accident," the other to "cause unknown."

"There's no question that this so-called 'cause unknown' was Dave Kliewer," said VMF-211's Sergeant Robert Bourquin, who kept a detailed diary covering every day of the battle beginning with the first day of the war. "And he definitely got the sub on the twelfth because I have the record of it in black and white. Normally, Dave was very reserved, but he was absolutely beside himself that afternoon."

Chapter 9

p. 168 *On December 9, Admiral Stark...* Stark's radio communication with Admiral Kimmel is quoted and Kimmel's subsequent actions described in Gregory Urwin's *Facing Fearful Odds: The Siege of Wake Island.*

p. 172 *At 3:00 P.M. on December 17, Kimmel's staff...* Commander Layton's remarks are quoted in Urwin's book.

Chapter 10

p. 180 *"Why doesn't this damn fool..."* This remark is mentioned in *Wake Island: The Heroic Gallant Fight* by Duane Schultz, but is attributed only to an unidentified "Marine flier."

p. 186 *By the time Bayler left the hospital...* Ensign Murphy's nervous habit of glancing from the eastern sky to his wristwatch is described in Bayler's *Last Man Off Wake Island.*

p. 196 *Aboard one of the Kates...* Noted World War II historian Gordon W. Prange, author of *At Dawn We Slept,* described Kanai's death as a "serious blow" to the Japanese navy, which needed every one of its combat-tested airmen. Men like Kanai were extremely hard to replace because, unlike the United States, Japan had no fast, efficient training program for turning out large numbers of pilots, bombardiers, and aerial navigators. Japan had plenty of ordinary soldiers and sailors, but she was critically short of young men with the kind of technical training or advanced education required by these high-skill jobs. In fact, Japanese officers had a difficult time even finding enlisted men who could drive a truck or automobile.

Chapter 11

p. 203 *But there were other reports as well...* Other reports indicated that part of the Japanese task force supporting the impending Wake invasion was spooked into firing at imaginary planes or "ghost ships" that didn't exist. Some historians have suggested that confused enemy gunners thought they were shelling Wake itself, but many of the Marines interpreted the display as a distinctly bad omen. "We knew those dudes flashing the lights were definitely not friends," said PFC Jesse Nowlin of Battery A on Peacock Point. Major Devereux, Commander Cunningham, and other officers familiar with the muzzle flashes of naval artillery were sure they were seeing distant gunfire, but they could no more explain the cause of the phenomenon than their men could.

p. 206 *But in the rough seas and rainy darkness...* This error may help explain some of the lights seen in that area, but it doesn't offer a complete explanation. The bombardment took place around 1 A.M., an hour or more after the first reports of light flashes on Wake. It also lasted only a few minutes, while many American observers described the flashes as continuing constantly for about an hour.

p. 207 *"Drink plenty of sake now..."* This incident was recounted by some surviving Japanese crewmen after the war and was mentioned in the book *Facing Fearful Odds: The Siege of Wake Island* by Gregory J. W. Urwin. The identity of the senior officer is not known.

Chapter 12

p. 223 *"The enemy put down a barrage..."* The Japanese correspondent's report of the barrage by Hanna's gun is quoted in Urwin's book.

p. 224 *"As we started to rise to our feet..."* A translation of this written account by a Japanese eyewitness to the landing on Wake appears in the book *Japan Fights for Asia* by John Goette, published in 1943.

Chapter 13

p. 242 *But by the light from the two blazing troopships...* To this day, no one knows for sure what happened to the 100 or so invaders from the two enemy landing craft that Poindexter found empty on the beach an hour earlier. If these troops had remained west of Poindexter's force, they could've attacked the Americans from the rear—and some of them may have. Others may have moved east through the brush and slipped past Poindexter's line in the darkness to link up with the men from *Patrol Boat No. 33*.

p. 247 *Devereux took the phone and listened to a faint voice...* The phone call from the unidentified American and Devereux's account of it are described in Devereux's *The Story of Wake Island*.

Chapter 14

p. 270 *"Even though each and every one of you fall..."* Historian Gregory Urwin cites the Japanese officer's exhortation to his men in *Facing Fearful Odds: The*

Siege of Wake Island. None of the officers who had come ashore with the Wilkes landing force survived.

Chapter 16

p. 300 *"I was amazed to see that they had brought..."* Correspondent Toshio Miyake's lengthy denunciation of the American "luxuries" found on Wake is quoted in its entirety in Gregory Urwin's *Facing Fearful Odds: The Siege of Wake Island.*

p. 302 *"You have one hour to live..."* The Japanese guard's threatening remark to Sergeant Malleck is cited in Urwin's book.

Chapter 17

p. 316 *"Twarn't nuthin..."* The guard's beating of Platt and Platt's comment are recounted in Cunningham's book *Wake Island Command.*

p. 319 *...in testimony before the Allied War Crimes Commission...* This eyewitness account is taken from a transcript of testimony before the Allied War Crimes Commission at the trial of Lieutenant Saito after the war, excerpts of which appeared in *Wake Island Command*. The *Nitta Maru* crewman offering the testimony is not identified.

Chapter 19

p. 355 *"All the incidents which took place on Wake Island..."* Details of Admiral Sakaibara's trial and convictions as well as his remarks during the trial were included in a February 1983 article written for the U.S. Naval Institute's *Proceedings* publication by retired Navy Captain Earl A. Junghans.

Afterword

p. 374 *"Kimmel was inclined to make up his mind..."* Morison's comments are taken from his book *History of United States Naval Operations in World War II, Volume III: The Rising Sun in the Pacific, 1931–April 1942.*

p. 375 Cunningham's remarks about the vulnerability of Japanese ships at Wake are from his book, *Wake Island Command.*

p. 375 The quotes attributed to Colonel Omar Pfeiffer, Admiral Harold Stark, and Navy Secretary Frank Knox appeared in Urwin's *Facing Fearful Odds: The Siege of Wake Island.*

SELECTED BIBLIOGRAPHY

BOOKS

Bayler, Walter L. J. *Last Man Off Wake Island*. Indianapolis: Bobbs-Merrill Co., 1943.

Cohen, Stan. *Enemy on Island. Issue in Doubt*. Missoula, Mont.: Pictorial Histories Publishing Co., 1983.

Cressman, Robert J. *A Magnificent Fight: Marines in the Battle for Wake Island*. Washington, D.C.: Naval Institute Press, 1995.

Cunningham, W. Scott. *Wake Island Command*. Boston: Little, Brown & Co., 1961.

Darden, James B. III. *Guests of the Emperor: The Story of Dick Darden*. Clinton, N.C.: The Greenhouse Press, 1990.

Devereux, James P. S. *The Story of Wake Island*. New York: J. B. Lippincott Co., 1947.

Goette, John. *Japan Fights for Asia*. New York: Harcourt Brace & Co, 1943.

Heinl, Robert D. Jr. *The Defense of Wake*. Washington, D.C.: U.S. Marine Corps, 1947.

Hough, Frank O., et al. *History of U.S. Marine Corps Operations in World War II, Vol. 1: Pearl Harbor to Guadalcanal*. Washington, D. C.: U.S. Government Printing Office/Historical Branch G-3, USMC, 1958.

Kinney, John W. *Wake Island Pilot: A World War II Memoir*. Washington, D.C.: Brassey's, 1995.

Morison, Samuel Eliot. *History of United States Naval Operations in World War II, Volume III: The Rising Sun in the Pacific, 1931–April 1942*. Boston: Little, Brown & Co., 1948.

Okumiya, Masatake, and Jiro Horikoshi with Martin Caidin. *Zero!* New York: E. P. Dutton, 1956.

Prange, Gordon W. *At Dawn We Slept: The Untold Story of Pearl Harbor*. New York: McGraw-Hill Book Co., 1981.

Schultz, Duane P. *Wake Island: The Heroic, Gallant Fight*. New York: St. Martin's Press, 1978.

Sherrod, Robert. *The History of Marine Aviation in World War II*. Washington, D.C.: Combat Forces Press, 1952.

Toland, John. *But Not in Shame: The Six Months After Pearl Harbor*. New York: Random House, 1961.

Urwin, Gregory J. W. *Facing Fearful Odds: The Siege of Wake Island*. Lincoln: University of Nebraska Press, 1997.

PERIODICALS

Andrews, Peter. "The Defense of Wake." *American Heritage*, July / August 1987.

Burroughs, J. R. "The Siege of Wake Island." *American Heritage*, June 1959.

"Col. Wesley M. Platt Funeral Rites Today in Fort Myer Chapel." *Washington Star*, January 11, 1952.

Cunningham, Winfield Scott. "The Truth Behind the Wake Island Marine Hero Hoax." *Cavalier*, May 1961.

"Flame of Glory: Wake's Hopeless, Gallant Fight." *Time*, January 19, 1942.

Frankes, Glen. "Wake Island." *Leatherneck*, December 1982.

Hood, Ernie. "Seven Idaho Wake Survivors Reach States." *Idaho Daily Statesman*, September 14, 1945.

"Isles of Valor." *Newsweek*, January 5, 1942.

Junghans, Earl A. "Wake's POWs." *U.S. Naval Institute Proceedings*, February 1983.

Keene, R. R. "Wake Island: The Corps Raised Its Name to Honor and Fame." *Leatherneck*, December 2001.

"Message from Wake." *Time*, December 29, 1941.

Miller, William Burke. "Flying the Pacific." *National Geographic*, December 1936.

Poindexter, Arthur A. "Our Last Hurrah on Wake." *American History Illustrated*, February 1992.

———. "Wake Island: America's First Victory." *Leatherneck*, December 1991.

Urwin, Gregory J. W. "The Wildcats of Wake Island." *Air Classics*, September 1977.

Wensyel, James W. "Odyssey of the Wake Island Prisoners." *World War II*, November 2000.

AUTHOR INTERVIEWS

Joseph E. (Ed) Borne: November 2001
Robert Bourquin: April 2002
Walter Bowsher: December 2001
Arlene Cemeris: January 2003
J. J. Coker: June 2001
John R. Dale: January 2003
Ed Doyle: May 2002
June Faubion: January 2002, May 2002
Richard S. Gilbert: February 2002
Bryghte D. Godbold: June 2001, December 2001
Paul Golden: June 2002
Franklin D. Gross: June 2001, December 2001
Robert M. Hanna: January 2002
Charles Harrison: October 2001
Edwin F. Hassig: January 2003
Jack Hearn: June 2001, March 2002
Ralph J. Holewinski: February 2002, September 2002
John S. Johnson: December 2001, June 2002
Walter T. (Tom) Kennedy: February 2002
John F. Kinney: January 2002
David D. Kliewer: October 2001, April 2002
Chalas Loveland: May 2002
Don Ludington: August 2002
William H. Manning: January 2003
Trudy McAnally: January 2003
Glenn Newell: May 2002
Shigeyoshi Ozeki: February 2002
Patricia Poindexter: October 2002
Ernest Rogers: January 2002
John Rogge: May 2002
Clifton A. Sanders: January 2002
Leroy Schneider: October 2001
Jack R. Skaggs: March 2002
Wiley W. Sloman: June 2001, January 2002, August 2002
Artie J. Stocks: January 2002, June 2002
Glenn Tripp: April 2002
Hisao Tsuji: April 2002
Glen Walden: January 2002
Mackie L. Wheeler: August 2002

INDEX

ABOUT THE AUTHOR

Bill Sloan is a native Texan, a graduate of the University of North Texas, and a former award-winning newspaper reporter who started trying to write his first book when he was in the fifth grade.

During more than forty years as a professional journalist, editor, and author, Sloan has helped cover some of the most significant stories of the second half of the twentieth century, and interviewed some of the period's most famous people. In 1972 he was nominated for a Pulitzer Prize in local reporting for a series of articles he wrote for the *Dallas Times Herald*.

He was working on the city desk of the *Times Herald* on November 22, 1963, when President John F. Kennedy was assassinated a few blocks away. His close proximity to this momentous event and his ongoing interest in it led him to interview many principals in the case and subsequently write three books on JFK's slaying and the ensuing investigation. Since 1977, he has been a full-time freelance writer.

Most of Sloan's previously published books have dealt in one way or another with some aspect of modern American history, but *Given Up for Dead* is his first "war book." In hopes that it won't be his last, he is currently researching another all-but-forgotten World War II battle in the Pacific.

Sloan lives in a well-preserved 1920s Arts and Crafts house on a wooded hillside in Dallas, Texas, with his wife, Lana—also an accomplished author and veteran journalist—and an incorrigible pet Pekingese named Gizmo.